ID0368679

FACE VALUE

THE HIDDEN WAYS

SHAPES WOMEN'S LIVES

Autumn Whitefield-Madrano

SIMON & SCHUSTER

NEW YORK LONDON TORONTO SYDNEY NEW DELHI

Simon & Schuster
1230 Avenue of the Americas
New York, NY 10020

First Simon & Schuster hardcover edition June 2016

SIMON & SCHUSTER and colophon are registered trademarks of Simon & Schuster, Inc.

For information about special discounts for bulk purchases, please contact Simon & Schuster Special Sales at 1-866-506-1949 or business@simonandschuster.com.

The Simon & Schuster Speakers Bureau can bring authors to your live event. For more information or to book an event, contact the Simon & Schuster Speakers Bureau at 1-866-248-3049 or visit our website at www.simonspeakers.com.

Manufactured in the United States of America

1 3 5 7 9 10 8 6 4 2

Library of Congress Cataloging-in-Publication Data

Names: Whitefield-Madrano, Autumn, author.
Title: Face value : the hidden ways beauty shapes women's lives / Autumn Whitefield-Madrano.
Description: New York : Simon & Schuster, [2016] | Includes bibliographical references and index.
Identifiers: LCCN 2015038730
Subjects: LCSH: Aesthetics—Social aspects. | Beauty, Personal—Social aspects. | Women—Psychology. | Body image in women. | Self-perception in women. | Appearance (Philosophy)
Classification: LCC HQ1219 .W45 2016 | DDC 111/.85—dc23 LC record available at http://lccn.loc.gov/2015038730

ISBN 978-1-4767-5400-0
ISBN 978-1-4767-5405-5 (ebook)

For Cam

Contents

Author's Note

THE EXPERIENCES OF MANY of the women and men I interviewed have remained private until now—and, for that reason, are mostly presented here with anonymity. Last names in this book have almost universally been omitted, with first names and identifying details changed upon request. The dozens of in-depth interviews I conducted were formal and recorded, but I also share a sprinkling of experiences I've heard in passing—cast-off anecdotes from women I've met at parties, stories I heard before I began writing about beauty that stuck with me through the years. (I'm also not above bursting into strangers' conversations on the subway to learn more if I happen to eavesdrop on a juicy morsel.) I made a point of interviewing a number of women who were demographically unlike me—that is, not white, heterosexual, middle-class, able-bodied urbanites. In doing so I was looking for the threads that bound us together. Certainly women of color navigate a different set of challenges in regard to beauty than white women do; black women, for instance, have historically been both desexualized and hypersexualized more than white women. Women of every ethnic group in America have faced, and continue to face, assumptions about their appearance and self-image in ways that intersect with stereotypes about their race. For example, the fetishization of Asian women plays into larger racist notions of East Asians as the model minority. As one woman of Korean descent told me, "I'm supposed to look like some sort of sex toy, and I'm supposed to be good at math too? It's like, don't I get a break?" When someone's personal information is pertinent to the themes of this book—like, say, when a queer woman talks about comparing her body with her girlfriend's, an experience straight women are less likely to be familiar with—I've included relevant details. Women, regardless of color, economic standing, and sexuality, face a matrix of choices, expectations, and stereotypes about personal presentation that revolve around the idea that women should try to be perfectly pretty at all times. *That* is the common thread I've explored here, and my hope is that this book will shed enough light on the conditions we share for each reader to see how it has played out in her or his own life.

INTRODUCTION

Beyond the Beauty Myth

Hand me my makeup kit, would you? Chat with me as I walk through my morning routine. Retinol cream first, then moisturizer. I'll mix together two shades of foundation to get just the right tone, perhaps getting annoyed at the extra step but also taking a second to think of the Irish-Scottish-Caddo-Cherokee family tree that's given me my particular complexion. Concealer is dotted around my nose and mouth, blush dusted onto the cheeks; bronzer if I feel like playing the golden girl that day, none if I feel more like the English rose. Purple liquid eyeliner; funny how once I switched from black, people started calling my eyes hazel, not brown. As my neighbor—a gifted makeup artist in whose chair I've talked feminism, race, relationships good and bad, and, of course, makeup—told me as she dotted violet onto my lash line for the first time, "That's color theory for ya." She also taught me to articulate my brows with pencil, and every time I do, I take quiet pleasure in how much more it makes me match the image of myself I have in my head. A swipe of mascara. Finally, the lips: nothing most days, a gentle rose on others. And on my boldest days—or on the days when I need to find my boldest self—it's unignorable, unoverlookable, unambiguous red. The name of the shade is Talk to Me.

That's six and a half minutes of my morning, and afterward I'm ready to give you my full attention. I feel prepared to show my public self. It's simple, really—until you look a little closer. Right there in my makeup caddy lies a knot of contradiction: Is my makeup routine about revealing my best self (purple eyeliner) or about hiding my flaws (concealer)? What about things like that eyebrow pencil—if it makes me appear more like the way I look in my mind's eye, am I wise to be fixing the brow line to match, or should I be adjusting my mental image of myself? And then there are the other story lines running through my head: I think of my neighbor nearly every time I reach for that eyeliner, and I relish the conversations we've had when I've sat in her chair for a quick haircut or makeup advice. But we rarely hang out otherwise, even as we always part ways by promising to grab a cocktail soon. Beauty has given us an inroad to connection, but have the limitations of that inroad limited our friendship as well?

Beauty invites gaps in our thinking. There's the gap between how people look and how we aspire to look, the gap between appearance standards for men and those for women, the gap between the words we use to describe ourselves and those we use to describe others. For decades, these inconsistencies have been acknowledged for their negative effect on our lives. We're told that appearance is fraught, forever leaving women feeling like beasts in the face of idealized, retouched, impossibly perfect images—or that beauty rituals are a trap, distracting women from what really matters.

But viewing women's relationship with beauty primarily as something we must overcome is problematic, and any black-and-white interpretation of how aesthetics shapes us is bound to be one-dimensional. In truth, the gaps in our thinking about beauty host rich possibilities: What about the gap between the theoretic competition and envy beauty breeds in women's relationships with one another, and the reality that shared experiences of beauty—pedicures with friends, complimenting a colleague on her skirt—give women a way to connect? Or the gap between conventional beauties and the people who become beautiful to us only as we fall in love with them? These gaps exist because we can't reconcile how we think we should be influenced by looks with our actual experiences. And when we gloss over these gaps, we overlook unexpected and often positive ways that beauty fashions our lives.

I want to close these gaps by challenging our assumptions, looking at beauty not only in terms of gender, power, and low self-esteem but sisterhood, ideology, and identity. We need to move the conversation beyond overtweezed brows, wriggling into Spanx, and duck-face selfies to consider instead how looks shape our lives in unexpected, often positive ways. We need to eschew clichés when speaking—even thinking—of our own habits and desires.

We've got a number of routes toward closing those gaps in understanding how beauty shapes us. Looking at language gives us a direct line to the surprisingly nuanced ways we regard appearance. Examining the pool of scientific data attempting to determine what exactly we find attractive tells us more about the desire to pin down beauty than it does about beauty itself. In the social sciences, we'll find that looks play a role in forging our relationships, but differently than we might expect. And we'll see that the media has been successful in linking good looks with other good things—sex appeal, power, wealth, happiness—but that those links aren't as straightforward as newsmakers would have you believe.

A new conversation about beauty frees us from either-or scripts, reframing our relationship with our looks not as a chronic struggle toward a nirvana of self-acceptance but as a lens that can help us identify our true values and desires. Beauty can help us connect with other women, serve as a barometer for our love lives, and center us through daily rituals. It's a powerful portal to a stronger relationship with the world. By simultaneously taking beauty at face value and looking beyond its superficial sheen, we can opt to go straight to that portal, allowing us to drop beauty rites when they don't serve us—while also allowing us to tease our hair and dab on cat's-eye eyeliner along the way if we wish.

~

I've spent more than a decade working in women's and teen magazines, where I've observed firsthand the crafting of mainstream messages about beauty. Those observations jockeyed alongside my feminist leanings; I'd grown up with a mother who took me to her NOW meetings, and the birth of my career was an internship at *Ms.* magazine, the flagship publication of the feminist movement. In short, beauty culture was a matrix of contradictions to me. In 2011 I started a blog, *The Beheld*—a mix of long-form interviews, essays, and critical takes on how we treat appearance in society at large—in the hopes that talking with other women about beauty might help me figure out my own thoughts on the matter.

Certainly *The Beheld* was helped along by my background in women's magazines, as it was by my journalism degree and focus on women's studies. But the more the blog grew and the more I was called on to publicly critique the way our culture regards women and beauty—and, eventually, when I began writing this book—I saw that I wasn't just drawing on my time at the back offices of the glossies or my reporting skills. Those were helpful, sure, but it was my wealth of personal experiences that informed what I had to say. More than that, it was the stories other women were willing to share with me. I talked with women whose experiences lent them a particular perspective on physical appearance, one that might illuminate the ways beauty shapes other women's lives too. I talked with, among others, a fashion photographer, a burlesque dancer, a professional bodybuilder, a mortician, a psychologist, a little person, a dominatrix, and a nun. In listening to the stories of women who couldn't be more different from one another I began to hear the same themes. These themes became even more evident when I redirected my focus from women with an extraordinary relationship with beauty to women who were—well, more like me, and maybe like you too.

Plenty of women were fluent in describing how the beauty imperative had made them feel bad. I'd expected this, to a degree; my interest in the subject had partly stemmed from my own bouts of discontent with the mirror. Most of the women I was talking with were of the generation that grew up in the era that made *The Beauty Myth*, Naomi Wolf's groundbreaking 1991 feminist polemic, a best seller. Even if they hadn't actually read the book, they were well versed in its argument—that increasingly impossible beauty standards were redirecting women's energy: Rather than beaming their focus outward, they were aiming their attention onto their own bodies. The end result—and I understood this viscerally—was that most of us felt crappy about the way we looked. Evidence of this was everywhere in my interviews: One woman talked of covering her bathroom mirror with newspaper so she wouldn't have to see herself, and another described adding an extra item into her bedtime prayers as a child: "Let me be pretty."

Many a woman who had suffered at the hands of the beauty imperative— refusing to leave the house without makeup, stifling sexual desire due to leg-hair stubble, quelling hunger with coffee as a weight-control measure— had worked her way to a place of peace. Indeed, "a place of peace" was the exact phrase used repeatedly by many women I talked with. But the more I listened, the more I'd hear glimmers of opposition to this neat story line. Even when women reported being in the midst of crisis, they had anecdotes about when beauty had made them feel *good*. Stories of vamping it up on Halloween, playing off their glamour as a joke but secretly feeling fierce. One woman tells me of how a friend nudged her to try an exfoliating scrub, and how the results not only pleased her sensually but also made her trust her friend just that much more. Another says that she knew to seek help for her depression when she stopped wearing her trademark bright-coral lipstick: "That color tends to get me a lot of comments, and I didn't want people to look at me. I knew that wasn't like me." And in these more complicated stories, unlike the tales when beauty made women feel *bad*, they didn't really know how to talk about it. I heard apologies ("I don't mean to sound superficial but . . ."), self-doubt ("This might be arrogant, but I've never had a problem with how I look"), even musings about whether *not* having a beauty crisis made them a traitor to other women.

There was an inherent contradiction in the ways women talked about beauty, and I began to wonder if the scholarly research on beauty reflected this contradiction. Sure enough, the material out there painted anything but a clear picture. Even when I turned toward an area I thought would offer some cold, hard facts about beauty—the field of science—I didn't see the straightforward story I'd expected. (That bit about how we find symmetrical faces the most attractive, for example? Not really the case.) Sure, there was plenty of evidence that our idea of beauty is basically biologically determined, but there was just as much support for the notion that beauty is a cultural construct. How could these both be true? And wasn't there something sort of bleak about framing our drive for beauty as being out of our hands, at the will of our genetic drive? It didn't jibe with the more joyous aspects of beauty I'd heard reported to me. But when I tried to chase down a neat origin story about those more celebratory ways of enacting prettiness, it was just as riddled with contradictions. I listened to women act as cheerleaders for makeup as a place of play—while using words like *rules* and *no-nos* to describe their makeup routines. Same thing with economics: Plenty of feminists have long pointed out that our beauty standards also serve capitalist standards. Buy enough creams, enough potions, enough lipsticks and lip balms and lip stains and lip glosses and lip liners, and maybe you'll wriggle into the narrow space of conventional prettiness—filling corporate pockets all the while. Yet the beauty practices of countries with other economic systems show that beauty culture hardly forms a neat equation with capitalism as its sum. Croatian writer Slavenka Drakulić reported hearing from women all across the Eastern Bloc under the blanket of Communism, "Look at us—we don't even look like women. . . . There is no fine underwear, no pantyhose, no nice lingerie. . . . What can one say except that it is humiliating?" When I asked my fortysomething Albania-born hairstylist about how women's lives changed after the fall of Communism, she laughed. "Women finally had time to pay attention to their looks! With Communism, women had jobs but still did everything in the home—*everything*. There was no time to care about putting lotion on your skin." What many American women the same age were beginning to consider a burden, women behind the Iron Curtain were longing for the time and tools to indulge in.

Eventually it became hard to find *any* way that beauty shaped women's lives without bursting with contradictions. Were we jealous of our particularly pretty friends? Not once we'd entered adulthood, for the most part— but the awareness of the possibility of envy still hovered like a shadow around many a female friendship. Did men really prize beauty as much as we'd been told? Studies reveal that many men *say* they do—but the truth of who winds up with whom is way more complicated than that. And the media (oh, the media!)—since I first began working in women's magazines, I'd seen those publications take a pretty strong beating from

Internet critics. The new line of thinking: Women's magazines were unrealistic, promoting perfect bodies that only Photoshop could achieve, leaving the rest of us feeling like dump trucks. I applauded this critique, but I also had to wonder why women kept buying ladymags and visiting like-minded websites if they just made us feel bad about ourselves. Did our self-loathing really run that deep, or was the new critique just as simplistic as the "10 Days to a Flat Belly" cover lines we were now jeering?

Some of these opposing story lines boil down to sexist stereotypes versus real, live people. More often, though, the contradictions come from women themselves. In fact, contradiction itself, not any sort of streamlined manifesto, is the marker of how so many women regard beauty. And these contradictions aren't lies—or if they are, they're lies of omission, a shearing of the sensations and experiences that don't fit into an acceptable narrative. There is plenty of overlap between what women "should" feel about beauty and what they reported to me. But there is a barrier too—apologies for saying something that "might be weird" or prefacing an opinion with "maybe it's just me." Women are easily able to articulate what is expected from them about beauty—both in their acquiescence to the beauty standard and in their critiques of it. But the "weird" little pockets of their relationship with appearance that aren't seamlessly integrated into the story? This is where so many women stumble.

We as a culture have become fantastic at identifying the troublesome aspects of beauty, and we're getting better at fighting it too. Hawk-eyed Internet critics in particular have shined a light on the ways the need to be pretty is reinforced from every angle. Sites like *Jezebel* call attention to the issue with such regularity that some skeptics have begun to call clickbait (witness the controversy over the site's 2014 offer of $10,000 to the first person to send along unretouched photos from Lena Dunham's *Vogue* shoot). Dismantling the beauty standard with these direct critiques is necessary, but it is not enough. Going at it again and again with a head-on approach risks forming a groove that doesn't allow for the richness of the ways women regard beauty in our everyday lives. It entrenches the idea that our relationship with beauty is something we must overcome. It allows us to talk of our experiences in terms of a therapeutic victory

("I didn't like how I looked but now I do"), obscuring the more complex, often contradictory truths that lie underneath.

Other writers have done a worthy job of directly, and brilliantly, attacking the rigidity of the beauty imperative. With this book, I want you to take a more roundabout approach with me. Let's ask not only the obvious questions about beauty but also the questions that form the foundation of our connection to it: questions of intimacy, politicization, identity. And let's look at the contradictions too. Only once we can acknowledge beauty's power to both hurt and heal, to both pit us against others and bond us together, to drain our energy and to amplify it, can we successfully loosen the hold that the beauty standard exerts on us.

Rigorous conversations about the ways beauty shapes us—conversations that I hope this book will trigger—can help us come to a more thorough understanding of what aspects of our relationship with our appearance we want to keep, and what we want to discard. It's not like the goal is to get rid of beauty culture wholesale—after all, we humans have been trying to make ourselves look better for millennia. While aspects of beauty culture are undeniably problematic, particularly for women, the reason we've kept our pots of makeup around is that on some level, it serves us. Decoding our connection to beauty ensures it will serve us better, and in ways that go beyond simply feeling better about putting on a little rouge (though it can do that too). For example, once we understand the connection between looks and love, we can use beauty as a barometer of romantic satisfaction if it suits us. Developing an appropriate skepticism about beauty science can fine-tune our reading of *all* pop-science data, particularly that surrounding gender. Taking an unblinking look at what we get out of sharing selfies can allow us to post without embarrassment—or to start looking away from the screen if we learn we're searching for something more than a quick "like."

Plenty of us have learned to tell a certain story about our relationship with beauty. As you read the following pages, I ask you to challenge those stories. There's no need to forget your beauty narrative, even if you could, but consider it from a different angle. By learning how other women experience beauty's influence in their everyday lives—their friendships, their romances, their late-night Internet surfing sessions, what they take away from flipping through a glossy magazine at the doctor's office, even something as pedestrian as the words they choose when offering a compliment to another woman—you might find echoes of yourself. You have lived a lifetime of being looked at; you've had your own struggles and pride and realizations and transformations surrounding appearance, each of which has left an imprint on you. Now it's time for you to do the looking.

I urge you to do that looking with me here through examining the base of your relationship to beauty, which goes far deeper than questioning how much makeup you wear or how pretty you feel today. Questions of beauty and friendship, beauty and language, and beauty and love are hardly tangential. They're veins that carry us to beauty's beating heart.

1

The Pencil Test

Quantifying the Unquantifiable

It *should* be a long story as to why I found myself standing with nickels between my upper thighs, knees, calves, and ankles. But the story isn't long at all: I'd read that the ability to hold coins at these juncture points (and not, of course, at any other place along your shapely gams) was a way to determine whether you had nice legs. I've also lain a ruler from my rib cage to my pelvic bone to see if the ruler touches my belly flesh (if it does, your middle could supposedly use some slimming), measured the distance between my eyes (it "should" be equidistant to the length of one eye), walked in wet sand to see how close together my right and left footsteps fall ("try walking with your feet closer together for a sexy sway!"), and placed a pencil underneath my breast to determine whether I was sagging yet (*ahem*). I'd collected these tidbits pretty much unintentionally, through reading magazines and books primarily aimed at women. I knew none of these algorithms were definitive, and that some were downright capricious (didn't the thigh gap controversy indicate that having nice legs meant *not* being able to hold a coin between your thighs?), but seeing an unambiguous measure of beauty written down in black and white immediately made me want to test what I was made of. I'd like to be able to report that I tested myself in these ways to prove their folly—I mean, what grown woman actually lies down with a ruler across her hips just because a magazine told her to? It wasn't that, though. I wanted to see if I passed.

Perhaps it seems like inverted logic to try to objectively measure qualities based in sensory appreciation, not facts and figures. In a way, though, that was exactly the point. Regardless of whatever truth it might contain, there's something unsatisfactory about that whole "eye of the beholder" bit. It's so assuring, so *nice*, so subjective. But beauty as a lived experience doesn't always *feel* subjective, particularly when you suspect you're lacking in it. A strictly subjective approach—eye of the beholder, whatever floats your boat, to each her own, and so on—can feel pat, even dismissive. The term *beautiful woman* may conjure a thousand different women, but who hasn't been curious to know whether the average person would place her among those ranks? A yes/no answer to beauty, which all my little tests purported to issue, was both reassuring and provocative. With a test, the question was out of my hands, as well as the hands of those who might be favorably biased or dubious about my allure. It now belonged to an objective third party, one that didn't care about aesthetics or the beholder but rather just the facts, ma'am. Beauty was now in the hands of science.

In 2013 alone, researchers conducted thousands of studies involving personal appearance. Whether in the "hard" sciences ("Influence on Smile Attractiveness of the Smile Arc in Conjunction with Gingival Display"), the "soft" sciences ("The Effects of Facial Beauty in Personnel Selection"), or somewhere in between ("Middle Temporal Gyrus Encodes Individual Differences in Perceived Facial Attractiveness"), few aspects of beauty have escaped researchers' investigations. While some of these studies have a distinctly contemporary feel, inquiries into the aesthetics of us Homo sapiens are hardly new. From the Aristotelian concept of the golden mean and its role in human beauty to the supposedly ideal human proportions of Leonardo da Vinci's *Vitruvian Man* to the "Anthropometric Laboratory" of Charles Darwin's cousin Sir Francis Galton, researchers have longed to pair rationality with beauty.

It's not that scientists are any more intrigued by beauty than the rest of us; the discipline's fascination with appearance echoes that of the population at large. What separates the scientist from the layperson is, ironically, the very thing that might help us reconcile the science of beauty with our lived experience: an understanding that science is conditional. Scientists tend to position their work as one contribution to a larger body of knowledge, as opposed to establishing a pure fact in and of itself—and as research in any one area develops, so too must our baseline understanding of that field. After all, the brightest scientific minds on earth once believed in spontaneous generation (the idea that, say, flies grew from rotting meat or moths from neglected clothes). It was observable fact. Today, of course, we understand this to be an example of how the "facts" of science can shift with our knowledge—but we might still be loath to apply that understanding to the "facts" of today. Yet when it comes to something as loaded and intensely personal as beauty, that's an understanding we must keep in mind if we're to make any sense out of the sea of data that's been collected on the way we look. At its best, the science of beauty may be able to illuminate why we find beauty where we do. But its lingering contribution may be the mere fact of its existence: The enormous pool of data tells us that we're eager—verging on desperate—to understand beauty and its draws. The fact that we keep searching for answers within the sciences indicates that we're unwilling to settle for easy, clichéd answers about the human drive for beauty.

Numbers Don't Lie (Right?)

Beauty is a concept, not a fact. But unlike with other concepts such as justice, truth, and honor, we believe that if we just investigate beauty thoroughly enough, we can come up with an objective measure of it. And in some ways, these measures can actually help us relieve beauty of some of its weight. The idea that beauty is an ineffable mystery is in many ways a misogynist trap, a way of circumscribing women to the realm of the mystical instead of allowing them to roam on terra firma, warts and all. This matter-of-fact approach characterizes the work of psychologist Nancy Etcoff, who probably didn't intend to drive legions of women to their tape measures and calculators with her work. Her 1999 book, *Survival of the Prettiest*, published eight years after *The Beauty Myth*, served as a response to Naomi Wolf's claim that the beauty imperative was a social construct meant to curb women's growing power in the world. Etcoff, an award-winning researcher and Harvard instructor, took a different tack, attempting to demonstrate that our conception of beauty is hardwired within us. The human eye, she argues, is drawn to physical characteristics that supposedly signal prime ability to propagate the species. Symmetrical bodies and facial features, the female waist-hip ratio of the classic hourglass figure, clear skin: All these, Etcoff explains, are tied to health and fertility. The entire human race finds these attributes beautiful not because anyone tells us to but because our Darwinian drive to reproduce propels us toward them. "[O]ur thoughts and our behaviors are ultimately under our control," Etcoff takes pains to make clear, but we simply can't help what our eye is drawn to.

The book made a splash, garnering favorable reviews from leading news outlets and going through several printings. It also gave women a scale they could use to measure aspects of their own beauty. When I asked around, I wasn't surprised to find that I wasn't the only woman who, upon learning the evolutionarily preferred waist-hip ratio (an hourglassy 0.70, for the record), did a few quick calculations. Turns out my hips are a hint too small for me to propagate the species (one could also say my waist is a hint too thick, but I'm happy to play my own spin doctor here), leaving me feeling somewhat as thirty-eight-year-old Cara did upon doing the same thing: "Not only was I not close to the ideal, but I wasn't even sure I was doing the math right! I felt more stereotypically stupid than evolutionarily beautiful."

But for every woman whose waistline theoretically destines her to dateless Saturday nights, there's another who learns she's been blessed with the perfect proportions. "I calculated my ratio in college after I read about it in a magazine, and it turns out my ratio was damn near perfect," reports Aliyah, thirty-five, a math teacher in the Pacific Northwest. "It was the first concrete reason I could find to help explain to myself why on earth men suddenly seemed to find me more attractive than I'd ever found myself, having grown up far from any beauty ideal. It was the beginning of a slow, decade-long shift in my perception about my physical self. And I think I allowed myself to believe it because it wasn't subjective. It was math."

The biological basis of beauty has, in the public mind, become fact. And why wouldn't it? Unlike *The Beauty Myth*, there were ostensibly no political underpinnings to *Survival of the Prettiest*; this is *science*, people, entirely based on facts and figures, arrived at by people whose worldview is shaped around impartiality and objectivity. I mean, you can't argue with the data, right?

Yet plenty of researchers have done just that, with data of their own, bringing into question the supposed facts about beauty that we've come to accept as truth. Let's look at one of the most oft-repeated claims about beauty: that facial symmetry is integral to good looks. In 1994 university researchers—including Judith Langlois, one of the field's preeminent scholars—found that while a degree of symmetry is a component of attractiveness, "symmetry does not solely determine perceived attractiveness in a range of normal faces with no craniofacial deformities." So if you're noticeably lopsided, your chances of stopping traffic dwindle, but the rest of us are doing all right even if our right eye is a couple of millimeters higher than our left. Langlois and her colleagues were hardly alone; at least two other studies the same year reached similar conclusions.

Another given of female beauty—the much-vaunted 0.70 waist-to-hip ratio (WHR)—turns out not to be such a given after all, once the data is examined more closely. The pioneering study on WHR, Devendra Singh's 1993 longitudinal survey of the measurements of *Playboy* centerfolds and Miss Americas, found that the overwhelming majority of the women's WHR fell within .02 points of 0.70. The study was widely reported, including in outlets such as *Newsweek*, *Time*, and even the *Weekly World News*, opposite a piece about blood banks for vampires.

Yet according to researchers Jeremy Freese and Sheri Meland, the study is an "academic urban legend." Upon examining Singh's data in 2002, Freese and Meland found that the 1993 study omitted nearly a third of all *Playboy* centerfolds from the years studied (1955 to 1965 and 1976 to 1990). Singh attributed this to unavailability of data; indeed, Freese and Meland found access to the missing measurements on the Internet, which was in its infancy at the time of Singh's research. As for the pageant contestants, the data had been rounded to the nearest half inch by Singh's primary source—insignificant when buying a pair of jeans, but quite significant when calculating specific waist-hip ratios to within 1/100 of an inch and drawing conclusions from the data. When *all* the measurements were accounted for and recorded accurately, the results didn't match those of the initial study. Only nine of the fifty-nine pageant winners had the WHR Singh claimed dominated the pool; similarly, only 31.4 percent of the centerfolds fell between the WHR of .68 and .71. Moreover, Singh had claimed that WHRs remained constant over time, even if the actual measurements themselves changed due to fluctuating fashions in women's body size. Freese and Meland found that the measurements *and* the ratio changed: The classic girdled 1950s look was reflected in the lower WHR of the measurements from the mid-twentieth century; as the years passed, the ratio increased. (Think the undulating Jayne Mansfield versus the willowy Gwyneth Paltrow.) Other researchers also found results contrary to the original report. And despite interpretations of Singh's research that claimed female WHR was more important than the overall size of a woman's body in attracting men, in 1998 psychologists at Texas A&M University found that weight and relative body size mattered more to men than waist-hip ratio, findings echoed in numerous other studies—including cross-cultural studies that skewer the notion that there's such a thing as a universally attractive WHR.

Let's also not forget that some of the data may have been artificially manipulated: Measurements of the *Playboy* centerfolds were self-reported. As Freese and Meland point out, this theoretically works in favor of Singh's conclusion, since centerfolds would have incentive to fudge their measurements to fit a preconceived ideal (36-24-36, anyone?). But that's just it: If the models are reporting dimensions to conform to a predetermined ideal, so too would the conclusion drawn from that data.

And yet the idea that there's a perfect waist-to-hip ratio has filtered into women's own beauty preconceptions—I've seen it referenced again and again, with little regard for these counterarguments. (A headline from *Glamour*'s website: "Dressing for Men? Avoid the Empire Waist," the idea being that "At all times, they want to see your 0.7 waist-to-hip ratio a la Cindy Crawford.")

The list of popular beauty maxims challenged by various researchers doesn't stop at WHR, of course. Have you heard that babies gaze longer at faces rated attractive by adults? This doesn't necessarily imply that children are born with innate knowledge of attractiveness per se—it could be that conventionally attractive faces are just more face-like because of their regularity, so babies seize onto them more readily. Or how about the one that says that the average face is considered the most attractive? Scientists in 1999 found that *actual* faces, as opposed to computer-generated composite faces, with features close to the mean size of populations studied were usually rated as average in attractiveness, not highly attractive. The "average is beautiful" effect applies only to generated composite faces, in which one person's flaws are canceled out by another's; in truth, the average face is, well, average. Then there's the study that ostensibly proves most people are attracted to faces that exemplify stereotypically masculine or feminine traits—that we prefer girlie girls and manly men. In truth, the relationship remains unclear at best: Clinically speaking, a woman who prefers a jaw of stone when she's at her most fertile might gravitate toward a more baby-faced man once she's past that stage of her menstrual cycle. Underneath many of these studies is a fact that's problematic for *all* sciences: The majority of people who participate in studies about appearance preferences are undergraduate students at the universities hosting the research—students who are disproportionately educated and middle-class. It's like studying a campus on Saturday night and determining that North America's favorite recreational activity involves beer bongs.

The social sciences get even murkier. Economist Daniel Hamermesh made waves in 2011 by analyzing five earlier studies measuring the impact of looks on life satisfaction and happiness. Of the five studies used, four relied on attractiveness ratings furnished by *one person*. That is, the bulk of the data about what constitutes beauty in this widely reported aggregate study was decided by one person alone. In one of them, the people doing the rating were elementary schoolteachers rating their own seven- and eleven-year-old students. In the lone study that had multiple people rating subjects' attractiveness, a panel of twelve people based their assessments on high school graduation photos taken thirty-five years prior.

It's troubling that a major study proclaiming the connection between beauty and happiness boils down to the opinion of only a handful of people, so a logical solution would appear to be to follow the scientific model and have beauty quantified by a larger pool of respondents. Surely if forty people rate a number of faces, we can trust that we're getting an accurate opinion by consensus, right? Perhaps, but that solution also presents a paradox of beauty research: When a large number of people rate beauty, the prevailing result is going to be *what we as a culture have agreed is beautiful*, not necessarily beauty as we experience it individually. At best it captures the average of beauty, not beauty itself. These studies are of conventional attractiveness, which may be related to beauty but doesn't constitute the fascination, intrigue, and sheer pleasure of the latter. Even the truth behind the "average is beautiful" fallacy of beauty—that computerized composite images made of several individual faces are consistently found more attractive than most individual faces—supports this. A composite face may be appealing because it is *familiar*, not because it is riveting.

And let's not forget that our perception of good looks may be more fickle than we'd like to believe. A 2011 report in *Psychological Science* demonstrated that men who had rated pictures of women on their looks were apt to change their ratings after seeing what they believed to be their peers' estimation of the women's beauty. And no, the men weren't just caving to peer pressure; MRI scans showed that the responses of their brains' pleasure centers were neurologically altered upon seeing other men's assessments. We may all have our preferences that stay level throughout our lives, but the fact that other people can so directly influence our brains' recognition of beauty makes it seem ever more like a construct, not a biological given.

At day's end, beauty is all about what gives us a visceral pleasure and fascination—so to a degree, what we collectively determine is beautiful really *is* beautiful. And it's not like we should look at the conflicting evidence about physical appeal and decide to throw it all out wholesale. (If anything, the contradictions contained within the science of beauty can serve as a guide to being appropriately skeptical of any science that attempts to classify human behavior by sex and gender.) Much of this research has its place in helping us understand why we humans do what we do—an endeavor that becomes all the more intriguing when investigating something as intangible as beauty. In fact, the enormous number of studies on attractiveness makes me wonder if the shroud of mystery that surrounds beauty is exactly what makes us want to decode it. Is it possible that beauty is seen as so genuinely powerful that we're willing to spend enormous resources on its investigation? Or is it that we're hungry to figure out whether beauty is as meritocratic as the beauty industry would have us believe (try hard enough, buy enough products, and you can be beautiful too!)—or if Mother Nature has retained her aristocracy by doling it out unevenly, and we've just got to learn to accept the facts?

Monkey See, Monkey Want: Attraction, Feminism, and Evolutionary Psychology

If Mother Nature has been doling out beauty unequally, evolutionary psychologists believe there's a pattern in the cards. As applied to beauty and attractiveness, the ev-psych theory goes something like this: In order to ensure that the human species stays strong, evolution has given us an innate preference for traits that indicate fertility and a strong likelihood of health and longevity. Those traits are the ones that have remained more or less steadily seen as appealing through time and across cultures—curvy hips on women, height in men, thick hair on everyone. The idea is that these attributes function as advertisements for reproductive fitness, and we can't help but be attracted to them.

Let's leave aside for the moment the potential shakiness of some of those findings due to research flaws, as described earlier. And let's also assume that the fact that narrow-hipped women and acne-prone men are able to reproduce just fine simply means that evolution is forgiving. Instead, let's look at the base premise here: that certain facets of beauty reliably advertise health. As with other scientific findings on beauty, this isn't necessarily airtight. In fact, a 1998 study reveals that while there is a modest correlation between people's health and health as perceived through attractiveness scoring, the relationship between perceived health and attractiveness far outweighed the actual connection between the two. That is, we *think* beautiful people are healthier than they are. It's a perfect example of how we retrofit ev-psych theories to conform to what we already believe, regardless of how much the grain of truth within might actually shape our mating choices. We may take comfort in the findings of evolutionary psychology because they confirm what we already believe.

Plenty of feminists would argue that whatever comfort stems from evolutionary psychology is a masquerade for comfort with the status quo. Indeed, evolutionary psychology at its worst has put forth theories that, even generously interpreted, aren't so friendly to the ladies—for example, the idea that rape is an unfortunate but natural behavior (man needs to spread his seed, after all). But even less loaded research, such as that surrounding beauty, is sometimes hardly satisfactory. Dr. Satoshi Kanazawa of the London School of Economics caused a bona fide shitstorm in 2011 when he published a blog post on *Psychology Today*'s website about his findings that women of African descent were objectively less attractive than white and Asian women. Kanazawa had published plenty of controversial research before—for example, a study indicating that attractive parents were likelier to produce female offspring than unattractive parents were—but it wasn't until the subject of race was introduced that protests began. And begin they did: The student union called for his dismissal, thousands signed a petition demanding that *Psychology Today* cease publishing that sort of article, and sixty-eight of his colleagues published an open letter distancing the field of evolutionary psychology from Kanazawa's work. He was let go from *Psychology Today*, temporarily banned by his employer from publishing in non-peer-reviewed outlets, and, perhaps most important, made to publicly acknowledge that this particular bit of research "may have been flawed," though he continues to evoke "political correctness" as the motivation behind those questioning his research. (Kanazawa declined to be interviewed for this book.)

The fiasco was a heightened example of the clash between feminism and evolutionary psychology. To a degree, this clash is inevitable. Feminists have worked for decades to show that sexism is a learned trait, and therefore a malleable one; introducing Darwin into the mix offers little more than a shoulder shrug to sexism, because, hey, it's in our genes, whatcha gonna do?

At an even more basic level, evolutionary psychology is concerned with accounting for what exists—like sex-based power imbalances—while feminism is concerned with both accounting for what exists and finding ways within the existing system to deepen women's perceived value and power. Put a shade antagonistically, feminism has an agenda. That agenda may at times include questioning or even dismissing evolutionary psychology, at least when it comes to the public's understanding of it. The public at large is already fairly entrenched in centuries of sexist attitudes and behaviors, so offering a biological explanation for those attitudes—especially when much of the public lacks a nuanced understanding of the sciences and may take research as more black-and-white than the researchers intended—can appear to justify malevolent attitudes toward women.

Yet just as with politicians and televangelists, it's the extremists among evolutionary psychologists who garner the most attention, while more moderate practitioners simply continue doing work that may lead to a synthesis of feminism, sociology, biological anthropology, and evolutionary psychology in understanding beauty. "At one point, evolutionary psychologists were sort of putting these controversial theories out there, but the field has [started] reining that in, and most practitioners have a more moderate stance," says Dr. David Perrett, a professor of psychology at the University of St Andrews in Scotland, whose research has focused on facial attributes, including attractiveness (his own book on the science of attraction, *In Your Face*, isn't entirely based in evolutionary psychology, but it touches on the field). "Attraction is enormously complex. [Evolutionary psychologists] aim to better understand one particular aspect of attraction, but our lived experience tells us that it's only one part of the whole. Sociology comes into play, culture comes into play, our learned behaviors come into play."

In fact, there is a growing number of practitioners who are aiming to show that a scientific approach to questions surrounding gender—including attraction and appearance—needn't be incompatible with feminism. Dr. Kathryn Clancy of the University of Illinois is an anthropologist, not an evolutionary psychologist, but she studies the evolutionary medicine of women's reproductive physiology. She's quick to point out that there's evolutionary psychology, and then there's *bad* evolutionary psychology—and that it's the latter that's problematic. "The reason that bad ev-psych is more likely to ignore human variables—like flexibility of environment, social behavior—is because the field's principle is to look for universality. If you're looking for ways in which all humans are the same, culture is going to really screw that up. Yet at the same time, people who do pay attention to those perspectives come up with these really beautiful, rich perspectives on how humans came to be. Culture is also biology." A comprehensive view of human evolution would encompass our lives as social creatures and a potential mate's suitability in areas that will help us not only propagate the species but make it thrive—communication skills, say, or intelligence. The wealth of factors that make a person *appealing* to us, not just physically beautiful, have a place in the ev-psych conversation.

What's more, bad evolutionary psychology sometimes—ironically enough—overlooks some aspects of evolution. "When we have just one perspective on one behavior of the suite of behaviors known to humans in a particular population, and we identify that behavior as the dominant one—the one most supported by evidence to give the most reproductive success—that crowds out the fact that that's not how evolution works," Dr. Clancy says. "There are always multiple, competing strategies, and this constellation of strategies is how we understand the richness of human behaviors. It's a lot easier to understand the richness of female responses to male strategies and vice versa when we understand that there are a lot of different phenotypes [observable traits resulting from genetics as well as environmental factors] instead of just the ones that women get lumped into." Evolutionary psychology can make for some glamorous conclusions, but like any discipline, it can be narrow in scope. Were women's waist-hip ratios definitively found to be an evolutionary boon to the species, that would be only one pixel in the larger picture that explains why we are the way we are.

Still, even when looking at ways that a more comprehensive view of ev-psych can comfortably exist alongside feminism, there's something deflating about this particular discipline. As a feminist who came of age in a nascent era of girl power, one of the core tenets of my upbringing was that

I could do anything I put my mind to. Put aside, for the moment, the more insidious aspects of ev-psych: Being told that there's just not that much we can *do* to be more beautiful—well, it's a passive, painful thought, and one with few antidotes.

So it's interesting to peruse some of the offshoot studies that stem from evolutionary psychology that might—*might*—offer, if not solace, at least the knowledge that some of the findings on beauty indicate it's not necessarily *all* out of our hands. Etcoff herself led a 2011 study on people's perception of varying makeup styles, showing that, among other findings, moderate cosmetics use makes women appear more likable and trustworthy. At first glance this is in the realm of neither feminism nor evolutionary psychology—not least because it spurs on the idea that women "should" wear makeup—but it pertains to both. The study's authors position makeup as an "extended phenotype," or genetic properties that extend beyond an organism's body (like the shell of a hermit crab or a spiderweb). Seen this way, makeup becomes an emblem not of vanity but of survival. That may seem like a dramatic term to describe swiping on some lipstick, but it goes some way toward explaining the fraught relationship many women have with cosmetics. Same thing with a 2008 study on how women's eyes and lips are darker than men's in contrast with skin tone; by using cosmetics on the eyes and lips, perhaps women aren't just passively embodying patriarchal notions of femininity but amplifying traits that signal their supposed femaleness.

I'm not about to argue that it's fair, or feminist, that today's artificial manipulation of the face and body is largely left to women, regardless of how loudly our Neolithic selves may be asking for just a *hint* of lipstick. Nor am I about to argue that makeup worn for biological reasons should somehow get a pass that it wouldn't if it were merely a creation of the Maybelline marketing department. But I will argue that studies that touch on the role of human agency within the confines of evolutionary biology may blaze a path toward potential compatibility between varying disciplines. The better our understanding of the complex matrix of attraction and beauty—incorporating biological drive, psychological incentives, cultural preferences, personal eccentricities and desires, popular imagery, and social and political mores—the better all of us will be able to critique, and eventually dismantle, the more troublesome parts of the beauty puzzle.

"Tell Us a Story": The Pitfalls of Science Journalism

"Can Being Attractive Make You Bad at Math?" blazed a 2011 headline at *NewBeauty*. The story was the same one heralded by *Psych Central* as "Are Good Looks Problematic for Women?" The answer, according to the pieces, was yes. But the study detailed in these pieces had literally *nothing* to do with how good-looking women are. It measured the effects of objectification: Study participants took a math quiz, and some of the female participants had been intentionally gawked at by a male "study partner" before taking it. Unsurprisingly, the women who had been subject to a leering gaze didn't do as well as women who were allowed to take the test in peace. But *nowhere* in the study were participants' looks measured. The entire premise of the two headlines simply didn't exist.

So here's a study that takes a stab at understanding the day-to-day impact of the male gaze, a classic feminist issue—yet the outcome was misrepresented in ways that reinforce stereotypes about women. And plenty of other studies examine biological, cultural, psychological, anthropological, and sociological factors in an attempt to form a holistic view of beauty—so why is that bounty frequently absent from the journalism on the subject of beauty science?

Part of the answer here rests in your Facebook feed. Journalists, particularly in an era when a story's page views may be taken into account when paying writers, are skilled in crafting attention-grabbing headlines and takeaways. At their best, these takeaways make for reader-friendly, high-traffic stories . . . and at their worst, they fall into the realm of sensationalist clickbait. And what's more sensational than seeming evidence that some of us are more beautiful than others—and therefore happier, better paid, and better laid? Responsible journalists incorporate flash into headlines that remain accurate, but sometimes we end up with just plain old bad reporting or bad headline writing.

But the crux of the oft-poor translation of science via media lies not within the world of science, or within the world of reportage, but in the uncomfortable pairing of the two. Laypeople depend on cultural translators like reporters to help them understand and assimilate scientists' findings—which, when the journalist is trained to accurately relay the experiment's implications, doesn't present a problem. But just as the average reader doesn't necessarily have the tools or background to place scientific findings in a broader context, the average journalist isn't necessarily trained in science reportage either. That's how we wind up with headlines like "More Beautiful Than Most? Your Higher Salary Makes You Happier" (the study established a correlation, not causation, invalidating the phrase *makes you happier*), "Beauty and Its Neural Reward Are in the Eye of the Crowd" (the study was about how the brain calculates *value*, not beauty), and "A Perfect Body? Women Would Swap a Year of Life" (more than two-thirds of women in the survey said they *wouldn't*).

David Brown, physician and twenty-four-year veteran reporter for *The Washington Post*, gave a 2008 lecture at the University of Iowa identifying key concerns about science reporting. First, he says, American journalists (and, I'd argue, the general public) are often intimidated by the sciences. Because of an undereducation in technical areas, journalists may revere scientists and are, as Brown pointed out, "often unwilling to bring their own natural (and legendary) skepticism to scientific topics." That is, writers often put aside their own "lived experience," which Perrett refers to as being key to his own understanding of the importance of beauty research. Second, journalists may conceive of science as being more black-and-white than it actually is. Third, journalists are trained to find authority figures to comment on events, whereas scientific findings specifically do *not* rely on commentary. The practice is evidence based, not political.

But the biggest obstacle to a healthier flow of strong science journalism may be one of writing's basic tenets. One of the things journalism students are repeatedly told is to find the *story* within any body of evidence or research. The idea is that the human mind craves a linear tale in order to make sense of the strands any one mess of information has to offer. Paint a picture for the reader, and the piece makes a stronger impact. "But for science writing, [narrative] is a hazardous form," said Brown. "Why? Because the narrative form makes an anecdote evidence." In the case of beauty research, the temptation to tease out a narrative may be downright irresistible—after all, looks are powerful enough to impact each of our own personal narratives in one way or another. The role of physical appearance can be so loaded with emotion that we'll do quite a bit to tease out a story line that explains its importance. Hence a single study on the ideal waist-hip ratio goes from an account of an actual study to a paean to supermodels and a tsk-tsk to women whose waistlines aren't deemed evolutionarily fit. Research based on women's perceptions of beauty is even more rife with narrative possibilities. For a reporter, a single experiment testing women's body image after exposure to idealized images becomes a chance to address far more than the study; it can quickly become a buffet of commentary on eating disorders, Photoshop, and the diseased relationship American women supposedly have with glossy magazines. In other words, it becomes evidence of a crisis, which makes for more intriguing journalism than the review of a single study of thirty-three white college students. A study is not a story. But humans have an urge to create a story out of an anecdote in order to understand its potential. And if crafting stories is your job, that urge becomes an imperative. A story is what readers want to read, and what writers try to tell.

The Science of Looks: Retro Edition

If evolutionary psychology has a public-relations problem, it's no different from a past field that linked appearance to other personal traits. Physiognomy, or the pseudoscience of assessing one's character through appearance—specifically the face—was invented by the ancient Greeks and was popular off and on throughout history until the nineteenth century. Firm lips signaled a firm character, weak lips a weak one; a retreating forehead was a sign of superior wit, and so on. Read today, the specific codes of physiognomy are laughably unscientific. Witness this passage on unibrows from Johann Kaspar Lavater, a Swiss pastor who became the field's authority with the 1775 publication of his book on the craft: "Meeting eyebrows, held so beautiful by the Arabs . . . I can neither believe to be beautiful, nor characteristic of such a quality. . . . [They] perhaps denote trouble of mind and heart."

Physiognomy wasn't necessarily about beauty per se; the point was to measure character, not aesthetic charms. Still, generally speaking, a good character was held to be reflected in an aesthetically pleasing face—and poor character manifested itself in the reverse. Lavater also took care to spell out the characteristics necessary for features to qualify as beautiful—a nose viewed in profile shouldn't exceed in width more than one-third its length, for example. Yet when reading the precision with which Lavater treated his diagnoses, it's hard not to be reminded of the exactness used by scientists studying beauty to describe their own subjects today. The careful measurement of waist-hip ratios, the anthropometrics of what constitutes facial symmetry, the assignation of numbers to rank photographs of people: The modern science of beauty parallels physiognomy, even if the disciplines purport to have different aims. And given that we overattribute certain characteristics to lovely appearances—including, as we have seen, physical health—it's not out of the realm of possibility to think that the science of beauty as we know it today might eventually wind up being viewed as we now regard physiognomy. It might be happening already, actually. In one of the studies disputing Singh's findings on the waist-hip ratio, the authors concluded, "We . . . suspect the WHR, not unlike the golden section or the grand mean, will eventually be understood to be a dimensionless number with great intuitive appeal but with highly circumscribed explanatory or predictive efficacy with respect to aesthetic judgments."

Not that everyone these days entirely disavows the possibilities of physiognomy. The pseudoscience is seeing a revival of sorts, with numerous researchers taking up the cause. While some studies simply test whether people make associations between physical and personality characteristics without measuring the accuracy of those associations, other experiments are explicitly designed to assess their veracity. Faces expressing introversion versus extroversion, openness to experience, and emotional stability— three of the Big Five in personality testing—were measured by British researchers (including Perrett) in 2006. A companion study looked at how desire for certain personality traits in a partner affected attraction (for example, if you like easygoing men, you'll be attracted to a different type of face than those who prefer their men a little more keyed up).

These modern incarnations aside, to most of us physiognomy seems like some sort of twisted parlor game. But at one point its importance went well beyond that. In 1878, Charles Darwin's cousin Sir Francis Galton started collecting and merging photographs of violent criminals in order to determine shared physiognomy among them. Not only did he become one of the first scientists to proclaim the "average is beautiful" maxim (he noted that the more faces added into a composite, the more appealing the result), he later began to wonder whether certain physical characteristics—and, correspondingly, their moral equivalents—could be eliminated through breeding. In 1883, Galton coined the word *eugenics*.

Even without the involvement of physiognomy, the testing and categorization of people has a historic link to eugenics. After all, one purpose of testing anything is to be able to divide and classify information, and once we get into dividing and classifying people, we tiptoe into dangerous territory. Consider in this light studies such as the 2011 one on the supposed unattractiveness of black women, and it begins to look less like political incorrectness and more like an alarm bell about where ranking human looks could lead. In fact, actual beauty contests—at least, the most well-known one, Miss America—started at the same time as the Fitter Family contest, an explicitly eugenics-minded competition in the 1920s that emphasized familial pedigrees (think the Westminster Dog Show, but for people). In the Miss America Pageant, the longer lasting and more popular of the two, contestants supposedly won not on beauty alone but also on charm, comportment, and, starting in 1935, talent. But Miss America took contestants' measurements, including those of the calf, upper and lower arms, wrist, thigh, ankle, and of course bust-waist-hip. Contestants' dimensions were recorded for posterity, and as with the 1993 waist-hip ratio study and its myriad offshoots, these were seen as a uniquely qualified measure of beauty. In another part of the hemisphere, not much later than the birth of Miss America, another group of specially selected citizens were also having their measurements recorded. The fascination with evaluating human bodies in Nazi Germany may have had a darker purpose than that of a group of Atlantic City suits trying to rally up some business, but the means remains uncomfortably similar regardless.

This is not to say that evolutionary psychology and its practitioners are necessarily eugenics-minded in any way. Indeed, most in the field are quick to point out that evolution can account for only so much of any human action or tendency. But the base concern remains: Measuring human beings on things they can neither help nor change contains an element of appraisal, and in such a situation it's near impossible to avoid introducing an assessment of human value. And once we introduce human value into the equation, isn't the next natural question, *How can we improve what we've already got?*

Hot or Not: Our Desire to Quantify Beauty

When I think through the various tests I've conducted on myself—pulling on strands of wet hair to see if it's thick enough to be considered "good," or tracing the reflection of my face in the mirror to determine, once and for all, if my face is round or oval—one in particular stands out. As I stood in my kitchen a few years ago placing a pencil underneath my breast, I remembered that I'd done this exact test before. Except that time I wasn't in my thirties and hoping the pencil would drop to prove my perkiness. No, the first time I'd conducted the pencil test I was eleven, and inspired by a tidbit in some teen novel, I was placing a pencil underneath my breast in the hopes that it would *stay put*. That, I'd learned, would mean I was developed enough to graduate to a *real* bra—maybe even the kind with wires!—instead of the stretchy training bra I'd donned since fourth grade.

It probably doesn't take a degree in women's studies to see the "damned if you do, damned if you don't" trap at play here. Standing there in my kitchen, I laughed out loud when I realized that I'd done the same thing twenty-odd years prior. It's ridiculous, right? This test was particularly ridiculous—I mean, what's the sweet spot? To indicate that its subject is properly breasted, should the pencil stay but shake loose after six seconds?

Dangle by the eraser? *Levitate?* But the test was just an exaggerated version of the problem with all these tests. I was looking for something concrete to provide a guideline of something aesthetic; I was searching for unassailable proof that some part of me was either acceptable or unacceptable. The result mattered, sure, but the true satisfaction came from merely *having* a result. I was looking to quantify something unquantifiable.

This desire to quantify beauty—to pin it down, put a number on it, check a yes/no box—is, I suspect, what lies at the base of the wealth of beauty science, both on the researchers' end and in the public eagerness for their findings. The wish to measure beauty is the logical follow-up to the wish to possess or embody it, and when treated cursorily, the sciences give us a veritable checklist against which we can measure our attractiveness. Once I know a defined standard exists, at some point I'm going to wonder how well I match it. I'm embarrassed to tell you that the first thing I did upon learning of the golden ratio that supposedly measures the perfect human face was find an online tool that would calculate how close my own features were to that ratio.

Rather, I'd be embarrassed to tell you about my calculation if I weren't surrounded by proof that I'm hardly alone. From the website Hot or Not to the iPhone app Model Potential (which tells you your chances of making it on the catwalk after you upload a photo of yourself and punch in your measurements) to the knowing nods I get whenever I mention the pencil test, it's clear that though plenty of people might eschew these admittedly ridiculous tests, a lot of us are hungry to know whether we're beautiful. And if all signs point to yes, the next logical question is, exactly how beautiful are we? We sometimes want a yes/no answer to queries that drive us to distraction; for all of that "eye of the beholder" stuff, sometimes we want firm, incontrovertible proof that we're pretty. We may even want proof that we're not.

Two women I know come to mind: a friend of mine who once pursued acting and a writer who goes by Charlotte Shane who also worked as an escort. On her first visit with an agent, my actress friend was told she wasn't pretty enough to be cast in the kind of roles that were appropriate for her age and stature. She reports it as being crushing—but also freeing.

"He sort of confirmed my worst fears, but from there it was like: *Well, now I know.* I didn't need to stress about it anymore—I had my answer." She quit performing shortly thereafter, a choice she says she doesn't regret. As for Shane, she told me about one of the reasons she first engaged in sex work: "In our culture, the majority of messages directed at women say: You're valuable for how you look. I think it's natural for most women to say, 'I want to know how much I'm worth in this world'—and that means, 'I want to know how much my looks are worth.' We're told we contribute by being attractive. How attractive am I? Am I attractive enough? Should I be more? *Could* I be more? There's a desire to quantify your appeal." An agent served as an expert opinion for the erstwhile actress, while the escort has an exact market price on her appeal, something she describes as "almost merciful"—a mercy few of us have. (Even if you accept the idea that men "buy" women's beauty by spending money on dates or gifts, it's still not as stark of a value assessment as actual money changing hands.) Science, with its waist-to-hip ratios and symmetrical features, may fulfill a similar function for the rest of us.

Parallel to the drive to quantify our beauty is a wish to distance ourselves from it, or at least separate it from our identity. Beauty is intensely personal, in both our relationship with our own looks and the way we see others. You know the throwaway phrase *nothing personal*? Putting a number on beauty makes it exactly that: nothing personal. Calculating our looks takes something that we embody and wrests it from judgment, whether our own or that of others. I didn't feel great after my waist-hip ratio revealed that I was hardly a top-notch specimen—but I also had a sense of relief upon seeing an actual number assigned to my figure. It wasn't that I wasn't *good* enough or pretty enough or thin enough. It was something definite, measurable, and more or less unchangeable—the ratio is no different now than it was when I was twenty pounds heavier—and casting it in these prewritten biological terms removed the sense of fault I'd previously had about my figure. Quantifying beauty erases opinion from the equation; it removes subjectivity from something that is inherently subjective.

Pinpointing the parameters of prettiness also removes our agency.

Normally I argue the need for women's exertion of personal power, and certainly it has a vital role in self-presentation. But with that agency comes responsibility—and with responsibility comes burden, at least sometimes. In the last century—particularly since the advent of feminism—the beauty industry has couched itself as a sort of secret weapon that any woman can use to enhance her looks, regardless of where she began on the scale of conventional attractiveness. But just because the beauty industry has attempted to democratize access to beauty doesn't mean that it *is* a democracy. The notion that beauty is something within our control also sets us up to believe that beauty is something we can fail at—don't hate her because she's beautiful, for you can be beautiful too. Maybe you're not trying hard enough. Introducing specific questions of beauty that can yield specific answers relieves us of that notion, of that burden of beauty. If science gives us relief from wondering where we fall on the scale, it also provides succor from the self-blame that accompanies failure. The research on attractiveness may not make us feel more or less appealing. But it can be a guidepost for where we want to focus our energies. My unsatisfactory waist-hip ratio didn't change how I felt about my waistline, but it *did* help me realize that there wasn't really much I could do about it. Did the energy I'd previously spent fretting over my belly suddenly go toward, say, learning Portuguese or developing my origami skills? Hardly. But having an answer was one little nudge toward freeing up the part of my brain that was devoted to chiding myself for not being quite enough in this particular way.

As your average seventh-grader learns in science class, one of the inherent characteristics of the practice of science is its requirement of isolating variables: the factors, traits, or conditions that are controlled or changed in an experiment. Experiments isolate variables so that they test only one at a time; an experiment on facial attractiveness might use head shots instead of full-body photographs in order to prevent participants from factoring below-the-neck appeal into their responses. In that vein, beauty researchers stress repeatedly that they are aiming not to define beauty itself but rather to define its physical characteristics. But because those characteristics must be defined in isolation from one another, the entity of beauty, which depends in part on the overall impression made, cannot itself be measured in its entirety. Even without introducing larger concepts like inner beauty or the relationship between beauty and charm (or beauty and love, or, for that matter, beauty and attraction), the very definition of beauty is that it's a quality or *aggregate of qualities* that is pleasing to the eye. Beauty science may indeed be able to someday tell us the exact waist-hip ratio that is "beautiful" or the exact distance between the eyes or the length of the nose in proportion to the mouth. But by its nature, it will never be able to tell us about the aggregate of qualities that each of us perceives as beauty. In fact, quantifying beauty can alert us to the places where we instinctually challenge beauty norms, revealing to ourselves that allure is more multifaceted than hitting all the right neurons. Talking with people about what they find appealing in others inevitably brings mentions of quirks. One friend of mine admits he's a sucker for "chicks in glasses"; another looks at what she calls "beard porn." Me, I've always been inexplicably drawn to men with acne scars from their youth. One man tells me that he's always been attracted to women who were larger than those his friends thought were hot. He points out that there is a sort of comfort in knowing what, and who, he finds beautiful. "My tastes are different than what's thrown at me as a guy, and I've always actually liked that," he says. "There's a lot of bullshit out there telling you what guys are supposed to like. You look at ads and half of them have these hot chicks trying to sell stuff to you because that's what businesses think my demographic likes. Knowing what I actually like, it sets me apart. It's not manipulated. My tastes are mine."

"Beauty can be looked at rationally, but it doesn't always *feel* rational," says Perrett. "It can drive humans to unimaginable things." The entire field of science sprang from the desire to make the irrational rational, to discover and explain what was once thought inexplicable. It's only logical that the people in a field that exists to demystify and classify knowledge would want to do just that with the ineffable essence of beauty. And it's just as logical that beauty's very ineffability ensures that it's an endeavor that can never be fulfilled.

2

Hotties, Foxes, and Cankles

Why We Use the Words We Do

My friend Sarah is decidedly not *cute*. Nearly six feet tall, alabaster-skinned, and possessing a face that would be at home alongside, say, Greta Garbo's, she still resembles the fashion model she briefly was in her teen years. Her modeling career was too short-lived to say in what niche she ultimately would have landed, but in my admittedly amateur view, of the ampersand brands, she's far more Dolce & Gabbana than Abercrombie & Fitch. Elegant, not peppy; classic, not trendy.

So when she relays this story revolving around the word *cute*, I understand its significance. Her husband had mentioned that an intern at his workplace had an obvious crush on him. He was more amused than troubled by this—it was harmless, even sweet, given that his devotion to Sarah (and to appropriate workplace conduct) precluded any inappropriate actions. But when Sarah met this intern at a work function, it was clear from her fawning—and touchy-feely—manner that the intern was taking her crush more seriously than Sarah's husband had realized.

Before we go any further, I should tell you that I first met Sarah through a feminist group. You'd be hard-pressed to find a fiercer advocate for women; she's the kind of woman who smiles at other women on the subway out of solidarity. Girl-on-girl cattiness isn't a part of her emotional vocabulary, at least not that I've ever witnessed. That said, like most women, she's seen plenty of cattiness, so when it came time for her to bare her claws, she knew what to do. "For the next work function, I went all out. I *worked it*. I put on my highest-cut shorts, did the whole pinup-girl hair and makeup. I wanted jaws to drop, you know?" Did I mention Sarah is a fashion designer? She's trained in the art of creating an effect; without having seen the outfit, I'm sure she looked like a Vargas pinup girl.

"So I'm standing at the bar, and this girl comes up to me, and she says, 'Sarah, you look *so cute*.' She used it like a dagger—*cute*. It was like she wanted to diminish me, diminish my importance to my husband, brush me aside. It was this clear attempt to belittle me. *Cute*." Sarah's lip visibly curls at this point, as if to embody the antithesis of cuteness: *threat*.

I thought of this story when another friend, telling me why she wore shapewear despite its discomfort, said, "If I'm wearing a dress without it, I just don't look as *cute*." I think of it when I hear myself utter it about a friend's shoes, dress, or earrings: "*Cute!*" I thought of it when a boyfriend, after having met my mother, said she was *cute*. I thought of it when, at a party at a ritzy address, I overheard a young doorman directly tell one of the building tenants—a soft-featured woman who looked no younger than eighty—that she was *cute*. For in each of these distinctly different instances, *cute*—ostensibly a complimentary term—had a covert meaning.

I'm guessing that any word to come out of that intern's mouth about Sarah's appearance would have taken on the sheen of malice. Yet she didn't choose just any word; she chose *cute*. My squeezed-into-shapewear friend favors a rock-and-roll aesthetic, complete with tattoos and heavy eyeliner. She's never aimed to look *cute* in her life, but it was as if calling herself the way she actually wanted to appear—*sexy*, perhaps, or *dramatic, striking*, or, for that matter, *beautiful*—was a step too far. Better to play it safe with *cute*. When I think back to some of the items I've squealed over as being "cute"—a pair of rainbow-striped platform heels beloved by a coworker, a ring featuring a sparkly emerald-colored skull—I find things that I recognize have aesthetic value for other people but I would never purchase for myself. That is, I find something that at day's end I personally find unsatisfactory. *Cute*, sure . . . just not for me.

As for *cute* in regard to my mother and the older tenant, we come back to my friend Sarah at the bar, even if the venomous tone of a misguided intern has little in common with that of a fellow expressing fondness for his girlfriend's mother or a doorman looking after the people who keep him employed. In each of these instances, *cute* dances with status and power. My then-boyfriend couldn't have called my mother *gorgeous* without raising my eyebrow; with *cute*, he was able to acknowledge her physical bearing while remaining appropriate to both me and the woman whose genes I inherited. The doorman may have believed he was doing much the same, but underneath his obsequious manner, I heard a barely perceptible note of dismissal—even contempt, as though he knew that the word *cute* was one of the only ways he, in his position of servitude, could exert even the slightest power over a rich old lady.

The words we use to describe beauty, its relatives, and its absence are deliberate. Lacking a formal classification system as one would find in the taxonomy of, say, plant species, we're left to shape the meanings of various appearance-related words ourselves. Each and every word we've ascribed to appearance—especially female appearance—carries weight and significance, and reflects our acute awareness of the effect beauty has on our social relationships, our self-image, and our place in the larger society. The careful yet intuitive calibration of beauty words that each of us tinkers with on an individual level is a result of a collective, ever-shifting mind-set about appearance. In looking at the language of beauty, we're looking at a larger web of history.

More than that, we're looking at how we individually and collectively manifest our attitudes toward beauty. While the way we talk about looks may be lip service on the most literal level, underneath clichéd phrases like *beauty comes from within* lies a go-to grab bag of language that each of us uses to reflect root beliefs about appearance. If we gloss over the importance of the words we choose, we rob ourselves of the opportunity to see not only how beauty shapes our language but how we choose our language to reflect contradictory desires—like how no matter how much we strive for sexual equality, we treat compliments from men differently than those shared between women. Or how we might want to celebrate one another's looks but only manage to coin new words that describe our not-so-pretty parts, reflecting a hesitancy to claim beauty. Language can be a signpost to understanding that hesitancy—and to understanding that the fact that we have an entire vocabulary to describe the way we look means that we are really, *really* eager to talk about it.

The Six-Letter Word: Beauty

In the language of appearance, a vague hierarchy emerges. I think of it as less of a sleek pyramid with the word *beautiful* perched at the top than as a ziggurat composed of miniature file drawers filled with caveats and exceptions, stories and histories, desires and limitations. Still, nestled there in a perch toward the top is *beautiful*, the queen bee of all the words we use to describe looks. Not everyone strives to be *beautiful* per se, but few among us actively work *against* it. Clustered around *beautiful* are nooks filled with words like *gorgeous* and slithering passageways that describe the effect on the viewer more than the object itself (*stunning, striking,* even *ravishing*—which, by the way, comes from *ravish,* i.e., *rape*).

From there the words resting in their caddies become a hair milder, a shade more open to interpretation. Take *pretty*: pleasant-looking but not necessarily beautiful. *Lovely*: purposefully indeterminate, in keeping with its root word of *love*. *Alluring*: Who hasn't met creatures whose magnetism gives them an unmistakable physical appeal that transcends conventional good looks—or lack thereof? Then there are the safe words we employ when describing something positively yet hedging our bets for a variety of reasons. Out of propriety I might not want to refer to a friend's husband as *hot*, but what's to stop me from acknowledging he's *nice-looking*? *Cute,* as we saw earlier, can be used as a weapon, but a generous reading of my utterance of "cute shoes" finds a simple wish to acknowledge someone else's taste without passing judgment on it myself. And perhaps the grand pooh-bah of all safe words is *attractive*. Given the fact that the word stems from the very thing that brings lovers together—attraction—it's ironic that we've drained it of sexual energy. Yet that's exactly what we've done. We use it to acknowledge everyone from children to friends' partners to mistake boyfriends from long ago, as a way of appraising a person's looks in a sup- posedly objective manner. To say "My ex was gorgeous" might imply a sense of continued longing. To say "My ex was attractive" makes for a businesslike description.

Attractive also comes in handy when describing ourselves. One of the greatest sins a woman can commit is letting other people know she's aware of her appeal, so to openly refer to oneself as *beautiful* requires a chutzpah that most of us don't have. *Pretty* isn't quite as shocking to hear as a self- descriptor, but it's still in the danger zone—like *beautiful*, it goes against the cultural script we've written that allows women to claim their visual appeal only after they've qualified it. *Attractive* is a modest alternative that allows the same detached appraisal that it offers when we use it to describe others. It's tidy, neutral, and matter-of-fact, which allows us to acknowledge our own appeal without seeming vain—unless, of course, one is aware enough of language to recognize that using the word *attractive* implies that others are attracted to you. Luckily for those linguistically minded souls, the word is easily downgraded. When asking women to describe their looks, I was struck by how often they used the word pairing of *reasonably attractive*. So encoded is the need not to sound *too* pleased with our own looks that we take pains to clarify that we're only attractive *within reason*. (Has anyone ever been described as "reasonably beautiful"?)

So the ziggurat of words is uneven, supported by social propriety and the need to be able to describe the variety of human physical appeal. Yet it's not until we look at the users of the little drawers and crevices of beauty words that we see how specific the language of looks really is. When I asked a handful of friends what words or terms they would most like to hear someone else use about their looks, I expected to hear small variations on the word *beautiful*. Instead, what I heard was a collectively uncanny understanding of each woman's own particular allure. Sarah (she of the not-cute hot pants) went with *glamorous*—apt for a woman who is skilled at the sleight of hand that creates an immediate effect. Lisa, who transforms from quite pretty to downright spellbinding once you enter her quippy, ani- mated world, chose *alluring*. Andrea, a statuesque friend from high school who commanded presence even at age fourteen, opted for *striking*. And

Ayoola, who, the first time we met, was wearing a demure tea-length dress and a babushka-style kerchief on her head, delighted in *fetching*. Just as each of these women, ranging in age from twenty-nine to forty-eight, had learned over the years how to emphasize her natural assets and draw out chosen aspects of herself through self-presentation, each had also zeroed in on words that could easily be used to describe her without stretching the imagination one bit. (It's also worth noting that many women proclaimed that the adjective didn't matter so much as long as it was preceded with a juicy adverb. *Absolutely* beautiful, *fucking* gorgeous, *totally* hot—anything as long as we're a superlative version of it.)

But why do any of us employ any particular word, whether as a standard-bearer for our own appearance or as a way of describing others? Part of the reason lies in etymology. It would be a mistake to think that the centuries-old origins of a word dictate how we use it today—but it would also be a mistake to think that a word's beginnings have no bearing on its present meaning. Take *gorgeous*, one of the few appearance-related words that rivals *beautiful* for sheer potency. Sharing its Old French root with the word *gorge*, *gorgeous* implies a showy excess—the grand buffet of beauty. From there, is it any accident that *gorgeous* became the most likely suffix to *drop-dead*? Why not *drop-dead beautiful*—or, for that matter, *drop-dead striking* or *drop-dead stunning*, both of which would make more immediate sense, as a strike or a stun can kill? With its connotations of over-the-top gorge-worthy opulence, *gorgeous* isn't used to describe one's inner riches, as with "inner beauty" or "a beautiful mind." Minds aren't gorgeous; faces are, and the sense of deadly exaggeration that is conveyed by *gorgeous* is part of what makes it a grand compliment.

As specific as *gorgeous* is to a sort of technical beauty, *lovely* relies on a sense of the indefinite. We speak of someone being "a lovely person," but we're hard-pressed to articulate exactly what that means. It's not a straight-up synonym for *pretty*, but neither is it a euphemism for *not-pretty*. It implies a certain delicacy, but one that echoes a person's overall sensibility, not only her exterior. It's just as vague and amorphous as its root word, *love*. In fact, *lovely*'s indeterminate quality has extended its usage not only to mean an overall sense of beauty but also to lend a weakened sense of approval—you might not find a woman physically attractive, but you can safely describe her as *lovely* without betraying your personal judgment of her looks. Stevie Wonder might have gotten some side-eye had he sung of his baby daughter, "Isn't She Gorgeous?"—but "Isn't She Lovely?" made the Top 40.

The trickiness of the word *cute* might stem in part from its origins, a shortening of *acute*. The direct meaning of *acute* here was a sharp, quick intelligence. But the other associated meanings of *acute* aren't exactly qualities one wants ascribed to oneself: pointed, irritating, inconstant. The sense of dissatisfaction surrounding *cute* lingers in its usage regarding appearance. (Try this: Log out of your search engine account to prevent tailored results and type in "I hate being called"; as of this writing, *cute* was the number-one term used to complete that phrase.) It was only a hundred years after *cute* first started to be used as an ostensible compliment that it was decried: "In this changing world, the 'sweet girl' and the 'cute girl' belong to the past," read ads for a 1936 mail-order "charm test."

And then there's the queen bee: *beautiful*. Tolstoy may have written that "It is amazing how complete is the delusion that beauty is goodness," but etymologically speaking, it's not a delusion at all. The word *beauty* shares a Proto-Indo-European language root with *bene-*, as in *beneficial* and *benevolent*. As in *good*.

Used as a concrete noun as opposed to an abstract one, *beauty* applies to women only: *She's quite a beauty.* (*He* certainly isn't.) Used as a proper noun, it can apply to both sexes, but guess which sex has a panoply of beauty terms available as a first name? In 2013, Bella was the 58th most popular baby name for girls in the United States; Beau, 270th for boys— quite a difference, even accounting for the *Twilight* effect, which saw a heroine named Bella lead a quartet of young-adult novels to the best-seller list. Not that most beauty-derived names are as literal a translation as the Italian *bella* or French *beau*. A partial offering of girls' names rooted in appearance includes Lana (Gaelic, meaning *attractive*), Belinda (Italian, *very beautiful*), Callista (Greek, *most beautiful*), Inga (Danish, *beautiful daughter*), Helen and its myriad variants (thousand ships and whatnot), Shana (Yiddish, *beautiful*), Jamille (Arabic, *beautiful*), Jolie (French, *pretty*), Leanne (Gaelic, *light, beautiful woman*), Alina (Polish, *beautiful*), Bonnie (Scottish dialect for, well, *bonny*), and what might again become popular if old-fashioned names continue their current upward trend, Mabel (Welsh, *my beautiful one*). Even companies are getting in on the action: Sephora (Israeli, *beautiful bird*) and our favorite know-it-all, Siri (Scandinavian, *beautiful victory*). Compare that with the paltry offerings of looks-oriented male names, all of which roughly translate to *handsome*, without the superlatives and specific connotations of their sister names: Hassan (Arabic), Kenneth (Celtic), Kevin (Gaelic), and a rather esoteric name sure to delight *Twilight* fans, Cullen (Celtic—and *Twilight* devotees will remember that the vampiric Edward Cullen was paired off with none other than Bella, making for a pair of beautiful creatures, not a stand-alone male).

Beauty can even be an adjective, if you're willing to forsake *Webster's* for *Cosmo*. When I started my first job in women's magazines, I was mystified by the title of "beauty editor." I understood what happened in the fashion department, the features department, the news department—but *beauty*? I mean, I'd read stories about *makeup* in ladymags; was that all it was? When I finally got up the nerve to ask the beauty editor what exactly her title meant, she shrugged. "There's just no other word that puts together hair and makeup and skin care." Fair enough, I suppose, and it satisfied me then. But as one beauty editor put it years later when I related this exchange to her, "The beauty department is the only place in women's magazines where you're describing the desired *outcome*, not the process. You don't call the fashion department the 'trim and polished department' or features 'the smart department.'" Beauty is presumed to be the unified goal of the magazine's readers—indeed, readers of all mainstream women's magazines—to the point that it can become an all-encompassing label and nobody thinks twice about it.

Now that the job of disseminating news of spring makeup collections has gone beyond the magazine world to the broader pastures of the Internet, it's unlikely that any editorial assistant would be remotely confused by the use of the word *beauty* in this sense. The word *beauty* in *beauty blogger* is understood by all to encompass not only hair, makeup, and skin care but the functions of noun (we blog on the entity of beauty), verb (*beauty* is shorthand for the process of creating the effect of beauty), and adjective (it's not *beautiful blogging*, it's *beauty blogging*). Some might decry this as sloppy language; I champion it. Language's purpose is to help us communicate, and if the morphing of any particular word helps us do that more effectively, then bring it on. Just as the six-letter word of b-e-a-u-t-y can expand to be as flexible as we need it to be, our vocabulary for physical description continues to expand, allowing us to note—if not always celebrate—the markers that make each of us notice one another.

He Says, She Says

On a flight of fancy in my early thirties, I spent a spring in Prague teaching English. I was assigned to lead a beginner-level lesson about how to describe people, and in addition to basic terms like how to express someone's height, build, coloring, and age, I taught a few terms of evaluation—*pretty, handsome, beautiful,* and *cute.* Everything was going fine until two students role-played a conversation in which a woman told a man he looked *pretty.* In reviewing the role-play, I pointed out the mistake—but was stumped when a student asked me why it was considered wrong. English is gender neutral in structure, meaning that our nouns aren't masculine or feminine, as they are in one-quarter of the world's languages (including Czech). So why would the English language have certain words that are applied only to men or women and that don't even have a balanced equivalent, as with *waiter/waitress?*

From an ESL teacher's perspective, the answer is simple: That's just not what English speakers say. From any other perspective, it's not nearly as simple as that. Just as words shape our idea of how any particular person might look, words can rigidly encode gender to the point where assigning words to the "wrong" sex can be used as a tool of belittlement. Being a "pretty boy" is rarely a good thing—let alone the nonexistent "pretty man." And what of the "handsome woman"? Until the twentieth century, *handsome* was used as a compliment for both sexes. (Lizzy Bennet of *Pride and Prejudice* was merely "pretty," while her more desirable older sister was known as "handsome.") When spoken of women as a compliment today, *handsome* is usually applied to older women who may have aged out of conventional beauty but not *too* much—women we've decided to desex, but whom we want to evaluate anyway.

Yet when uttered of men, *handsome* is unambiguously a compliment, as it implies a well-built sense of sturdiness that we're more eager to assign to men. (*Handsome's* sense of development and construction may be why we used it more readily for women 150 years ago, before widespread vaccinations ensured that common disease wouldn't make a notable percentage of the population appear *not* well-built.) Because *handsome* carries an assumption of fine construction, not refined aesthetics, is it any surprise that we use it primarily for men? Just as we'll take our women dainty and demure (is it possible to be aggressively pretty?), we'll take our men solidly developed. The rough equivalent of a feminine adjective to *handsome*— *beautiful*—implies a sort of divine harmony, a grace that must be inspired, not constructed. We want our men well-built; we want our women magical.

Then there are the words we use to describe ourselves to potential partners. A study of personal ads revealed that 45 percent of straight women in the sample identified themselves as—you guessed it—"attractive" when advertising themselves to men. Good thing, too, since 27 percent of ads from straight men are seeking women who are exactly that. (And is it a coincidence that the same percentage of men—27 percent—self-identify as "attractive" as well?) Given *attractive's* handy purpose as a confident yet humble catchall term, it's not terrifically surprising that the word shows up so frequently when one is blindly casting a net into fish-filled seas. As Celia Shalom, the author of the personal-ads study, writes, "We all like to think we are attractive, and the reader is more likely to include herself or himself in the category *attractive* than in the category of one of its more specific near-synonyms (*pretty, good-looking, handsome, beautiful,* and the ambiguous *lovely*)."

Attractive has another important characteristic: It's unisex. *Attractive, cute, sexy*—these are some of the words applied unilaterally to both sexes. They're also the words that have a weakened or vague use. We may sign up to find attractive partners, but we also use the same word to write off potential partners who don't have anything *wrong* with them per se but who simply aren't our type ("I mean, she's attractive, but . . ."). *Cute* is positive enough but, as we've seen, is also the mark of someone easily dismissed. As for *sexy*—hardly an anemic term—it's also one of the more subjective words we can use to describe someone, and it's simultaneously more specific and all-encompassing than gendered words like *handsome* and *pretty*. For while sexiness has plenty of attached iconography—deep cleavage, rippling muscles, and other romance-novel-cover imagery—we also use it when describing someone who isn't conventionally attractive but who, for whatever reason, just *does it* for us. (*People's* annual "Sexiest Man Alive" feature, after all, is separate from its "Most Beautiful" list.) These unisex terms, by virtue of being unisex, must cast a wider net. Their ambiguity, subjectivity, and openness to interpretation are what make them considered suitable to be applied to men and women alike—and also what make them harder to pin down. We *need* these words to be vague if we're going to uphold the status quo of gender roles. Were we to have more words to describe specifically how men look, it would signal that we care more about how men look. Limiting the vocabulary to a small cluster of words keeps the discussion off men's faces and bodies. And it's not hard to see how having a smorgasbord of words for women's appearance keeps the cultural conversation right on their looks.

Matters get a little more complex—and just as revealing—when looking at words selected by queer users of personal ads. While men seeking women wanted an *attractive* woman, and, farther down the list, a *pretty* or *beautiful* one, gay women sought out women who were *good-looking*—a term often associated with a male object. That's not to say that lesbians look for masculine-appearing women, though butch-femme roles may indeed play into lexical choices here (*feminine* was one of the most-used words in lesbian ads, a term that didn't show up for men seeking women). It's more that, as study author Shalom puts it, "its use to describe a woman implies a strong, assertive kind of beauty that is distinct from the heterosexually marked terms *pretty* and *beautiful*." It's a subtle but important differentiation that tells us more about the gender markings of words like *pretty* and *beautiful* than it does about gay women—for don't plenty of partners come to find their beloved beautiful, regardless of either person's sex? Yet *beautiful* carries a weight not just of womanhood but of *conventional* womanhood. (To wit, the word *beautiful* was thrown about like confetti to describe Caitlyn Jenner's 2015 *Vanity Fair* cover, confirmation of her transition into womanhood—and of many people's eagerness to combat transphobia by using the same words to describe her as they would anyone who was born a woman.) And conventional womanhood is still considered to be heterosexual womanhood. A straight man might be attracted to the exact same good-looking woman that a lesbian lusts for—but for all the equality strides of the LGBT movement, the attraction is still coded differently.

"No, *You're* So Pretty!"

Woman-to-woman words thrive in another setting: the compliment. Sweet nothings given by one woman to another are the most frequent configuration of compliments, followed by man-to-woman compliments. (Unsurprisingly, man-to-man compliments are the least frequent type.) And you'll hardly be shocked to learn that the number-one *topic* of compliments given to women by either sex is appearance. The most common topic of compliments doled out to men? Skill.

Women use more words than men do when issuing a compliment—think "I love that coat!" as opposed to "Great coat!" In keeping with this verbosity, linguists have repeatedly noted that women are more prone to taking an indirect approach to communication—for example, couching reprimands in terms of questions ("Why didn't you tell me earlier that you couldn't find the file?" instead of "You should have told me earlier that you couldn't find the file"). This also holds true in compliments. Women are more likely than men to begin compliments with "I like" and "I love," which hedges the compliment a bit. Proclaiming a coat to be "great" is direct, with no filters; proclaiming that "I love that coat" is both more intimate (here's what *I* think) and more roundabout (I'm not making a value judgment here, it's just my two cents).

But more revealing than how women give compliments to one another is how women *receive* them. There are a number of ways we respond to compliments—like giving a compliment in return, refuting the kindness, or simply saying "thank you." But the number-one response women give to a compliment coming from another woman is what language researchers call "comment history," and what the rest of us call conversation. Women treat compliments from other women as gateways to connection, and rightfully so: Isn't the easiest way to break the ice with a female stranger to compliment something she's wearing? As I write this, I'm thinking of the last compliment I received, a kind word from an acquaintance about a beautiful mauve scarf I own. It was knitted for me by my brother's then-girlfriend, a fact I relayed to my acquaintance—surprising her, for she hadn't known that I have a brother. It led me to ask about her siblings, and soon we found ourselves in a conversation about how our family structures have shaped the way we pursue friendships—all because she told me she liked my scarf.

The woman-to-woman compliment is a convenient linguistic tool, one I'm glad to have—but it's easy to become dependent on it as a way to reach out to other women. I once found myself at a dinner party seated next to a woman whose professional accomplishments both intrigued and intimidated me. Unsure of how to get to what I *really* wanted to know about her—how she developed her steely self-assurance, how she managed to always know something about every topic under the sun, and most of all, how I could become just a little more like her—I started with what had worked so well for me with other women: "I love your shoes." She smiled graciously and said, "Thank you," and then neither of us had anything further to say to one another. Rather, I didn't know how to get to that further point—at least not without her doing some of the heavy lifting along with me. I'd expected her to help me out, which isn't an outrageous expectation; that's how conversations work. But in expecting her to help me out by saying anything other than the logical, polite response—"thank you"—I was attempting to direct her attitude. Toward herself, toward me, toward womanhood itself; I was expecting her to volley back a bit of "comment history" that would have revealed something I could latch on to in order to help me build the scaffolding of the conversation I *wanted* to have.

I'd relied on small talk to lead to big talk—but small talk works only when we presume the talkers share a common condition (which is why the weather is the foremost example of small talk). I'd assumed that what we had in common was a desire to talk about shoes, not because I actually like to talk about shoes all that much but because I knew that *women are expected to talk about shoes*. I'm guessing she knew this too, and that that's exactly why she didn't take my friendly bait—a fact I admire, even if it left me adrift at that dinner. In a way, her noncompliance with girl talk served as an answer to my larger questions about her. Part of the self-confidence I'd admired from afar may well have been shaped by a reluctance to have conversations women are "supposed" to have, saving her energies for the talks she *wanted* to have. My momentary inability to go against the expected line of conversation kept me in the same loop I'd been in—the same loop I'd wanted her advice on escaping. That moment is lost, but it was instructive: Compliments can be powerful tools of connection, but relying on them means relying on traditional roles. Which, depending on the person you're trying to connect with, might be a dead end to any potential alliance.

Linguistics studies show that my dinner companion's type of response—"thank you" or its rough equivalent—happens only 10 percent of the time in woman-to-woman compliments. Yet we teach children that "thank you" is the correct response to a compliment. It's a bit of a paradox, but not as much as it initially appears. When linguist Robert K. Herbert conducted his leading study on compliments, he found that upon hearing a compliment, study participants often reported that *they didn't know what to say*. Human humility prevents us from always giving the "correct" response of "thank you." And if women sense that another woman is using a compliment as a way of reaching out in quiet sisterhood, that humility can easily turn to tender embarrassment or just plain tenderness. Compliments temporarily shift the power toward the recipient, and when it's a compliment about looks—a topic we widely believe to be especially touchy for women—we may rush to equalize that power as quickly as possible, and a simple "thank you" doesn't do the trick. So we come up with other ways to acknowledge the shared bond of womanhood: "comment history," for starters, but also reassigning the compliment ("Oh, my hairdresser is amazing—here's her card"), returning the compliment ("I was just about to say that *your* hair looks fantastic"), agreeing ("I know, I love it too!"), disagreeing ("Ugh, I can't wait for it to grow back"), downscaling ("The color's nice but I don't know about the cut"), qualifying ("Well, I just got back from the salon"), and questioning ("Really?"). The relative infrequency of a straightforward "thanks" points to how we've framed the cultural story around women and beauty. We *expect* a woman to downgrade, qualify, or reassign a compliment. What we don't expect her to do is simply accept it.

But none of this explains why women in the study used "thank you" to respond to compliments from men a whopping *66 percent* of the time. (Remember, the "thank you" rate between women is 10 percent.) Where women suffuse compliments from other women with overtures of friendship or connection, they hear a compliment from a man and manage to come up with the "correct" response. Herbert attributed the vastly different responses to a sense of maintaining social order. Compliments can be indicators of social status. People with a greater degree of status can compliment those with less status, but it's more readily understood by both parties as a gift of sorts—the equivalent of "giving down" to office assistants at Christmas, while giving one's boss a gift is trickier. Since men as a class are usually seen as having more social status, the theory goes, women treat compliments from them as coming from a social superior.

I follow this argument well enough, but when I think of how I interpret compliments from heterosexual men versus those from women, something else comes to mind: expectation. Even when a man complimenting me is out of the realm of romance—a work superior, say, or a friend's husband—I still understand his words about my appearance as coming from him *as a man* and being directed to me *as a woman*. The relationship itself has a degree of codification that isn't there in my relationships with women. And true to the template, I'm likely to affirm that codification by responding to a compliment with a symbol of my own: "Thank you." When it comes to women, the field is more open. A woman could be complimenting me because she wants to get to know me, because she wants to butter me up, because she's trying to elicit information about me, because she wants to ask me out, because she wants to make a good impression, or just because she really likes my shoes. (They're Clarks, for the record.) A man could be issuing a compliment for any of those reasons too, of course. But with most straight men, by dint of our sex, there's a loose blueprint: He is a man, I am a woman, and we're so trained to think that man plus woman equals romance—or at least a faint impression of it—that even when the relationship has nothing to do with courtship, I have a rough beginning point of reference. With women, I don't necessarily have that—and so the reaction is more tailored to the specific woman and more generous with the number of words in order to establish a reference point for whatever might come next.

There's another reason women's responses to men's compliments are more standardized and don't necessarily extend the conversation. Women just might understand intuitively that men don't place the same nuance on the language of compliments as women do. I think of an old boyfriend who never complimented me, and when I suggested that he might want to give it a whirl, he started saying things like, "That's a nice dress." It was touching that he was trying, but I was still dissatisfied. He didn't understand that I didn't want to hear from my beloved that my dress was pretty; I wanted to hear that *I* was pretty. It was a subtle distinction that was clear as day to me and utterly lost on him.

Now, you could look at this as an instance of me being demanding or of him being a bit withholding. Perhaps both are true to a degree. But years later, what I see in our series of exchanges on compliments is a case study of how women are more careful with and sensitive to the particulars of language because our social position is somewhat less secure. This sensitivity is expected of us in what sociologist Arlie Russell Hochschild terms the "emotion work" of romantic relationships, which generally falls to women in heterosexual pairings. Women are the ones who say, "We need to talk," or who conjure just the right words of apology. The flip side of mastering the nuances of language well enough to shape emotional relationships is a vulnerability to the subtleties of language. This vulnerability may explain why my then-boyfriend's well-meaning compliments fell short of what I wanted to hear. As thirty-year-old Natalie puts it, "'You look nice' or 'you look pretty' just don't cut it—both feel so banal." Indeed, if I was being a tad particular with that man, I was hardly alone. Research shows that even though men appreciate the role compliments play in a relationship just as much as women do, women are likelier to notice the presence or absence of compliments from partners. A cynical take on this finding is that women are keeping score with compliments. A more forgiving approach is that men have the luxury of not weighing their words as carefully as women traditionally have. It then falls to the ladies to intuitively parse men's words—even words of appreciation and care—for what they "really" mean.

My, What Curvy Cankles You Have

We're exquisitely sensitive to the implications of beauty, so we've carefully calibrated our language to reflect how comfortable—or uncomfortable— we are with various aspects of appearance. And as a society, we're not very comfortable with fatness. But let's begin not with *fat* but with *curvy*. If I describe a woman as *curvy*, you might summon an image of slender yet bosomy Scarlett Johansson or of plus-size Octavia Spencer or of a slim-hipped but cartoonishly silicone-breasted adult film star named Kandy. Perhaps you'd think of a muscular athlete along the lines of Venus Williams, a figure straight out of a Rubens painting, or your own body—even the slimmest of frames can't help but curve in places. I applied it to myself for a while, even though I hardly cut an hourglass figure. What I was at the time was *soft*, but that didn't have quite the same ring. I eventually started lifting weights and in the process developed undulating muscle that hadn't been visible before, and I also lost some body fat, including in my breasts—leaving me both curvier and *not* curvier than I'd been. So was I curvy before my gym-rat days, or am I curvy now? The flexibility of *curvy*—the very thing that makes it so appealing—has wound up making it meaningless.

Compare that with *fat*, a word generally understood to have none of the approval of *curvy*. It's considered an insult, perhaps the worst thing you could say to a woman. To wit, female writers of all sizes are regularly called "fat" by online commenters who happen to disagree with the writer's opinion. *Fat* is used as a term of dismissal, the idea being that anyone fat is clearly a stupid, misinformed, blithering idiot. And never mind if the woman in question happens to be slender; we'll call her fat anyway, because "stupid, slim bitch" just doesn't pack the same wallop. *Skinny* comes closer to being an insult, but a "skinny bitch" brings to mind a different sort of bitchiness than that of a "fat bitch"—a fact capitalized on by the writers of the best-selling *Skinny Bitch*, the first of a series of Skinny Bitch diet books.

The irony here is that *fat* has potential to be a nonjudgmental descriptor. If you're someone who is indeed fat, you've simply got more than the average amount of body fat—medically speaking, a type of tissue composed chiefly of adipocyte cells. Robbed of its social wrist-smacking, the word could be as neutral as *tall*. It's only once a culture has decided that a certain percentage of body fat is a no-no that it becomes a term of abuse. And once a word is a term of abuse, you need other, "nicer" words (like *curvy*) to refer to the trait in question. As fat activist Marilyn Wann writes in her book *FAT!SO?*, "[Y]ou only need a euphemism if you find the truth distasteful."

Curvy and *fat* stand on opposite sides of the mirror. One is sometimes used as a gentle euphemism for a body that exceeds the size to which we've given the cultural thumbs-up; the other is often used to stigmatize that same body. And that's exactly the point: *The bodies are the same.* As powerful as the word *fat* (and, to a lesser extent, *curvy*) may be, the actual word means little. It's only when coupled with the strong reaction fat people provoke in our society that the word takes on any potency beyond *tall* or *brown-haired* or *broad-shouldered*. Because they're adjectives, *fat* and *curvy* are ostensibly descriptive words. In truth they're evaluative ones.

So what do we do about things we want to either elevate or stigmatize? We come up with new words. We go from having fleshy waists to having *love handles*—no, make that *muffin top*. Our thick ankles are now *cankles*. Where we once had hips, we now have *saddlebags*. Our loose upper arms are now *bat wings*, which sit nicely next to that bulge above the bra strap, aka *back bacon*. Let's not even get into *FUPA*. Lucky enough to have a body with none of these? Congratulations, o ye of perfect body—but you'd better look great from the neck up, lest you be known as a *butterface* (". . . but her face!"). For everyone knows that kind of woman goes beyond being just ugly—she's *fugly*, don't you think?

We keep coming up with these terms to describe body parts that are perfectly normal to have, and we've gotten quicker to name and meaner about our wobbly bits too. *Love handles*, a term that originated around 1970, is generous to those gentle mounds of flesh above the hips. The term implies that they're to be loved, and then handled. Its usage, applied to both men and women, connotes affection, even when we might wish to diet or exercise them away, as shown in the term's appearance in a 1974 diet book: "His girlfriend grabbed the rolls around his middle and playfully christened them love handles." *Love handles* indicates, well, *love*, which is hardly suitable for a nation now supposedly in the midst of an obesity epidemic. Enter *muffin top*—a term that, while similarly cutesy, is also point-and-laughable.

Now take a look at the collection of newly coined terms here. *Cankles. Saddlebags. Butterface. Fugly. Back bacon.* Notice anything? *None of them make us sound better-looking.* Where are the portmanteaus that glorify us? Where are *absolovely, beautifoxy, ravishapely*? We're more creative in our terms of derision than we are with terms of acclaim because as much power as beauty carries in this world, ugliness still carries more. The sheer repellent force of ugliness means that we need more labels for it. And because women have more cultural permission to talk about the parts of their bodies that they *don't* like compared with the parts they *do*, we've had to develop a broader vocabulary for our less-appealing features than we have for our assets.

If the old maxim is true that everyone has something beautiful about them, this contemporary collection of vicious little terms attempts to prove the opposite: Everyone has something ugly about them too. Even the leanest of women will get a muffin top if her pants fit incorrectly. These words were developed to create awareness where there might not have been any, which is their neat mental trick. For how do we really ever *know* if we possess back bacon or cankles or if we're butterfaces? Do I have saddlebags or plain old hips? My arms are toned, but you can still easily pinch their flesh; are those bat wings, then? Do I have back bacon, rolls of porcine flesh spilling out over my bra band—or do I just need a proper bra fitting?

Invented words become a form of body policing, a way of letting women know they are being watched—true even of supposedly desirable terms, like *thigh gap.* Thick ankles have never been a trait that we've valued in women in the West. But it wasn't until we named them something distasteful—*cankles*—that, ahem, *ankles of size* became enough of a concern to warrant "Cankle Awareness Month," as Gold's Gym declared July dictionary folks made it up. It was included because it had guest starred in enough media outlets that it had actually *become* a word that, in turn, should be defined by the leading word reference book in the United States. We develop our language collectively. We might talk of the Internet as being the "hive mind," but language was the original hive mind. Whatever words we have, we came up with together. That's sort of depressing when considering that we came up with dozens of words to describe women's looks, yet still have just a mere handful for men—but it also means that if our hive mind begins to think of beauty differently, our language will shift accordingly. For example, *Merriam-Webster* lexicographer Kory Stamper points out that one of the newest appearance-centric words to make it into the dictionary is *hottie*, which can be used to describe both sexes. "Since the second wave of feminist writers, we've been so much more aware of how we use language for any sort of marginalized group of people," Stamper says. "We're much more embarrassed by racial slurs, we're much more aware of the language we use for women. When we look at the use of some of the newer words like 'hottie,' there's more gender parity in their uses. You're chatting with the 'hottie barista.' That doesn't say if the barista is a man or a woman. We see more and more of that with informal words." *Hottie* reflects heightened gender awareness; it's also a reflection of the ways we're increasingly objectifying men. Similarly, we've largely dropped old-fashioned words like *comely* from our vocabularies. We've been developing our lexicon for beauty for centuries, and it's up to us to shift our language to allow for the ways we're chiseling away at the omnipotence of the beauty standard. Changing the words we use en masse to describe the way we look has the potential to change the ways we *think* about how we look. If we want to drop *fugly*, or begin collocating terms like *pretty man*, we can.

Yet . . . we haven't, for the most part. And maybe that's because we don't want to. Perhaps our hive mind prefers to skew beauty discussions toward women. Or perhaps we've developed the vocabulary of beauty in the ways we have because the nature of beauty is still a mystery to us. Even as each word that evaluates beauty carries its own specificity, it also carries a sense of ambiguity. Both *gorgeous* and *lovely* are used approvingly, and it's not like *gorgeous* is a magnification of the simpler *lovely*. Yet most of us would agree that in the ziggurat of beauty words, *gorgeous* is nestled

2009. The words *thick ankles* describe something undesirable in neutral language. *Cankles* takes that undesirable feature and escalates it into an insult.

In her 1979 essay "Words and Change" about the impact of feminism, Gloria Steinem wrote, "We have terms like *sexual harassment* and *battered women*. A few years ago, they were just called *life*." Her point was that developing lingo for these problems was a positive development. The inverse intent holds true too: If naming domestic violence allows us to go about fixing it, what does that do for cankles, which were once just called life? Every time we use a word like *cankles* to describe bodies—our own or other women's—we add power to the phenomenon of thick ankles, which wasn't a phenomenon until we named it. The point of these cagey words isn't nullification of women's extraordinary awareness of our bodies. The point is to amplify it. And if we refuse to use language designed to intensify that self-consciousness, we take a small step toward eroding the self-consciousness itself.

Most of the time, we invent words to label an existing phenomenon that requires discussion. Think back to the days and weeks after September 11, 2001, when people called that day anything from "the attacks" to "September 11" to "nine-one-one" to simply "Tuesday"—and now consider how we've collectively settled upon "9/11" as the handiest term. Same with "the Internet" over "World Wide Web" or "the information superhighway." Now, both 9/11 and the Internet were new; obviously we didn't have the words before they existed. But thick ankles, ample waistlines, and fleshy upper arms have existed as long as the human body. Still, it wasn't until the past decade or so that their monikers came into use. Part of that could be because of democratized access to the collective consciousness, courtesy of the information superhighway. If someone dreams up a clever term for something that's currently unlabeled, it can go viral in a matter of hours.

More likely, though, these terms stuck because they serve a larger purpose. They give us a language that allows us to bond while discussing our physical appearance. Women are *expected* to talk of their bodies in derogatory terms. And we're rewarded for wielding this particular lexicon. If I tell you I have cankles, chances are you'll respond with something like, "Shut up, you do not." The language of the put-down gives birth to the language of support.

But we also need to look at why the vocabulary of self-deprecation came to be in the first place, which goes back to the beauty myth itself. As women's minds become more free to roam, the status quo can maintain its stability through the ways women keep their own bodies in line. (Not that it's only women who have more and more labels slapped on them: A man with anorexia nervosa requires treatment just as urgently as his female counterpart, but when we're able to dismiss his behavior as *manorexia*, he goes from having a clinical illness to merely being a little too vain.) If you can't name it, you can't shame it. And if you can't shame it, then there goes Cankle Awareness Month, jeans designed to prevent muffin top, and entire segments of the $60-billion-a-year weight-loss industry. There goes the pride a not-terrifically-pretty woman might feel upon developing her physique to its top form. All those hours at the gym, all those refusals of after-work beers and nachos, all those mornings of rising early to go for a run—they have their own rewards, yes, she knows this. Still, the word *butterface* lingers at the periphery of her mind.

Naming the Unnameable

Feminists have long pointed out the double standard of sexuality shown in language. A sexually promiscuous woman can be any of dozens of words—*slut, tramp, ho, easy, loose,* and so on—but the only word we have that's specific to male promiscuity is *stud*, which carries a positive connotation. But this formidable list is dwarfed by the number of words we have to describe women's bearing and beauty—or lack thereof. Women are consumable (*sugar, juicy*) and in need of care (*babe, doll*). We're haughty and distant (*queen, princess*) and untouchable (*goddess, angel, siren*). We're animals, able to be owned (*chick, cow, mousy*). We are here to be looked at: Has a man ever been described as being "pretty as a picture"? And when women's protests about being classified by their looks are actually heard, the language might shift in accommodation, but barely. Before the UK's Sex Discrimination Act of 1975 was passed, the word *attractive* was regularly used in help-wanted ads to describe desired female candidates for secretarial positions. Once the law stepped in to provide employment protection for people of all sexes, *attractive* continued to be used almost

as frequently—but to describe the office environment, not th[…] it. The law had nothing to do with the word *attractive*, but onc[…] were unable to specify the desired sex of their secretaries, the[…] use the word in regard to candidates. But decision makers co[…] use the word in other applications proved that the *idea* of attract[…] was important enough to remain in the strategy for gathering[…] even if its literal emphasis had to be displaced.

Just as women's cultural status is reflected in the languag[…] that language becomes a repository for cultural concerns. Th[…] word *bombshell*, which rose in popularity to describe good-looki[…] along with America's anxieties over the atomic bomb. We litera[…] the two in the first bomb tested after World War II by painting[…] *Gilda* on the side of it, after Rita Hayworth's 1946 bombshell rol[…] bigger our anxieties about actual bombs became, the emptier th[…] as-bombshell categorization had to become in order to nullify[…] threat. Who was taken more seriously as an actress during he[…] Jean Harlow, the original bombshell, whose 1933 *Bombshell* can[…] fore the idea of the atomic bomb had even been patented—or[…] enduring bombshell of all time, Marilyn Monroe, whose infam[…] tion of "Happy Birthday" was sung to JFK the same year as t[…] Missile Crisis? The more serious the threat, the more we need[…] the bombshell. Meanwhile, on the other side of the arms race, Ru[…] to regard its word for beauty, *krasota*, as the value of beauty—m[…] quality, not its worth on any sort of market. But in the years after[…] the meaning of the word expanded to match the ways Russians[…] able to think in overtly capitalist terms. *Krasota* can now refer to s[…] that can be bought and sold, akin to how drugstores have "beau[…] meaning products that enhance beauty, not beauty itself. The valu[…] to accommodate the advent of capitalism.

We can track the changing meaning of words over time with dic[…] But even as we may turn to dictionaries to verify the exact meaning[…] the makers of dictionaries turn to *us* to find out how words are be[…] and then shape dictionaries accordingly. When, for example, *f-bomb*[…] included in *Merriam-Webster* in 2012, it wasn't dropped in there bec[…]

somewhat higher than *lovely*, and that "a gorgeous woman" and "a lovely woman" bring two different women to mind—but we'd be hard-pressed to articulate precisely *why*. We can take a stab at it—indeed, *beautiful* is one of the words in *Merriam-Webster* that has an entire synonym breakdown devoted to it—but ultimately each of us is going to associate a different set of qualities with the word *beautiful*, even as we simultaneously understand the collective definition of the word.

If beauty is in the eye of the beholder, it's also on the beholder's lips. Not only does a beautiful woman vary from a lovely woman in my mind's eye, but my image of a beautiful woman may well vary from yours. Other terms of description allow us to be more precise—*dark-haired* or *blond*, *tall* or *petite*, *fair-skinned* or *olive-complected*. Yet the terms of evaluation— *beautiful, lovely, striking, gorgeous*—remain vague, even as each word carries its own specificity. We need the language of beauty to be mystifying in order to maintain an enigmatic shroud over the *concept* of beauty.

Still, despite this mystification, we're easily able to distinguish what is gorgeous from what is, say, cute. Beauty's glossary, simultaneously specific and vague, mirrors the way that we tend to regard beauty: We know both what we personally consider appealing, and what we understand is considered appealing by society at large. So we've compiled an arsenal of words that expands to accommodate our individual interpretations of beauty but that can also be shrink-fitted to the template we all recognize at a glance. I use the word *beautiful* to describe my best friend, not only for her inner beauty but for her creamy skin, sparkling eyes, and hourglass curves. I'd also employ *beautiful* to describe someone like Nicole Kidman. While I'm using the same word to describe them, I don't mean that they share the same kind of beauty, nor am I necessarily proclaiming that they're both objectively beautiful, if such a thing as objectivity exists with beauty. I can see the parts of my best friend that don't adhere to the rigid template of conventional beauty—just as I can look at Kidman and understand her appearance as something we *as a culture* have decided is beautiful, regardless of my personal evaluation of her looks. Yet the same word applies to both of them, with the same truth.

The ways each of us experiences the sheer variety of beautiful people indicate exactly why we've constructed our ziggurat of words to describe appearance. I've seen beautiful women and had to look away because it practically *hurt* to look at them. I've seen beautiful men and felt something physically altered within me; once, upon unexpectedly running into a particularly good-looking suitor, I literally felt my knees go weak. Who among us hasn't lain next to a lover and felt our hands reach out, seemingly of their own will, to touch the beautiful body next to us—or rather, the body that has *become* unalterably beautiful to us?

We may be able to distinguish *gorgeous* from *pretty*, *handsome* from *cute*, *lovely* from *striking*. But *beauty*? Beauty compels us; beauty moves us. Beauty can even leave us speechless. And when we're left without words, we have the illusion that we've lost control. The unnameable power of beauty is exactly what drives us to name it. This mystification can be downright romantic, and far be it from me to rap anyone's knuckles when they want to revel in the glorious mystery of beauty. But if we keep the shroud of beauty affixed too firmly, rarely peeking at what lies underneath, we rob ourselves of an opportunity to challenge assumptions about beauty—assumptions we've collectively manifested by compiling a vast vocabulary of words to describe looks. When we pick up the corner of that shroud, we see our assumptions laid bare. We learn that women aren't supposed to refer to themselves with words bolder than *reasonably attractive*; we learn that the same words that favorably describe a woman can be manipulated to bring shame to a man, revealing a rigid gender binary that we subtly reinforce by calling men *handsome* but women *pretty*. We learn that we might be even more preoccupied with ugliness than we are with beauty. Only when we understand what lies beneath our words can we begin to reshape those words to reflect the ways we want beauty to be a part of our lives. Women have already begun this linguistic reconnaissance mission, with things like the annual "No Fat Talk" week initiated by the Tri Delta sorority, which has gone national on college campuses and beyond. These are the beginnings of a critical examination of the ways we manifest assumptions about beauty through our words. The next step—understanding the implications of the words that come from our lips and keyboards, and choosing words that align with the role each of us wants beauty to play in our lives—is yours.

3

Lipstick Isn't Cubist

The Artifice of Beauty

When I finally got permission to wear makeup in seventh grade, I took it as a symbol of my entrance into womanhood, or at least into not being quite so girlish anymore. I tried all the makeup instructions in *Seventeen*, but the only one I ever mastered was covering the occasional pimple; the wild blues and greens of 1980s eye shadows eluded me. Instead I settled on eye makeup you might call *tasteful*, even as *tasteful* isn't a likely aesthetic goal for many twelve-year-old girls. Taupe eye shadow for the upper lids, a deeper brown closer down, and a hint of mascara—that was it. (Besides the foundation, blush, and Dr Pepper Lip Smacker, that is.)

On the bus ride home one day, I had the good fortune to sit next to Ryan O., a bona fide Cute and Popular Boy who had retained enough schoolboy decency to talk with those of us further down on the social register of Simmons Junior High. We had a conversation—let's say it was about Bon Jovi, just to channel the moment—but it hit a lull. Ever the raconteur, I had a filler ready: "I can't wait to get home to fix my makeup," I said in what I hoped was a slightly jaded, exasperated tone that conveyed my womanly sophistication.

"You don't *wear* makeup," he said. Now, if someone said that to me today, I'd smile smugly and consider my sleight of hand well-done—I want people to see me, after all, not my makeup. But in 1988, at age twelve, coming from a Cute and Popular Boy Who Was Talking to Me, it was *devastating*. How could he not see my declaration of worldliness, elegance, glamour? How could he overlook my grand entrée into womanhood? *How dare he call me a child?*

"I *am* wearing makeup, I'm wearing *lots* of it," I said, taking off my Sally Jessy Raphael glasses so he could see my eye shadow handiwork unobscured.

He leaned closer, squinted, then leaned back. "I don't see any makeup." By this point, blush would have been redundant; my cheeks were aflame with embarrassment. I quickly changed the subject (Def Leppard, perhaps?) and did my best to recover. But privately, silently, I made a vow: Ryan O. would see my makeup. And not just Ryan O. but his whole gang of Cute and Popular Boys, not to mention their cohorts, the Pretty and Popular Girls. They would see my makeup. They would see *me*.

Of course, after a few days of piling on eye shadows in the moss-seafoam-aqua color family, I went back to my taupe. After all, the whole reason I was wearing taupe eye shadow in the first place was because I wasn't comfortable with anything flashier. But the lesson stuck. Makeup wasn't just something to enliven my eyes, bring a flush to my cheeks, punch up my lips. It meant something more, something deeper. When Ryan O. announced that he couldn't see my makeup, it sliced me to the core; it felt like he was pointing out something far more loaded than the fact of my makeup being subtle to begin with. That's all he *was* telling me, of course, but what I heard was this: *You have not yet matured. Your efforts to be noticed by Cute and Popular Boys such as myself are in vain. You are, in truth, invisible.*

Since then I've had plenty of motivations for wearing makeup, which I've done nearly every day for more than twenty years. During the grunge years, I followed the lead of my high school's alternaqueen and drew on thick black eye pencil that had been melted with a match; I wanted to look cool. During a bout of bad acne in my early twenties, I wore opaque foundation in an attempt to not visibly ooze; I wanted to look normal. Today I alternate between bronzer and blush; I want to look more vibrant. Yet no matter what I tell myself about why I'm wearing makeup, attempting to break down the reasons any of us do so is an exercise in futility. After all, our motivations for doing *anything* are rarely clear and singular. And when it comes to cosmetics, it's even murkier. We usually think about motivations for wearing makeup as being sociological—but even though women are subject to similar social conditions, not all women wear makeup (though the majority in America do, 63 percent as of 2010). And attempting to look at individual motivations for wearing makeup means that we're relying on self-reporting, which contains a bevy of blind spots. Then there are differences of degree: One woman's definition of makeup might mean tinted lip balm and mascara, while another's involves three shades of eye shadow plus eye shadow *primer*—while yet another goes for lip balm and mascara one day and a thirty-five-minute face the next. Our motivations for wearing cosmetics are as varied as the tools themselves.

In fact, looking at the individual differences in why women wear makeup is a handy portal to the larger question about why so many of us bother with the stuff. Research published in the *Journal of Cosmetic Science* had seventy women answer questions about their makeup usage and also had them complete psychometric tests—think clinical versions of the personality quizzes you might take online. They found two distinct groups of makeup wearers: one who wore makeup primarily to conceal flaws, and another who wore it as a way of revealing or enhancing themselves. What they found was that women who reported wearing makeup to conceal flaws had lower self-esteem and higher levels of anxiety, and were less extroverted and assertive than women who reported wearing makeup as a method of attraction. The idea here is that women who don't have the greatest self-image use makeup as a defense mechanism to normalize their appearance—even though there wasn't anything in particular to normalize. There was no difference in the baseline of conventional beauty between the groups of women.

As for the women who wore makeup as a means of alluring as opposed to concealing, they fell into three groups: women who valued their natural face more than their made-up face, women who valued their made-up face more than their natural face, and women whose valuation fluctuated depending on context. This last group had the highest rates of all the good stuff—optimism, emotional stability, assertiveness, self-esteem—followed closely (and unsurprisingly) by women who valued their natural face over their painted one.

But here's where things get really interesting: The ways women valued themselves and their makeup was reflected *in the makeup itself*. The women who wore makeup for attraction but valued their made-up face more than their au naturel self? They tended to do the same makeup routine all the time. Contrast that with the women who valued their natural face more than their cosmeticized self: These women used makeup in a playful manner, creating a variety of "looks" that changed day to day. As for the women who used makeup as a means to conceal, they used fewer colors on the face than their counterparts. Forgive me the analogy, but I can't help but think of a moth and a butterfly. A moth's strategy for survival is to be neutrally colored so as to neatly fit into its surroundings, while a butterfly displays vivid colors to attract mates and repel predators.

Of course, we're neither moths nor butterflies—we're women, with motivations more complex than survival. But what I like in this study is less the idea of being able to locate oneself on any sort of linear scale—makeup wearers with low self-esteem to the left, buoyant butterflies to the right—and more the idea of finding a framework of varied motivations within women's reported experiences. Confronting assumptions about makeup and the reasons women use it is the only way to assure that it can ever *truly* be a choice made freely instead of a societal siphoning of women's time and money. The idea isn't to squarely pin any one person into any one category—and it's certainly not to determine the totality of any individual person's motivations for wearing makeup. It's a starting point, not an end, to examining why any of us do or don't carve out time in our day to finger-paint ourselves.

"I Do It for Me": Internal and External Motivators for Wearing Makeup

Let's begin with a big ol' "duh" here: We wear makeup because it makes us look better. Yes, yes, "better" is subjective, and there are all sorts of arguments for a truly naked face being the most beautiful any of us can get—but, c'mon, don't most of us look better, at least by the terms of conventional beauty, when our blemishes are concealed and our eyes more luminous? Research supports this: Women are consistently rated as more attractive by both sexes when wearing makeup, with eye makeup having the greatest impact. In fact, for some women this is a reason *not* to wear makeup. Upon seeing a dancer friend of mine backstage after a performance, I commented on how nice her eyes looked rimmed with the black eyeliner she'd swiped on for the show. "I know," said the normally eyeliner-free woman, mildly exasperated. "I love how I look with it, but I only wear it for shows—if I started wearing it as myself I'd never be able to leave the house without putting it on. I'd begin to think I looked less like myself without it." It's the flip side of something other women have pinpointed as a reason they dab on the stuff: "Wearing makeup allows me to look the way I imagine I look all the time," says an English professor from upstate New York.

But that's just the end result of makeup. The process itself brings other internal rewards. "I like the ritual," says twentysomething Signe. "It feels like I'm really getting ready for the day." Indeed, the six-minute makeup ritual I perform before leaving the house functions like a second cup of coffee in the morning—it's a wake-up tool, tangible evidence that this day is *on*. (And given that many cite "Not looking so tired" as a reason for wearing makeup, particularly eye makeup, perhaps it's more like a *first* cup of coffee.) Plus, after twenty years of applying makeup almost every day, for me it's become habit, as much a part of my morning as putting in my contact lenses. I do it on autopilot. Some non-makeup-wearers report the same in their reasoning for not wearing it. "I never got in the habit of it," says Gabriela from Albany, New York. "I'm feeling more interested in makeup now that I'm getting older, but experimenting with it is work I don't care to invest in. Playing with makeup isn't fun for me like I think it is for a lot of women."

And it *is* fun for some. In the makeup motivation study, researchers found that the specific type of makeup wearer who views cosmetics as play not only has more variability in her routine than other women—think sixties mod one day, nineties au naturel the next, bold red lipstick on the third—but has a distinct psychological profile too. In addition to having high self-esteem and being assertive, this type of woman is least likely to say she uses makeup to control her self-image or to feel more like herself. Instead she wears it to channel a particular state of being, whether that's glamorous, gentle, artistic, rebellious, and so on. Makeup doesn't express the self for this kind of wearer; it expresses the moment. "I'm an actress at heart," says one thirtysomething blogger. "Makeup is a part of the roles I slip into every day."

Before we all start rushing to do our makeup Lady Gaga–style in hopes of capturing this psychological resilience, let's look at the factor that lies under this approach to cosmetics—which, not coincidentally, is one of the biggest buzzwords surrounding the beauty industry today: confidence. "Like chugging a Red Bull, makeup gives me energy and confidence," says Elyssa, a writer in her twenties. "When I'm going out, I'm heading off into my battle with the night, and I will win by looking absolutely fabulous. Makeup is my drag." Study after study has shown that women report feeling more self-confident when wearing makeup. What's unclear is whether this confidence applies only to women who already wear makeup on a regular or semiregular basis, or whether the maxim could extend to women who don't usually wear it. Non-makeup-wearing women often mention feeling distinctly uncomfortable in it: "Yes, I've tried that stuff that 'feels like nothing.' It still feels like something, and I hate it," says one woman who shuns cosmetics. I imagine it's similar to the feeling I have when I try out a lipstick that's too bright for me. How can you feel confident when you're too busy feeling conspicuous?

It's also difficult to feel confident when stressed-out, and makeup comes in handy here too. In a study of 140 women, researchers in France determined that when faced with stress, women applied more makeup than usual. Smart thinking too: When placed in a tense situation, women who were wearing makeup had lower signs of physiological stress like heightened skin temperature and restrained vocal pitch than their non-makeup-wearing counterparts, an effect that was exaggerated in women with higher levels of anxiety. Other studies have shown similar benefits. By literally concealing our anxieties and fears, makeup can arm women with a sort of shield against the flurry of stresses any of us go through every day. Applying makeup becomes an act of self-care not only through its motions—the act of simply touching oneself has therapeutic benefits—but through its results. It's a connection that hasn't gone unnoticed by the beauty industry, which has successfully linked cosmetics with confidence and self-care through advertising ("I use [makeup] to show the world who I truly am," says beauty vlogger Cassandra Bankson in an ad for Dermablend, which she uses to cover up severe acne scars) and even product names (MAC's Supremely Confident lipstick shade).

That confidence isn't limited to the person in it; makeup can make *other* people see its wearer as more confident. It can also drive others to find her more competent, more likable, and more alluring than those with a makeup-free face. The real-life benefits of this go beyond the conceptual: The makeup wearer isn't just abstractly *seen* as being more attractive; she's approached more frequently by men. If she's a waitress, she may get more tips from her male customers than her barefaced counterpart. Even absent these tangible effects, a woman may actually be able to change how the people around her feel, simply by putting on a little makeup: People exposed to pictures of makeup-wearing women experienced a decrease in stress hormones and an uptick in hormones supporting the immune system, as compared with people shown photos of barefaced women. That's also part of what makes makeup potentially problematic. If wearing makeup helps a woman seem more confident, more appealing, and more helpful to those around her, it frames the one-third of women who don't wear it as noncompliant, unwilling to perform the most basic of acts that could boost herself and others.

Of course, as with anything, it's impossible to neatly divide reasons for wearing makeup into internal and external motivations—money is an external reward, but we have internal reasons for wanting more cash, right? Still, some makeup motivations do an especially nice job of straddling that line, like using makeup to honor special occasions. My false-eyelash kit sees the light of day only during wedding season. I wear them to look just a little nicer, sure, but it's also a tiny way of acknowledging the importance of one of our last cultural rites—few other occasions warrant that extra bit of time and care. Some Latina women may have a particularly good grasp of this, as pointed out by Rosie Molinary, author of *Hijas Americanas: Beauty, Body Image, and Growing Up Latina.* "You might run into a woman of a non-Latina background and say she looks great, and she'll say, 'Oh, I just threw myself together this morning,' like it's this effortless perfection," she says. "But if you run into a Latina woman and say, 'You look really nice,' her reaction will be, 'Oh, thanks! I worked overtime to buy this dress, I've got on this girdle, it took me three hours to get my hair like this.' She'll own up to the effort, because part of it is wanting people to know they thought this event warranted that effort and respect. I see some truth in that."

Makeup can also function as a symbol of belonging to certain urban tribes or subcultures. Rockabilly women sport their cat's-eye eyeliner, goth kids make their skin ethereally pale, lip gloss and bronzer seems to be the look among the gym bunnies in my neighborhood, and there's a certain breed of magazine editrix who wears no makeup whatsoever except fire-engine-red lipstick. In occupations that see a growing number of women in positions of power, the ability to flash, say, a Chanel compact becomes a status symbol. Hairstyles come into play too: For some black women, wearing one's hair in a "natural" style versus a relaxed or straightened look can signal politicization and resistance to the idea that straight, fine, white-girl hair is preferred. "Wearing my hair textured, for me, is a way of affirming my African heritage," says Crystal, thirty-eight. "I grew up looking at pictures of Pam Grier from the seventies and thinking how beautiful she looked, and how her hair was a part of that. I don't do the Afro thing but having textured hair is a tribute to that period of awakening." (Of course, imbuing black women's hair with politics can be problematic, as Chicago journalist Britt Julious writes: "I don't like the idea that my hair is political . . . We rarely—if ever—require this of non-black women.")

But the biggest tribe that makeup signals membership in is the tribe simply marked *women.* Cosmetics can mark the transition from childhood into young-adult life—getting permission to wear makeup to school is a hallmark of adolescence for many women. Soon enough after I started wearing makeup, I began to understand that visible makeup signaled not just womanhood but a certain *kind* of womanhood, one that adheres to at least one convention of femininity. "This is what we do," says a friend of mine who once disliked makeup but grew into wearing it daily in her thirties after deciding on a career path. "This is what we've decided looks good, or professional, polished, normal. If all the other ladies are doing it, then I should also, so that we're all on the same playing field." Unlike other forms of cultural capital—i.e., non-monetary assets that aid social mobility, like education, speech patterns, etc.—makeup skill signals membership not in a socioeconomic class but in a gender class.

Within that gender class, though, we can learn even more about makeup as a mechanism instead of a signal. Dana, a fortysomething woman who dresses almost exclusively in traditional men's clothing—every time I've seen her, she's been in a perfectly cut suit—shuns conventional femininity in most ways, and yet: "I wear [makeup] every day, but subtly, and with the aim of just tweaking things to look a little better." It's a sentiment not much different from what plenty of girlie girls might say about their style, and in the hands of someone expressing a non-feminine identity, makeup reveals itself to be even more of a strategic tool, not a trap that wastes women's time. A hint of gray eye shadow, a dab of concealer—if Cary Grant had worn makeup, he'd have borrowed Dana's look. Conscious use—and non-use—of makeup can signal a strategy surrounding gender identity. "A new haircut is a butch accessory," says "boi" comedian Kelli Dunham, who identifies as a woman but favors conventionally masculine clothes and hairstyles. When I asked her if she ever got flak for not wearing makeup, her "no" surprised me at first. But her explanation made sense: "A friend of mine who transitioned [from being a woman to being a man] said, 'Wow, being a fat man is so much easier than being a fat woman.' There are ways in which there's a protective space formed around masculinity, and butch women have some masculine privilege. I mean, we're also liable to get beat up or knifed on the street, but there is some masculine privilege. Even when people think I'm a fifteen-year-old boy, there are benefits to that." And some transgender women report cosmetics as being crucial to their development as women. "I want to do what women do," says Ally, a fortysomething trans woman. "The very act of wearing makeup in our society is a gender marker. And I want to be on the girl side."

The Female of the Species:
Evolution, Attraction, and Makeup

I spent more than a decade making a living by reading women's magazines as a copy editor. Nowhere in those thousands of hours spent poring over the glossies have I once seen a beauty tip designed to make a woman's eyes look *smaller*. Same with making the eyes look lighter (save for the once-in-a-blue-moon flirtation with, say, yellow mascara) or tinting the cheeks to look paler than the rest of the face. And though the nude lip—think Twiggy—goes in and out of fashion, the majority of lipsticks are designed to make lips look rosier, if not always darker.

As it happens, all of these more or less consistent makeup rules run parallel to universal facial traits that distinguish women's faces from men's, a quality known as sexual dimorphism. Women's pupils are slightly larger than men's, giving the impression of larger eyes; plus, since men tend to be taller than women, women's eyes are closer to men's field of vision, making them appear disproportionately large to men. Women across races also have skin that's a shade lighter than that of their male counterparts, making their eyes and lips appear darker by contrast, a trait called "facial luminance." And what makes eyes and lips appear darker? Virtually every eye makeup on the market, and a good number of the lip products too. That includes lipstick specifically designed for women of color that tend to focus on the deeper end of the spectrum, keeping the facial luminosity maxim consistent across varying skin hues.

Not only do cosmetics tend to reinforce facial differences between the sexes; they also tend to mimic traits that signal women's ability to reproduce. That vibrant complexion and unlined skin? Signs of youth (and what beauty product ever promises to make a woman over the age of twenty-one appear *older*?), which translate to signs of fertility. And to stretch the makeup-as-signal argument a bit further, have you ever heard that bit about how lipstick was invented to make a woman's lips more closely resemble her inner labia, which become flushed and engorged when she's sexually aroused? (Never mind that men don't actually find reddish labia more alluring, according to a 2012 study.) The idea caught on after zoologist

Desmond Morris theorized the connection in his 1967 book, *The Naked Ape*, but there's no actual evidence that this was ever the drive behind lip coloration. Still, the idea became popular enough to become a naughty little beauty tip of sorts. "Match your lipstick to the color of your labia," advises a character in the 2011 film *Sleeping Beauty*—a tip then echoed throughout the beauty blogosphere, and hinted at every time a women's magazine floats the lipstick-labia theory.

Sound far-fetched? Perhaps. (Though imagine the possibilities for lipstick shades: Labial Lavender! Cunty Coral!) After all, when other animals show off their reproductive fitness, they simply strut the stuff they were born with, and everything seems to have worked out evolutionarily for *them*. But let's consider makeup as what evolutionary biologists call an "extended phenotype," a concept we touched on earlier. The idea is that the extended phenotype of makeup, just as with the spider's web or the bird's nest, becomes an advertisement for features that make us reproductively suitable. In other words, lipstick, eyeliner, and blush are just an externalized version of the fully opposable thumb that allowed our predecessors a firm grip on primitive tools. They're a feature that allows the human species to grow. And to a degree, it works. While there's no evidence that women who wear makeup are more fertile, a 2012 study showed that ovulating women wore more makeup than they did when they weren't at their monthly peak of fertility. (And since men have been shown to be quicker to approach makeup-wearing women in social situations, those efforts aren't in vain.)

There's an appeal to thinking that my paleo beauty ritual is as humanly necessary as eating, sleeping, and having sex. It enriches the ritualistic aspect of cosmetics. Not only are we partaking in a personal practice that centers us for what lies ahead in our day, but we're participating in a collective custom that's written into our genes, one that signals not just our womanness but our humanness. When seen as something that has helped the species flourish, makeup, so easily accused of being for the vain, can be considered a bona fide human development along the lines of agriculture or written language—call it the Mascara Age. The theory becomes even more satisfying when looking at some appearance customs outside the

Western world. Kayan women in Myanmar are famous for their neck rings, coils of brass that create the appearance of a lengthened neck. It's an awkward fashion to those outside the Kayan community. But it's an example of how sexual dimorphism is exaggerated by something that could theoretically be considered an extended phenotype: Generally speaking, women's necks appear somewhat longer than men's (in part because women's heads tend to be larger in proportion to the neck, giving the illusion of a longer, slimmer stem). Place brass rings around your neck, then, and you're exaggerating the look of the lengthy neck that sets women apart from men.

But before we leap into tutorials on creating a smoky cavewoman eye, let's look at another aspect of human behavior that we attribute to evolution: mating cost. Since it takes nine months for a woman to reproduce (as opposed to a man's short-lived contribution to the matter), women's mating cost is higher—which, according to some researchers, translates to women being choosier about whom they mate with. After all, if you're going to spend nine months housing a baby in utero, wouldn't you want that baby to have the strongest genes possible? So if we take mating cost and its fallout of feminine choosiness to be fact, why aren't *men* the ones adorning themselves with the extended phenotype of makeup to ensure they're not overlooked by those famously picky women? *Esquire* should be running step-by-step instructions on how to apply highlighter to give the illusion of a prominent square jaw, so that women—the shorter of the species—can gaze up to them and select the man with this classic testosterone marker. Twiggy's nude lip should be adopted by the gents to *decrease* facial luminosity and lip size, "nasal illuminators" should line drugstore shelves to help men get the coveted prominent masculine nose, and every eyebrow waxer in America should also be skilled in the art of eyebrow implants, to give male clients the heavy brow that distinguishes the male face from the female. In short, why aren't men peacocking around like . . . well, like peacocks? After all, those glorious iridescent tail feathers belong solely to the male peafowl and are put on display when attempting to woo the peahen, who is just as choosy as her human counterpart when it comes to mating.

Actually, historically speaking, men *did* do more of that peacocking than most do today. It's only in the last two hundred years or so that upper-class Western men dropped rouge, high heels, and ornamental clothing in favor of a bare face and the standard suit, a change that came about not because the ruffles of the aristocracy were seen as foppish but because it echoed the new ideals of democracy—poor men couldn't buy velvet coats, but many could afford a basic three-piece. Before that shift, things like wearing tinted face powders, and even painting one's head to mask baldness, were common. (And, of course, humans of all genders have worn painted-on embellishments for millennia—many an ancient Egyptian was buried alongside his cosmetics collection.) Even today, conventional men's grooming does allow for some evolutionary artifice. The classic five o'clock shadow gives weight to the lower half of the face, for example. But chalking up cosmetics use to evolution is Darwinian cherry-picking, justifying a mainstream vision of beauty that excludes a good portion of human history—and indeed, a good portion of the world today. Perhaps you could work backward from attractiveness cues like the famed lip plates of the Mursi women of Ethiopia, or the blackened teeth of some ethnic minority women in the hills of Vietnam—or the neck rings of the Kayan women of Myanmar—to find an evolutionary justification. But we tend to speak of such beauty traditions as being socially constructed. Indeed, lip plates and blackened teeth survived for centuries as symbols of the wearer's sexual maturity. Because these looks fall so far outside Western beauty norms, it's less tempting to claim that the relationship between a woman's sexuality and how black her teeth are is decided by her biology.

Most evolutionary psychologists do concede that beauty is defined by social and cultural norms as well as our genes. But whenever evolution is credited for something that costs women, *and not men*, a good deal of money—a projected $265 billion spent on cosmetics, hair care, skin care, and perfume by 2017 globally—it requires critical scrutiny.

Facing the World

While some women wear makeup when alone with no intention of leaving the home, most tend to reserve it for public use. The superficial reason here is obvious: Just as we might save the good china for company while eating off everyday plates ourselves, we're familiar enough with our own unadorned features to forgo the betterment makeup offers. We might wear makeup for ourselves, but in this way, it's actually something we do for other people, an acknowledgment of the ways we enhance ourselves when we're in plain sight.

But there's more to the public face of makeup than its end result. My paternal grandmother spoke of the act of applying makeup as "putting on her face," a turn of phrase that puzzled me as a kid, as it implied that the makeup *was* her face, the mass of skin tissue beneath it not even worthy of the word. As I got older and entered the workforce—specifically, the workforce in an urban area boasting the highest population density in the nation—I began to understand what she meant. It wasn't that the makeup was her face; it was that the made-up face is what one "puts on" for public occasions, even if the occasion is just going to work or a dentist appointment. It's what we put on to face the world. For makeup wearers, a layer of lipstick or blush can function as a boundary marker, one that helps us define exactly what we consider home and not-home.

Makeup can help us organize our public selves, making it a part of what sociologists would call our social "performances." But it's not just a signal to others; it can be a signal of public life for the person wearing it as well. As I write this from my home office, my hair is knotted in a messy bun, and I'm makeup free. I'm wearing a bra, though: The physical sensation of having parts of my body contained puts me in a "professional" writing mind-set that my pajamas can't match. I might be at home, but I'm working, and the bra serves as a tactile reminder of this, helping me keep on task. When the bra comes off, it's the end of the day, and I'm more easily found lounging on the sofa than pounding away on my laptop. I have another work-from-home friend who can't work unless she's wearing shoes. In the same way, when I meet up with some friends later this evening, I'll put on makeup—not because my friends care how polished I look, but because it will help me transition from writer-at-home mode into gal-about-town mode. It psychs me up, basically, and every time I catch a glimpse of myself in the mirror wearing lipstick that was absent earlier in the day, it's a reinforcement of the automatic adjustments any of us make depending on a change of setting or ambience. Cosmetics, clothing, and hairstyle all aid us in approaching various social performances with earnest belief.

And the opposite is true as well: Ill-fitting self-presentation is a quick route to discomfort. And discomfort—especially discomfort with stereotypes that accompany the various guises any of us might slip into—can foster a cynicism toward our own social performances. I think of an acquaintance who talked of feeling like she was "wearing a bear suit" when she uncharacteristically donned a dress to serve as her sister's maid of honor. It's not that she didn't want to stand by her sister as she wed, just as it's not that non-makeup-wearers are unable to transition into gal-about-town mode. It's that the expectations that might accompany those signals feel like a bad fit. As sociologist Erving Goffman writes, "[A] given social front tends to become institutionalized in terms of the abstract stereotyped expectations to which it gives rise, and *tends to take on a meaning and stability apart from the specific tasks which happen at the time to be performed in its name.*" (Emphasis mine.) The stereotypical signals makeup sends— makeup emphasizes femininity, and feminine people are supposed to be sexy yet demure, alluring yet coy, sparkling yet supportive—spur some of the discomfort its non-wearers may feel. That's not to say that women who wear makeup actually embody those stereotypes. Some might just be more willing to brush aside the larger implications of makeup and femininity, or might want those implications at their disposal to use at will.

So clearly the act of wearing makeup in public is, well, public. Yet it's the *private* side of wearing makeup in public that alerts us to its true importance. Once upon a time, applying makeup in public spaces was socially verboten, with women's advice columns tut-tutting the practice in the early twentieth century. If the number of women dabbing on eye shadow during the average morning subway commute is any measure, the stigma has lessened, but it's still seen by many as a no-no, or at least questionable. (The top companion search term on Google for "applying makeup in public" is "etiquette," and indeed Miss Manners herself has registered her thoughts against the act.) But the question is: *Why* is it objectionable? Concerns of safety aside—I've seen more than one woman get poked in the eye with a mascara wand when the subway comes to a sudden halt—it's not really hurting anyone, it's silent, and most concoctions are scentless to passersby. Yet I've heard plenty of people grumble about the practice, and I admit that when I see a woman preening in public, I feel a rush of something between anger and embarrassment. Not embarrassment for her but embarrassment of my own: the embarrassment of having one's secrets exposed.

Sociologically speaking, my secrets *are* being exposed. A "dark secret," in Goffman's terms, is something about a person that's incompatible with the impression she or he is hoping to make—the scandal surrounding former New York governor Eliot Spitzer is a prime example, as he admitted to soliciting a prostitute despite having signed legislation that heightened punishment for doing so. The way to keep dark secrets hidden is to expose them only in places we might call "backstage." So when we're talking about makeup, drawing back the curtain to allow anyone to see the work that goes into self-presentation casts a harsh light on those secrets. The work, products, practice, and effort behind a made-up face clash with the effect of *that's just how women look.* This is doubly true for the so-called natural look of subtle makeup meant to make the wearer look like she's wearing no makeup at all—but even for makeup that calls attention to itself as artificial, the idea is usually to enhance one's appearance, not to showcase a fabulous eye shadow. It's the wearer, not the product, that the public is supposed to see. Revealing the suppressed facts of the feminine performance—time, products, money, skill, *trying*—lets the public see precisely what many a makeup wearer doesn't want anyone else to directly observe. When my neighbor gets on the subway car and proceeds to give herself a six-stop makeover, she's revealing not only her own performance but mine as well. The act of womanhood is a shared one. "[A] team whose vital secrets are possessed by others will try to oblige the possessors to treat these secrets as secrets that are entrusted," writes Goffman. My silent embarrassment is the only way I can "try to oblige" other women to keep our secrets hidden, as I'm not about to admonish anyone for whipping out a lipstick at the bus stop. (And I don't need to admonish them, as in 2015 the New York City transportation system ran a series of public service announcements about proper transit etiquette, including a wrist slap to subway primpers.)

My anger and embarrassment are irrational feelings, ones I wish I didn't have—intellectually, I like the idea of letting non-makeup-wearers (specifically men) know exactly how much work goes into creating the effect of beauty. I wish I could be more like one woman who tasks her husband with letting her know if her lipstick is smudged: "I'm the one who puts it on every day, and if he wants me to keep wearing it, let him take some responsibility for it," she says. Beauty work isn't effortless, it's not always easy, and it can take a good amount of time and supplies to craft an "oh, I just woke up looking this way" appeal. I'd like to showcase this as a skill instead of tucking it away, but the truth is, I dearly protect the truths of artifice because revelation feels too risky. The as-is self, stripped not only of makeup but of all easily understood guises, reveals itself to be complex, messy, human. The public self that's undergone the private, unobserved ritual of putting on one's face—*that* self is more easily communicated and more easily understood. As Simone de Beauvoir wrote in *The Second Sex*, the made-up woman "does not present *herself* to observation; she is, like the picture or statue, or the actor on the stage, an agent through whom is suggested someone not there—that is, the character she represents, but is not. It is this identification with something unreal, fixed, perfect as the hero of a novel, as a portrait or a bust, that gratifies her . . ."

As it happens, we can find gratification in the opposite too: witnessing something "unreal, fixed" without its usual veil of perfection. Who doesn't get a smidge of satisfaction from those paparazzi slideshows of celebrities without makeup? We take immense joy in seeing proof that our contemporary idols engage in beauty's dirty work by catching a glimpse of them that we're not supposed to see. In turn, the appeal behind the celebrity trend of makeup-free selfies exposes a wish to break free of the "fixed" public persona that celebrities wear.

But for all the ways that makeup serves women in public, the private face of cosmetics serves us equally well at home. "Meditate for ten minutes a day" perennially tops my list of New Year's resolutions, and I perennially fail at it. But when I look at the essence of meditation—taking time to clear the mind, temporarily freeing oneself from tasks and to-dos and all the business that otherwise occupies our time—I wonder whether I've been meditating all along through the quiet solitude of my makeup ritual. My day-to-day look rarely varies, so my fingers automatically find their way around my face, to the point where I can apply a decent face of makeup without looking in the mirror if need be. You know how some people say they do their best thinking in the shower? I do my best *non*-thinking in front of the mirror. Dabbing on rouge and mascara gives me a place of pause. It prepares me for the day ahead—or, when I amp it up for a big evening, the night ahead. Most of this is the mere act of doing something that I've done so many times that I don't need to pay conscious attention to it, allowing my mind to drift in a meditative fashion. Physiology has its role too: The fragrance of some cosmetics can decrease heart rate, calm the nervous system, and increase the ability to feel pleasure. But it's something specific to cosmetics that makes this feel so ritualistic. I go on autopilot when I'm washing dishes too, but I don't fall into the same meditative mind-set as I do with makeup. Seeing the process, and then the result, of a transformation is a quiet daily reminder that I consciously create my persona. I wouldn't go so far as to say my morning rite is empowering. But it is a part of how I articulate myself, and the prep work involved in that articulation is crucial to its outcome.

Perhaps we can best understand the ways cosmetics channel our energies for public performance by looking at face paint in a different context. Army veteran Miyoko Hikiji barely wore makeup during her stints in Iraq and Afghanistan—"I maybe had a stick of concealer, for the sand flea bites," she says—but she's skilled in creating effects with military tools that amount to makeup. "Camouflage is like a little eye shadow pack. It's extremely thick, almost like clay; you sweat in it and it's just there. It's kind of miserable," she says. "But if you look at yourself in the mirror after doing these exercises with the camouflage paint on, it's hard to look at yourself the same way. There's something to putting on the camouflage, or the uniform, or just the effect you have when you're holding a loaded weapon. All that contributes to your behavior. So yeah, I definitely feel different when I wake up and put my regular makeup on. I approach the world differently, and the world treats me differently." The act of applying camouflage—whether it's tinted to match the Arabian Desert or your complexion—becomes not only a way of making yourself *look* the part but also a way of actually *becoming* the part.

Hikiji had a defined purpose in applying her camouflage—in fact, the goal was to literally camouflage herself. But in doing exactly that, she also embodied the role of soldier, just as a stage performer might wear exaggerated makeup to embody the role of starlet. Those of us whose livelihoods don't appear to be directly tied to the paint on our faces are stepping not into the public role of soldier or professional beauty but simply of *woman*. "My mother used to call it 'putting on your war paint,'" my college roommate Annie told me when we were musing about why we considered canceling our garbage service to save money but still managed to buy makeup. "I wonder—what kind of war am I in that I need makeup to have an advantage?"

Concealing and Revealing: Makeup Motivation and Lipstick Feminism

There's an idea floating around out there—partly born from a one-dimensional interpretation of *The Beauty Myth*—that makeup universally signals a strain of low self-esteem particular to women. The #nomakeupselfie movement popular in 2015 was applauded on social media as an act of bravery. The National Eating Disorders Association hosts a "Barefaced and Beautiful" campaign as an awareness-raising measure, in which women are urged to post makeup-free selfies. A certain kind of well-meaning man will urge women not to wear makeup, claiming that "you don't *need* it." Morning talk show hosts from Katie Couric to the cast of *The Talk* have gone barefaced for the cameras, framing their experience in terms of a crutch they had to summon bravery to go without. There's even an entire subgenre of women's writing revolving around abstaining from makeup and other vanity practices, as exemplified by *The Beauty Experiment* author Phoebe Baker Hyde's yearlong cosmetics-free experiment and Rachel Rabbit White's "No Make-Up Week," which dozens of bloggers participated in. Hyde and White both took pains to explain that their projects weren't designed to demonize makeup, but rather to help themselves understand the complex relationship they—and we—have with it. But that complexity was often lost in discussion once it left the hands of the creators.

The "barefaced and beautiful" attitude zooms in on the camouflaging aspect of makeup, ignoring other reasons women wear it. That's not to say that insecurity *isn't* a part of the makeup matrix: Plenty of women told me that at some point in their lives, they felt so unsure of how their natural face looked that they felt unable to do the most pedestrian of acts without a full face of makeup—go to the gym, walk outside to check the mail, run to the grocery store. The crossroads of self-esteem and beauty is indeed a troubling issue, and one that affects women disproportionately. Women's self-esteem is shown to be consistently lower than men's, beginning in early adolescence—the same age when body consciousness begins. And people with higher levels of anxiety about their appearance tend to have lower self-esteem and reduced ability to enjoy social situations.

But the number of makeup wearers I talked with who framed makeup foremost in terms of self-esteem? Zero. It came up in discussion, sure: "I guess you could call it insecurity, because on the days I'm not wearing any makeup, I catch myself thinking about the probability of looking bad," says Signe. On my end, I tend to pay particular attention to my makeup when I don't feel so great about my looks—it saves me the anxiety I might other-wise have regarding what others might think is "wrong" with my face. Now, self-reporting isn't necessarily a reliable gauge of motivations for wearing makeup. But for all the framing of cosmetics as a way of exploiting women's low self-esteem, and for all the ways women frame their relationship with beauty as an ongoing arc of self-acceptance, not once did this reason stand alone or even loom largely when I listened to what women said about their approach to makeup.

In fact, there were so few women who focused on this angle at all—or who spoke of makeup with the sort of hesitancy that implies that there's more to the story than what they're saying—that I began to wonder whether a sassier thread of talk has begun to replace the low-self-esteem conversation where makeup is concerned. The newer line of thinking goes something like this: We've spent so long denigrating the feminine—you don't throw like a *girl*, do you?—that for women to cast something particularly feminine like makeup in a negative light is equivalent to admitting that femininity is weak after all. Why not embrace makeup as a way of owning the feminine *and* the strong? Constructing cosmetics use as a form of self-articulation and even resistance might give us a broader perspective.

This mind-set has seeped out of the circles of academic postmodern feminist thought into popular culture. Two popular women's websites, *Jezebel* and *xoJane*, launched beauty-specific subsites; the Boobtique of feminist magazine *Bust* proffers cheek tints; and BuzzFeed, the marker of all things hive-minded, ran "14 Women Tell Us Why They Wear Makeup," with all participants framing their cosmetics use as joyful or empowering. There's defiance to this line of thought, which I've seen repeatedly in explicitly feminist circles as well as the more mainstream "postfeminist" culture that regards women's equality as something already achieved. Think of the playful way makeup images are arranged in women's magazines—wild eye shadow adorning haute couture models, artistic dribbles and splashes of various products covering the glossy pages. It echoes what thirtysomething Shannon says: "It's fun in the same little-girl way that coloring is fun—that crayons in themselves are fun. It's like coloring, but on your face." Framed this way, makeup is fun, a choice, a source of pleasure.

And as for that whole "women wear makeup because society pressures us" frame of mind? Few can deny the truth of its history. Less than seventy years ago, girls in high school home-economics classes were instructed in skillful makeup application, the idea being that makeup was as essential a part of womanhood as cooking and housekeeping. Employment handbooks regularly outlined what type of makeup female employees should wear; some still do. And in 2000, Darlene Jespersen was fired from Harrah's Casino in Reno, Nevada, for not wearing makeup; the Ninth Circuit Court of Appeals initially sided with Harrah's by ruling Jespersen's firing as legal after she took the casino to court. Across the pond, Melanie Stark, who worked in the music department at a Harrods store in London, suffered the same fate. But the fact is, we know about Jespersen's and Stark's cases because they were *news*, and news is what's outstanding, not what's run-of-the-mill. Workplaces mandating that women wear makeup seems outrageous, even when the courts disagree. The more established women's equality becomes, the more the idea that makeup is something thrust on us by the looming patriarchy begins to seem outdated. Old-fashioned, second wave, stodgy. *Boring.*

Indeed, there are plenty of numbers to support the idea that the makeup situation isn't quite so glum. According to research published in the *International Journal of Cosmetic Science*, women report feeling more self-confident and more sociable when wearing their usual makeup as opposed to none at all. Their body image is better when they're wearing makeup, and as for hairstyling, women's mood improves on nearly all measures after a visit to the hairdresser. And in a finding that might give makeup-championing feminists a moment of triumph, heavy makeup wearers have been found to be more pro-feminist in belief and attitude than women who wore less of it or none at all. As for women who *do* have low self-esteem, makeup isn't merely a veil for them to stay hidden behind; as we've seen, women with iffy regard for themselves actually have a decrease in signs of stress after applying cosmetics.

Yet despite these facts championing makeup as something far beyond flypaper that sticks women to our makeup kits for hours each month, something holds me back from being a wholehearted makeup evangelist—even though I wear it nearly every day. I can't help but question how "empowering" makeup can truly be when the vast majority of us use it fully within the boundaries that have been presented to us. It smacks of "choice feminism": the idea that if a woman *chooses* an action, as opposed to being shunted into it by patriarchal standards, it becomes feminist or at least symbolic of the hard-won options American women now have. In the case of makeup, though, not all of us *can* opt out. The firings of Darlene Jespersen and Melanie Stark are extreme in their consequences, but they're only a logical end point of research suggesting that women wearing light makeup are likelier than barefaced ones to be seen as competent in the workplace. And choice feminism in many ways is a euphemism for consumer feminism. While plenty of makeup is low cost and accessible to pretty much anyone who wants it, the fact is that to "choose" to wear makeup is to "choose" an ongoing expense that, at this point in time, is primarily drawn from women's bank accounts, not men's.

One of the pro-lipstick arguments that its cheerleaders defend most staunchly is the concept of makeup as self-expression. For if we decorate ourselves out of a desire to articulate that most sacred of beings—the self, unknowable to anyone but the subject—how can anyone decry it? It's as though if we're applying makeup because of a personal drive, it's okay, but if we do it because that's just what the majority of women *do*, we're caving in. It's a particularly American mind-set, as exemplified by one of the United States' standout writers: "Whenever you find that you are on the side of the majority, it is time to reform (or pause and reflect)," said Mark Twain. We're the country that invented the pioneer, the cowboy, the rebel outsider—hell, we're the country that turned Ayn Rand's self-above-all books into best sellers. We elevate the individual to the point where we just might be willing to work backward to justify any action as being about an iconoclastic vision, not about our collective or social sensibilities— including wearing makeup. The country that created the Lone Ranger is more willing to nod with approval when a woman claims to wear makeup "for me" than if the same woman, wearing the same makeup, meekly admits she wears it because it's expected of her by others. Marry our love of individualism with the legitimate complaints raised by feminists about the immense pressure on women to look good—and how this pressure makes us susceptible to the lures of the beauty industry—and it's not hard to see why we might denigrate any groupthink connected with makeup.

But here's the thing: Individuality exists in tandem with conformity. No society can be formed without a degree of collectivity, and we express that collectivity via aesthetic norms. We may have plenty of latitude within those norms, of course, but viewing makeup as an individual choice conveniently ignores the ways in which individual—even iconoclastic—

identities are formed in response to our collective ideal. For the most part, the majority of us wear makeup in ways that are more similar than different. When was the last time you pulled out green lipstick or red eyeliner? If a woman's face is a canvas for some sort of personal artistry, then frankly, we're making some pretty repetitive art. Where are the abstract expression- ists, the conceptual artists, the cubists? Outside of high fashion magazines and the occasional club night, where is *anyone* but the realists, minimalists, and a handful of dabblers in pointillism or pop art?

We've worked ourselves between a rock and a hard place, cosmetically speaking, simultaneously framing makeup as a place of individualism, play, and expression *and* as a shameful covering-up of our authentic selves. With the latter narrative of makeup as balm for culturally instilled insecurity, we paint makeup as something for the milquetoast. In doing that, we mute the palette of reasons that women wear cosmetics. In fact, many women I talked with did speak of justifying their makeup use by discussing the ways they enjoy cosmetics, as though they were aware of some of their own negative motivations—or were aware that because we've been so success- ful in calling attention to the dark side of makeup, they were *expected* to have some sort of justification for it. Enter the mind-set of makeup as play, which eschews insecurity in favor of the active celebration of cosmetics. Given that we've cast women's relationship to beauty as being pathological, there's something refreshing about seeing young women revel in the play- ful, expressive possibilities of makeup—witness the wildly colorful ads for makeup line MAC or the work of YouTube beauty vloggers. But these dual mind-sets carry the risk of an either-or opposition: Either you use makeup as play or you use it to cover up the parts of yourself you're ashamed of. The way we actually use makeup, of course, is hardly so delineated—a fact reflected in the tools themselves. We may wear eyeliner to emphasize a gorgeous pair of eyes, but we may also dot on concealer to hide imperfec- tions; we may define kinky hair with pomade but cover up our grays with dye. The best we can do by looking not only at our reasons for makeup but also at our eagerness to label some reasons as good (and others as not so good) is come closer to understanding the complexity of human beautification.

In doing so, we can adjust the disproportionate weight that makeup carries in popular feminist conversation. Going over the "is makeup feminist or not?" ground ad nauseam can serve as a distraction from other political concerns. It's a handy token point of debate for feminists in the Western world: Most of us have worn makeup, or considered wearing it, or have been challenged about why we don't wear it—or, as feminists, are simply hyperaware of the enormity of the messages we receive about expected feminine behavior. It makes sense that makeup is a locus of feminist-oriented conversation; after all, who is looking at the day-to-day lives of women more than feminists? But the extraordinary focus on whether wearing makeup makes one a "bad feminist" makes it all the easier for contemporary feminism to be written off as trivial. Look at the term *lipstick feminism*, the idea that young feminists base their political identity on tools of feminine power such as lipstick . . . and then ask yourself how many women you know who define themselves as lipstick feminists. In my case, the answer is zero.

Makeup, Femininity, and Power

A few years ago, I received an e-mail from Siobhan O'Connor, coauthor with Alexandra Spunt of the natural beauty guidebook *No More Dirty Looks* and coproprietress of the associated website. Earlier that year, the duo had issued a challenge to their blog readers: Send in photographs of themselves without a drop of makeup on. O'Connor and Spunt would then post them on the website, and one of the participants would win a raffle prize. The no-makeup gimmick that was popular online at the time worked particularly well for the No More Dirty Looks ethos, as the site focused on earth-friendly, cruelty-free, nontoxic beauty products; by showcasing themselves sans makeup, site users would see that "natural beauty" products were just an extension of the natural beauty they themselves possessed. The challenge was a hit. Dozens of readers sent in photos of themselves makeup free, comments were stuffed full of "wow!" and the like, and the four-month-old site found itself established in the natural beauty community.

Why not do another challenge? the duo reasoned a few months later. This time, they chose the opposite tack, asking readers to send in photos of themselves wearing a *lot* of makeup. "We want you to go wild . . . It's your going-out face we're looking for, not your doing-groceries face." This was a community of makeup lovers, remember, and the site's readership had expanded considerably since the initial challenge, so they expected this challenge to be even bigger than the last one.

So they waited a couple of weeks for photos to come in . . . and waited . . . and *waited*. That's where the e-mail I received came in. In an effort to prevent the challenge from being a total bust, O'Connor sent an e-mail to other beauty bloggers asking them to send in pics. I happily complied, of course, and in the end the challenge appeared to be a success. But the question raised by the scenario stuck with me: Why were women—specifically women who frequented a site devoted to makeup—far more eager to post public photos of themselves wearing no makeup than going all-out glam with the stuff?

"We had people privately e-mailing us and saying, 'I just can't do it,'" O'Connor says when I ask what she made of the lack of response. "I guess the mentality was, *Well, if I look bad with no makeup, no big deal.* But if you look bad with makeup, it's like you've said to the world, 'This is the best I can do,' and then if it doesn't work out you feel foolish."

Indeed, though I rarely leave my neighborhood without some makeup on, I *have* done it, and save for the occasional moment of self-consciousness, it's been fine. I compare that with the time I got a purposefully over-the-top makeover and then took the subway to a friend's place. I avoided eye contact with people, and if I happened to spot someone looking at me I wanted to rush over and say, *This is an experiment, this isn't the real me—I know it looks like I'm asking you for your attention, but I'm not.* What I take from this, and from the unexpected lack of response from the No More Dirty Looks readers about the glamour challenge, is this: Makeup can take courage. It's not necessarily an act of courage to dab it on, nor is refraining from using cosmetics an act of cowardice. The trouble is that the public conversation about makeup too often focuses on the self-esteem angle, regarding cosmetics as a crutch that women use to paper over negative

way to wriggle out of a different comfort zone, the one of perfect
erence to feminine codes. Challenging the assumptions surrounding
ty means challenging the rituals that make up our mornings and the
phrases that run through our heads: *Will I look too aggressive if I wear
lack eyeliner* and *the red lipstick? Does this meeting warrant the expensive
dation? I don't feel like shaving my legs today—how much do I care what
ht's date might think, and how much do I care that he's someone who
t care? I love this plum lipstick a friend made me try, but will my coworkers
 I'm "trying too hard" if I start dolling myself up all of a sudden?* It means
enging our complacency level with public and private life, letting the
her vane of our discomfort alert us to factors that run deeper than the
tion of makeup itself.

feelings about ourselves. Going makeup free is seen as a brave embrace of
one's own natural self—which, depending on the woman, it can be. But
praising that as a stroke of fortitude overlooks the ways in which asking
for attention—*here is my face, painted in a way that makes you likelier to
look at me*—can take a fortitude of its own. When we frame makeup as
something we do to cover ourselves up out of fear that we're not good
enough as is, we sell women's resilience short. We sell *women* short. When
women try—when women *strive*—we put ourselves on the line, more so
than men because our purpose is still so often presumed to be *You are here
to be looked at*. We should change the paradigm that led to this condition,
yes. But in changing it we can't afford to cast sidelong glances at women
who seize power through being seen or who take the traditionally passive
role of being looked at and transform it into an act of agency.

Makeup artists might stress another moral of the story here: When
it comes to makeup, moderation is key. And where there is moderation,
something is being moderated. That something is the wearer's relationship
to the world around her. Makeup helps us modulate our public image, our
sense of self, our levels of stress. It helps us keep a sense of order—fitting,
given that the word *cosmetics* comes from the Greek *cosmos*, meaning *order*.
And of course that's just the problem with it in many a mind. Why should
face paint be the way we organize ourselves—rather, how women organize
ourselves?

Part of the answer here comes from the current inseparability of cosmetics from womanhood. Until men wear makeup in numbers as strong
as women, we won't really know how much our cultural attitudes have to
do with makeup itself as opposed to the people who wear it. A side note
in a study on cosmetics and impressions in the workplace points to the
trouble in collapsing the two. Makeup-wearing women were judged negatively in occupations that are stereotyped by sex. So if you're a secretary
or a nurse, wearing makeup could actually hurt you—but if you're, say,
an insurance agent, it won't. What this suggests is that as many associations as we make with makeup, ultimately its relationship to femininity
matters more. Amp up the makeup, and you amp up the womanness
of its wearer. As long as we associate womanhood with qualities that

have little to do with sex—like competence (or lack thereof), compliance (or stubbornness; *you know women*), moodiness (is it that time of the month?)—anything associated exclusively with women is going to carry more weight than it would alone.

Frustrating as that is, it's not as frustrating as the limits of makeup. For no matter how skillfully we apply our eyeliner or how carefully we arrange our hair, some people are going to be more conventionally beautiful than others. Makeup can act as a sort of beauty democratizer: Not born with colorful lips, smooth skin, and a vibrant complexion? Fake it, my dear. But at the end of the day, no matter how skilled our makeup technique might be, *beauty is not a meritocracy*. It's not as though she who tries the hardest (or spends the most money, or has the most charm or even the most sex appeal) is the most beautiful. And if we assign that expectation to makeup, it will forever fall short.

Yet as much as we tie makeup to beauty, we've seen that beauty in and of itself is far from the only reason we bother with it. My hope is that by considering a more complex relationship with makeup, we can consider our real expectations surrounding it. Makeup is the ultimate placebo effect; it's a cosmetic change in every sense of the word, and our expectation that it will work—whatever that might mean to the wearer—is the only thing that keeps the beauty industry afloat. I think of what that English professor said about why she wears it: "Wearing makeup allows me to look the way I imagine I look all the time." I hear resilience in this statement, not capitulation. It's not that she wears makeup because she feels bad without it. She wears it because she thinks she looks pretty damn good, and makeup helps her realize that more fully. With makeup, we are not aiming to be transformed into someone else; we're trying to present our best selves. It's an articulation of the psychological drive to be seen. Makeup literally increases our visibility in the world.

In this light, both makeup fasts and over-the-top makeup challenges like the one posed by the No More Dirty Looks team take on a different importance than they might if looked at alone. We're in an unusual time, womanwise. More women than ever are entering public office, leading corporations, and outearning their male domestic partners. At the same

time, women in the public eye are under ever-more [attractive] at all times, and the US cosmetics industry c[ontinues] the point of $58.3 billion, taking a larger and larger ch[unk] earnings. Women's visibility has increased—accompa[nied] magnifying glass. But when presented with tools availa[ble] sixteen dollars to assemble a basic makeup kit, wome[n] perspective, personality, and opportunity—are able to sh[ape] in a way that speaks to their own visions of themselves. [ ] the basic question here: Is makeup quite literally a tool of [ ] an instrument of women's self-articulation? And it's here t[hat] and challenges and everything in between serve their pur[pose] not to swear off all forms of artifice forever, or to embrace [ ] our disposal, or even to give a point-by-point on why you [ ] or don't, or wore it yesterday but not today. Nor is it to r[ ] of choice feminism: *Hey, it's fine to wear makeup as long as* [ ] Yet it might be something just as personal: finding, and cha[llenging] comfort zone.

Plenty of women don't wear makeup because it never in[ ] ("I'll wear it if I have to, like if it's expected of me because i[ ] or a work event or whatever, but I've never been drawn to it [ ] that changing," says Cheryl, a woman in her late forties). Bu[t] adhere to a wash-and-go face report a deep discomfort with t[ ] makeup can bring. "It's like, who am I, to think you should l[ ] says one mother of three. This whisper of *Who am I to ask for yo[ur]* goes to the core of nice-girl syndrome, the condition that ha[s] many a woman from speaking out on everything from job discrim[ination] unwanted sexual advances to just contradicting the blowhard w[ho] women at parties, asks them what they do for a living, then proce[eds] them everything *he* knows about their industry. Certainly makeu[p] secret voice box that allows women to utter words like *No* or *Th[ ]* or *You're wrong*. But if staying in one's comfort zone means holdi[ng] with the ever-polite monster of *Who am I to ask for your attention* leaving that zone, no matter the route, is crucial. For some wom[en] ning makeup might be one of those routes. For others, dropping [ ]

4

The Eye of the Beholder

Sex, Dating, and Romance

One of the most endearing stories about love and beauty I know begins with pornography. A friend of mine worked at what's affectionately known in the industry as a "stroke mag"—i.e., a magazine with stories and images designed with a purpose-driven mission for their gentleman readers. This particular magazine didn't accept reader submissions, but that didn't stop a persistent handful of men from attempting to make their own contributions. Each month, my friend would receive dozens of photos from male subscribers. Not of the men themselves, but of their wives and girlfriends, with notes attached about how these women absolutely *needed* to be featured in an upcoming issue—I mean, isn't she *lovely?*—and if the editors had any business sense at all, they would send over a photo crew immediately to capture this woman in all her glory.

"And here's the thing," my friend told me over lunch. "These women— I'm sorry, but they're not all that!" (She dated women, so she was particularly qualified to make the assessment.) "The pictures are terrible, they're at awkward angles, and even when the women are attractive they just don't look like anything special to me. I don't get it." I took an odd sort of assurance from her report. These men were convinced that the utterly normal-looking women in their lives were *so* stunning, *so* alluring, that to deny them a spot in a stroke mag would be a gross disservice to masturbators nationwide. I pictured an average middle-age man gazing on his average middle-age wife and seeing not her crow's-feet or ashy skin or doughy thighs or any of the things the run-of-the-mill woman has that fall outside the realm of conventional beauty. No, he sees a *queen*. The eye of the beholder indeed.

It's interesting that what these particular men did in their private lives flies in the face of so much of the conventional thinking surrounding beauty and love. Men are visual creatures, we're told, so looks are the first thing they notice about a woman. It's a bit of wisdom that feels true at times: I've experienced the humiliation of watching a man I was on a date with stop talking midsentence to stare at a stunning leggy blonde walking through the room. I've seen male friends go gaga over a particularly pretty female friend of mine. And I've adjusted my behavior accordingly—taking special care with my makeup before dates, and then, when I've been in a relationship, making sure not to "let myself go."

But I also knew that the whole "men love beautiful women" thing was shortsighted. For starters, it didn't recognize the fact that we women are rather visual creatures ourselves. (The old saw that women go for personality, men for looks? It's not quite that simple, as we'll soon see.) It also didn't explain why I knew so many women who were average-looking, or even plain, who constantly had men sniffing after them—or why that particularly pretty friend of mine didn't date anyone until her mid-twenties. And where did this whole thing leave queer women? It wasn't like the lesbian and bisexual women I knew lived in some sort of utopia where they were romantically evaluated on their inner beauty alone.

I saw enough evidence of both of these lines of thought to know that chances were some men prized conventional beauty above other qualities, others had more unique ideas about beauty, and still others might not particularly care what a woman looked like as long as he felt attracted to her. Maybe some really didn't care at all. Most of all, I knew there wasn't much I could do about it—there wasn't some bulletproof way to ensure that anyone I wanted to find me attractive would do so. I could try to look my best, sure, but as thirtysomething Rob put it, "I'm pretty much attracted to someone or I'm not. And if I'm not attracted to someone, it's not like it's because I don't like how she does her hair or something—it's because there's *just not an attraction*. I can think a woman is really pretty and just not be attracted to her."

So I knew this rationally. But what these two competing schools of thought on beauty and attraction did was create not a spectrum but two parallel tales. One was that beauty was in the eye of the beholder, and that I could safely assume that if someone was drawn to me, he found me attractive as is. The other was that conventional beauty was the surest route toward landing a quality partner, and that the best way to maximize my chances of finding a match was to maximize my beauty. I feared that at some point, those two parallel lines would turn perpendicular and crash. Someone could fall for me and find me beautiful—and then one day, he'd switch tracks and realize that I wasn't actually as pretty as he'd once found me. I'd never had a problem attracting men, but that fact failed to give me much protection from the fear that if I found myself single when I didn't want to be, it would be my looks that were to blame. It was insecurity, sure, but within my fears dwelled something more potent—more intimate—than mere insecurity. I just wasn't sure what.

When I think of all the ideas floating around out there about how beauty shapes our intimate relationships, I picture something resembling an awkward party. In one corner is the dude going on about how, duh, *of course* the purpose of beauty is to attract mates, and men are just more *visual* than women, so can he help it if he wants to be with the most gorgeous woman in the room? Meanwhile, he looks knowingly at the woman on his arm—who *isn't* conventionally beautiful but who has that ineffable quality known as "it," and who, when you catch her in the ladies' room later on, says, "Sex appeal is an *attitude*," winks at you, and wiggles her way back into the fray. Then there's the frowsy couple who dress alike and seem utterly enchanted with one another; when the woman goes to get a drink, her fellow's eyes trail after her and he sighs, "Isn't she beautiful?" And then there are the women like me, and maybe like you, who are watching the party and wondering where exactly their own brand of allure fits into the smorgasbord of attraction.

Will the following pages answer that question definitively? Probably not. But I will tell you this: Several years ago, a coworker told me about a woman he'd met at a party the night before. There were dozens of women at the soiree whom he found prettier, but as he put it, "I couldn't stop watching her. It was like my body was making the choice for me—I had to make myself not follow her around all night, but I wanted to be near her." And at night's end, when he asked for her number and they wound up canoodling, "It was unbelievably sexy. And I *still* don't think she's all that pretty." At the time I didn't know whether to cheer him or raise my eyebrow—this was a man well into his thirties, and he was only *now* discovering that someone's presence could outshine her plain wrapper? I've shared this anecdote plenty of times since that conversation, and nearly everyone who hears it nods in recognition or chimes in with their own similar tales, including people who have strict physical preferences they prefer not to stray from. *He* was the outlier for not recognizing this earlier, not me. As much as we as a society have pushed the idea that physical appeal is the key to attracting romantic attention, particularly for women, we intuitively challenge that assumption all the time simply by being attracted to whomever we're attracted to. There's no guarantee that the person we see under a special golden light will see us in the same way, of course. But most of us, wherever we fall on the spectrum of conventional beauty, have had moments of being glimpsed through that golden lens of attraction. To me, that's a comfort.

A word on sexual orientation: Most of the themes I'm covering here are common to people all over the spectrum of sexual orientation—the proverbial rose-colored glasses, for instance, and the role of personality in defining who catches our eye. However, much of the clinical and academic research on those themes focuses on heterosexual attraction. It's difficult and dangerous enough to draw broad generalizations from studies and interviews, let alone apply those generalizations to the LGBT community. All might be fair in love and war, but the gender differences that play into some of those generalizations make it impossible to assume that relationship templates between men and women apply to romances between women. As the saying goes, take what you like, and leave the rest.

I'll Tell You What You Want:
Physical Preferences in the Dating Market

If barroom wisdom is to be believed, the best thing a woman can do to snag a date is be irresistibly good-looking—and the best thing a man can do is have a fat wallet. And sure enough, the leading study on the matter, which surveyed more than ten thousand people around the globe, upholds the beauty-and-money maxim. Men reported valuing physical attractiveness more than women did, and women were likelier than men to say they wanted a mate with high earning potential. The theory here is an echo of what we looked at in chapter 1: Beauty is prized, particularly in women, because it signals reproductive fitness. That is, our evolutionary drive pushes a man to seek out the most attractive partner to bear his children while leading women to find the man with the greatest resources to provide for those children.

Let's leave aside concerns about the validity of this theory for the moment. For whatever the science behind the "men want beauty, women want money" line of thinking might reveal, we certainly *act* as though it's true. When it comes to "mate retention practices," or the things we do to keep our lovers around, heterosexual women are likelier than men and gay women to gussy themselves up in hopes of holding on to a partner. And the more conventionally attractive a straight woman is, the more of those practices her fellow will engage in, particularly "resource display," or flashing cash. The prizing of beautiful women can reach the point of lunacy: In one study, men were likelier to pursue women whose online dating profiles featured an attractive picture—even when they were explicitly told that the photo wasn't actually of the woman whose profile it was paired with. The mere *thought* of beauty, it seems, can blind men to reason.

So is it any wonder that women sometimes believe the route to love is lined with beauty rites? "I wish I had more time to put into my appearance so I could make men I'm dating prouder to be seen with me," says Jasmin, a thirty-eight-year-old paralegal. Elyssa, a twenty-six-year-old writer, has slept with her makeup on when spending the night with paramours. YouTube is littered with first-date makeup tutorials (one of which specifies using a primer from Benefit named, aptly enough, Stay Don't Stray). As for me, my pre-date checklist consisted of cash, credit cards, ID, keys, phone—and a stick of concealer. Not that it's just first-date jitters that have women connecting relationships with appearance; I've heard three different women craft their marriage-proposal tales in a way that specifically includes self-consciousness about something being wrong with their appearance at the moment the question was popped. (One woman had just come home from the gym and uttered a sweaty, red-faced "Yes," while another had a piece of salami caught between her teeth as her boyfriend went down on bent knee.)

There's a problem with believing that men pursue relationships with beauty foremost in mind. It's not true. That study of more than ten thousand people? It asked men and women about their *preferences* in dating, not their *experiences*. In fact, most empirical data on "what men want" is actually data on what men *think* they want. Truth is, we humans aren't so great at knowing what we truly want when it comes to partners. In a study that examined people's choices in speed dating, both in the moment and in long-term follow-up, researchers found little correlation between people's stated preferences and their actual choices. (Case in point: A boyfriend once mentioned that I fit his type—short brunettes—to a T. I've got brown hair, but I'm also three inches taller than the average American woman. When I pointed this out, his retort was, "I mean shorter than *me*." He's six-foot-one.) One way to interpret this finding is that our preferences make for a sort of wish list, but we're willing to settle for less. That makes a certain sense—why *wouldn't* we all want to pair off with people we think are good-looking? Indeed, most studies that support the men-love-hotties idea show that women say they want physically appealing partners too; they just don't rank it as high in importance as men do. Instead, women tend to place value on earning potential—or at least, in keeping with the idea that we don't know what we really want, women *think* they place more value on the wallet than on the face of its holder.

The speed-dating study authors add a crucial twist to the wish-list theory. We make those lists in a state of cool rationality—but when faced with a real, live human, what we find ourselves attracted to may have little to do with what's on that oh-so-rational checklist. It might not be so much that a man "settles" for a woman with pedestrian looks, or that a woman "settles" for a man with a modest income, but that the intoxication of attraction instantly realigns our stated priorities into something that more accurately reflects our deeper longings. Attraction might follow some forms of logic, sure. That doesn't mean that it's a logic we can manipulate at will. You've heard the term *perfect on paper*, right? We all know what trumps that person who checks every box on our wish list: the one we're *actually* attracted to.

Still, there is a phenomenon that, at first glance, looks like support for the idea that men pursue beautiful women: the matching effect. Men who meet society's definition of conventionally good-looking do indeed tend to pair off with similarly attractive women. Crudely put, a ten is likelier to marry a ten, while fours wind up with one another. (Of course, one person's four might be another person's ten, but most of us are able to recognize what makes a person traditionally attractive, and that's what the research we're looking at here considered.) But the matching effect in relationships extends to most areas of our lives: education, income, temperament, personal interests. Similarities predict how satisfying a relationship is to the people in it—as much as we say that opposites attract, statistically speaking, they don't. So yes, rich, good-looking men do gravitate toward rich, good-looking women—just as rich, average-looking men gravitate toward rich, average-looking women, and low-income hotties wind up with one another.

Theories on why we humans love to match our partners in looks range from evolutionary (good-looking people want good-looking babies) to market-based (since we prize beauty, it becomes a form of currency that people can exchange with one another on the fair market of love), from commonsense (matching is satisfying) to Freudian (we pick people who resemble our parents, and who therefore somewhat resemble ourselves). Where things get really interesting is in looking at not just how objectively good-looking people are but how good-looking people *think* they are. Researchers theorize that conventional attractiveness simply sets a baseline for how good-looking a person can reasonably expect his or her sweetheart to be. But people who rate themselves as highly attractive have a better chance of pairing up with good-looking people—even if, objectively speaking, they're not terrifically attractive themselves. It boils down to this: If you think a person is out of your league, you're less likely to try to go to bat. But if you think you're both playing in the major leagues, you've at least got a chance to hit a home run.

Does all this talk of fours and tens and home runs seem a bit crude? It might, but there's good news here for the average-looking person—i.e., most of us. And it's something that lies at the heart of many a feel-good romantic comedy, to the point where there's no way to say this without seeming cheesy, so bear with me: Inner beauty counts too. Most of us have had the experience of meeting someone average-looking and finding him or her more attractive the more we get to know the person—or of meeting someone stunning and finding him or her *less* appealing the more we're exposed to that person's disagreeable personality. This isn't limited to the occasional *Beauty and the Beast* anecdote; it's backed by research as well. Men given positive general information about women's personalities rated a wider range of female body sizes as attractive, as compared with a group of men told that the women they were rating were unpleasant. Same with general attractiveness, for both sexes—in fact, in one study, people rated the subjects of *the exact same photos* as more or less attractive than they had only minutes before, depending on the kind of information they were given about the people in the pictures. And when researchers looked at participants' diaries, they found recorded evidence that this sensation isn't unusual. My own journals reflect this truth, whether the proclamation is 1989's "I can't believe I ever thought he was hot! GROSS!!!" or 2007's "How is it that he's become beautiful to me?"

If you're feeling particularly cunning, you could even reverse engineer these findings, as people with better education, more likable personalities, and higher grooming standards are likelier to land themselves an objectively good-looking partner. (And yes, that goes for women as well as men—we're just as likely to trade our own education to snag a good-looking date as the guys.) Being Miss Congeniality may be construed as being runner-up, but it needn't be. Taking steps to improve other aspects of your life—your job, your life satisfaction, your temperament, your wit—

can actually make you be seen as more physically beautiful. Challenging the notion that inner beauty is by necessity different than the skin-deep variety allows us to see that beauty isn't just some extraneous force that's left up to the whim of genetics. It's a malleable concept, one we can tailor to our strengths. The no-makeup makeover might not be easy—and just as with physical beauty, it might not even be fair—but it's an option. And depending on your perspective, it just might be a good one.

Rose-Colored Glasses: Positive Illusions in Relationships

I'd tell you I once fell in love with a handsome man, but that's not exactly what happened. What happened was more like this: I met a man whose looks were . . . well, more than one person suggested that were we to have children, it would be a stroke of misfortune were they to inherit their father's looks. When I first met him, I'd have agreed. It's been ages since I've seen him, but I can recall what a disinterested party might refer to as his flaws: limbs disproportionate to his body, tightly curled hair of a color he once referred to as "opossum," unnaturally smooth skin that lent him an oddly childlike quality tempered by the tufts of opossum-colored facial hair that he never seemed to quite depilate correctly. I saw those things, and when I met his stunning pocket Venus of a girlfriend, I thought, *Wow, how'd he wind up with her?*

Our love story itself is fairly unremarkable: Time passed, our friendship developed, his relationship disintegrated, then mine—in part because, while attending the wedding of a friend whose vows included "waking up every morning next to my favorite person," my mind went not to the person I was seeing but to this other man. What made it remarkable (to me, anyway) was what happened to him. He went from being odd-looking to cute to—I still couldn't call him *handsome*, what with its connotations of square jaws and Clooney eyes and rugged yet genteel masculinity. *Beautiful*, though—*that* he became.

Coming to find him beautiful was a series of fits and starts: watching him crack a good joke and loving the glint that came into his eyes, finding myself softening ever so slightly when I'd catch his profile at a particular angle. It didn't feel like I was talking myself into finding him more attractive, nor did it feel like I was superimposing his inner beauty onto his looks. I knew he hadn't physically changed—and yet, *he had*. He was beautiful to me, and he hadn't been before; surely my taste hadn't changed so dramatically in a matter of months, had it? I'd heard the term *rose-colored glasses* before, but in regard to relationships I'd thought of it as a mental trick, a way of fooling ourselves—or is the better term *deluding* ourselves?—into thinking we're with someone better-looking than we actually are. I hadn't known that when those glasses were calibrated by affection, it could change your vision. It felt like a slower, more gradual version of what happened the first time I put on a pair of glasses to correct my nearsightedness. The eye doctor placed the pair of pink plastic frames onto my nine-year-old face, I looked over to where my mother was sitting, and I thought, *Oh, that's what you look like.* For the first time, I could see the small details that made her *her*—the hair not only a mass of red but individual strands; the skin not a smear of pink but made up of curves and lines and pores and a small, pale mole I'd never seen before. Twenty-some years later, the way my vision had been altered when it came to this man wasn't as sudden, but it felt just as dramatic. And the first time I found myself being held in his arms, I tilted my head up from his chest, saw his care-softened features, and thought the same: *Oh, that's what you look like.* Were you to tell me this story about you, I'd find it sweet, but I'd know that of course *he* didn't change a bit; it was all you. Yet to this day I am not fully convinced that the shift was mine alone. *He changed.*

The sensation of someone becoming more attractive over time is hardly a quirk unique to me—at least half the people I interviewed about this said they'd had some sort of similar experience. It's so common that it has a name of its own: positive illusions. The general idea behind positive illusions is that our minds will fool themselves into thinking things are better than they actually are, or that we're more exceptional than we really are, so that we can go about our day-to-day business with a sense of optimism. It's part of why so many of us still buy into that "till death do us part" business in the face of high divorce rates, why the majority of us think of ourselves as better-than-average drivers, and even what allows some terminally ill

2009. The words *thick ankles* describe something undesirable in neutral language. *Cankles* takes that undesirable feature and escalates it into an insult.

In her 1979 essay "Words and Change" about the impact of feminism, Gloria Steinem wrote, "We have terms like *sexual harassment* and *battered women*. A few years ago, they were just called *life*." Her point was that developing lingo for these problems was a positive development. The inverse intent holds true too: If naming domestic violence allows us to go about fixing it, what does that do for cankles, which were once just called life? Every time we use a word like *cankles* to describe bodies—our own or other women's—we add power to the phenomenon of thick ankles, which wasn't a phenomenon until we named it. The point of these cagey words isn't nullification of women's extraordinary awareness of our bodies. The point is to amplify it. And if we refuse to use language designed to intensify that self-consciousness, we take a small step toward eroding the self-consciousness itself.

Most of the time, we invent words to label an existing phenomenon that requires discussion. Think back to the days and weeks after September 11, 2001, when people called that day anything from "the attacks" to "September 11" to "nine-one-one" to simply "Tuesday"—and now consider how we've collectively settled upon "9/11" as the handiest term. Same with "the Internet" over "World Wide Web" or "the information superhighway." Now, both 9/11 and the Internet were new; obviously we didn't have the words before they existed. But thick ankles, ample waistlines, and fleshy upper arms have existed as long as the human body. Still, it wasn't until the past decade or so that their monikers came into use. Part of that could be because of democratized access to the collective consciousness, courtesy of the information superhighway. If someone dreams up a clever term for something that's currently unlabeled, it can go viral in a matter of hours.

More likely, though, these terms stuck because they serve a larger purpose. They give us a language that allows us to bond while discussing our physical appearance. Women are *expected* to talk of their bodies in derogatory terms. And we're rewarded for wielding this particular lexicon. If I tell you I have cankles, chances are you'll respond with something like, "Shut up, you do not." The language of the put-down gives birth to the language of support.

But we also need to look at why the vocabulary of self-deprecation came to be in the first place, which goes back to the beauty myth itself. As women's minds become more free to roam, the status quo can maintain its stability through the ways women keep their own bodies in line. (Not that it's only women who have more and more labels slapped on them: A man with anorexia nervosa requires treatment just as urgently as his female counterpart, but when we're able to dismiss his behavior as *manorexia*, he goes from having a clinical illness to merely being a little too vain.) If you can't name it, you can't shame it. And if you can't shame it, then there goes Cankle Awareness Month, jeans designed to prevent muffin top, and entire segments of the $60-billion-a-year weight-loss industry. There goes the pride a not-terrifically-pretty woman might feel upon developing her physique to its top form. All those hours at the gym, all those refusals of after-work beers and nachos, all those mornings of rising early to go for a run—they have their own rewards, yes, she knows this. Still, the word *butterface* lingers at the periphery of her mind.

Naming the Unnameable

Feminists have long pointed out the double standard of sexuality shown in language. A sexually promiscuous woman can be any of dozens of words—*slut, tramp, ho, easy, loose,* and so on—but the only word we have that's specific to male promiscuity is *stud*, which carries a positive connotation. But this formidable list is dwarfed by the number of words we have to describe women's bearing and beauty—or lack thereof. Women are consumable (*sugar, juicy*) and in need of care (*babe, doll*). We're haughty and distant (*queen, princess*) and untouchable (*goddess, angel, siren*). We're animals, able to be owned (*chick, cow, mousy*). We are here to be looked at: Has a man ever been described as being "pretty as a picture"? And when women's protests about being classified by their looks are actually heard, the language might shift in accommodation, but barely. Before the UK's Sex Discrimination Act of 1975 was passed, the word *attractive* was regularly used in help-wanted ads to describe desired female candidates for secretarial positions. Once the law stepped in to provide employment protection for people of all sexes, *attractive* continued to be used almost as frequently—but to describe the office environment, not the people in it. The law had nothing to do with the word *attractive*, but once recruiters were unable to specify the desired sex of their secretaries, they ceased to use the word in regard to candidates. But decision makers continuing to use the word in other applications proved that the *idea* of attractive women was important enough to remain in the strategy for gathering new talent, even if its literal emphasis had to be displaced.

Just as women's cultural status is reflected in the language of looks, that language becomes a repository for cultural concerns. Think of the word *bombshell*, which rose in popularity to describe good-looking women along with America's anxieties over the atomic bomb. We literally merged the two in the first bomb tested after World War II by painting the word *Gilda* on the side of it, after Rita Hayworth's 1946 bombshell role. And the bigger our anxieties about actual bombs became, the emptier the woman-as-bombshell categorization had to become in order to nullify a very real threat. Who was taken more seriously as an actress during her lifetime: Jean Harlow, the original bombshell, whose 1933 *Bombshell* came out before the idea of the atomic bomb had even been patented—or the most enduring bombshell of all time, Marilyn Monroe, whose infamous rendition of "Happy Birthday" was sung to JFK the same year as the Cuban Missile Crisis? The more serious the threat, the more we need to defuse the bombshell. Meanwhile, on the other side of the arms race, Russia used to regard its word for beauty, *krasota*, as the value of beauty—meaning its quality, not its worth on any sort of market. But in the years after glasnost, the meaning of the word expanded to match the ways Russians were now able to think in overtly capitalist terms. *Krasota* can now refer to something that can be bought and sold, akin to how drugstores have "beauty" aisles, meaning products that enhance beauty, not beauty itself. The value shifted to accommodate the advent of capitalism.

We can track the changing meaning of words over time with dictionaries. But even as we may turn to dictionaries to verify the exact meaning of words, the makers of dictionaries turn to *us* to find out how words are being used, and then shape dictionaries accordingly. When, for example, *f-bomb* was first included in *Merriam-Webster* in 2012, it wasn't dropped in there because the dictionary folks made it up. It was included because it had guest starred in enough media outlets that it had actually *become* a word that, in turn, should be defined by the leading word reference book in the United States. We develop our language collectively. We might talk of the Internet as being the "hive mind," but language was the original hive mind. Whatever words we have, we came up with together. That's sort of depressing when considering that we came up with dozens of words to describe women's looks, yet still have just a mere handful for men—but it also means that if our hive mind begins to think of beauty differently, our language will shift accordingly. For example, *Merriam-Webster* lexicographer Kory Stamper points out that one of the newest appearance-centric words to make it into the dictionary is *hottie*, which can be used to describe both sexes. "Since the second wave of feminist writers, we've been so much more aware of how we use language for any sort of marginalized group of people," Stamper says. "We're much more embarrassed by racial slurs, we're much more aware of the language we use for women. When we look at the use of some of the newer words like 'hottie,' there's more gender parity in their uses. You're chatting with the 'hottie barista.' That doesn't say if the barista is a man or a woman. We see more and more of that with informal words." *Hottie* reflects heightened gender awareness; it's also a reflection of the ways we're increasingly objectifying men. Similarly, we've largely dropped old-fashioned words like *comely* from our vocabularies. We've been developing our lexicon for beauty for centuries, and it's up to us to shift our language to allow for the ways we're chiseling away at the omnipotence of the beauty standard. Changing the words we use en masse to describe the way we look has the potential to change the ways we *think* about how we look. If we want to drop *fugly*, or begin collocating terms like *pretty man*, we can.

Yet . . . we haven't, for the most part. And maybe that's because we don't want to. Perhaps our hive mind prefers to skew beauty discussions toward women. Or perhaps we've developed the vocabulary of beauty in the ways we have because the nature of beauty is still a mystery to us. Even as each word that evaluates beauty carries its own specificity, it also carries a sense of ambiguity. Both *gorgeous* and *lovely* are used approvingly, and it's not like *gorgeous* is a magnification of the simpler *lovely*. Yet most of us would agree that in the ziggurat of beauty words, *gorgeous* is nestled somewhat higher than *lovely*, and that "a gorgeous woman" and "a lovely woman" bring two different women to mind—but we'd be hard-pressed to articulate precisely *why*. We can take a stab at it—indeed, *beautiful* is one of the words in *Merriam-Webster* that has an entire synonym breakdown devoted to it—but ultimately each of us is going to associate a different set of qualities with the word *beautiful*, even as we simultaneously understand the collective definition of the word.

If beauty is in the eye of the beholder, it's also on the beholder's lips. Not only does a beautiful woman vary from a lovely woman in my mind's eye, but my image of a beautiful woman may well vary from yours. Other terms of description allow us to be more precise—*dark-haired* or *blond*, *tall* or *petite*, *fair-skinned* or *olive-complected*. Yet the terms of evaluation—*beautiful, lovely, striking, gorgeous*—remain vague, even as each word carries its own specificity. We need the language of beauty to be mystifying in order to maintain an enigmatic shroud over the *concept* of beauty.

Still, despite this mystification, we're easily able to distinguish what is gorgeous from what is, say, cute. Beauty's glossary, simultaneously specific and vague, mirrors the way that we tend to regard beauty: We know both what we personally consider appealing, and what we understand is considered appealing by society at large. So we've compiled an arsenal of words that expands to accommodate our individual interpretations of beauty but that can also be shrink-fitted to the template we all recognize at a glance. I use the word *beautiful* to describe my best friend, not only for her inner beauty but for her creamy skin, sparkling eyes, and hourglass curves. I'd also employ *beautiful* to describe someone like Nicole Kidman. While I'm using the same word to describe them, I don't mean that they share the same kind of beauty, nor am I necessarily proclaiming that they're both objectively beautiful, if such a thing as objectivity exists with beauty. I can see the parts of my best friend that don't adhere to the rigid template of conventional beauty—just as I can look at Kidman and understand her appearance as something we *as a culture* have decided is beautiful, regardless of my personal evaluation of her looks. Yet the same word applies to both of them, with the same truth.

The ways each of us experiences the sheer variety of beautiful people indicate exactly why we've constructed our ziggurat of words to describe appearance. I've seen beautiful women and had to look away because it practically *hurt* to look at them. I've seen beautiful men and felt something physically altered within me; once, upon unexpectedly running into a particularly good-looking suitor, I literally felt my knees go weak. Who among us hasn't lain next to a lover and felt our hands reach out, seemingly of their own will, to touch the beautiful body next to us—or rather, the body that has *become* unalterably beautiful to us?

We may be able to distinguish *gorgeous* from *pretty*, *handsome* from *cute*, *lovely* from *striking*. But *beauty*? Beauty compels us; beauty moves us. Beauty can even leave us speechless. And when we're left without words, we have the illusion that we've lost control. The unnameable power of beauty is exactly what drives us to name it. This mystification can be downright romantic, and far be it from me to rap anyone's knuckles when they want to revel in the glorious mystery of beauty. But if we keep the shroud of beauty affixed too firmly, rarely peeking at what lies underneath, we rob ourselves of an opportunity to challenge assumptions about beauty—assumptions we've collectively manifested by compiling a vast vocabulary of words to describe looks. When we pick up the corner of that shroud, we see our assumptions laid bare. We learn that women aren't supposed to refer to themselves with words bolder than *reasonably attractive*; we learn that the same words that favorably describe a woman can be manipulated to bring shame to a man, revealing a rigid gender binary that we subtly reinforce by calling men *handsome* but women *pretty*. We learn that we might be even more preoccupied with ugliness than we are with beauty. Only when we understand what lies beneath our words can we begin to reshape those words to reflect the ways we want beauty to be a part of our lives. Women have already begun this linguistic reconnaissance mission, with things like the annual "No Fat Talk" week initiated by the Tri Delta sorority, which has gone national on college campuses and beyond. These are the beginnings of a critical examination of the ways we manifest assumptions about beauty through our words. The next step—understanding the implications of the words that come from our lips and keyboards, and choosing words that align with the role each of us wants beauty to play in our lives—is yours.

3

Lipstick Isn't Cubist

The Artifice of Beauty

When I finally got permission to wear makeup in seventh grade, I took it as a symbol of my entrance into womanhood, or at least into not being quite so girlish anymore. I tried all the makeup instructions in *Seventeen*, but the only one I ever mastered was covering the occasional pimple; the wild blues and greens of 1980s eye shadows eluded me. Instead I settled on eye makeup you might call *tasteful*, even as *tasteful* isn't a likely aesthetic goal for many twelve-year-old girls. Taupe eye shadow for the upper lids, a deeper brown closer down, and a hint of mascara—that was it. (Besides the foundation, blush, and Dr Pepper Lip Smacker, that is.)

On the bus ride home one day, I had the good fortune to sit next to Ryan O., a bona fide Cute and Popular Boy who had retained enough schoolboy decency to talk with those of us further down on the social register of Simmons Junior High. We had a conversation—let's say it was about Bon Jovi, just to channel the moment—but it hit a lull. Ever the raconteur, I had a filler ready: "I can't wait to get home to fix my makeup," I said in what I hoped was a slightly jaded, exasperated tone that conveyed my womanly sophistication.

"You don't *wear* makeup," he said. Now, if someone said that to me today, I'd smile smugly and consider my sleight of hand well-done—I want people to see me, after all, not my makeup. But in 1988, at age twelve, coming from a Cute and Popular Boy Who Was Talking to Me, it was *devastating*. How could he not see my declaration of worldliness, elegance, glamour? How could he overlook my grand entrée into womanhood? *How dare he call me a child?*

"I *am* wearing makeup, I'm wearing *lots* of it," I said, taking off my Sally Jessy Raphael glasses so he could see my eye shadow handiwork unobscured.

He leaned closer, squinted, then leaned back. "I don't see any makeup." By this point, blush would have been redundant; my cheeks were aflame with embarrassment. I quickly changed the subject (Def Leppard, perhaps?) and did my best to recover. But privately, silently, I made a vow: Ryan O. would see my makeup. And not just Ryan O. but his whole gang of Cute and Popular Boys, not to mention their cohorts, the Pretty and Popular Girls. They would see my makeup. They would see *me*.

Of course, after a few days of piling on eye shadows in the moss-seafoam-aqua color family, I went back to my taupe. After all, the whole reason I was wearing taupe eye shadow in the first place was because I wasn't comfortable with anything flashier. But the lesson stuck. Makeup wasn't just something to enliven my eyes, bring a flush to my cheeks, punch up my lips. It meant something more, something deeper. When Ryan O. announced that he couldn't see my makeup, it sliced me to the core; it felt like he was pointing out something far more loaded than the fact of my makeup being subtle to begin with. That's all he *was* telling me, of course, but what I heard was this: *You have not yet matured. Your efforts to be noticed by Cute and Popular Boys such as myself are in vain. You are, in truth, invisible.*

Since then I've had plenty of motivations for wearing makeup, which I've done nearly every day for more than twenty years. During the grunge years, I followed the lead of my high school's alternaqueen and drew on thick black eye pencil that had been melted with a match; I wanted to look cool. During a bout of bad acne in my early twenties, I wore opaque foundation in an attempt to not visibly ooze; I wanted to look normal. Today I alternate between bronzer and blush; I want to look more vibrant. Yet no matter what I tell myself about why I'm wearing makeup, attempting to break down the reasons any of us do so is an exercise in futility. After all, our motivations for doing *anything* are rarely clear and singular. And when it comes to cosmetics, it's even murkier. We usually think about motivations for wearing makeup as being sociological—but even though women are subject to similar social conditions, not all women wear makeup (though the majority in America do, 63 percent as of 2010). And attempting to look at individual motivations for wearing makeup means that we're relying on self-reporting, which contains a bevy of blind spots. Then there are differences of degree: One woman's definition of makeup might mean tinted lip balm and mascara, while another's involves three shades of eye shadow plus eye shadow *primer*—while yet another goes for lip balm and mascara one day and a thirty-five-minute face the next. Our motivations for wearing cosmetics are as varied as the tools themselves.

In fact, looking at the individual differences in why women wear makeup is a handy portal to the larger question about why so many of us bother with the stuff. Research published in the *Journal of Cosmetic Science* had seventy women answer questions about their makeup usage and also had them complete psychometric tests—think clinical versions of the personality quizzes you might take online. They found two distinct groups of makeup wearers: one who wore makeup primarily to conceal flaws, and another who wore it as a way of revealing or enhancing themselves. What they found was that women who reported wearing makeup to conceal flaws had lower self-esteem and higher levels of anxiety, and were less extroverted and assertive than women who reported wearing makeup as a method of attraction. The idea here is that women who don't have the greatest self-image use makeup as a defense mechanism to normalize their appearance—even though there wasn't anything in particular to normalize. There was no difference in the baseline of conventional beauty between the groups of women.

As for the women who wore makeup as a means of alluring as opposed to concealing, they fell into three groups: women who valued their natural face more than their made-up face, women who valued their made-up face more than their natural face, and women whose valuation fluctuated depending on context. This last group had the highest rates of all the good stuff—optimism, emotional stability, assertiveness, self-esteem—followed closely (and unsurprisingly) by women who valued their natural face over their painted one.

But here's where things get really interesting: The ways women valued themselves and their makeup was reflected *in the makeup itself.* The women who wore makeup for attraction but valued their made-up face more than their au naturel self? They tended to do the same makeup routine all the time. Contrast that with the women who valued their natural face more than their cosmeticized self: These women used makeup in a playful manner, creating a variety of "looks" that changed day to day. As for the women who used makeup as a means to conceal, they used fewer colors on the face than their counterparts. Forgive me the analogy, but I can't help but think of a moth and a butterfly. A moth's strategy for survival is to be neutrally colored so as to neatly fit into its surroundings, while a butterfly displays vivid colors to attract mates and repel predators.

Of course, we're neither moths nor butterflies—we're women, with motivations more complex than survival. But what I like in this study is less the idea of being able to locate oneself on any sort of linear scale—makeup wearers with low self-esteem to the left, buoyant butterflies to the right—and more the idea of finding a framework of varied motivations within women's reported experiences. Confronting assumptions about makeup and the reasons women use it is the only way to assure that it can ever *truly* be a choice made freely instead of a societal siphoning of women's time and money. The idea isn't to squarely pin any one person into any one category—and it's certainly not to determine the totality of any individual person's motivations for wearing makeup. It's a starting point, not an end, to examining why any of us do or don't carve out time in our day to finger-paint ourselves.

"I Do It for Me": Internal and External Motivators for Wearing Makeup

Let's begin with a big ol' "duh" here: We wear makeup because it makes us look better. Yes, yes, "better" is subjective, and there are all sorts of arguments for a truly naked face being the most beautiful any of us can get—but, c'mon, don't most of us look better, at least by the terms of conventional beauty, when our blemishes are concealed and our eyes more luminous? Research supports this: Women are consistently rated as more attractive by both sexes when wearing makeup, with eye makeup having the greatest impact. In fact, for some women this is a reason *not* to wear makeup. Upon seeing a dancer friend of mine backstage after a performance, I commented on how nice her eyes looked rimmed with the black eyeliner she'd swiped on for the show. "I know," said the normally eyeliner-free woman, mildly exasperated. "I love how I look with it, but I only wear it for shows—if I started wearing it as myself I'd never be able to leave the house without putting it on. I'd begin to think I looked less like myself without it." It's the flip side of something other women have pinpointed as a reason they dab on the stuff: "Wearing makeup allows me to look the way I imagine I look all the time," says an English professor from upstate New York.

But that's just the end result of makeup. The process itself brings other internal rewards. "I like the ritual," says twentysomething Signe. "It feels like I'm really getting ready for the day." Indeed, the six-minute makeup ritual I perform before leaving the house functions like a second cup of coffee in the morning—it's a wake-up tool, tangible evidence that this day is *on*. (And given that many cite "Not looking so tired" as a reason for wearing makeup, particularly eye makeup, perhaps it's more like a *first* cup of coffee.) Plus, after twenty years of applying makeup almost every day, for me it's become habit, as much a part of my morning as putting in my contact lenses. I do it on autopilot. Some non-makeup-wearers report the same in their reasoning for not wearing it. "I never got in the habit of it," says Gabriela from Albany, New York. "I'm feeling more interested in makeup now that I'm getting older, but experimenting with it is work I don't care to invest in. Playing with makeup isn't fun for me like I think it is for a lot of women."

And it *is* fun for some. In the makeup motivation study, researchers found that the specific type of makeup wearer who views cosmetics as play not only has more variability in her routine than other women—think sixties mod one day, nineties au naturel the next, bold red lipstick on the third—but has a distinct psychological profile too. In addition to having high self-esteem and being assertive, this type of woman is least likely to say she uses makeup to control her self-image or to feel more like herself. Instead she wears it to channel a particular state of being, whether that's glamorous, gentle, artistic, rebellious, and so on. Makeup doesn't express the self for this kind of wearer; it expresses the moment. "I'm an actress at heart," says one thirtysomething blogger. "Makeup is a part of the roles I slip into every day."

Before we all start rushing to do our makeup Lady Gaga–style in hopes of capturing this psychological resilience, let's look at the factor that lies under this approach to cosmetics—which, not coincidentally, is one of the biggest buzzwords surrounding the beauty industry today: confidence. "Like chugging a Red Bull, makeup gives me energy and confidence," says Elyssa, a writer in her twenties. "When I'm going out, I'm heading off into my battle with the night, and I will win by looking absolutely fabulous. Makeup is my drag." Study after study has shown that women report feeling more self-confident when wearing makeup. What's unclear is whether this confidence applies only to women who already wear makeup on a regular or semiregular basis, or whether the maxim could extend to women who don't usually wear it. Non-makeup-wearing women often mention feeling distinctly uncomfortable in it: "Yes, I've tried that stuff that 'feels like nothing.' It still feels like something, and I hate it," says one woman who shuns cosmetics. I imagine it's similar to the feeling I have when I try out a lipstick that's too bright for me. How can you feel confident when you're too busy feeling conspicuous?

It's also difficult to feel confident when stressed-out, and makeup comes in handy here too. In a study of 140 women, researchers in France determined that when faced with stress, women applied more makeup than usual. Smart thinking too: When placed in a tense situation, women who were wearing makeup had lower signs of physiological stress like heightened skin temperature and restrained vocal pitch than their non-makeup-wearing counterparts, an effect that was exaggerated in women with higher levels of anxiety. Other studies have shown similar benefits. By literally concealing our anxieties and fears, makeup can arm women with a sort of shield against the flurry of stresses any of us go through every day. Applying makeup becomes an act of self-care not only through its motions—the act of simply touching oneself has therapeutic benefits—but through its results. It's a connection that hasn't gone unnoticed by the beauty industry, which has successfully linked cosmetics with confidence and self-care through advertising ("I use [makeup] to show the world who I truly am," says beauty vlogger Cassandra Bankson in an ad for Dermablend, which she uses to cover up severe acne scars) and even product names (MAC's Supremely Confident lipstick shade).

That confidence isn't limited to the person in it; makeup can make *other* people see its wearer as more confident. It can also drive others to find her more competent, more likable, and more alluring than those with a makeup-free face. The real-life benefits of this go beyond the conceptual: The makeup wearer isn't just abstractly *seen* as being more attractive; she's approached more frequently by men. If she's a waitress, she may get more tips from her male customers than her barefaced counterpart. Even absent these tangible effects, a woman may actually be able to change how the people around her feel, simply by putting on a little makeup: People exposed to pictures of makeup-wearing women experienced a decrease in stress hormones and an uptick in hormones supporting the immune system, as compared with people shown photos of barefaced women. That's also part of what makes makeup potentially problematic. If wearing makeup helps a woman seem more confident, more appealing, and more helpful to those around her, it frames the one-third of women who don't wear it as noncompliant, unwilling to perform the most basic of acts that could boost herself and others.

Of course, as with anything, it's impossible to neatly divide reasons for wearing makeup into internal and external motivations—money is an external reward, but we have internal reasons for wanting more cash, right? Still, some makeup motivations do an especially nice job of straddling that line, like using makeup to honor special occasions. My false-eyelash kit sees the light of day only during wedding season. I wear them to look just a little nicer, sure, but it's also a tiny way of acknowledging the importance of one of our last cultural rites—few other occasions warrant that extra bit of time and care. Some Latina women may have a particularly good grasp of this, as pointed out by Rosie Molinary, author of *Hijas Americanas: Beauty, Body Image, and Growing Up Latina.* "You might run into a woman of a non-Latina background and say she looks great, and she'll say, 'Oh, I just threw myself together this morning,' like it's this effortless perfection," she says. "But if you run into a Latina woman and say, 'You look really nice,' her reaction will be, 'Oh, thanks! I worked overtime to buy this dress, I've got on this girdle, it took me three hours to get my hair like this.' She'll own up to the effort, because part of it is wanting people to know they thought this event warranted that effort and respect. I see some truth in that."

Makeup can also function as a symbol of belonging to certain urban tribes or subcultures. Rockabilly women sport their cat's-eye eyeliner, goth kids make their skin ethereally pale, lip gloss and bronzer seems to be the look among the gym bunnies in my neighborhood, and there's a certain breed of magazine editrix who wears no makeup whatsoever except fire-engine-red lipstick. In occupations that see a growing number of women in positions of power, the ability to flash, say, a Chanel compact becomes a status symbol. Hairstyles come into play too: For some black women, wearing one's hair in a "natural" style versus a relaxed or straightened look can signal politicization and resistance to the idea that straight, fine, white-girl hair is preferred. "Wearing my hair textured, for me, is a way of affirming my African heritage," says Crystal, thirty-eight. "I grew up looking at pictures of Pam Grier from the seventies and thinking how beautiful she looked, and how her hair was a part of that. I don't do the Afro thing but having textured hair is a tribute to that period of awakening." (Of course, imbuing black women's hair with politics can be problematic, as Chicago journalist Britt Julious writes: "I don't like the idea that my hair is political . . . We rarely—if ever—require this of non-black women.")

But the biggest tribe that makeup signals membership in is the tribe simply marked *women.* Cosmetics can mark the transition from childhood into young-adult life—getting permission to wear makeup to school is a hallmark of adolescence for many women. Soon enough after I started wearing makeup, I began to understand that visible makeup signaled not just womanhood but a certain *kind* of womanhood, one that adheres to at least one convention of femininity. "This is what we do," says a friend of mine who once disliked makeup but grew into wearing it daily in her thirties after deciding on a career path. "This is what we've decided looks good, or professional, polished, normal. If all the other ladies are doing it, then I should also, so that we're all on the same playing field." Unlike other forms of cultural capital—i.e., non-monetary assets that aid social mobility, like education, speech patterns, etc.—makeup skill signals membership not in a socioeconomic class but in a gender class.

Within that gender class, though, we can learn even more about makeup as a mechanism instead of a signal. Dana, a fortysomething woman who dresses almost exclusively in traditional men's clothing—every time I've seen her, she's been in a perfectly cut suit—shuns conventional femininity in most ways, and yet: "I wear [makeup] every day, but subtly, and with the aim of just tweaking things to look a little better." It's a sentiment not much different from what plenty of girlie girls might say about their style, and in the hands of someone expressing a non-feminine identity, makeup reveals itself to be even more of a strategic tool, not a trap that wastes women's time. A hint of gray eye shadow, a dab of concealer—if Cary Grant had worn makeup, he'd have borrowed Dana's look. Conscious use—and non-use—of makeup can signal a strategy surrounding gender identity. "A new haircut is a butch accessory," says "boi" comedian Kelli Dunham, who identifies as a woman but favors conventionally masculine clothes and hairstyles. When I asked her if she ever got flak for not wearing makeup, her "no" surprised me at first. But her explanation made sense: "A friend of mine who transitioned [from being a woman to being a man] said, 'Wow, being a fat man is so much easier than being a fat woman.' There are ways in which there's a protective space formed around masculinity, and butch women have some masculine privilege. I mean, we're also liable to get beat up or knifed on the street, but there is some masculine privilege. Even when people think I'm a fifteen-year-old boy, there are benefits to that." And some transgender women report cosmetics as being crucial to their development as women. "I want to do what women do," says Ally, a fortysomething trans woman. "The very act of wearing makeup in our society is a gender marker. And I want to be on the girl side."

The Female of the Species:
Evolution, Attraction, and Makeup

I spent more than a decade making a living by reading women's magazines as a copy editor. Nowhere in those thousands of hours spent poring over the glossies have I once seen a beauty tip designed to make a woman's eyes look *smaller*. Same with making the eyes look lighter (save for the once-in-a-blue-moon flirtation with, say, yellow mascara) or tinting the cheeks to look paler than the rest of the face. And though the nude lip—think Twiggy—goes in and out of fashion, the majority of lipsticks are designed to make lips look rosier, if not always darker.

As it happens, all of these more or less consistent makeup rules run parallel to universal facial traits that distinguish women's faces from men's, a quality known as sexual dimorphism. Women's pupils are slightly larger than men's, giving the impression of larger eyes; plus, since men tend to be taller than women, women's eyes are closer to men's field of vision, making them appear disproportionately large to men. Women across races also have skin that's a shade lighter than that of their male counterparts, making their eyes and lips appear darker by contrast, a trait called "facial luminance." And what makes eyes and lips appear darker? Virtually every eye makeup on the market, and a good number of the lip products too. That includes lipstick specifically designed for women of color that tend to focus on the deeper end of the spectrum, keeping the facial luminosity maxim consistent across varying skin hues.

Not only do cosmetics tend to reinforce facial differences between the sexes; they also tend to mimic traits that signal women's ability to reproduce. That vibrant complexion and unlined skin? Signs of youth (and what beauty product ever promises to make a woman over the age of twenty-one appear *older*?), which translate to signs of fertility. And to stretch the makeup-as-signal argument a bit further, have you ever heard that bit about how lipstick was invented to make a woman's lips more closely resemble her inner labia, which become flushed and engorged when she's sexually aroused? (Never mind that men don't actually find reddish labia more alluring, according to a 2012 study.) The idea caught on after zoologist

Desmond Morris theorized the connection in his 1967 book, *The Naked Ape*, but there's no actual evidence that this was ever the drive behind lip coloration. Still, the idea became popular enough to become a naughty little beauty tip of sorts. "Match your lipstick to the color of your labia," advises a character in the 2011 film *Sleeping Beauty*—a tip then echoed throughout the beauty blogosphere, and hinted at every time a women's magazine floats the lipstick-labia theory.

Sound far-fetched? Perhaps. (Though imagine the possibilities for lipstick shades: Labial Lavender! Cunty Coral!) After all, when other animals show off their reproductive fitness, they simply strut the stuff they were born with, and everything seems to have worked out evolutionarily for *them*. But let's consider makeup as what evolutionary biologists call an "extended phenotype," a concept we touched on earlier. The idea is that the extended phenotype of makeup, just as with the spider's web or the bird's nest, becomes an advertisement for features that make us reproductively suitable. In other words, lipstick, eyeliner, and blush are just an external-ized version of the fully opposable thumb that allowed our predecessors a firm grip on primitive tools. They're a feature that allows the human species to grow. And to a degree, it works. While there's no evidence that women who wear makeup are more fertile, a 2012 study showed that ovulating women wore more makeup than they did when they weren't at their monthly peak of fertility. (And since men have been shown to be quicker to approach makeup-wearing women in social situations, those efforts aren't in vain.)

There's an appeal to thinking that my paleo beauty ritual is as humanly necessary as eating, sleeping, and having sex. It enriches the ritualistic aspect of cosmetics. Not only are we partaking in a personal practice that centers us for what lies ahead in our day, but we're participating in a col-lective custom that's written into our genes, one that signals not just our womanness but our humanness. When seen as something that has helped the species flourish, makeup, so easily accused of being for the vain, can be considered a bona fide human development along the lines of agriculture or written language—call it the Mascara Age. The theory becomes even more satisfying when looking at some appearance customs outside the

Western world. Kayan women in Myanmar are famous for their neck rings, coils of brass that create the appearance of a lengthened neck. It's an awkward fashion to those outside the Kayan community. But it's an example of how sexual dimorphism is exaggerated by something that could theoretically be considered an extended phenotype: Generally speaking, women's necks appear somewhat longer than men's (in part because women's heads tend to be larger in proportion to the neck, giving the illusion of a longer, slimmer stem). Place brass rings around your neck, then, and you're exaggerating the look of the lengthy neck that sets women apart from men.

But before we leap into tutorials on creating a smoky cavewoman eye, let's look at another aspect of human behavior that we attribute to evolution: mating cost. Since it takes nine months for a woman to reproduce (as opposed to a man's short-lived contribution to the matter), women's mating cost is higher—which, according to some researchers, translates to women being choosier about whom they mate with. After all, if you're going to spend nine months housing a baby in utero, wouldn't you want that baby to have the strongest genes possible? So if we take mating cost and its fallout of feminine choosiness to be fact, why aren't *men* the ones adorning themselves with the extended phenotype of makeup to ensure they're not overlooked by those famously picky women? *Esquire* should be running step-by-step instructions on how to apply highlighter to give the illusion of a prominent square jaw, so that women—the shorter of the species—can gaze up to them and select the man with this classic testosterone marker. Twiggy's nude lip should be adopted by the gents to *decrease* facial luminosity and lip size, "nasal illuminators" should line drugstore shelves to help men get the coveted prominent masculine nose, and every eyebrow waxer in America should also be skilled in the art of eyebrow implants, to give male clients the heavy brow that distinguishes the male face from the female. In short, why aren't men peacocking around like . . . well, like peacocks? After all, those glorious iridescent tail feathers belong solely to the male peafowl and are put on display when attempting to woo the peahen, who is just as choosy as her human counterpart when it comes to mating.

Actually, historically speaking, men *did* do more of that peacocking than most do today. It's only in the last two hundred years or so that upper-class Western men dropped rouge, high heels, and ornamental clothing in favor of a bare face and the standard suit, a change that came about not because the ruffles of the aristocracy were seen as foppish but because it echoed the new ideals of democracy—poor men couldn't buy velvet coats, but many could afford a basic three-piece. Before that shift, things like wearing tinted face powders, and even painting one's head to mask baldness, were common. (And, of course, humans of all genders have worn painted-on embellishments for millennia—many an ancient Egyptian was buried alongside his cosmetics collection.) Even today, conventional men's grooming does allow for some evolutionary artifice. The classic five o'clock shadow gives weight to the lower half of the face, for example. But chalking up cosmetics use to evolution is Darwinian cherry-picking, justifying a mainstream vision of beauty that excludes a good portion of human history—and indeed, a good portion of the world today. Perhaps you could work backward from attractiveness cues like the famed lip plates of the Mursi women of Ethiopia, or the blackened teeth of some ethnic minority women in the hills of Vietnam—or the neck rings of the Kayan women of Myanmar—to find an evolutionary justification. But we tend to speak of such beauty traditions as being socially constructed. Indeed, lip plates and blackened teeth survived for centuries as symbols of the wearer's sexual maturity. Because these looks fall so far outside Western beauty norms, it's less tempting to claim that the relationship between a woman's sexuality and how black her teeth are is decided by her biology.

Most evolutionary psychologists do concede that beauty is defined by social and cultural norms as well as our genes. But whenever evolution is credited for something that costs women, *and not men*, a good deal of money—a projected $265 billion spent on cosmetics, hair care, skin care, and perfume by 2017 globally—it requires critical scrutiny.

Facing the World

While some women wear makeup when alone with no intention of leaving the home, most tend to reserve it for public use. The superficial reason here is obvious: Just as we might save the good china for company while eating off everyday plates ourselves, we're familiar enough with our own unadorned features to forgo the betterment makeup offers. We might wear makeup for ourselves, but in this way, it's actually something we do for other people, an acknowledgment of the ways we enhance ourselves when we're in plain sight.

But there's more to the public face of makeup than its end result. My paternal grandmother spoke of the act of applying makeup as "putting on her face," a turn of phrase that puzzled me as a kid, as it implied that the makeup *was* her face, the mass of skin tissue beneath it not even worthy of the word. As I got older and entered the workforce—specifically, the workforce in an urban area boasting the highest population density in the nation—I began to understand what she meant. It wasn't that the makeup was her face; it was that the made-up face is what one "puts on" for public occasions, even if the occasion is just going to work or a dentist appointment. It's what we put on to face the world. For makeup wearers, a layer of lipstick or blush can function as a boundary marker, one that helps us define exactly what we consider home and not-home.

Makeup can help us organize our public selves, making it a part of what sociologists would call our social "performances." But it's not just a signal to others; it can be a signal of public life for the person wearing it as well. As I write this from my home office, my hair is knotted in a messy bun, and I'm makeup free. I'm wearing a bra, though: The physical sensation of having parts of my body contained puts me in a "professional" writing mind-set that my pajamas can't match. I might be at home, but I'm working, and the bra serves as a tactile reminder of this, helping me keep on task. When the bra comes off, it's the end of the day, and I'm more easily found lounging on the sofa than pounding away on my laptop. I have another work-from-home friend who can't work unless she's wearing shoes. In the same way, when I meet up with some friends later this evening, I'll put on makeup—not because my friends care how polished I look, but because it will help me transition from writer-at-home mode into gal-about-town mode. It psychs me up, basically, and every time I catch a glimpse of myself in the mirror wearing lipstick that was absent earlier in the day, it's a reinforcement of the automatic adjustments any of us make depending on a change of setting or ambience. Cosmetics, clothing, and hairstyle all aid us in approaching various social performances with earnest belief.

And the opposite is true as well: Ill-fitting self-presentation is a quick route to discomfort. And discomfort—especially discomfort with stereotypes that accompany the various guises any of us might slip into—can foster a cynicism toward our own social performances. I think of an acquaintance who talked of feeling like she was "wearing a bear suit" when she uncharacteristically donned a dress to serve as her sister's maid of honor. It's not that she didn't want to stand by her sister as she wed, just as it's not that non-makeup-wearers are unable to transition into gal-about-town mode. It's that the expectations that might accompany those signals feel like a bad fit. As sociologist Erving Goffman writes, "[A] given social front tends to become institutionalized in terms of the abstract stereotyped expectations to which it gives rise, and *tends to take on a meaning and stability apart from the specific tasks which happen at the time to be performed in its name.*" (Emphasis mine.) The stereotypical signals makeup sends— makeup emphasizes femininity, and feminine people are supposed to be sexy yet demure, alluring yet coy, sparkling yet supportive—spur some of the discomfort its non-wearers may feel. That's not to say that women who wear makeup actually embody those stereotypes. Some might just be more willing to brush aside the larger implications of makeup and femininity, or might want those implications at their disposal to use at will.

So clearly the act of wearing makeup in public is, well, public. Yet it's the *private* side of wearing makeup in public that alerts us to its true importance. Once upon a time, applying makeup in public spaces was socially verboten, with women's advice columns tut-tutting the practice in the early twentieth century. If the number of women dabbing on eye shadow during the average morning subway commute is any measure, the stigma has lessened, but it's still seen by many as a no-no, or at least questionable. (The top companion search term on Google for "applying makeup in public" is "etiquette," and indeed Miss Manners herself has registered her thoughts against the act.) But the question is: *Why* is it objectionable? Concerns of safety aside—I've seen more than one woman get poked in the eye with a mascara wand when the subway comes to a sudden halt—it's not really hurting anyone, it's silent, and most concoctions are scentless to passersby. Yet I've heard plenty of people grumble about the practice, and I admit that when I see a woman preening in public, I feel a rush of something between anger and embarrassment. Not embarrassment for her but embarrassment of my own: the embarrassment of having one's secrets exposed.

Sociologically speaking, my secrets *are* being exposed. A "dark secret," in Goffman's terms, is something about a person that's incompatible with the impression she or he is hoping to make—the scandal surrounding former New York governor Eliot Spitzer is a prime example, as he admitted to soliciting a prostitute despite having signed legislation that heightened punishment for doing so. The way to keep dark secrets hidden is to expose them only in places we might call "backstage." So when we're talking about makeup, drawing back the curtain to allow anyone to see the work that goes into self-presentation casts a harsh light on those secrets. The work, products, practice, and effort behind a made-up face clash with the effect of *that's just how women look.* This is doubly true for the so-called natural look of subtle makeup meant to make the wearer look like she's wearing no makeup at all—but even for makeup that calls attention to itself as artificial, the idea is usually to enhance one's appearance, not to showcase a fabulous eye shadow. It's the wearer, not the product, that the public is supposed to see. Revealing the suppressed facts of the feminine performance—time, products, money, skill, *trying*—lets the public see precisely what many a makeup wearer doesn't want anyone else to directly observe. When my neighbor gets on the subway car and proceeds to give herself a six-stop makeover, she's revealing not only her own performance but mine as well. The act of womanhood is a shared one. "[A] team whose vital secrets are possessed by others will try to oblige the possessors to treat these secrets as secrets that are entrusted," writes Goffman. My silent embarrassment is the only way I can "try to oblige" other women to keep our secrets hidden, as I'm not about to admonish anyone for whipping out a lipstick at the bus stop. (And I don't need to admonish them, as in 2015 the New York City transportation system ran a series of public service announcements about proper transit etiquette, including a wrist slap to subway primpers.)

My anger and embarrassment are irrational feelings, ones I wish I didn't have—intellectually, I like the idea of letting non-makeup-wearers (specifically men) know exactly how much work goes into creating the effect of beauty. I wish I could be more like one woman who tasks her husband with letting her know if her lipstick is smudged: "I'm the one who puts it on every day, and if he wants me to keep wearing it, let him take some responsibility for it," she says. Beauty work isn't effortless, it's not always easy, and it can take a good amount of time and supplies to craft an "oh, I just woke up looking this way" appeal. I'd like to showcase this as a skill instead of tucking it away, but the truth is, I dearly protect the truths of artifice because revelation feels too risky. The as-is self, stripped not only of makeup but of all easily understood guises, reveals itself to be complex, messy, human. The public self that's undergone the private, unobserved ritual of putting on one's face—*that* self is more easily communicated and more easily understood. As Simone de Beauvoir wrote in *The Second Sex*, the made-up woman "does not present *herself* to observation; she is, like the picture or statue, or the actor on the stage, an agent through whom is suggested someone not there—that is, the character she represents, but is not. It is this identification with something unreal, fixed, perfect as the hero of a novel, as a portrait or a bust, that gratifies her . . ."

As it happens, we can find gratification in the opposite too: witnessing something "unreal, fixed" without its usual veil of perfection. Who doesn't get a smidge of satisfaction from those paparazzi slideshows of celebrities without makeup? We take immense joy in seeing proof that our contemporary idols engage in beauty's dirty work by catching a glimpse of them that we're not supposed to see. In turn, the appeal behind the celebrity trend of makeup-free selfies exposes a wish to break free of the "fixed" public persona that celebrities wear.

But for all the ways that makeup serves women in public, the private face of cosmetics serves us equally well at home. "Meditate for ten minutes a day" perennially tops my list of New Year's resolutions, and I perennially fail at it. But when I look at the essence of meditation—taking time to clear the mind, temporarily freeing oneself from tasks and to-dos and all the business that otherwise occupies our time—I wonder whether I've been meditating all along through the quiet solitude of my makeup ritual. My day-to-day look rarely varies, so my fingers automatically find their way around my face, to the point where I can apply a decent face of makeup without looking in the mirror if need be. You know how some people say they do their best thinking in the shower? I do my best *non*-thinking in front of the mirror. Dabbing on rouge and mascara gives me a place of pause. It prepares me for the day ahead—or, when I amp it up for a big evening, the night ahead. Most of this is the mere act of doing something that I've done so many times that I don't need to pay conscious attention to it, allowing my mind to drift in a meditative fashion. Physiology has its role too: The fragrance of some cosmetics can decrease heart rate, calm the nervous system, and increase the ability to feel pleasure. But it's something specific to cosmetics that makes this feel so ritualistic. I go on autopilot when I'm washing dishes too, but I don't fall into the same meditative mind-set as I do with makeup. Seeing the process, and then the result, of a transformation is a quiet daily reminder that I consciously create my persona. I wouldn't go so far as to say my morning rite is empowering. But it is a part of how I articulate myself, and the prep work involved in that articulation is crucial to its outcome.

Perhaps we can best understand the ways cosmetics channel our energies for public performance by looking at face paint in a different context. Army veteran Miyoko Hikiji barely wore makeup during her stints in Iraq and Afghanistan—"I maybe had a stick of concealer, for the sand flea bites," she says—but she's skilled in creating effects with military tools that amount to makeup. "Camouflage is like a little eye shadow pack. It's extremely thick, almost like clay; you sweat in it and it's just there. It's kind of miserable," she says. "But if you look at yourself in the mirror after doing these exercises with the camouflage paint on, it's hard to look at yourself the same way. There's something to putting on the camouflage, or the uniform, or just the effect you have when you're holding a loaded weapon. All that contributes to your behavior. So yeah, I definitely feel different when I wake up and put my regular makeup on. I approach the world differently, and the world treats me differently." The act of applying camouflage—whether it's tinted to match the Arabian Desert or your complexion—becomes not only a way of making yourself *look* the part but also a way of actually *becoming* the part.

Hikiji had a defined purpose in applying her camouflage—in fact, the goal was to literally camouflage herself. But in doing exactly that, she also embodied the role of soldier, just as a stage performer might wear exaggerated makeup to embody the role of starlet. Those of us whose livelihoods don't appear to be directly tied to the paint on our faces are stepping not into the public role of soldier or professional beauty but simply of *woman*. "My mother used to call it 'putting on your war paint,'" my college roommate Annie told me when we were musing about why we considered canceling our garbage service to save money but still managed to buy makeup. "I wonder—what kind of war am I in that I need makeup to have an advantage?"

Concealing and Revealing: Makeup Motivation and Lipstick Feminism

There's an idea floating around out there—partly born from a one-dimensional interpretation of *The Beauty Myth*—that makeup universally signals a strain of low self-esteem particular to women. The #nomakeupselfie movement popular in 2015 was applauded on social media as an act of bravery. The National Eating Disorders Association hosts a "Barefaced and Beautiful" campaign as an awareness-raising measure, in which women are urged to post makeup-free selfies. A certain kind of well-meaning man will urge women not to wear makeup, claiming that "you don't *need* it." Morning talk show hosts from Katie Couric to the cast of *The Talk* have gone barefaced for the cameras, framing their experience in terms of a crutch they had to summon bravery to go without. There's even an entire subgenre of women's writing revolving around abstaining from makeup and other vanity practices, as exemplified by *The Beauty Experiment* author Phoebe Baker Hyde's yearlong cosmetics-free experiment and Rachel Rabbit White's "No Make-Up Week," which dozens of bloggers participated in. Hyde and White both took pains to explain that their projects weren't designed to demonize makeup, but rather to help themselves understand the complex relationship they—and we—have with it. But that complexity was often lost in discussion once it left the hands of the creators.

The "barefaced and beautiful" attitude zooms in on the camouflaging aspect of makeup, ignoring other reasons women wear it. That's not to say that insecurity *isn't* a part of the makeup matrix: Plenty of women told me that at some point in their lives, they felt so unsure of how their natural face looked that they felt unable to do the most pedestrian of acts without a full face of makeup—go to the gym, walk outside to check the mail, run to the grocery store. The crossroads of self-esteem and beauty is indeed a troubling issue, and one that affects women disproportionately. Women's self-esteem is shown to be consistently lower than men's, beginning in early adolescence—the same age when body consciousness begins. And people with higher levels of anxiety about their appearance tend to have lower self-esteem and reduced ability to enjoy social situations.

But the number of makeup wearers I talked with who framed makeup foremost in terms of self-esteem? Zero. It came up in discussion, sure: "I guess you could call it insecurity, because on the days I'm not wearing any makeup, I catch myself thinking about the probability of looking bad," says Signe. On my end, I tend to pay particular attention to my makeup when I don't feel so great about my looks—it saves me the anxiety I might other-wise have regarding what others might think is "wrong" with my face. Now, self-reporting isn't necessarily a reliable gauge of motivations for wearing makeup. But for all the framing of cosmetics as a way of exploiting women's low self-esteem, and for all the ways women frame their relationship with beauty as an ongoing arc of self-acceptance, not once did this reason stand alone or even loom largely when I listened to what women said about their approach to makeup.

In fact, there were so few women who focused on this angle at all—or who spoke of makeup with the sort of hesitancy that implies that there's more to the story than what they're saying—that I began to wonder whether a sassier thread of talk has begun to replace the low-self-esteem conversation where makeup is concerned. The newer line of thinking goes something like this: We've spent so long denigrating the feminine—you don't throw like a *girl*, do you?—that for women to cast something particularly feminine like makeup in a negative light is equivalent to admitting that femininity is weak after all. Why not embrace makeup as a way of owning the feminine *and* the strong? Constructing cosmetics use as a form of self-articulation and even resistance might give us a broader perspective.

This mind-set has seeped out of the circles of academic postmodern feminist thought into popular culture. Two popular women's websites, *Jezebel* and *xoJane*, launched beauty-specific subsites; the Boobtique of feminist magazine *Bust* proffers cheek tints; and BuzzFeed, the marker of all things hive-minded, ran "14 Women Tell Us Why They Wear Makeup," with all participants framing their cosmetics use as joyful or empowering. There's defiance to this line of thought, which I've seen repeatedly in explicitly feminist circles as well as the more mainstream "postfeminist" culture that regards women's equality as something already achieved. Think of the playful way makeup images are arranged in women's magazines—wild eye shadow adorning haute couture models, artistic dribbles and splashes of various products covering the glossy pages. It echoes what thirtysomething Shannon says: "It's fun in the same little-girl way that coloring is fun—that crayons in themselves are fun. It's like coloring, but on your face." Framed this way, makeup is fun, a choice, a source of pleasure.

And as for that whole "women wear makeup because society pressures us" frame of mind? Few can deny the truth of its history. Less than seventy years ago, girls in high school home-economics classes were instructed in skillful makeup application, the idea being that makeup was as essential a part of womanhood as cooking and housekeeping. Employment handbooks regularly outlined what type of makeup female employees should wear; some still do. And in 2000, Darlene Jespersen was fired from Harrah's Casino in Reno, Nevada, for not wearing makeup; the Ninth Circuit Court of Appeals initially sided with Harrah's by ruling Jespersen's firing as legal after she took the casino to court. Across the pond, Melanie Stark, who worked in the music department at a Harrods store in London, suffered the same fate. But the fact is, we know about Jespersen's and Stark's cases because they were *news*, and news is what's outstanding, not what's run-of-the-mill. Workplaces mandating that women wear makeup seems outrageous, even when the courts disagree. The more established women's equality becomes, the more the idea that makeup is something thrust on us by the looming patriarchy begins to seem outdated. Old-fashioned, second wave, stodgy. *Boring.*

Indeed, there are plenty of numbers to support the idea that the makeup situation isn't quite so glum. According to research published in the *International Journal of Cosmetic Science*, women report feeling more self-confident and more sociable when wearing their usual makeup as opposed to none at all. Their body image is better when they're wearing makeup, and as for hairstyling, women's mood improves on nearly all measures after a visit to the hairdresser. And in a finding that might give makeup-championing feminists a moment of triumph, heavy makeup wearers have been found to be more pro-feminist in belief and attitude than women who wore less of it or none at all. As for women who *do* have low self-esteem, makeup isn't merely a veil for them to stay hidden behind; as we've seen, women with iffy regard for themselves actually have a decrease in signs of stress after applying cosmetics.

Yet despite these facts championing makeup as something far beyond flypaper that sticks women to our makeup kits for hours each month, something holds me back from being a wholehearted makeup evangelist—even though I wear it nearly every day. I can't help but question how "empowering" makeup can truly be when the vast majority of us use it fully within the boundaries that have been presented to us. It smacks of "choice feminism": the idea that if a woman *chooses* an action, as opposed to being shunted into it by patriarchal standards, it becomes feminist or at least symbolic of the hard-won options American women now have. In the case of makeup, though, not all of us *can* opt out. The firings of Darlene Jespersen and Melanie Stark are extreme in their consequences, but they're only a logical end point of research suggesting that women wearing light makeup are likelier than barefaced ones to be seen as competent in the workplace. And choice feminism in many ways is a euphemism for consumer feminism. While plenty of makeup is low cost and accessible to pretty much anyone who wants it, the fact is that to "choose" to wear makeup is to "choose" an ongoing expense that, at this point in time, is primarily drawn from women's bank accounts, not men's.

One of the pro-lipstick arguments that its cheerleaders defend most staunchly is the concept of makeup as self-expression. For if we decorate ourselves out of a desire to articulate that most sacred of beings—the self, unknowable to anyone but the subject—how can anyone decry it? It's as though if we're applying makeup because of a personal drive, it's okay, but if we do it because that's just what the majority of women *do*, we're caving in. It's a particularly American mind-set, as exemplified by one of the United States' standout writers: "Whenever you find that you are on the side of the majority, it is time to reform (or pause and reflect)," said Mark Twain. We're the country that invented the pioneer, the cowboy, the rebel outsider—hell, we're the country that turned Ayn Rand's self-above-all books into best sellers. We elevate the individual to the point where we just might be willing to work backward to justify any action as being about an iconoclastic vision, not about our collective or social sensibilities— including wearing makeup. The country that created the Lone Ranger is more willing to nod with approval when a woman claims to wear makeup "for me" than if the same woman, wearing the same makeup, meekly admits she wears it because it's expected of her by others. Marry our love of individualism with the legitimate complaints raised by feminists about the immense pressure on women to look good—and how this pressure makes us susceptible to the lures of the beauty industry—and it's not hard to see why we might denigrate any groupthink connected with makeup.

But here's the thing: Individuality exists in tandem with conformity. No society can be formed without a degree of collectivity, and we express that collectivity via aesthetic norms. We may have plenty of latitude within those norms, of course, but viewing makeup as an individual choice conveniently ignores the ways in which individual—even iconoclastic—

identities are formed in response to our collective ideal. For the most part, the majority of us wear makeup in ways that are more similar than different. When was the last time you pulled out green lipstick or red eyeliner? If a woman's face is a canvas for some sort of personal artistry, then frankly, we're making some pretty repetitive art. Where are the abstract expressionists, the conceptual artists, the cubists? Outside of high fashion magazines and the occasional club night, where is *anyone* but the realists, minimalists, and a handful of dabblers in pointillism or pop art?

We've worked ourselves between a rock and a hard place, cosmetically speaking, simultaneously framing makeup as a place of individualism, play, and expression *and* as a shameful covering-up of our authentic selves. With the latter narrative of makeup as balm for culturally instilled insecurity, we paint makeup as something for the milquetoast. In doing that, we mute the palette of reasons that women wear cosmetics. In fact, many women I talked with did speak of justifying their makeup use by discussing the ways they enjoy cosmetics, as though they were aware of some of their own negative motivations—or were aware that because we've been so successful in calling attention to the dark side of makeup, they were *expected* to have some sort of justification for it. Enter the mind-set of makeup as play, which eschews insecurity in favor of the active celebration of cosmetics. Given that we've cast women's relationship to beauty as being pathological, there's something refreshing about seeing young women revel in the playful, expressive possibilities of makeup—witness the wildly colorful ads for makeup line MAC or the work of YouTube beauty vloggers. But these dual mind-sets carry the risk of an either-or opposition: Either you use makeup as play or you use it to cover up the parts of yourself you're ashamed of. The way we actually use makeup, of course, is hardly so delineated—a fact reflected in the tools themselves. We may wear eyeliner to emphasize a gorgeous pair of eyes, but we may also dot on concealer to hide imperfections; we may define kinky hair with pomade but cover up our grays with dye. The best we can do by looking not only at our reasons for makeup but also at our eagerness to label some reasons as good (and others as not so good) is come closer to understanding the complexity of human beautification.

In doing so, we can adjust the disproportionate weight that makeup carries in popular feminist conversation. Going over the "is makeup feminist or not?" ground ad nauseam can serve as a distraction from other political concerns. It's a handy token point of debate for feminists in the Western world: Most of us have worn makeup, or considered wearing it, or have been challenged about why we don't wear it—or, as feminists, are simply hyperaware of the enormity of the messages we receive about expected feminine behavior. It makes sense that makeup is a locus of feminist-oriented conversation; after all, who is looking at the day-to-day lives of women more than feminists? But the extraordinary focus on whether wearing makeup makes one a "bad feminist" makes it all the easier for contemporary feminism to be written off as trivial. Look at the term *lipstick feminism*, the idea that young feminists base their political identity on tools of feminine power such as lipstick . . . and then ask yourself how many women you know who define themselves as lipstick feminists. In my case, the answer is zero.

Makeup, Femininity, and Power

A few years ago, I received an e-mail from Siobhan O'Connor, coauthor with Alexandra Spunt of the natural beauty guidebook *No More Dirty Looks* and coproprietress of the associated website. Earlier that year, the duo had issued a challenge to their blog readers: Send in photographs of themselves without a drop of makeup on. O'Connor and Spunt would then post them on the website, and one of the participants would win a raffle prize. The no-makeup gimmick that was popular online at the time worked particularly well for the No More Dirty Looks ethos, as the site focused on earth-friendly, cruelty-free, nontoxic beauty products; by showcasing themselves sans makeup, site users would see that "natural beauty" products were just an extension of the natural beauty they themselves possessed. The challenge was a hit. Dozens of readers sent in photos of themselves makeup free, comments were stuffed full of "wow!" and the like, and the four-month-old site found itself established in the natural beauty community.

Why not do another challenge? the duo reasoned a few months later. This time, they chose the opposite tack, asking readers to send in photos of themselves wearing a *lot* of makeup. "We want you to go wild . . . It's your going-out face we're looking for, not your doing-groceries face." This was a community of makeup lovers, remember, and the site's readership had expanded considerably since the initial challenge, so they expected this challenge to be even bigger than the last one.

So they waited a couple of weeks for photos to come in . . . and waited . . . and *waited.* That's where the e-mail I received came in. In an effort to prevent the challenge from being a total bust, O'Connor sent an e-mail to other beauty bloggers asking them to send in pics. I happily complied, of course, and in the end the challenge appeared to be a success. But the question raised by the scenario stuck with me: Why were women—specifically women who frequented a site devoted to makeup—far more eager to post public photos of themselves wearing no makeup than going all-out glam with the stuff?

"We had people privately e-mailing us and saying, 'I just can't do it,'" O'Connor says when I ask what she made of the lack of response. "I guess the mentality was, *Well, if I look bad with no makeup, no big deal.* But if you look bad with makeup, it's like you've said to the world, 'This is the best I can do,' and then if it doesn't work out you feel foolish."

Indeed, though I rarely leave my neighborhood without some makeup on, I *have* done it, and save for the occasional moment of self-consciousness, it's been fine. I compare that with the time I got a purposefully over-the-top makeover and then took the subway to a friend's place. I avoided eye contact with people, and if I happened to spot someone looking at me I wanted to rush over and say, *This is an experiment, this isn't the real me—I know it looks like I'm asking you for your attention, but I'm not.* What I take from this, and from the unexpected lack of response from the No More Dirty Looks readers about the glamour challenge, is this: Makeup can take courage. It's not necessarily an act of courage to dab it on, nor is refraining from using cosmetics an act of cowardice. The trouble is that the public conversation about makeup too often focuses on the self-esteem angle, regarding cosmetics as a crutch that women use to paper over negative feelings about ourselves. Going makeup free is seen as a brave embrace of one's own natural self—which, depending on the woman, it can be. But praising that as a stroke of fortitude overlooks the ways in which asking for attention—*here is my face, painted in a way that makes you likelier to look at me*—can take a fortitude of its own. When we frame makeup as something we do to cover ourselves up out of fear that we're not good enough as is, we sell women's resilience short. We sell *women* short. When women try—when women *strive*—we put ourselves on the line, more so than men because our purpose is still so often presumed to be *You are here to be looked at*. We should change the paradigm that led to this condition, yes. But in changing it we can't afford to cast sidelong glances at women who seize power through being seen or who take the traditionally passive role of being looked at and transform it into an act of agency.

Makeup artists might stress another moral of the story here: When it comes to makeup, moderation is key. And where there is moderation, *something is being moderated.* That something is the wearer's relationship to the world around her. Makeup helps us modulate our public image, our sense of self, our levels of stress. It helps us keep a sense of order—fitting, given that the word *cosmetics* comes from the Greek *cosmos*, meaning *order*. And of course that's just the problem with it in many a mind. Why should face paint be the way we organize ourselves—rather, how women organize ourselves?

Part of the answer here comes from the current inseparability of cosmetics from womanhood. Until men wear makeup in numbers as strong as women, we won't really know how much our cultural attitudes have to do with makeup itself as opposed to the people who wear it. A side note in a study on cosmetics and impressions in the workplace points to the trouble in collapsing the two. Makeup-wearing women were judged negatively in occupations that are stereotyped by sex. So if you're a secretary or a nurse, wearing makeup could actually hurt you—but if you're, say, an insurance agent, it won't. What this suggests is that as many associations as we make with makeup, ultimately its relationship to femininity matters more. Amp up the makeup, and you amp up the womanness of its wearer. As long as we associate womanhood with qualities that have little to do with sex—like competence (or lack thereof), compliance (or stubbornness; *you know women*), moodiness (is it that time of the month?)—anything associated exclusively with women is going to carry more weight than it would alone.

Frustrating as that is, it's not as frustrating as the limits of makeup. For no matter how skillfully we apply our eyeliner or how carefully we arrange our hair, some people are going to be more conventionally beautiful than others. Makeup can act as a sort of beauty democratizer: Not born with colorful lips, smooth skin, and a vibrant complexion? Fake it, my dear. But at the end of the day, no matter how skilled our makeup technique might be, *beauty is not a meritocracy*. It's not as though she who tries the hardest (or spends the most money, or has the most charm or even the most sex appeal) is the most beautiful. And if we assign that expectation to makeup, it will forever fall short.

Yet as much as we tie makeup to beauty, we've seen that beauty in and of itself is far from the only reason we bother with it. My hope is that by considering a more complex relationship with makeup, we can consider our real expectations surrounding it. Makeup is the ultimate placebo effect; it's a cosmetic change in every sense of the word, and our expectation that it will work—whatever that might mean to the wearer—is the only thing that keeps the beauty industry afloat. I think of what that English professor said about why she wears it: "Wearing makeup allows me to look the way I imagine I look all the time." I hear resilience in this statement, not capitulation. It's not that she wears makeup because she feels bad without it. She wears it because she thinks she looks pretty damn good, and makeup helps her realize that more fully. With makeup, we are not aiming to be transformed into someone else; we're trying to present our best selves. It's an articulation of the psychological drive to be seen. Makeup literally increases our visibility in the world.

In this light, both makeup fasts and over-the-top makeup challenges like the one posed by the No More Dirty Looks team take on a different importance than they might if looked at alone. We're in an unusual time, womanwise. More women than ever are entering public office, leading corporations, and outearning their male domestic partners. At the same time, women in the public eye are under ever-more scrutiny to look attractive at all times, and the US cosmetics industry continues to grow to the point of $58.3 billion, taking a larger and larger chunk from women's earnings. Women's visibility has increased—accompanied by a critical magnifying glass. But when presented with tools available to anyone with sixteen dollars to assemble a basic makeup kit, women—depending on perspective, personality, and opportunity—are able to shape that visibility in a way that speaks to their own visions of themselves. So we're back to the basic question here: Is makeup quite literally a tool of the patriarchy, or an instrument of women's self-articulation? And it's here that makeup fasts and challenges and everything in between serve their purpose. The goal is not to swear off all forms of artifice forever, or to embrace all the tools at our disposal, or even to give a point-by-point on why you wear makeup, or don't, or wore it yesterday but not today. Nor is it to reach the nexus of choice feminism: *Hey, it's fine to wear makeup as long as you* choose *it!* Yet it might be something just as personal: finding, and challenging, one's comfort zone.

Plenty of women don't wear makeup because it never interested them ("I'll wear it if I have to, like if it's expected of me because it's a wedding or a work event or whatever, but I've never been drawn to it and don't see that changing," says Cheryl, a woman in her late forties). But others who adhere to a wash-and-go face report a deep discomfort with the attention makeup can bring. "It's like, who am I, to think you should look at me?" says one mother of three. This whisper of *Who am I to ask for your attention?* goes to the core of nice-girl syndrome, the condition that has prevented many a woman from speaking out on everything from job discrimination to unwanted sexual advances to just contradicting the blowhard who corners women at parties, asks them what they do for a living, then proceeds to tell them everything *he* knows about their industry. Certainly makeup isn't the secret voice box that allows women to utter words like *No* or *That's unfair* or *You're wrong.* But if staying in one's comfort zone means holding hands with the ever-polite monster of *Who am I to ask for your attention?*—then leaving that zone, no matter the route, is crucial. For some women, donning makeup might be one of those routes. For others, dropping it might be a way to wriggle out of a different comfort zone, the one of perfect adherence to feminine codes. Challenging the assumptions surrounding beauty means challenging the rituals that make up our mornings and the little phrases that run through our heads: *Will I look too aggressive if I wear the black eyeliner* and *the red lipstick? Does this meeting warrant the expensive foundation? I don't feel like shaving my legs today—how much do I care what tonight's date might think, and how much do I care that he's someone who might care? I love this plum lipstick a friend made me try, but will my coworkers think I'm "trying too hard" if I start dolling myself up all of a sudden?* It means challenging our complacency level with public and private life, letting the weather vane of our discomfort alert us to factors that run deeper than the question of makeup itself.

4

The Eye of the Beholder

Sex, Dating, and Romance

One of the most endearing stories about love and beauty I know begins with pornography. A friend of mine worked at what's affectionately known in the industry as a "stroke mag"—i.e., a magazine with stories and images designed with a purpose-driven mission for their gentleman readers. This particular magazine didn't accept reader submissions, but that didn't stop a persistent handful of men from attempting to make their own contributions. Each month, my friend would receive dozens of photos from male subscribers. Not of the men themselves, but of their wives and girlfriends, with notes attached about how these women absolutely *needed* to be featured in an upcoming issue—I mean, isn't she *lovely*?—and if the editors had any business sense at all, they would send over a photo crew immediately to capture this woman in all her glory.

"And here's the thing," my friend told me over lunch. "These women— I'm sorry, but they're not all that!" (She dated women, so she was particularly qualified to make the assessment.) "The pictures are terrible, they're at awkward angles, and even when the women are attractive they just don't look like anything special to me. I don't get it." I took an odd sort of assurance from her report. These men were convinced that the utterly normal-looking women in their lives were *so* stunning, *so* alluring, that to deny them a spot in a stroke mag would be a gross disservice to masturbators nationwide. I pictured an average middle-age man gazing on his average middle-age wife and seeing not her crow's-feet or ashy skin or doughy thighs or any of the things the run-of-the-mill woman has that fall outside the realm of conventional beauty. No, he sees a *queen*. The eye of the beholder indeed.

It's interesting that what these particular men did in their private lives flies in the face of so much of the conventional thinking surrounding beauty and love. Men are visual creatures, we're told, so looks are the first thing they notice about a woman. It's a bit of wisdom that feels true at times: I've experienced the humiliation of watching a man I was on a date with stop talking midsentence to stare at a stunning leggy blonde walking through the room. I've seen male friends go gaga over a particularly pretty female friend of mine. And I've adjusted my behavior accordingly—taking special care with my makeup before dates, and then, when I've been in a relationship, making sure not to "let myself go."

But I also knew that the whole "men love beautiful women" thing was shortsighted. For starters, it didn't recognize the fact that we women are rather visual creatures ourselves. (The old saw that women go for personality, men for looks? It's not quite that simple, as we'll soon see.) It also didn't explain why I knew so many women who were average-looking, or even plain, who constantly had men sniffing after them—or why that particularly pretty friend of mine didn't date anyone until her mid-twenties. And where did this whole thing leave queer women? It wasn't like the lesbian and bisexual women I knew lived in some sort of utopia where they were romantically evaluated on their inner beauty alone.

I saw enough evidence of both of these lines of thought to know that chances were some men prized conventional beauty above other qualities, others had more unique ideas about beauty, and still others might not particularly care what a woman looked like as long as he felt attracted to her. Maybe some really didn't care at all. Most of all, I knew there wasn't much I could do about it—there wasn't some bulletproof way to ensure that anyone I wanted to find me attractive would do so. I could try to look my best, sure, but as thirtysomething Rob put it, "I'm pretty much attracted to someone or I'm not. And if I'm not attracted to someone, it's not like it's because I don't like how she does her hair or something—it's because there's *just not an attraction*. I can think a woman is really pretty and just not be attracted to her."

So I knew this rationally. But what these two competing schools of thought on beauty and attraction did was create not a spectrum but two parallel tales. One was that beauty was in the eye of the beholder, and that I could safely assume that if someone was drawn to me, he found me attractive as is. The other was that conventional beauty was the surest route toward landing a quality partner, and that the best way to maximize my chances of finding a match was to maximize my beauty. I feared that at some point, those two parallel lines would turn perpendicular and crash. Someone could fall for me and find me beautiful—and then one day, he'd switch tracks and realize that I wasn't actually as pretty as he'd once found me. I'd never had a problem attracting men, but that fact failed to give me much protection from the fear that if I found myself single when I didn't want to be, it would be my looks that were to blame. It was insecurity, sure, but within my fears dwelled something more potent—more intimate—than mere insecurity. I just wasn't sure what.

When I think of all the ideas floating around out there about how beauty shapes our intimate relationships, I picture something resembling an awkward party. In one corner is the dude going on about how, duh, *of course* the purpose of beauty is to attract mates, and men are just more *visual* than women, so can he help it if he wants to be with the most gorgeous woman in the room? Meanwhile, he looks knowingly at the woman on his arm—who *isn't* conventionally beautiful but who has that ineffable quality known as "it," and who, when you catch her in the ladies' room later on, says, "Sex appeal is an *attitude*," winks at you, and wiggles her way back into the fray. Then there's the frowsy couple who dress alike and seem utterly enchanted with one another; when the woman goes to get a drink, her fellow's eyes trail after her and he sighs, "Isn't she beautiful?" And then there are the women like me, and maybe like you, who are watching the party and wondering where exactly their own brand of allure fits into the smorgasbord of attraction.

Will the following pages answer that question definitively? Probably not. But I will tell you this: Several years ago, a coworker told me about a woman he'd met at a party the night before. There were dozens of women at the soiree whom he found prettier, but as he put it, "I couldn't stop watching her. It was like my body was making the choice for me—I had to make myself not follow her around all night, but I wanted to be near her." And at night's end, when he asked for her number and they wound up canoodling, "It was unbelievably sexy. And I *still* don't think she's all that pretty." At the time I didn't know whether to cheer him or raise my eyebrow—this was a man well into his thirties, and he was only *now* discovering that someone's presence could outshine her plain wrapper? I've shared this anecdote plenty of times since that conversation, and nearly everyone who hears it nods in recognition or chimes in with their own similar tales, including people who have strict physical preferences they prefer not to stray from. *He* was the outlier for not recognizing this earlier, not me. As much as we as a society have pushed the idea that physical appeal is the key to attracting romantic attention, particularly for women, we intuitively challenge that assumption all the time simply by being attracted to whomever we're attracted to. There's no guarantee that the person we see under a special golden light will see us in the same way, of course. But most of us, wherever we fall on the spectrum of conventional beauty, have had moments of being glimpsed through that golden lens of attraction. To me, that's a comfort.

A word on sexual orientation: Most of the themes I'm covering here are common to people all over the spectrum of sexual orientation—the proverbial rose-colored glasses, for instance, and the role of personality in defining who catches our eye. However, much of the clinical and academic research on those themes focuses on heterosexual attraction. It's difficult and dangerous enough to draw broad generalizations from studies and interviews, let alone apply those generalizations to the LGBT community. All might be fair in love and war, but the gender differences that play into some of those generalizations make it impossible to assume that relationship templates between men and women apply to romances between women. As the saying goes, take what you like, and leave the rest.

I'll Tell You What You Want:
Physical Preferences in the Dating Market

If barroom wisdom is to be believed, the best thing a woman can do to snag a date is be irresistibly good-looking—and the best thing a man can do is have a fat wallet. And sure enough, the leading study on the matter, which surveyed more than ten thousand people around the globe, upholds the beauty-and-money maxim. Men reported valuing physical attractiveness more than women did, and women were likelier than men to say they wanted a mate with high earning potential. The theory here is an echo of what we looked at in chapter 1: Beauty is prized, particularly in women, because it signals reproductive fitness. That is, our evolutionary drive pushes a man to seek out the most attractive partner to bear his children while leading women to find the man with the greatest resources to provide for those children.

Let's leave aside concerns about the validity of this theory for the moment. For whatever the science behind the "men want beauty, women want money" line of thinking might reveal, we certainly *act* as though it's true. When it comes to "mate retention practices," or the things we do to keep our lovers around, heterosexual women are likelier than men and gay women to gussy themselves up in hopes of holding on to a partner. And the more conventionally attractive a straight woman is, the more of those practices her fellow will engage in, particularly "resource display," or flashing cash. The prizing of beautiful women can reach the point of lunacy: In one study, men were likelier to pursue women whose online dating profiles featured an attractive picture—even when they were explicitly told that the photo wasn't actually of the woman whose profile it was paired with. The mere *thought* of beauty, it seems, can blind men to reason.

So is it any wonder that women sometimes believe the route to love is lined with beauty rites? "I wish I had more time to put into my appearance so I could make men I'm dating prouder to be seen with me," says Jasmin, a thirty-eight-year-old paralegal. Elyssa, a twenty-six-year-old writer, has slept with her makeup on when spending the night with paramours. YouTube is littered with first-date makeup tutorials (one of which specifies using a primer from Benefit named, aptly enough, Stay Don't Stray). As for me, my pre-date checklist consisted of cash, credit cards, ID, keys, phone—and a stick of concealer. Not that it's just first-date jitters that have women connecting relationships with appearance; I've heard three different women craft their marriage-proposal tales in a way that specifically includes self-consciousness about something being wrong with their appearance at the moment the question was popped. (One woman had just come home from the gym and uttered a sweaty, red-faced "Yes," while another had a piece of salami caught between her teeth as her boyfriend went down on bent knee.)

There's a problem with believing that men pursue relationships with beauty foremost in mind. It's not true. That study of more than ten thousand people? It asked men and women about their *preferences* in dating, not their *experiences*. In fact, most empirical data on "what men want" is actually data on what men *think* they want. Truth is, we humans aren't so great at knowing what we truly want when it comes to partners. In a study that examined people's choices in speed dating, both in the moment and in long-term follow-up, researchers found little correlation between people's stated preferences and their actual choices. (Case in point: A boyfriend once mentioned that I fit his type—short brunettes—to a T. I've got brown hair, but I'm also three inches taller than the average American woman. When I pointed this out, his retort was, "I mean shorter than *me*." He's six-foot-one.) One way to interpret this finding is that our preferences make for a sort of wish list, but we're willing to settle for less. That makes a certain sense—why *wouldn't* we all want to pair off with people we think are good-looking? Indeed, most studies that support the men-love-hotties idea show that women say they want physically appealing partners too; they just don't rank it as high in importance as men do. Instead, women tend to place value on earning potential—or at least, in keeping with the idea that we don't know what we really want, women *think* they place more value on the wallet than on the face of its holder.

The speed-dating study authors add a crucial twist to the wish-list theory. We make those lists in a state of cool rationality—but when faced with a real, live human, what we find ourselves attracted to may have little to do with what's on that oh-so-rational checklist. It might not be so much that a man "settles" for a woman with pedestrian looks, or that a woman "settles" for a man with a modest income, but that the intoxication of attraction instantly realigns our stated priorities into something that more accurately reflects our deeper longings. Attraction might follow some forms of logic, sure. That doesn't mean that it's a logic we can manipulate at will. You've heard the term *perfect on paper*, right? We all know what trumps that person who checks every box on our wish list: the one we're *actually* attracted to.

Still, there is a phenomenon that, at first glance, looks like support for the idea that men pursue beautiful women: the matching effect. Men who meet society's definition of conventionally good-looking do indeed tend to pair off with similarly attractive women. Crudely put, a ten is likelier to marry a ten, while fours wind up with one another. (Of course, one person's four might be another person's ten, but most of us are able to recognize what makes a person traditionally attractive, and that's what the research we're looking at here considered.) But the matching effect in relationships extends to most areas of our lives: education, income, temperament, personal interests. Similarities predict how satisfying a relationship is to the people in it—as much as we say that opposites attract, statistically speaking, they don't. So yes, rich, good-looking men do gravitate toward rich, good-looking women—just as rich, average-looking men gravitate toward rich, average-looking women, and low-income hotties wind up with one another.

Theories on why we humans love to match our partners in looks range from evolutionary (good-looking people want good-looking babies) to market-based (since we prize beauty, it becomes a form of currency that people can exchange with one another on the fair market of love), from commonsense (matching is satisfying) to Freudian (we pick people who resemble our parents, and who therefore somewhat resemble ourselves). Where things get really interesting is in looking at not just how objectively good-looking people are but how good-looking people *think* they are. Researchers theorize that conventional attractiveness simply sets a baseline for how good-looking a person can reasonably expect his or her sweetheart to be. But people who rate themselves as highly attractive have a better chance of pairing up with good-looking people—even if, objectively speaking, they're not terrifically attractive themselves. It boils down to this: If you think a person is out of your league, you're less likely to try to go to bat. But if you think you're both playing in the major leagues, you've at least got a chance to hit a home run.

Does all this talk of fours and tens and home runs seem a bit crude? It might, but there's good news here for the average-looking person—i.e., most of us. And it's something that lies at the heart of many a feel-good romantic comedy, to the point where there's no way to say this without seeming cheesy, so bear with me: Inner beauty counts too. Most of us have had the experience of meeting someone average-looking and finding him or her more attractive the more we get to know the person—or of meeting someone stunning and finding him or her *less* appealing the more we're exposed to that person's disagreeable personality. This isn't limited to the occasional *Beauty and the Beast* anecdote; it's backed by research as well. Men given positive general information about women's personalities rated a wider range of female body sizes as attractive, as compared with a group of men told that the women they were rating were unpleasant. Same with general attractiveness, for both sexes—in fact, in one study, people rated the subjects of *the exact same photos* as more or less attractive than they had only minutes before, depending on the kind of information they were given about the people in the pictures. And when researchers looked at participants' diaries, they found recorded evidence that this sensation isn't unusual. My own journals reflect this truth, whether the proclamation is 1989's "I can't believe I ever thought he was hot! GROSS!!!" or 2007's "How is it that he's become beautiful to me?"

If you're feeling particularly cunning, you could even reverse engineer these findings, as people with better education, more likable personalities, and higher grooming standards are likelier to land themselves an objectively good-looking partner. (And yes, that goes for women as well as men—we're just as likely to trade our own education to snag a good-looking date as the guys.) Being Miss Congeniality may be construed as being runner-up, but it needn't be. Taking steps to improve other aspects of your life—your job, your life satisfaction, your temperament, your wit—

can actually make you be seen as more physically beautiful. Challenging the notion that inner beauty is by necessity different than the skin-deep variety allows us to see that beauty isn't just some extraneous force that's left up to the whim of genetics. It's a malleable concept, one we can tailor to our strengths. The no-makeup makeover might not be easy—and just as with physical beauty, it might not even be fair—but it's an option. And depending on your perspective, it just might be a good one.

Rose-Colored Glasses: Positive Illusions in Relationships

I'd tell you I once fell in love with a handsome man, but that's not exactly what happened. What happened was more like this: I met a man whose looks were . . . well, more than one person suggested that were we to have children, it would be a stroke of misfortune were they to inherit their father's looks. When I first met him, I'd have agreed. It's been ages since I've seen him, but I can recall what a disinterested party might refer to as his flaws: limbs disproportionate to his body, tightly curled hair of a color he once referred to as "opossum," unnaturally smooth skin that lent him an oddly childlike quality tempered by the tufts of opossum-colored facial hair that he never seemed to quite depilate correctly. I saw those things, and when I met his stunning pocket Venus of a girlfriend, I thought, *Wow, how'd he wind up with her?*

Our love story itself is fairly unremarkable: Time passed, our friendship developed, his relationship disintegrated, then mine—in part because, while attending the wedding of a friend whose vows included "waking up every morning next to my favorite person," my mind went not to the person I was seeing but to this other man. What made it remarkable (to me, anyway) was what happened to him. He went from being odd-looking to cute to—I still couldn't call him *handsome*, what with its connotations of square jaws and Clooney eyes and rugged yet genteel masculinity. *Beautiful*, though—*that* he became.

Coming to find him beautiful was a series of fits and starts: watching him crack a good joke and loving the glint that came into his eyes, finding myself softening ever so slightly when I'd catch his profile at a particular angle. It didn't feel like I was talking myself into finding him more attractive, nor did it feel like I was superimposing his inner beauty onto his looks. I knew he hadn't physically changed—and yet, *he had*. He was beautiful to me, and he hadn't been before; surely my taste hadn't changed so dramatically in a matter of months, had it? I'd heard the term *rose-colored glasses* before, but in regard to relationships I'd thought of it as a mental trick, a way of fooling ourselves—or is the better term *deluding* ourselves?—into thinking we're with someone better-looking than we actually are. I hadn't known that when those glasses were calibrated by affection, it could change your vision. It felt like a slower, more gradual version of what happened the first time I put on a pair of glasses to correct my nearsightedness. The eye doctor placed the pair of pink plastic frames onto my nine-year-old face, I looked over to where my mother was sitting, and I thought, *Oh, that's what you look like.* For the first time, I could see the small details that made her *her*—the hair not only a mass of red but individual strands; the skin not a smear of pink but made up of curves and lines and pores and a small, pale mole I'd never seen before. Twenty-some years later, the way my vision had been altered when it came to this man wasn't as sudden, but it felt just as dramatic. And the first time I found myself being held in his arms, I tilted my head up from his chest, saw his care-softened features, and thought the same: *Oh, that's what you look like.* Were you to tell me this story about you, I'd find it sweet, but I'd know that of course *he* didn't change a bit; it was all you. Yet to this day I am not fully convinced that the shift was mine alone. *He changed.*

The sensation of someone becoming more attractive over time is hardly a quirk unique to me—at least half the people I interviewed about this said they'd had some sort of similar experience. It's so common that it has a name of its own: positive illusions. The general idea behind positive illusions is that our minds will fool themselves into thinking things are better than they actually are, or that we're more exceptional than we really are, so that we can go about our day-to-day business with a sense of optimism. It's part of why so many of us still buy into that "till death do us part" business in the face of high divorce rates, why the majority of us think of ourselves as better-than-average drivers, and even what allows some terminally ill people to thrive in the face of certain death. It's also what saw 75 percent of heterosexual married folks rating their partner a seven or above on a one-to-ten scale when asked to rate them objectively, with the average physical attractiveness rating landing at 8.06. In fact, people consistently rate their partners as more attractive than other people do and as better-looking than the partners rate themselves (even though, consistent with the idea of positive illusions, most of us rate ourselves as being better-looking than the average person).

As if positive illusions weren't enough, people in love also exaggerate the appeal of their beloved with a bit of mental chicanery known as the derogation effect. With the derogation effect, people in relationships tend to see other people as less attractive than single folks do. So a group of committed people and a group of single folks might look at the same person, and on average, the single people will find the target better-looking than their paired-off counterparts do. What's more, committed women *remember* the faces of conventionally attractive people as being less attractive than singletons do. The derogation effect isn't just in the moment. It lasts.

Positive illusions and the derogation effect have the same goal: Our minds want to protect a good thing. What simpler way to protect a happy relationship than to suddenly dim the appeal of everyone else? Sure enough, there is a correlation between relationship satisfaction and these mental tricks. When a group of partnered people were presented with a number of images that had been digitally manipulated to make their partner appear both more and less conventionally attractive, the people who rated their relationships as more satisfying were likelier to finger a beautified photo as being unretouched. On the other end, attached people who reported being romantically unhappy chose an "uglified" picture of their partner as being unretouched. (Meanwhile, most participants were easily able to identify the non-manipulated photos of a celebrity.) It's unclear whether positive illusions help keep us happier in relationships or if people in happy relationships more easily generate such relationship safeguards. Whatever the case, they're a predictor not only of romantic satisfaction but of a relationship's longevity—the stronger the illusion at the birth of a relationship, the longer the pairing is likely to last. You could take these findings and use them as one measure of your satisfaction in a relationship. Secretly finding your partner a little lacking in the looks department lately? Could be that your positive illusion is eroding to reveal a deeper dissatisfaction and that the more reasoned part of your brain simply hasn't caught up yet.

Alas, there's a catch. While both men and women engage in positive illusions, they may do it differently. For a straight man to adopt such an illusion, he's got to not only be happy in a relationship but be committed to it. Heterosexual women, on the other hand, seem to do it as long as they're reasonably content, regardless of how committed they are to the partnership. (As for queer couples, research suggests that lesbians and gay men engage in positive illusions just as much as their straight counterparts, though it's unclear how commitment factors into it.) This could be because women may be likelier than men to derive a sense of identity from being in a relationship, which would nudge their perception favorably toward their beloved, since the stakes—one's own identity—are higher. It could be because women are more likely to approach relationships with a mind-set of commitment. It could be because women are just more willing to give the benefit of the doubt.

But perhaps the most satisfactory explanation of the gender discrepancy with positive illusions comes from someone whose livelihood depends on successfully decoding what men "really" want: a sex worker. Charlotte Shane, a writer and prostitute, puts it this way: "I'm sure there are men who hire escorts and they just want the most attractive thing they can find. They want *things*, and a person is a thing for them, and they want the thing to be announcing its attractiveness. But I don't think most men want that. You know those articles that are always so hysterical about men watching porn who don't want real women now? Do you *know* any men like that? The men I've spent time with usually genuinely love women. There are some neurotic guys with strict preferences, or they're afraid of women or whatever. But usually they seem really delighted to be around a female." Clearly, a paid sexual relationship will have a dynamic that differs to some degree from those done on a strictly volunteer basis. But what I take from Shane's musings is this: *Men like how women look.* And it's true: Statistically speaking, men en masse consistently rate women as being better-looking than women rate men. As thirty-eight-year-old Han says with a shrug when I ask about his relationship with women on the whole, "I like to look at them."

Indeed, women have been seen as decorative objects throughout history, and one of the fallouts from this is that prettiness is presumed to be a default setting of womanhood. Now, there are plenty of valid arguments about why we should sever the automatic association between women and physical attractiveness. For this moment, though, let's put those aside and take a generous look at one of its implications: If women are seen as perfectly lovely simply by dint of being women, perhaps men don't have as great a need for those proverbial rose-tinted glasses. And then once a man is in a relationship that feels right in the long term, those positive illusions come into play as a safeguard.

It would be naive to believe that men are in perpetual delight whenever a woman is within their field of vision, just as it would be naive to believe that once you're in love, your significant other will only have eyes for you, and vice versa. Plus, few of us want to attract a partner who sees no further than skin-deep. But what I see in the research surrounding positive illusions is an eagerness to love—an eagerness that means that once things click, most of us are happy to slip on those rosy spectacles as long as they still seem to fit. It's a picture that's out of sync with some of the fears I've heard from other women—and felt myself—about maintaining our allure over time. That fear has driven many a purchase of, say, fifty-eight-dollar glycolic acid facial smoothing cream. What I'd wish for more of us to understand is that the human eye can be more generous than we give it credit for—and that a tint of rose can do more for one's complexion than any cream around.

Lesbian Chic: Appearance and Queer Women

Buzz cuts, bow ties, straight-cut jeans, überfemme sequined wiggle dresses, a flash of hair flopping over shorn sides, plaid shirts, no makeup, over-the-top makeup—just as there's no singular queer look for women, queer women can't necessarily be spotted by their style. But as with any community, there is a loose, unofficial set of LGBT style guidelines, whether it's reflected in Ellen DeGeneres dapper, Beth Ditto rock-star fabulous, Rachel Maddow "soft butch," or the gender fluidity of *Orange Is the New Black*'s Ruby Rose. And as with any community, there's a reason for those guidelines: They signal a group identity, both to members of the group and to those outside of it. While identifying one another might be a nice boost to some subcultures—like, say, fitness enthusiasts or rockabillies—in the queer community there's a uniquely practical use for appearance standards, in that one's look announces, *Hey, I'm interested in people of my own gender.* Which, given that the majority of American adults identify as heterosexual, is pretty important to telegraph in order to widen the dating pool.

But as with so many aspects of women's physical appearance, there's a double bind here. The fluidity of gender within the LGBT world means that, to a certain degree, traditional beauty norms can be subverted. "I don't have to worry about hiding from the male gaze or about stepping in front of it either," says Christy, a soft-butch lesbian in her forties. Likewise, Cara, age thirty-eight, says that it was only when she started dating women that she began to question things like why she wore makeup every day and spent substantial money coloring her hair: "I really felt that [my first girlfriend] saw me for me, and that helped me start to see myself more clearly as well. I found that my makeup choices started to become more subtle and less sexualized the more we hung out—certainly attracting a male gaze was the last thing I was thinking about. I didn't care if men looked at me, which made me care more about how I saw myself." On the flip side, within the queer community there are still plenty of ways to get a style "wrong," and scrutiny of one's appearance is hardly limited to straight folks. "When things ended with this one woman I dated, she started telling me stuff she didn't like, and she said, 'I feel like I want to be with someone more boi,'" says Christy. "She'd bought me this men's flannel shirt, but I've got a forty-three-inch bust—a shirt cut for a man isn't ever going to fit me right. It felt like she was saying, *This is my idea of you.* But I couldn't wear it. My body type wasn't ever going to let me wear it. It was like I wasn't quite butch enough to be *truly* butch. I felt like I'd failed."

"I really think women can look at your shoes and lose interest," says

Nicole Kristal, coauthor of *The Bisexual's Guide to the Universe* and founder of the #StillBisexual campaign. "I'm serious! I remember reading about a study that said there are really only a handful of reasons a guy wouldn't go on a second date with a woman, but there are hundreds of reasons why a woman wouldn't go on a second date with a guy. That pickiness applies to women dating women too, so that factors into my appearance—I don't want the way I look to be one of the reasons a woman wouldn't want to go out with me."

Actually, the question of self-presentation does get more complicated when looking specifically at bisexual women. While queer women across the spectrum are easily able to identify a variety of lesbian styles, many are stumped when it comes to identifying a distinctly bisexual look. The result? Bi women are often assumed to be straight. On a political level, this plays into a broader concern of bisexuals: silencing and dismissal. (Plenty of straight and gay people believe there's no such thing as bisexuals, just people who are halfway out of the closet—or sexual dilettantes who will go back to being straight once they've experimented enough.) And on a personal level, it can make bi women invisible to one another. "In the 1920s, didn't men wear a red necktie or something like that to signal to one another that they were gay?" says Kristal. "It would be great if bisexuals had something like that."

Not that bisexual women are the only ones who are consistently mistaken for straight. Amy, a thirty-year-old with long, wavy hair who describes herself as a clothes hoarder, took to purposefully adopting edgier fashions into her wardrobe in hopes of being seen as gay more frequently. "You know how in nature animals will undergo adaptation in order to survive?" she says. "My style had to sort of do that to be seen by women I was interested in—Doc Martens, or other things that have a hint of gay to them—especially once I moved to Florida, where there isn't as much of a lesbian scene as there was where I'm from. I was like, *Do I need to wear a freakin' rainbow bracelet and wave my arm out every time I want to meet a girl?* It's hard out there for a femme." She theorizes that these assumptions of straightness are where the queer term *aggressive femme* comes from. "I think people assume that I'm this passive pillow princess or that I'm not 'really' gay and am just trying it out, so I've actually started saying to more masculine-looking women I'm interested in, 'I'm probably gayer than you are.' I've had to become a lot more outgoing, a lot more aggressive and sort of in your face, in order to make it clear that, yes, I'm 'really' gay."

Looks come into play in another way unique to same-sex relationships: comparison. The woman who said that Christy wasn't butch enough for her was butch herself. "She's five nine, really skinny—she could shop in the men's department without a problem," says Christy. "But with the way my body is shaped, if I wear men's underwear it's like I have a diaper tucked into my pants. That feeling of failure came because she could pull off the butch thing more successfully and consistently than I did. She'd beat me in that arena." On the flip side, Amy, who prefers to date more androgynous or masculine-looking women, reports feeling fat when with athletic women. "Weight has always been a problem for me," she says. "I'm confident in all sorts of other ways, but it's sometimes hard for me to even go to the beach with my girl-friend, because she and her friends will look a certain way in their bathing suits, and I feel huge." In this way, a queer woman can feel caught—protected from some patriarchal expectations by dint of her sexual orientation, but still subject to their influence in the most private spaces of her world.

Researchers have come to varying conclusions about whether queer women are cushioned against conventional beauty standards—where one study says that lesbians internalize conventional beauty norms less than straight women, another finds that they're at similar risk as straight women for having a poor body image. The truth is likely a synthesis of the two. After all, gay women, even those who spend much of their time in queer communities, also exist in the world at large and deal with many of the same factors that could lead a heterosexual woman to not feel so great about her looks. This dual-pronged set of cultural expectations shows up in body image: Overall, compared with straight people and gay men, lesbi-ans tend to find bodies with a higher BMI more attractive, suggesting that there's more social latitude in body size among women who date women. But heavier queer women like Amy may still internalize comparisons with thin partners. Just like heavy straight women who date slender men, portly lesbians are likelier to think of themselves as overweight when involved with a thin partner, a comparison that dwindles when fat women of any orientation partner up with similarly sized people.

Wherever things stand now with queer women and appearance, it'll be interesting to see where things go as LGBT rights become more and more of a given in our culture. In order to avoid discrimination, gay women in the past had to carefully code their visible queerness so they appeared straight to everyone but those in the know. Certainly discrimination today still exists for queer women; in fact, one backhanded benefit of there being a lack of a bisexual visual code is that bisexual women report less workplace discrimination than lesbians. But in an era when the US Supreme Court has proclaimed same-sex marriage legal in all states, queer women are increasingly able to opt into a luxury that many straight women have taken for granted: the ability to present authentically as an individual. Indeed, when I asked two married femme lesbians what they tried to project with their appearance, their answers had nothing to do with queer visibility. Jen speaks of how, as a nurse, she seeks to telegraph a level of professional competence to soothe her patients. Her wife replies, "I'm just me. My appearance reflects that." Visible "gaydar" signs may be a part of any queer woman's self-presentation but needn't be limited to it.

"Dear Girls": Exploiting Insecurity

Not long ago, as I was walking home from the grocery store, a car pulled up beside me in a way that made it clear I was about to be either asked for directions or subjected to street harassment. I braced myself for a "Hey, baby" or some variation thereof. What I heard was this: "Don't worry, baby, you've still got it."

Don't worry, baby, you've still got it. I was in my late thirties when this happened—far from my crone years, but past the age of being a "young woman." Intended to be simultaneously elevating and degrading (as are all catcalls), it was as if the fellow in the car was making a direct appeal to how I might feel about myself due to my advancing age. I shouldn't "worry," after all; I still had "it," even after all these years. Left unspoken was the base premise of his words: I *must* feel bad about myself because I was edging rapidly toward forty, and therefore I'd welcome his assertion of my appeal. Also left unspoken was the base premise of every catcall: This gentleman believed he had the right to tell me something about myself. How I looked, how I should behave, even how I should feel about myself. And as the public success of activist groups like Hollaback! and Stop Street Harassment has shown in recent years, this isn't just my interpretation of catcalls—women in general are fed up with it.

Now, words hurled from moving vehicles are hardly the same thing as advances made in situations where both parties might be able to express attraction. A catcall is not a date. But still, I knew what had happened. I'd been negged.

The Game, the 2005 best seller chronicling author Neil Strauss's adventures within the pickup artist community, laid bare a basic set of guidelines that supposedly allowed any man who followed them to become a pied piper of babes. Among those guidelines was a technique known as the neg, in which the fellow offers his female target a light insult, usually about her looks, disguised as a compliment. It's meant to keep her a bit vulnerable, and therefore more receptive to his advances—and to make him stand out from other men, who presumably offer straightforward compliments. Sample negs from an online pickup artist forum: "I like your look—beauty is common but you seem like you have character," "That's lovely long hair—are they extensions?" and "You're cute, just like my nine-year-old cousin." Sample neg from life: Don't worry, baby, *you've still got it.*

The tactic only works, of course, if the target has an unsteady self-appraisal. If her opinion of herself is too high, she'll just write off the guy as a jerk. Frankly, I'm not convinced the neg works at all, but that hasn't stopped it from being one of the most discussed aspects of *The Game*; it was the lead of Strauss's 2004 *New York Times* essay. But it doesn't matter if the neg actually works—the point is that enough of us *think* it works for the editors of the nation's paper of record to mention it. And we think it works because we so often presume that when it comes to the crossroads of beauty and self-worth, women perennially come from a position of injury.

The neg is a case study of how this assumption can play out in the dating realm, but it's not the only example. At its heart, the neg takes the way a woman feels about her looks (or is presumed to feel about her looks) and uses that as a tool against her. That can play out in other ways—the straight-up put-down, for example, which is a red flag for intimate partner violence. But a compliment—ostensibly the opposite of a put-down—has the potential to be another form of manipulation, as it sets up its speaker to be a woman's savior from low appearance esteem.

The Internet saw this sentiment go viral with the "Dear Girls" meme of 2011, in which young male fashion model Cole Mohr wore a somber, soulful expression and implored girls to feel better about themselves by holding up a sign that read:

> Dear Girls
> DONT [*sic*] BE INSECURE
> you dont need make-up & nice clothes
> you're *all* fucking *beautiful*

Undoubtedly Mohr was well-meaning, but plenty of women took issue with it nonetheless. As the viral responses of young women holding up signs reading "Don't tell me what to do" showed, he'd made the mistake of thinking that women primarily wear makeup as a means to cover up insecurity. Moreover, he'd positioned himself as savior, rescuing women (or rather, girls) from the worries over their appearance that presumably plagued them. Though Mohr appeared to be earnest in his plea, the tactic can also be used cynically. Nicole Kristal tells of observing a queer friend's apparent luck with women: "I watched this friend of mine pick up woman after woman, and I was jealous because I couldn't. I finally said, 'How do you get so many women?' She was like, 'I just figure out what they're most insecure about, and I tell them I love that the most.' That was something sort of evil I thought only a certain kind of guy would do. I feel like that's dishonest." The thing is, as a tactic, it worked. "Then this woman I started dating was like, 'I'm going to lose some weight,' and I started doing that a little, telling her how much I loved her body," Kristal says. "And yeah, I think her body's amazing, but when I'd tell her, 'Your body is amazing, I think about it all the time,' that's a bullshit line."

Is there something inherently manipulative about complimenting someone you care about, or even someone you just want to bed for a night? Not necessarily; compliments are nice to hear, after all. And to be sure, plenty of girls and women do have enormous gaps in their appearance esteem and could take heart in messages such as Mohr's. Compliments can be a part of mending insecurities, even more so for women than men. (In heterosexual relationships, women report being more aware of the presence—and absence—of compliments than men are.) What's more, those sweet nothings aren't nothings at all; there's a correlation for both sexes between the number of compliments received and relationship satisfaction. Straight men who heartily compliment their partners just might be onto something, and those compliments don't have to signal some sort of manipulation of a woman's heart.

But compliments based on appearance aren't necessarily just about someone having beautiful eyes. Because women are so often assumed to have a fraught relationship with their looks, compliments on those looks take on a meaning that's larger than the words themselves: They can paint women as creatures who need to be rescued from psychological crisis. If one half of a duo presumes that the other half is in constant need of an ego boost, it creates the appearance of a chronic power imbalance. Now, not all relationships actually *have* that imbalance, and certainly it's not like all men think that their female partners need to hear they're gorgeous in order to get out of bed in the morning. But when we as a culture view women's feelings about their own looks as something to approach with caution, we set up a paradigm that sees women as needy, and men (or canny queer women) as white knights. In other words, it replicates the exact romantic dynamic that plenty of women have worked hard to cast off in the past couple of generations. Challenging the supposition that women's relationship with their appearance is inherently poor can ultimately make compliments more meaningful. If we erase their power as a dark currency that feeds a woman's wounded self-esteem, we're left with the sincerity that we yearn to find behind every sweet nothing.

"You'll See Through Me": Self-Consciousness

"I'd stayed up the whole night before our first date texting the girl, and in the middle of our date I was so tired I had to take a nap," reports nineteen-year-old Camille, a university student. "She nestled my head in her lap and I sort of arranged my body so that I lay on my side, with the dip of my waist showing—I wiggled a little to get into the best viewing position. It wasn't comfortable. It didn't occur to me to be comfortable."

When Camille painted this picture for me, I flashed to one of the many times I'd done a quick, artful arrangement of bedsheets when a lover would rise from bed. The idea was to drape myself just so, strategically covering parts that I felt required control of some sort—belly, pubis—while exposing just enough of my flesh to evoke hazy nineteenth-century erotica. It wasn't that I was anxious about the way I looked; it was more that I was *aware*. Self-consciousness, not lack of confidence or poor appearance esteem per se, has been at the heart of many an uncertain moment in my own relationships—and the more I listened to women whose beauty woes were enmeshed with their love lives, the more I saw that this sensation wasn't particular to me.

To be clear, this feeling of hyperawareness of being in my own skin is different from the times when I feel bad about how I look. I'm just as likely to feel self-conscious when I'm feeling particularly attractive as when I'm not so convinced of my own allure, yet it's still a sense of discomfort, as Camille points out. It's led me to suck in my gut and check my reflection nearly every time I'm in front of a mirror; it's prompted a friend of mine to adopt a particular posture when she's picking up an object off the floor if a man is around, to ensure she looks dainty while doing so. It's a monitoring that goes double for little slips that might contradict the assigned role one plays within a pairing, as when Christy felt inadequate for not being able to wear the men's flannel shirt her girlfriend gave her: "It was proof I wasn't ever going to be butch enough for her." Similarly, twenty-six-year-old Rebecca has no problem with her husband seeing her apply makeup, but when it comes to things that appear to pose a threat to her status as a woman, like plucking stray hairs on her chest, she stays behind closed doors.

As I listened to woman after woman share tales of self-consciousness within relationships, I thought back to something Ashley, thirty-three, had told me: "This might be strange, but I've noticed that I feel prettier when I'm single than I do when I'm in a relationship." It didn't seem strange at all to me. The point in my life when I felt the most attractive also happens to have been during an extended stint of singlehood. I was twenty-nine and had just ended an unhappy long-term relationship; the direct uptick in my happiness certainly showed up in how I carried myself and how I felt. I also started casually dating for the first time in my life, and the thrill of having multiple suitors didn't hurt how I regarded my own looks. But I knew I felt particularly attractive at that time for reasons that went beyond the simple math of having more admirers. There was something else there, and the more I heard women talk about self-consciousness in relationships, the more I began to understand it through that lens.

When I was single and just casually dating, it was easy enough to adopt the persona of a single girl about town. Not that I was acting per se or putting up a front; it was more that if I entered a fling knowing it was just that, a fling and nothing more, there was only so much of myself I needed to reveal. That persona wouldn't have served me well in a committed relationship, but it worked just fine for Friday nights out—I wasn't thinking about getting to know someone well enough to reveal my full self. But having a persona of any sort—even one as unremarkable as Woman Who Casually Dates—made me all the more aware of the gap between the idealized person I presented to dates and the warts-and-all person I really am. It was just a variation on one of my long-standing fears about beauty and dating—not that I wasn't pretty enough to attract amorous attention, but that once I'd gotten someone's attention, he'd soon see through me. I'd thought it stemmed from the collision of the two parallel story lines I'd heard surrounding beauty and attraction: "the eye of the beholder" as the optimistic narrative, with "but what men *really* prize is beauty" hovering just underneath. To some extent my apprehension of being seen through might indeed have stemmed from those clashing tales. But if self-consciousness was the pulse behind many a story about appearance and dating, it only made sense that it was the pulse behind mine as well.

" *[F]alling in love' is no more than the process of alteration of male vision— through idealization, mystification, glorification—that renders void the woman's class inferiority,"* writes Shulamith Firestone in *The Dialectic of Sex* (italics in the original). "However, the woman knows that this idealization, which she works so hard to produce, is a lie, and that *it is only a matter of time before he 'sees through her.'"* (Emphasis mine.) When Firestone linked feminine glorification with love, she was doing so with the notion that women are considered second-class citizens, so in order for a man to be able to love a woman, he must glorify her in order to reconcile his feelings with the fact of loving someone "beneath" him. Interesting as the theory is, it's not one I subscribe to. But haven't I worked for years to produce a more ideal version of myself? Being kinder and better read, sure, but also going through the daily work of plucking my brows, moisturizing my face, tinting my cheeks. And hasn't that work partly been a result of the same self-consciousness I was hearing about from so many women? Being seen through in regard to looks lies at the heart of what I've come to think of as a beauty impostor syndrome—a specialized strain of impostor syndrome, which is a chronic self-doubt that leads plenty of competent people (particularly women) to believe that they're not competent at all, but rather that they've just fooled people around them into *thinking* they're competent. The sensation I'd been feeling was a sister to that self-doubt: the fear that a partner might find me beautiful for a while—and then would suddenly see that I wasn't that attractive after all, just that I'd fooled him into *thinking* I was pretty. At its core, it was the fear of being discovered to be inauthentic.

Beauty's artifice is too complex to be written off as an exercise in inauthenticity. Still, the fact remains that when you put on cream to smooth your skin, foundation to even its tone, blush to enliven your complexion, and eyeliner to make those proverbial windows to the soul look more engaged, you're presenting an enhanced version of yourself. Which, in a certain light—specifically, the light of love, in which we hope to be embraced unconditionally for nothing other than being ourselves—can be construed as a *manipulated* version of yourself. And if there's a part of a woman that believes she's maneuvering to make herself more idealized in a lover's eyes—or, as Firestone writes, that she's played a part in the "alteration of male vision"—she may well feel that "it is only a matter of time before he 'sees through her.'"

Being seen through has a semiliteral interpretation—many women express nervousness about being seen by a partner without makeup for the first time, some to the point of wearing makeup on camping trips. But my own fear goes well beyond the apprehension of being seen without makeup. It's the fear of someone seeing through the near-unconscious ways I maneuver myself within the dating realm to be seen as an attractive woman. That includes the vigilance paid to my appearance, yes, but also to things I find myself doing that aren't intentional but that tickle me with muffled discomfort, like holding eye contact with a man I'm interested in, making sure to laugh at his jokes even if they're sort of weak, and, eventually, placing a lover's hand on my hip when we're spooning so he doesn't feel my little belly roll. It's Camille's arrangement of her body to emphasize the curve of her waist while napping with her date; it's the friendly hand touch a friend of mine has mastered that creates a physical connection between her and anyone she's interested in; it's the engineered facial expression twenty-year-old Aliza adopts to capture her features at their most flattering.

Sometimes these measures may be conscious—perhaps, at their most cunning, even a hair manipulative. But for all the overt training plenty of women have received in the art of self-presentation, the biggest form of training we've had is the kind that's unconscious and internalized. A man once told me, in the midst of a harrowing separation, that he thought I'd manipulated him by physically mirroring his actions in order to make us seem simpatico. I hadn't done so consciously, but the fact was that I *knew* mirroring was well documented as a phenomenon that happens organically when people are in sync. Had I taken this psychological tidbit and incorporated it into my feminine "act"? I wondered if something about me that I didn't even know existed had been exposed. In other words, I wondered whether he'd seen through me.

That fear of being seen through is an entirely human fear of being seen as is. It's the fear of the first time a partner sees me truly angry, not in a "she's so cute when she's mad" way or even a "hell hath no fury" way, but in a way that makes me entirely unappealing: red-faced, inarticulate, inaccessible, mean. It's the fear of being with someone long enough to unwittingly tell the same story twice (or more) and immediately shattering the illusion of being perpetually fascinating company. It's the fear that if the mystique of what it supposedly means to be a woman is dropped, enchantment would vanish as well. Hell, it's the fear of farting in the company of a lover. It's the fear that whatever work I've put into being attractive, once revealed, will look less like work and more like a trick. And once a trick is exposed, it's an invitation for judgment—or worse, dismay. A trick isn't something that was included in the original bargain.

Here's the thing about that bargain: Chances are, the person any of us has bargained with doesn't know about the deal you've made. When I talked with men about how they regarded the tricks of conventional femininity, the truth was that most of them hadn't given much thought to the matter. Neither, for that matter, had queer women—including those who professed to indulge in such tricks themselves. There's the occasional person who's going to hurl accusations of manipulation through things like mirroring or makeup, but there are plenty more who are eager not to see through but simply to *see*. "It wouldn't occur to me to think a woman had deceived me. I mean, you can't really hide what you look like," says forty-two-year-old Neal. For all the effort some women might put into getting eyeliner just so before a date, the only illusion present might not be the illusion that makeup's sleight of hand can give but the positive illusion lent by the light of attraction.

Meeting the Cool Girl

In the summer of 1985, I wrote a letter to Ann Landers, the advice columnist, for help on a pressing issue in my marriage. My husband at the time had an unfortunate habit of, as I articulated to Ms. Landers, inviting "women in skimpy bikinis" over to our home, where he would have them "parade" around in front of the two of us. His purpose in doing so, presumably, was to goad me into looking as nice as these women in skimpy bikinis; were I to transform myself into one of them, he wouldn't be forced to do such awful things. I was nine years old at the time.

I laugh this off as one of those weird kid things now; where I got the idea that this had ever happened to anyone, let alone me in my lonely, nonexistent marriage, is an utter mystery. (Certainly neither of my parents was prone to inviting "women in skimpy bikinis" to our home for any reason, much less for emotional sadomasochism.) But here's the thing: I remember sitting down to write that letter on my thick-rule three-punch notebook paper, and I remember being convinced in that moment that *this was real.* If memory serves, a miniature waterfall of tears ran down my cheeks, so pained was I at the image, so hurt was I at my husband—and so anguished was I by the knowledge that I'd never be pretty enough for him.

This is to say, of all the arenas in which appearance has shaped my life, romance has been the most fraught with anxiety. (Ann Landers would probably agree.) At some point in nearly every relationship I've had, there's come a point where I've become convinced the fellow doesn't *really* find me attractive. Reading Firestone's work helped me on this front, and I'm better able to interpret the Ann Landers episode as equal parts psychological quirk and manufactured gender expectations. Simple maturity is what's helped me most here, though. I can't say that I don't still start down the same path that led the nine-year-old me to righteously complain about her terrible husband; I do. But what I'm able to do now is understand that the certainty I feel from time to time that any minute now my beloved will peek behind the gauze of love and see someone he doesn't actually find attractive has nothing to do with him, and everything to do with me. I mean, I'd fashioned an entire *marriage* out of this set of fears. My worries as an adult not only had nothing to do with reality; they had nothing to do with any actual partnership. This wasn't about relationships; this was about me, and it was about me specifically as a woman.

When I was talking with people to gather material for this chapter, I'd entered these interviews on how appearance affects romantic relationships expecting to hear more about . . . well, romantic relationships. What I heard instead were stories about women, specifically about women's consciousness of their own looks. Even when I was talking with men and asking them about their own lives, it was the women whose experiences took center stage. When I asked thirty-four-year-old Rob whether anything about the appearance of a significant other had ever bothered him, he automatically answered from the perspective of his girlfriend: "My girlfriend has apologized for not having had time to shave her legs, and it's not something that's important to me—but *I could tell it bothered her.*" (Emphasis mine.) Matt kept apologizing to me for having a difficult time articulating his thoughts but had little trouble expressing how his girlfriend's exes had shaped *her* perspective on beauty: "She's gone out with one too many assholes, so she's sort of sensitive about how she looks." And before I even asked Neal a single question, he asked, "Are we talking about my perception of women, or my perception of women's perception of themselves?" I said I'd like to focus more on the former, and he responded that he'd be happy to—but that he'd had far more prompts to consider women's perception of themselves than he'd had to consider his own thoughts on the matter.

It makes sense that men might flounder when talking about appearances—indeed, the fact that these particular men seemed hesitant to expound on their own thoughts confirms that this is an area where women are the experts. To wit, queer women seemed to have an easier time than men talking about their own experiences as well as the experiences of women they'd dated. But even when talking with women about their same-sex romances, little was shared about the actual relationships. The reports I heard were of internal experiences: "*I* loved her body," "*I* felt like I wasn't butch enough for her." In other words, the greatest impact your appearance has on relationships is the impact it has on *you*. Whatever self-consciousness one party brings into a partnership colors the way that person behaves—which, in turn, colors the relationship itself.

As we've seen, anxiety about one's looks isn't the only way self-consciousness can color romantic relationships. But when that anxiety is there, it casts a long, dark shadow, blocking the light from the very things that have the potential to lift it, like love, satisfying sex, and intimacy. Anxiety about looks is often a smoke screen for more inarticulate longings. We all want to be loved, but getting there can be complicated, and we pepper the path with our own neuroses and worries. We take the intensely personal phenomenon of love and layer it with thoughts about beauty. In a way it can be a distancing tool—better to worry about styling your hair before a date than to worry about whether you'll be sexually compatible, whether your tempos will match, whether this is the person you'll be happy to make room for in your life. Of course, men want to be loved just as much as women, and have plenty of looks-based anxiety of their own. But traditionally men's appearance worries haven't been as supported by the culture at large, so they don't seep as easily into their psychological cracks.

When I look at the ways my own beauty fears have played out in relationships, I see a series of tiny red flags staked by a part of myself that my romantic yearnings couldn't bear to listen to. In one relationship that was doomed from its start, I expressed to him my concern that he wouldn't find me attractive *decades down the line*. With another man, one who cheated on me, I spent as much time fretting about the fact that the woman was strikingly pretty as I did about the betrayal itself. Now that these relationships are in past tense, I can see what my beauty miseries were masking: an understanding that we had the potential to make it decades down the line but would be unhappy if we did so, an unwillingness to examine the factors that drove him to stray from our commitment. By turning my focus to my looks, I was temporarily—if ineffectively—able to ignore the inevitable end of these pairings. Masochistic? Perhaps. (Let's not forget about that letter to Ann Landers, people.) But it was a buffer from reality that I needed at the time.

Today I live with a loving, loyal partner in domestic harmony, and I'd love to report that those anxieties have evaporated. They haven't. They're far fainter, but they're there. I'll still find myself rearranging my body to avoid thigh spread when we're hanging out watching television. I still feel a flicker of tension when a woman I know fits his type passes us on the street. And yes, I still occasionally muse on the day when he'll suddenly wake up and realize he's made a terrible mistake in ever having found me attractive. What's changed isn't so much the thoughts but, rather, how

I regard them. Taking cues from earlier relationships, I can see that the low, barely perceptible hum these thoughts form is, for me, a vessel for the minor, day-to-day emotional maintenance that commitment asks for. Easier to worry about thigh spread than to express my concern that we haven't had a date night in a month, or at least that seems easier some-times. I'm wired in a way that makes beauty a more manageable container for normal relationship anxieties than the bare facts themselves. I wish I weren't, but the girl who wrote to Ann Landers still lives. The difference between the me of today and the girl who wrote that letter is that I can identify those beauty woes as a mask for something else, and act—or not act—accordingly. Challenging the idea that my fears about how I look *were* actually about how I look opened up a more genuine awareness. I'm content in my relationship, and the low volume of my anxieties reflects that. Perhaps someday the hum will dwindle away forever. Until then I can simply see it for what it is: a Trojan horse for something that's harder for me to look at head-on.

Beauty, romantic relationships, and insecurity are triangulated for me in a particularly precarious fashion, and I've tried to avoid the mistake of thinking that what's true of me is true of women at large. (Presum-ably most fourth graders aren't as plagued by marital woes as I was.) At the same time, the workings of women's private lives have traditionally remained private in part because isolation prevents the kind of communi-cation that disrupts the status quo. Whenever I'm talking about insecurity in relationships with other women, inevitably the phantom of the Cool Girl shows up—the girl who doesn't give a damn about how she looks but just happens to be stunningly gorgeous anyway. None of us want to be saddling our partners with the chorus of "Do I look fat in this?"; we'd all rather be free of those worries, and free of expressing those worries. Certainly there are plenty of women who don't carry this weight with them in their intimate relationships. But their existence doesn't mean the Cool Girl exists. She doesn't, even as she continues to nudge plenty of us into a guilty silence about these fears. Until those of us who have this sort of weight on our hearts are able to understand this insecurity for what it is—a veil that prevents us from seeing the true contents of a relationship in full daylight—the best I can do is see the Cool Girl as not a bully or an ideal but a distorted model of what life might be like if we *did* stop giving a damn, or at least stopped giving as many damns about how looks play out in our couplings. Those of us who have wished to be the Cool Girl admire her not because she's pretty but because *she's having fun.* Fun isn't the only goal of a committed partnership. But if it's absent—well, then, what's the point?

5

The Prettiest Girl in the Room

Bonding, Competition, and Other Women

I f you want to find out what many people first think of when looking at how beauty plays out in relationships among women, you don't need to look much further than Disney. Cinderella's stepsisters? Oh, women are so jealous of beautiful ladies, they'll do *anything* to keep them down. Hell, if things get bad enough—like if an aging woman suddenly finds out she's no longer the fairest in the land—she might even kill her own stepdaughter, à la *Snow White*. Some might decide to take whatever they can from a pretty woman out of spite—like a hundred years of her life, which the poor beauty will be forced to spend sleeping. Not that the beautiful characters are always good. Didn't the evil sea witch in *The Little Mermaid* disguise herself as a lovely maiden to thwart our heroine Ariel?

I bring up fairy tales not because they accurately reflect women's experiences but because the morals we're supposed to take from them mirror the common conception of how beauty defines relationships among women. Jealousy, competition, rivalry, acting out, poison apples—it's a trope of reality TV and rom-coms, and the knee-jerk response of many a person whenever the topic of beauty and female friendship comes up. And as with many women's stories, the message has become unduly streamlined because of its teller. Change the storyteller, and you change the story.

When novelist Carolyn Turgeon penned a retelling of Hans Christian Andersen's "The Little Mermaid" for her 2011 book *Mermaid*, she took Andersen's neutral account of the relationship between the mermaid and the princess in the opposite direction that Disney did. In Andersen's original tale, the two rivals for the love of the prince barely meet; in Turgeon's novel, their relationship becomes pivotal for both characters. "You have these two beautiful protagonists who are competing for the love of the prince, but who are longing for what the other one represents," she says. "They're both beautiful, but they are literally different species, and I wanted to explore that complicated relationship." The pair don't exactly become friends in Turgeon's retelling, but there's a pulse of empathy between them in a way that rarely shows up in the fairy tale retellings we now refer to as Disneyfied. Challenging the assumption that looks are inherently competitive for women—or even that women are competitive about beauty not inherently but as a response to a sexist culture that overvalues them for their looks—reveals that women take the tools beauty culture has laid out for them and repurpose them as powerful tools of connection, compassion, curiosity, and understanding.

We presume female beauty fascinates men. The quieter truth is that it fascinates other women too. The tales that pit women against one another form only one part of the mosaic of how beauty plays out in friendships between women. And while jealousy and rivalry may have a hand in the enchantment of women's beauty, even those are more multifaceted than they appear. Jealousy will be little more than fleeting unless it's paired with fascination—and where there's fascination, more often than not, there's something resembling affection. What's more, as we'll see, that affection is often a sign of recognition: of other women, and of ourselves.

Beauty Contests: Looks and Competition

It's easy to assume that the poison-apple scenario of competition is the foremost lens through which women see their friendships in regard to appearance. In truth, though, not one single woman I talked with said that competition was the first thing that came to mind when asked to think of how beauty affected her relationship with other women. If a woman brought up competition right off the bat, it was either to say specifically that she *didn't* generally feel competitive about her looks or that she did when she was younger but had grown out of it. "Once I learned that someone else being pretty didn't take away anything from me, I chilled out about it," says Gina, a New Yorker in her late twenties.

Those interviewees echo my own experience. Do I compete with my friends on looks—or on anything else, for that matter? Not really. I have friends who are prettier than I am by conventional standards, but rarely do I resent their beauty or feel like I'm jockeying against them for attention. I'm in my late thirties, after all, and have better gauges of my life's successes and failures than my looks—and isn't all that the realm of twelve-year-old girls anyway? Cattiness, rivalry, put-downs subtle and straightforward—how many adults act that way?

Plenty, actually, if the studies on the matter are to be believed. Women are likelier to use indirect aggression on a beautiful woman than on a less-attractive one. (For "indirect aggression," think gossip, social exclusion, betrayals of confidence; in short, mean-girl stuff.) The inverse holds true as well, at least online. While men were likelier to accept a Facebook friend request from a stranger if the profile boasted an attractive photo, women were less likely to hit "Confirm" on a friend request from an unknown woman with a good-looking photo than they were if the profile came from a plainer one.

Will you be shocked to hear that evolutionary psychologists have an explanation for this phenomenon of women hating on pretty ladies? The idea is that in order to boost our own chances of reproductive success with a high-quality mate, we'll do whatever it takes to make ourselves seem like the best option around, an act researchers call "intrasexual competition." Putting down potential rivals theoretically makes us seem all the more attractive by comparison, so cattiness is just nature taking its course. And there are some strands of evidence supporting this line of thought: Mean-girl behavior toward particularly attractive girls doesn't start until adolescence—i.e., when girls first become fertile. Plus, ovulating women rate other women's faces as less good-looking than they do when they're not at their monthly height of reproductive fitness, and might therefore be particularly aware of competition on a primal level.

Of course, biology doesn't explain the entirety of the situation; self-esteem, which didn't exactly have the biggest role on the savannah, is a defining factor here. Women who most frequently engage in indirect aggression also compare their own looks more with other women's. And what's one of the biggest predictors of making looks-based comparisons? Satisfaction with one's *own* appearance. So women who are nasty to beautiful women might well be doing so not because of any *actual* evolutionary threat but because they simply *believe* there's a threat, so they think they need the boost that putting down a rival might bring. The story line of competition is what keeps it alive, not biological imperative. (In truth, though, conventionally beautiful women don't do anything different than plainer women to get attention, while their attractive male counterparts *do* use different strategies than homelier men.) Likewise, women who don't make such comparisons are less likely to be catty, regardless of their actual looks. Self-esteem, not evolutionary tactics, may well be the driving factor behind competition—hardly news to the women I interviewed. "Most of the time I feel pretty, so I don't feel bad about what other people have," says Gina.

This matter-of-fact assessment speaks to a recurrent theme I heard over and over when talking to women about their friendships: *No, really, I don't compete.* And in fact there's an underlying thread of noncompetition among women, even in studies that supposedly demonstrate the opposite. A 2011 study had independent reviewers estimate how much makeup female test subjects wore. The women were then asked to come back on another day and were told they would meet one of four people: an attractive man, an unattractive man, an attractive woman, or an unattractive woman. At the follow-up, reviewers estimated how much makeup the women wore to meet with the anticipated person. Women wore more makeup when anticipating a meeting with an attractive woman, while women who were supposed to meet an unattractive woman wore the same amount of makeup as they did in their initial interview. Now, one way to interpret the findings is that women use makeup to make themselves appear more attractive when meeting a "rival" in the form of a beautiful woman—that they're doing their best to compete. Indeed, that's what the researchers framed as one takeaway from the study. But what stands out to me is not that women wore more makeup when expecting to meet a particularly pretty peer, but that they wore their *usual* amount of makeup when expecting to meet a plain one. What this says is that when women walk through the world— a world we know is filled with women who are beautiful as well as those who aren't—we *don't* expect to compete with other women; we *don't* feel the need for some special reinforcement above and beyond whatever our personal norm might be. Indeed, women adjusted their levels of makeup in both directions for men—they wore more makeup when meeting an attractive man, less when expecting to meet an unattractive one. Being primed to meet a pedestrian, everyday, run-of-the-mill woman led participants to do what they already do most of the time. Even if we might see particularly beautiful women as competition, we don't see *women on the whole* as competition.

So women don't compete on looks as much as we're reputed to . . . but that doesn't change our reputation itself one bit. "I might be different from other women you're interviewing—I don't see beauty as a competition," says one woman. Another, who lived in a commune-style intentional community, told me the same thing, explaining that her cooperative living situation precluded the competition "other women" might feel. Competition is still presumed to be an overriding factor in beauty and female friendship. We just assume that it's something *other women* do, even if our own experience doesn't match up. As a result, the idea that women want to tear one another to pieces continues to thrive. This free-floating, unproven "truth" undermines solidarity using a woman made of straw—one who regards other women first and foremost as rivals. After all, if we believe other women think of appearance as a competition even if we ourselves don't see it that way, we're still letting the threat of a beauty contest cast a shadow over our friendships.

In fact, we may prefer to think of beauty and friendship as a host for cattiness because it's ultimately more comfortable than looking at the ways women actually *do* compete. Whatever beauty rivalries we actually experience are often a funnel for other sorts of competition—competitions that "good girls" aren't supposed to have. It's surprising in some ways that women don't spar more over their appearance, given the paradox of female rivalry: It's not ladylike to compete, but when we *are* culturally permitted to do so, it's about looks. (And not just in subtle ways either—call them pageants if you will, but we still hold literal beauty contests.) This little loophole means that we often channel other sorts of competition into the well of appearance. As the ev-psych crowd has maintained, beauty as a route to attracting partners—particularly male partners—is the competition women are usually quickest to identify. "It was hard being best friends with Sherry in college," says Candace, a thirtysomething sales director. "Being around someone as pretty as she was didn't matter when it was just us, but whenever we'd go out, it was like I was invisible. Guys would line up to talk to her, and *then* they'd talk to me." Today, Sherry acknowledges that she was "a bit of a catch" back then—but insists that Candace was equally popular with men. This mismatched perception is hardly unusual. A study of pairs of female friends found that women who judged themselves as less attractive than their friend reported higher levels of romantic rivalry than women who rated themselves as being at least as attractive as their pal. (For comparison: Differences in self-rated intelligence had no effect.)

But jockeying for male attention isn't the only thing we displace onto beauty. Ashley, a thirty-three-year-old digital consultant, tells me about how she felt when a stunning girl joined the theater department when she was in high school. "It was like, what is this girl doing in my freak zone when she could be prom queen?" Ashley says. Having grown up as an outcast, she was particularly protective of her "freak zone": "I felt excluded from the mainstream sort of stuff because I didn't look the part, and I wasn't really interested anyway, but to have someone from that world try to be a part of this niche I'd carved out for myself just felt unfair." When the girl started literally winning competitions by landing plum roles in school plays, Ashley was hesitant to attribute it to talent; she and her friends gossiped about how the other girl must have been giving sexual favors to the drama teacher. "That was the first time I bonded with other girls over making fun of someone," she says. "You'd think that having been made fun of my whole life, I'd be more sensitive, but having someone turn to me to make fun of someone else instead of being the butt of the joke—I mean, it felt kind of good."

As an adult she still feels regret about her mistreatment of the girl—but though she wishes this weren't the case, some of the underlying assumptions of her high school years refuse to budge. "I still make the mistake sometimes of assuming that beautiful women get things because of their beauty, not because of who they are or what they can do," says Ashley. Known in her field as a gifted strategist, she's been rewarded for her creative professional savvy, which she's worked hard to establish. It makes sense she might cast some side-eye at people who seem to have gotten ahead for other reasons—regardless of the fact that, as her various career-related television appearances reveal, she herself is vibrantly attractive. "It's hard to let go of these mental equations: *Okay, she's really pretty, but I'm successful or smart or funny.* We're sort of set up to think that there has to be this trade-off, and it can work out okay until someone who's really pretty *and* successful comes along, and then it's like whatever threat was there is doubled."

When I think of times I've felt competitive about my looks—or rather, when I *thought* I felt competitive about my looks—I picture myself suddenly small, sniffing around for bits of consolation. As with Ashley, those consolations have often taken the form of reminding myself of other gifts I'm lucky to have, as though some cosmic judge is doling out qualities that all even out in the end. We might be doing this because we believe it will soothe us. What it *actually* does is turn those other gifts—success, intelligence, charisma, talent—into bronze medals that fall forever short of the gold of beauty, instead of being features in and of themselves. Think of the clichés about inner beauty you've heard or read throughout your life. How often are reminders of inner beauty's merits meant as a healing balm for not feeling so great about the way you look?

Even as we might regard our inner qualities as a trade-off for beauty, it's often those other gifts that we're truly after. Beauty is a route to them, not strictly a reward in and of itself. One of my role models as a teenager was an exceedingly talented and well-liked acquaintance from another school who, like Ashley's nemesis, nabbed all the leads in her school plays. The difference was, she didn't fit the template of "the pretty girl." She wasn't extraordinarily beautiful, just extraordinarily gifted. Recognizing that she had earned recognition simply through skill made me want to throw up my hands in resignation. My nice-enough looks didn't even out my middling talent. She had what I really wanted—talent, recognition—so you'd think I'd have felt competitive with her, right? Instead, being faced with her lack of conventional beauty put a halt to any jockeying for first place I might have felt with her otherwise. I knew there was nothing I could do to re-create her innate talent; I didn't have the "it" factor, and I never would. But beauty, in my mind, was a way of generating a facsimile of that it factor. And while I knew there was only so much I could do to change how I looked, at least there was a template of sorts: Lose a little weight, smooth out your hair, clear up your skin, get to know your makeup kit. So my girlish competitive instincts stayed focused on girls who were more in the same boat as me—talented *enough*, pretty *enough*, but unremarkable in both ways—and I continued my daily beauty routine while failing to develop any formal practice that would have actually added to my actor's arsenal. Scurrying about for the crumbs of beauty felt somehow easier, somehow more acceptable, than fighting for the cake itself.

"What Does She Have That I Don't?": Envy and Similarity

When I was talking with women about how beauty plays into their friendships with other women, I wasn't surprised that certain themes popped up repeatedly. Nor was I surprised when many women minimized whatever envy they might feel about other women's appearance. After all, "she's just jealous" is one of the quickest ways to dismiss conflict among women. What did surprise me was how many women used the *exact same phrase* in describing those bouts of envy: "What does she have that I don't?"

Envy is commonly understood as the longing to possess something that belongs to someone else. So logically, you'd think we'd be likelier to envy people who are *different* from ourselves, right? Short people should envy the tall while the tall envy the petite; blue-eyed blondes should envy sultry brunettes while the latter's eyes turn green over their fair sisters. But a closer look at envy reveals the opposite: We envy not those who are different from us but those who are *similar* to us. Similar, but better, or at least "better" by our own definition of it, or "better" in one particular aspect. The refrain of "What does she have that I don't?" implies that both parties share many qualities, but that the speaker is unable to finger the precise characteristic that the other woman has that gives her an advantage. Were it not for this elusive appeal, both parties would be on equal footing. Few of us would wonder "What does she have that I don't?" about, say, Hillary Clinton or Tina Fey or Beyoncé; it's clear that each of those women has world-class leadership skills, wit, or talent. We *know* what she has that we don't. But I've wondered it about a friend whose similarities to me make our friendship possible—and whose indefinable charm leaves all who meet her utterly dazzled, while I stand to the side wishing I had a sliver of her charisma. Each time I heard a woman ask, "What does she have that I don't?" she was referring to a woman with whom she otherwise felt a kinship.

Though many close friends report that their differences make for a relationship Velcro that allows them to stick together, long-term friendships are often marked by the similarities between people. Indeed, the more satisfied we are with a friend, the more we see similarities between her and ourselves, and similarities are one of the most reliable ways to predict a friendship's strength. Beauty is no exception: Pairs of female friends are rated by neutral parties as being more equal on an attractiveness scale than women who are randomly paired together. Actually, it's something I keep in mind when I start to feel down about my looks—*Hey, my friends are a damned good-looking bunch, ergo . . . !* But just as easily, intuitive knowledge of this phenomenon can breed a painful self-consciousness, as with Ashley. "I've always been friends with women I felt were sort of 'in my league,' so to speak," she says. "I never really had friends who were conventionally pretty." Changing schools upwards of forty times before graduating high school, she had to learn shortcuts to making friends if she wanted to have any sort of social circle for the few months she'd be at any given school. "When the teacher would introduce me in front of the classroom on my first day at whatever new school I was going to, I'd survey the room to see if I was the fattest person there, and I'd be so excited if there was someone who was fatter than I was. And I was huge! I'd gravitate toward the least conventionally pretty girls, and toward fat girls, thinking they'd be less likely to reject me. My mom used to say 'Birds of a feather flock together,' meaning that if I only hung out with fat girls I'd never lose weight. But I felt threatened by anyone else."

Purposefully choosing conventionally unattractive friends protected Ashley from envy as a teen, but as an adult who had stopped "looking around the room like a heat-seeking missile, trying to find other people who weren't super attractive," the natural similarities between her and her friends generated resentment. "I have this friend who rocks the [burlesque entrepreneur] Dita Von Teese look—insanely thick lashes, bright lipstick, super formfitting dresses that show off these huge boobs and hips. If she walks into a bar, everyone turns and looks at her, because she looks like she stepped out of the movies," she says. With her porcelain skin, cherry-red lips, architectural cheekbones, and 1920s-movie-star bob, Ashley herself has created a look that isn't far from that—which is exactly what gets to her. "It's a lot of effort to do that all the time, a lot of maintenance, and I'm just not willing to do that. And because that look gets you a lot of attention, you have to have a certain level of confidence to pull it off. Confidence sort of comes and goes for me, but she seems to harness the look into this almost otherworldly character who's loud and brassy and smart and funny and extroverted and all of these things that roll up to make her super charismatic." The Old Hollywood look is Ashley's boyfriend's "type," making her hyperaware of other women who successfully cultivate that aesthetic. "I fit it more or less, but still, if we go to a restaurant and I see a woman who has that look, the hair on the back of my neck goes up. It's come up before with women I've worked with, and it's like, 'We can be work friends, but we're not going to be social friends because if I'm honest about it I just don't want you near my boyfriend.'" The idea is that if only Ashley felt she could channel the "it" of the It Girl look, she'd more closely resemble the women she envies. Absent the "if only" factor, she feels she's *almost* there, but not quite—a tension greater than that of observing someone whose physical gifts are entirely different from her own.

Our similarities allow us to view a friend as a mirror, and those same similarities highlight the gaps between us. Exquisitely sensitive to the role appearance plays in our lives, some women experience those gaps as envy of another woman's looks. And the more demographically similar a woman is to her female friends, the higher the likelihood that she feels beauty-based resentment. The inverse holds true as well: Women whose friends were more dissimilar in areas like ethnicity, religion, age, and sexual orientation report less envy of their friends' looks.

Yet you don't have to scratch too far beneath the surface of envy to see a more resonant truth: When we find ourselves coveting someone else's looks, chances are it's not actually her looks we're after. In fact, many women I asked about the green-eyed monster first mentioned not a gorgeous pal but a friend who *wasn't* conventionally beautiful. For instance, I asked thirty-five-year-old Farah whether she'd ever envied friends specifically for their beauty. Her answer: "My friend Jess is the sexiest woman I know. But to be honest, you probably wouldn't look twice at her if you just saw a photograph of her—she's no prettier than the next girl. But if you're in a room with her you can't take your eyes off her. Guys fall all over themselves around her. She just has this confidence that makes her so appealing to watch."

Catch what happened here? Even when asked directly about beauty, Farah's answer *wasn't about beauty at all*. Sex appeal, confidence, magnetism—*that's* what Farah covets, not Jess's appearance. But really, what else are our brains supposed to do when we as a culture mentally yoke all sorts of positive qualities to beauty? We assume good-looking people are happier, richer, more successful, *better*. We even coined the term *beautiful people* to mean exactly that. The thing is, for all the talk about how much better off beautiful people are, the actual statistics aren't overwhelming. Particularly good-looking people have indeed been found to be roughly 10 percent happier than people ranked as being in the bottom tenth percentile of the population. But most people aren't at the tip-top or the very bottom of the appearance scale—most of us reside in the middle, where our looks have a smaller impact on happiness. And for women, beauty's effect on workplace success amounts to a double bind. While being attractive does appear to increase income, good-looking men benefit from this more than good-looking women. Depending on the job, particularly attractive women may even be penalized for their looks.

Even when we're able to stop displacing envy of other assets like confidence, wealth, and even luck onto looks, our envy may still be associated with appearance. "I've never felt threatened by a picture in a magazine, but I feel threatened by real people, especially if they have some sort of physical obstacle they've managed to overcome," says Ashley. "The friend I'm most jealous of is two times my size, but she just *works* it. I know that by societal standards my body is considered 'better,' but I don't have her confidence. I see her walk into a room like she owns it, and her weight becomes a part of that, like it's just nobody's business but her own. It's amazing—if looking the way you're supposed to as a woman gets you all this attention, how can she be twice my size but so much prettier?" And then: "What does she have that I don't?"

When I first noticed the pattern of women (myself included) masking life envy as beauty envy, a wave of sadness hit me: So now that women are encouraged to be hungry for successes beyond our looks, we still harness one to the other? Fantastic. But if we catch ourselves indulging in that form of false envy, it can illuminate those deeper yearnings. When I found myself feeling envious of the luminous looks of a friend I'd known for years, it was only when I remembered that we'd been friends for more than a decade without me having a whiff of jealousy that I had to look deeper. I'd always appreciated her lustrous hair, toned figure, and French-girl style—but it was only in the past year that I'd gone from seeing those as a part of her to seeing them as a reflection of something I lacked. I started to feel downright unimportant in her presence, even as her attitude toward me hadn't changed, and at first I attributed it to her seemingly effortless success in weathering the physical changes our mid-thirties had brought both of us. My skin felt dull, my hair lifeless, my face somehow just not *right*, whereas she looked as vibrant as she had at age twenty-three. I actually went out and purchased a face cream she recommended with the hopes it would lend me a bit of her light. It was only once I articulated it that way to myself—*I want a bit of her light*—that I saw *that* was what I really wanted, not just the smooth skin. She'd spent years nurturing a close circle of local friends;

two of my best friends had just moved across the country. She'd recently been promoted at work and gotten serious praise from her mentor; as a freelancer, I had a daily support system that was loose at best. Community and mutual support—things that give us an inimitable inner light—were thriving in her life at a time when my own reserves were dwindling. That network was what I *sensed* about her, but what I *saw* was blinding beauty. I was reacting to my paucity of things she had in abundance, but what I acted on was appearance.

The neat resolution here would be that I traded in my face cream for actively building a support network, right? And yes, once I identified the real source of my envy, I was better able to focus on the root problem. But I kept the face cream. It became a talisman, a small symbol of the ways we cultivate successes. It became a conductor for the current of desire. As Virginia Postrel puts it in her 2013 book *The Power of Glamour*, the things we suffuse with glamour give "otherwise inchoate longings an object of focus." I regarded the face cream as a badge of beauty, not of glamour per se, but in this instance the two are conflated. By imbuing a tiny jar of lotion with the power to transform me, I was articulating my longing to change. And instead of being the chimera that hope in a jar so often is, the cream became the kick-starter to real change.

I'm hardly unique in attaching that sort of symbolism to the physical markers of beauty and style—many an ad campaign hinges on consumers making exactly that association. Where this becomes a potential source of power is when we recognize ourselves making that connection. "I have a friend who always looks amazing," says thirtysomething Mara. "For a long time I told myself, 'Well, you're good at a lot of things, but looking stylish isn't one of them.' But I found myself thinking of these sort of symbols of hers—lipstick, bangle bracelets, these drapey sort of outfits—and I was like, 'You know, I can have those things too. I can choose to prioritize those things in my life if I want.'" Neither Mara nor I dismissed the role beauty played in our pangs of envy. Instead, we listened to its message. "It led me to chase things that light me up," she says. "Envy can be the best teacher we have."

Girl Talk: Beauty Bonding

In the midst of one of those breakups where you think you'll never feel okay again, I got my first pedicure. I'd taken to spending as many nights as possible outside the emptiness of my own apartment, and this night's destination was the couch of a friend who lived in the depths of Brooklyn. I didn't need to talk about the breakup any more than I already had; I craved distraction and a way to pass long stretches of time, not counsel. We'd watched two *Lord of the Rings* movies plus the "making of" featurettes, gathered supplies for and then baked scrumptious chocolate chip cookies, curated a photo album of our college years, and played endless rounds of "Who'd you rather?" We were batting around a skein of yarn with her cat when the idea occurred to her: "Let's go get pedicures." I'd never had one before and didn't really see the point—it was December and nobody would be seeing my feet except me, and I wasn't particularly bothered by the state of my naked toenails, but it was a way to pass an hour or so without despair.

The nail salon was less posh than I'd envisioned. It was one of those clean, cheaply constructed, vaguely clinical salons that dot the city; the workers were bustling around in white coats to make themselves look authoritative, and surgery-style face masks to protect themselves from the fumes of their handiwork. My friend, her roommate, and I hopped into three adjacent pedicure chairs and paged through glossy magazines, sometimes talking, sometimes not, while the workers sometimes chatted with one another in Korean, and sometimes stayed silent. The easy, casual rhythm of everyone's conversation echoed something I'd commented on earlier, when we were lying on the living room floor playing with their cat. I'd noticed that though my friend and her roommate held a comfortable warmth between them, they didn't actually talk all that much, especially as compared with the nervous chatter of someone—me—who'd been living alone for a while and wasn't used to sharing space with people except in explicitly social situations. "So when you have roommates, you don't necessarily talk all the time?" The pair exchanged glances. "We don't need to," my friend said. "We know where we're at." She left it at that.

Their laconic way had rattled me ever so slightly at their apartment, but in the salon I understood: We were having a shared experience that would offer one brick of the foundation of friendship I was eager to build. Just as I couldn't have cared less about Frodo's plight when we'd watched *Lord of the Rings*, it wasn't that any of us wanted a pedicure so much as it was that it would provide a conduit for the relaxed connection of ostensibly doing one activity (getting our nails done) while truly doing another (strengthening our friendship). My friend's goal in suggesting we get pedicures wasn't making our feet look nice. It was that we'd pass the time, together, and in a way that might provide a moment of tranquil relief from the stresses of my breakup.

It worked. To this day, when I recall the quiet kindness of that friend who took in a refugee of heartbreak, the first image that comes to mind is that nail salon. By spending a little bit of money, I could have someone tend to hidden, neglected parts of myself that I'd never bothered to care for before. And as it was, it wasn't me who spent that money—my friend insisted on paying for my pedicure, at a point in both of our careers where every dollar was carefully meted out. I accepted the gift as graciously as I could, for I knew what she was saying with it was not *Let me treat you* but *Let me care for you. Let me give you solace.*

But today when I examine that small act of nurturing through beauty, I'm forced to work around the uncomfortable truth that beauty bonding depends on a certain kind of assumption of what it means to be a woman. At its best, beauty culture creates a sort of secret land for women: women gossiping with their hairstylists while getting their color touched up; friends wandering through Sephora on a quest for the perfect long-lasting red matte lipstick; aunts taking nieces for their first manicure; strangers on the subway sharing hairstyling tips after an artfully placed compliment. (Some hair salons have extended this "secret land for women" to activism. Hundreds of salons nationwide participate in Cut It Out, a program that trains salon professionals—i.e., people who work in female-dominated spaces—to recognize warning signs of domestic abuse among clients and colleagues.) But at its worst, it's a translation of fundamental inequalities between the sexes—women, and not men, can be brought together by their concern for their looks.

First, the good news: Several women I talked with spoke of beauty as a way they were able to connect with other women and develop friendships, and not always deliberately. "It's not like we go get pedicures together," says Gina. "It's more like it's something I'm able to learn from them over time." She'd long noticed that a friend of hers seemed to have a limitless wardrobe. Gina commented on this to her friend, who then offered to come to her apartment and go through Gina's clothes with her to assemble a mix-and-match wardrobe from her existing items that would allow for more outfits with no spending required. "It made me appreciate her and her skills—I mean, it took an entire afternoon, and she's a busy person," Gina says. "Trusting her with this let me know that I was right to trust her in other areas of my life that are ultimately more important. And it made me appreciate her and her skills in a way I didn't really know about before." In fact, Gina encouraged her friend to try her hand at professional styling—a career path her friend is now embarking on. The connection went both ways. Gina got a bevy of new looks, and her friend came away with the whisper of a professional calling.

Gina's experience may have been more explicit than most beauty bonds, but it's far from unusual. In her study of friendship, *Connecting: The Enduring Power of Female Friendship*, author Sandy Sheehy found that physical appearance was one of the most frequently mentioned qualities that attracted one friend to another, trailing only behind sense of humor and shared interests. Sometimes it's a quiet intrigue that leads us to want to know more about the woman in general. "Mariana is always so playful with her makeup—it's like she's got a hundred people inside her, and a different one will come out every day," says Jessica, a Philadelphia-based yoga teacher. "I saw all these different facets of her through how she presented herself and it made me think she was pretty multifaceted as a person. And she is, but I wouldn't necessarily have made the effort to find that out if she hadn't shown it through her playfulness first." Sometimes physical appearance forms an overt connection in a budding friendship, as with thirty-one-year-old Nancy, who complimented a total stranger at a party on her hair and eventually befriended the woman. Sometimes it's an admiration that simply warms the space between two strangers. I once complimented a woman on the subway on her lipstick shade, and she took a receipt out of her wallet and scribbled the name of the lipstick on the back of it. If the way we choose to style ourselves is on some level self-expression, the chatter around beauty is an articulation of that expression. Jessica's friend Mariana and Nancy's now-friend with the fantastic hair were revealing some part of themselves—something that might have been difficult to demonstrate verbally, or that would have taken more time spent together to show itself—and were duly rewarded for doing so. Beauty made for a shortcut to friendship.

"There's something safe about makeup and hair stuff as opposed to fashion," says Ashley. "Makeup never makes you feel fat. There's less of that idea of competition; it's more about sharing. I don't comment very often on how strangers look, but when I do compliment their hair or makeup or whatever, you want them to give away their secret—and a lot of times they do." The accoutrements of beauty support a subtle leveling of the playing field among women—with skill and effort most of us can approximate some semblance of prettiness—creating a safer place than the realm of fashion, which necessitates talk of bodies, generally a touchier area. It's also more affordable than fashion across economic classes. While it's possible to blow hundreds of dollars in an hour at Sephora, it's equally possible to assemble a makeup kit for under twenty dollars at the drugstore.

Intimate knowledge of the skill and effort behind self-enhancement can also make beauty work itself a form of silent communication. "Grooming yourself can be a way of saying, 'Oh, I know I'm not pretty enough without this,'" says multidisciplinary artist Lisa Ferber. "I go through phases of not wearing makeup and I had someone say to me, 'I noticed you don't wear makeup, how come?' I remember feeling like, *Should I wear makeup just to show that I don't think I'm okay without it?* There's this idea that you need to show that you're making the effort, that you know it's not okay to just show up." The belief that women are, or should be, unhappy with their appearance is so imprinted on us that when a woman appears to be just fine with how she looks, it can provoke questions. It's not the most empowering notion, but sticking to the rules of subtle self-deprecation can help a woman be seen as someone who plays by the rules of womanhood. In this way, actively highlighting her own beauty work communicates the idea that a woman places herself on the same level as the makeup-wearing majority. Ferber recalls complimenting the aesthetic of a woman who was costarring in a play with Ferber's then-boyfriend. "I said she was really pretty and she said, 'It's amazing what a good lipstick and a great dress can do.' It made me like her more because I felt like she was saying, 'I know I'm in a show with your boyfriend, but I am not a threat to you.'"

If playing by the rules helps a woman stay in harmony with other women, breaking those rules can bring punishment. A 2011 study brought in female test subjects two at a time and had them wait in a common room before entering the area where the experiment was supposedly taking place. What the women didn't know was that the waiting room was the actual research space. An undercover researcher dressed in either provocative clothing (short skirt, high boots, low-cut top) or conservative clothing (slacks and a button-down shirt) sat with the women, posing as another test subject. The two actual test subjects were observed to see how often they "checked in" with one another by exchanging looks or words about the third woman (the undercover researcher). Sure enough, subjects were far likelier to issue glances or comments to one another when the third woman was all sexed up, noting how her "boobs were about to pop out" or that she was dressed to have sex with one of the researchers. What's more, this held true regardless of whether the two women were friends or randomly paired strangers. (As Ashley put it about how she and her friends bonded over gossiping about another girl in high school, scrutinizing women *with* other women—well, it's hardly noble, but it can feel "kind of good.") The study also had observers record the facial expressions of the study participants. Women were perceived as being "happy" in the company of the plainly dressed peer, "angry" in the company of the *Pretty Woman* look-alike. The solidarity women might feel over appearance can come at the expense of another woman, but that doesn't change the fact that the women in the study *did* reach out to one another in reaction to appearance. Women still bonded over beauty; they just did so in a segregated manner. The tribal mind-set of ladies versus whores allows sisterhood, but only to some. To others it offers exclusion—an exclusion that can happen without the excluders uttering a single word to one another.

Still, even when women pit themselves against other women, they ultimately do so *because they are both women*. I hate to stereotype, but based on anecdotal research (i.e., bar nights), I imagine that if men were used as test subjects in that experiment, they'd be likelier to try to exchange looks with the provocatively dressed woman instead of with one another. When women who play by the rules of appropriate appearance ally themselves against those who appear not to, their agreeableness to the status quo becomes the tighter bond—but it's a bond that would not exist if there weren't a strict code about what ladies should and shouldn't do. Womanhood is the ultimate connection here. "[W]omen are bound together by a kind of immanent complicity. And what they look for first of all among themselves is the affirmation of the universe they have in common," writes Simone de Beauvoir in *The Second Sex*. Because women have a somewhat different set of cultural rules than men do, she continues, women enlist other women "to help define a set of 'local rules,' so to speak, a moral code specifically for the female sex. It is not merely through malevolence that women comment on and criticize the behavior of their friends interminably; in order to pass judgment on others and to regulate their own conduct, women need much more moral ingenuity than do men."

And here we have the larger problem of beauty as bonding: It assumes that the shared condition of womanhood *by necessity* includes attention to makeup, hair, clothing, and the like. As we've seen, this provides a much-needed alliance for women who stick to the guidelines of conventional femininity, and de Beauvoir would agree:

> With other women, a woman is behind the scenes; she is polishing her equipment, but not in battle; she is getting her costume together, preparing her makeup, laying out her tactics; she is lingering in dressing-gown and slippers in the wings before making her entrance on the stage; she likes this warm, easy, relaxed atmosphere. . . . In such circumstances women help one another, discuss their social problems, each creating for the others a kind of protecting nest; and what they do and say is genuine.

We as humans care about our appearance, so to a degree beauty talk is indeed universal. That's what makes it a mainstay of small talk. But when we assume that an active interest in beauty is universal among womankind, a good number of women may feel alienated, and not only women who shun makeup and conventional hairstyling. After all, women who actively reject mainstream standards may find a level of beauty bonding within their own communities. One self-identified butch woman I talked with says she doesn't remember the last time someone tried to engage her in diet talk—but she'll sometimes go with other butch women to a barbershop to make the experience less intimidating. But even those who participate in this form of "girl talk" often have mixed feelings about doing so. "I catch myself using compliments and makeup talk or whatever as a way to get to know other women, and I'm like, why can't I say something else?" says Gina. "It's such a cliché subject, women talking about looks, and I feel stupid when I do that. Like, I'm such a 'woman.'"

The "womanness" of beauty talk is both what makes it effective as a bonding mechanism and what makes it troublesome. A number of women I talked with about the ways they used beauty as a method of bonding with other women took pains to say that though they did it, they found it silly. A woman who described herself as a "makeup junkie" e-mailed me after our interview to emphasize that she and her friends didn't focus on their appearance when they were together. "That's the province of *Real Housewives*–type women," she wrote. Disowning the possibility of beauty bonding's importance seemed essential to many women, even those who could readily articulate the ways such chatter had provided inroads to friendships and professional connections. (Shunning the importance of beauty talk may actually be self-protective; there may be a negative correlation between how much a woman talks with her friends about appearance and her body satisfaction—the more beauty talk, the unhappier she might be with her body.)

Some women might dismiss beauty chatter because of its feminine essence. It's easy to dismiss "girl stuff" as trifling, so distancing oneself from it may well help a woman be taken more seriously. But in statements like Gina's—"Why can't I say something else?"—the wish to fast-forward to the meatier substance of friendships rides alongside a hesitancy to do exactly that. What *would* happen if we skipped this form of small talk more often? What sorts of conversations might we find ourselves having at the start of bridal showers, bachelorette parties, birthday dinners? How might our assumptions about the shared condition of womanhood change, and how might that shift our relationships with other women? For that matter, how might it shift our relationships with men, if the small talk we shared with them were to more closely resemble the small talk we share with women?

There's a sort of catch-22 going on here. Those of us who use beauty talk as a proxy for deeper forms of communication with other women might want to stop doing so—but one of the quickest routes to getting to those more thoughtful exchanges is to engage in the lingua franca of girl talk. Rejecting the clichés of womanhood means rejecting its conventions, but friendships are usually formed conventionally—you start with small talk and, if there appears to be mutual interest, hopscotch from small talk to medium talk to big talk over the course of time. Offering a form of particularly feminine currency to another woman displays a wish to find common ground. In truth, makeup or hair may be no more of a shared interest between them than, say, music, literature, or corgi breeding. Yet absent a context, you don't usually start a conversation with a potential friend by jumping into suddenly asking about her favorite bands. Plenty of women do, of course, and even those who do use girl talk as a way of reaching out have other conversational skills; creative chatting is hardly a skill limited to men or to women who make a point of avoiding beauty chatter. But especially in the adult years, it can be hard enough to make new friends without robbing oneself of an easy conversational "in" whose prompt is literally right in front of you. The way we look gives us an ever-present context.

As much as I use and even champion beauty talk as an entrée to connecting with other women, it's hard to ignore that conversational nods to beauty ultimately reinforce the beauty standard. Even conversations that, on the surface, tear down the beauty imperative are still a capitulation to the power it has to regulate women's lives. But, of course, we can't dismantle the beauty standard without taking a thorough inventory of the ways it's shaped us—which necessitates conversation. There's another catch-22 about women, beauty talk, and connection, which is that the conversations that take place among women are the only way the beauty standard can change, but part of the standard's hold is in those very conversations.

I saw this paradox most clearly in a framework removed from beauty. At a family reunion, I noticed that even though the men of the family are a helpful bunch, when it came time to clear the dinner plates, it was only the women who rose. I noted this aloud to my mother—a longtime feminist—and she laughed, saying to my aunts and grandmother, "Should we tell her the secret? This is when women *really* get to talk." It reframed "women's work" not as drudgery but as opportunity for connection. Because I knew my mother's politics, I saw it as subversive, not a kowtowing to the patriarchy. But our hands were the ones getting smeared with half-eaten potato salad nonetheless.

The Adolescent Within: Vulnerability and Friendship

You may have noticed something in reading the friendship anecdotes throughout this chapter: Many of them relate tales of *girlhood*, not womanhood. A variation of "When I was younger, but not anymore" was the most common response to inquiries into the nastier side of beauty—competition, jealousy, exclusion, and the like. Such behavior is called mean-*girl* stuff for a reason. Just as many of us indulge in some catty behavior as tweens and teens, most of us grow out of it, usually as young adults. The extraordinary self-consciousness of adolescence dwindles, leaving us with merely ordinary self-consciousness—and a heightened awareness of how such behavior does a disservice to all women. As forty-two-year-old Kerry stated when I asked how she transitioned from the intense competition she felt in high school into her relatively unfettered existence of today, "I grew out of it, that's all." Even if we find ourselves lapsing into competitiveness or jealousy surrounding looks, we're likelier to spot it early and nip it in the bud or dismiss our own emotions as silly. An acquaintance in her sixties put it this way when we were casually talking about feeling jealous of beautiful women: "I still get that way, but I can't be bothered to dwell on it anymore," she said, fluttering her hand as if shooing the thought away. "Who has the time?"

Yet maturity and its lack thereof aren't usually accounted for in the glut of studies about women, beauty, and competition. Solid as the research I've cited in this chapter may be, we're still seeing a participant pool of mostly college students. So when it comes to examining women's triangulated relationship with appearance and friendship, these studies reflect not a sample of the general adult female population but the attitudes of educated women ages eighteen to twenty-three who are taking their first tentative steps into the waters of adulthood. Were these studies conducted at the average workplace or, say, senior centers, the results might well be different. (Or maybe not, as I found when I visited my grandparents at their retirement community. A woman in her eighties told me over dinner that my grandmother has exquisite taste—"not like *some* of the women around here," she added in a whisper, looking to me for a chuckle.)

Still, it would be a mistake for adult women to dismiss the intensity surrounding female friendship in the teen years as strictly a thing of the past. The last time I moved apartments, I asked a friend for advice on paring down the enormous box of mementos I've been collecting for thirtysomething years. His advice: "Go through the box, item by item, and get rid of anything that doesn't make you feel something." I did this successfully, whittling down the collection of playbills and concert tickets to the size of a shoe box—until I hit the notes. I'd kept nearly every single note written to me by friends from sixth grade onward, and though my intention had been to keep just a handful of the particularly of-the-era ones (like the one where my friend had cut and pasted *Teen Beat* photos of New Kids on the Block), were I to have followed my friend's guidelines, I'd have kept every last one. Unfolding each note and seeing the looped handwriting of 1989 unfurled a small blossom inside me, until I was sitting on the hardwood floor, face coated with bittersweet tears, surrounded by piles of notes telling of crushes, mean math teachers, and babysitting woes; drawings of dolphins; and MASH results. There was the eighty-two-page note given to me by my best friend after our school's winter break (I'd written her a measly sixty-three pages). There was the note scribbled on a Gitano ad because "it made me think of you"; the note consisting of nothing but the name of my locker partner's crush written over and over again; the note in which a friend ran around the fact of her father's physical abuse of her. When I think of the friends I had between ages eleven and seventeen, the word that comes to mind to categorize our mutual devotion is *fierce*.

I haven't written a note to a friend for years, just the odd postcard. But when you're so fervent about a relationship, so intensely attached, so instinctually present—well, that sticks with you. "Are we always going to be our twelve-year-old selves?" proposed a friend during a late-night, wine-fueled discussion about how we make new friends as adults. No, of course we're not just overgrown versions of ourselves from several years back. But that girl who chronicled sixty-three pages of winter-break minutiae to her best friend in 1990? She still exists. She thrives on receiving a witty text from a new friend, and she recoils when an old friend quietly ignores a suggestion of a Skype date. She lives.

"Much has been written recently about the 'child within'—the still-whole, clear-sighted, outspoken innocence within us," write Terri Apter and Ruthellen Josselson in *Best Friends: The Pleasures and Perils of Girls' and Women's Friendships*. "Adolescence, by contrast, is regarded as a painful, awkward phase that we pass through and leave behind. . . . But the adolescent within us is also alive and well—the insecure, confused self, recurrently pinned on the horns of relational dilemmas." The exquisite sensitivity of our preteen years can continue in adult friendships. We may no longer pass notes or stay up all night chatting on the phone, but the lessons we learn about female friendship at that age create a scaffolding we tenuously scale for the rest of our lives. It's not so much that we replicate connections we had at that age or forever play the same social roles. It's more that the role looks play in many youthful friendships—an intense mixture of competition, pride, envy, and insecurity—echoes the larger cultural narrative of how adult women are assumed to feel about their appearance. The idea that women don't like how we look reverberates through our culture, and one of the larger prices women pay for stepping outside of that legend is the knowledge that we've broken the unspoken "girl code" that we wrote long ago. The price itself has shifted, though. Instead of exclusion and other forms of indirect aggression, we pay with our own silent worries.

Relationships of all sorts are marked by power, and in a world where a woman's perceived power is so frequently linked to her beauty, our looks can distort a friendship's dynamic. And as painful as it can be to envy a friend, it can be just as uncomfortable to accidentally provoke jealousy in other women. Doing anything that resembles such a provocation violates the code so many of us imprinted on ourselves long ago—jealousy is the realm of those bitchy, hopelessly insecure women, not *us*—just as admitting feelings of envy or competition might make us feel like we're in a cheap reality show instead of our own lives. To be sure, there's an obvious upside to the expectation that we'll go to great lengths to avoid conjuring negative emotions in other women (female solidarity, yo!). But there is a downside: It leads women to monitor themselves. It echoes another form of self-monitoring, that of the beauty imperative itself. Women's self-surveillance is the most insidious fallout of the beauty imperative. We usually think of that surveillance as manifesting itself physically: putting on makeup, sucking in the belly, mastering the perfect selfie smile. But in our relationships with other women, the surveillance is seen in what is said, or what is withheld, in women's conversations—the very conversations that have the potential to free us from self-monitoring.

One way most of us have monitored ourselves at some point is negating a compliment from another woman. As we saw earlier, women's most frequent response to a compliment from other women was to use it as an entryway to further conversation—but the second most popular response was to negate the compliment. Think of the things you may have murmured upon hearing a compliment from a friend: "Oh, come on, I look exhausted," "Yeah, but you should have seen how long it took me to get my hair to look this way," "Shut up, *you* look fantastic." Comic Amy Schumer brilliantly satirized the phenomenon with a sketch in which woman after woman responds to compliments with lines like "Are you *drunk*?" When one woman dares to respond to a compliment with a simple "thank you," the other women immediately kill themselves out of sheer shock. Like the saying goes, it's funny because it's true. When I asked women how they felt upon hearing compliments from friends, they reported feeling pleased, sure—and "weird," "uncomfortable," or "awkward." Compliments can temporarily tilt the delicate power balance between two friends, uneasily shifting the vibe. Negating a compliment is a woman's way of moving the fulcrum of power back to center. It's a way of saying, "We're on equal footing here"—something that felt crucial to establish during our teen years, and that can feel crucial to recall in adulthood. Add to that fragile scale the assumed narrative of how women feel about their looks—that is, that we don't really like our appearance all that much—and the ways women can maintain power balances in friendships becomes winnowed down further and further, until we're left with "Shut up, I look awful." As long as it's more permissible for a woman to neg herself than it is to show how she's all that, beauty talk will uncomfortably teeter on the edge of harm, ready to topple over anytime. We've built a story line around women and beauty that allows women far more space to talk about ways they don't like their looks than to talk about the ways they do. In the confines of that drama, we must strive toward beauty while never being able to comfortably, openly claim it as our own. The more we reinforce that theme, the more we obscure our relationship with our looks. And the more we do that, the more we complicate relationships with other women—who, after all, are largely under the same cultural forces, making them powerful potential allies in dismantling the beauty narrative.

It's one thing to refuse a compliment in an effort to keep the balance of power equal, but it indicates a larger phenomenon of womanhood: Looking *too* good, shining *too* brightly, gathering *too* much attention is dangerous. The assumed marriage of insecurity and beauty creates an expectation that we stick to a particular story line—we can admit we look good only if we've already paid our dues of *not* liking how we look. The irony here is that privately, plenty of women believe they *do* shine more brightly than their dearest friends. Pairs of female friends, when independently questioned, generally agree on which one is considered more attractive. But in cases where friends disagree, it was more often the case that each woman found *herself* to be the more attractive of the two. This despite the fact that when asked to rate themselves and their friend compared with other women their age, women generally scored their friends *higher* than they rated themselves! So we find our friends beautiful, generally speaking—but when it comes to looking at beauty within a friendship, we're more likely to see ourselves as having a leg up.

Seems mighty contradictory, eh? It is—and those contradictions are part of beauty's shape-shifting power. Most of us fluidly cast ourselves as both "the pretty one" and "the ugly one" in different friendships, even if we don't utter those exact words to ourselves. And we may deploy various tactics in an effort to maintain our friendships. I remember making a point of being particularly welcoming to a stunning former model who had been introduced to one of my social circles. I'd sensed by the way she down-played her looks that her sensational appearance might have caused her some discomfort in the past, so I did the little things you do when you're trying to be warm: ask follow-up questions without putting the new girl on the spot, take care not to casually interrupt, and, in this case, specifically *not* engage in beauty talk. My efforts were rewarded and we did indeed become friends, but it was only years later that I stopped to think about how in my effort to show a new friend—and myself—how little her beauty mattered, I'd actually altered my behavior to do so, proving that her looks *did* matter. Still, my hunch was at least partly accurate, as I learned when she told me that in junior high she'd threatened to stop hanging out with one particular friend unless the girl stopped telling her how pretty she was. Research backs up the ways we subtly adjust our behavior to match how we think others might see us. For example, though the cinematic trope of the fat, funny friend of the slim heroine may be rooted in fat stigma and stereotypes, research does show that many obese women report compensating for their size by being more likable and socially skilled.

Yet despite our intimate knowledge of the quiet role appearance can play in our friendships, we insist it doesn't matter. "I love my friends for who they are, not what they look like," said one twenty-nine-year-old—just a moment after stating, "My friends are beautiful inside and out, and that's why I love them." This in an interview specifically about how physical beauty affects her friendships! Other women shared similar sentiments: "I don't think about it all that much," said one woman at the beginning of a seventy-minute conversation about appearance and friendships. "I might be different from other women you're talking to—appearance doesn't really matter to me," said another, who then went on to discuss the physical self-consciousness she feels around certain friends. I point out these contradictions not to catch anyone in a game of "gotcha" but to reinforce the idea that contradictions, not linear attitudes, are what form the backbone of women's relationship to beauty. It's an effect that's only magnified when applied to female friendship, which in and of itself often manages to be strong yet vulnerable to nicks and dents that last.

We need to confront the popular narrative of women, appearance, and jealousy, of course. But in doing so we also need to acknowledge that beauty isn't simply a playground of manicures and carefree bonding. Challenging assumptions about beauty means looking at the uncomfortable grains of truth in those assumptions. In this case, that means acknowledging that envy can jockey alongside admiration, and that the tenderness of female friendship can easily loop in the dark side of beauty—the hesitancy to openly claim beauty as our own, the need to constantly calibrate power through tactical handling of compliments and complaints.

For all the ways appearance can serve as a conduit for conversation, it's not as though we are immune from seeing other women's beauty in a more primal, visceral way: as something to behold. Yet even when we look at another woman with the sort of detachment one might label "the male gaze," we see something beyond a beautiful or plain face, a lovely or ungainly frame. We see how she has chosen to navigate the juxtapositions of beauty that so many women face head-on every day: how to emphasize one's gifts without seeming vain; where to aim on the comfort-versus-style spectrum; whether to perform the daily work of beauty without revealing the amount of effort it took or to revel in an overt display of artifice. We may even see how she handles questions of beauty and other women—how does she balance her desirability with the urge to avoid provoking envy? Her use of girl talk with a wish to be taken seriously? In other words, we see a wealth of answers to questions some of us ask ourselves every day.

6

Who's Afraid of the Big Bad Media?

Skinny Models, Idealized Images, and Why Maybe It's Not Such a Big Deal

In the midst of one of my ever-rotating teenage schemes to Lose Weight and Become Prettier, I followed a classic piece of advice: Find a photo of someone you'd like to look like and hang it in a prominent place, preferably the refrigerator, to remind you exactly why you're denying yourself peanut butter. Today we might call it "thinspo" or "thinspiration" but this was the nineties and we hadn't invented Tumblr yet. I just called it what it was supposed to be: inspiration.

The photo I chose was from *Self* magazine and featured a long-legged brunette with an impeccable tan. She appeared to be leaping out of the ocean, mermaid-style, in a sleek black one-piece with cutouts nipping in at the waist. Her shoulder-length hair was wet but adorably styled, and her teeth were gleaming; the picture, on the whole, was one of a woman brimming with surfer-girl health and well-being. I ripped the page out of *Self*, folded it into vertical thirds so the text was hidden and all I could see was the model, and Scotch-taped it to the left of my bathroom mirror.

The idea here should be obvious: I was supposed to look at this aspirational image every day, multiple times a day, and this would push me that much harder to stick to the weight-loss plan I'd half-assedly concocted for myself. (The "plan" consisted of a breakfast of Diet Coke and doing jumping jacks in my bedroom, door closed.) The more I'd see this model, the more I'd note the differences between the current me and the current her, the more I'd want to look like her, and the more I'd stick to the hard work of diet and exercise. Maybe the motivation would be positive, as in, "Wow, if I work hard enough I'll look like her"—or maybe it would be negative, as in, "Aw, man, she looks great and I look awful by comparison, so I'd better get myself in shape." Either way, it was motivation, right?

It didn't work, either in the sense of its effect on the desired outcome—I stuck to the "plan" as much as I had before, i.e., haphazardly—or in that looking at the image didn't make me want to look like her at all. Sure, in the abstract sense I wanted to have that healthy, energetic look and the lean body that went along with it. But when I looked at the picture, I didn't feel inspired or encouraged—or *dis*couraged, for that matter. I just felt blank. The gap between me and that model felt insurmountable, and it was. She looked *nothing* like me. I too was white, brunette, and in possession of two X chromosomes, but our resemblance stopped there. Where she was California tan, I was Pacific Northwest pasty; where she was long-legged, I was just short-waisted; where she was teeming with health, I was exhausted and anemic. The differences between us meant that I knew no matter how hard I exercised, no matter how much food I denied myself, no matter how much I lay out on our deck slathered with baby oil, I was never, *ever* going to look like her. I might look better, conventionally speaking—my thighs might lose a bit of their fleshiness, and my moon face might come to more closely resemble her angular one. But my legs would never be that long, my hips would never be that narrow, my teeth would never be that straight and white, and the odds of me frolicking about on a sandy beach were approximately zero. My instinct was to identify with the model somehow, but the baseline differences between us meant that I couldn't. I may as well have put up a picture of a cartoon character for inspiration. Indeed, later that year I decided I wanted a prom dress that would make me look like Jessica Rabbit. That served as greater fantasy inspiration than the *Self* photo that lived on my wall for months, until I finally admitted it was useless and took it down.

A few years later, when I thought about that aborted mission to look like a *Self* model, I coded the experience as vague proof of my resilience. It wasn't that my self-esteem was buoyant; it was that I thought I might have some sort of Teflon coating that repelled the media dog pile of unrealistic beauty standards. Sure, I desperately wanted to look like people in the images with which I was bombarded every day—clear skin, lithe body, shiny hair—but rather than wanting to look like someone else, I wanted to look like the best version of myself. I still understood that the media was harmful to women—I'd learned this in my women's studies and communication theory classes, and plenty of discussions with friends had confirmed it—but I thought I'd stumbled into a personal wormhole that allowed me not to be deeply affected by idealized images.

I carried this belief through much of my tenure working at women's and teen magazines. My feminist friends would occasionally question various aspects of a career in the glossies: Did I feel conflict over framing women's lives as one big self-improvement project? (Sometimes.) What about all the "how to please a man in bed" nonsense? (Outdated critique; magazines are generally more focused on the reader's pleasure now.) And then all the various permutations of "But what about the pictures?" Did I witness extreme retouching? (Yes.) Did I ever speak up about glamorized images of painfully thin women? (Occasionally.) And did it ever bother me? Did being surrounded by images of professional beauties eight hours a day ever *get* to me? I never had to ask them to clarify the question; the assumption that idealized images harm the women viewing them was taken as fact, to the point that I began to feel downright rebellious that my standard answer was anything other than a resounding *Yes, it's awful.* In fact, my answer was usually that I didn't like it on a political level but that I hadn't noticed any change in how I felt about my looks since I'd joined the industry. It was the truth.

Fast-forward a few years: I'd been working in women's and teen magazines for nearly a decade when the magazine I was working for folded during the 2008 financial collapse. I promptly found work freelancing at—ironically enough—a finance magazine. Interest rates, municipal bonds, and equity funds now filled my days instead of lipstick tutorials and "quick de-stressing tips." Just as I'd done with the ladymag advice I'd been reading for years, I applied some of the wisdom from my new gig to my own life. I transferred my short-term savings to an account with a higher interest rate; I double-checked my bank fees. And I kept an eye on my savings account. No, I kept a *microscope* on my savings account. I went from looking at my balance every month or so, just to make sure things were as they should be, to checking it daily. Sometimes multiple times a day. Not because I was going to do anything to the account, but because I just wanted to make sure that what I *thought* was there was *actually* there. It wasn't a conscious decision. It was just that midway through an article on long-term savings, I'd have an irrepressible urge to peer at my own numbers to make sure nothing had changed in the past eighteen hours.

It's probably taken you far less time than it took me to figure out what was going on. My change of habit was directly correlated to what I was reading all day. Immersing myself in personal finance materials for eight hours a day for only a few weeks had *done* something to me. It had removed my basic trust in my own abilities to manage my finances and replaced it with a fruitless vigilance. Was it harmful? No, not really. But was it helpful? Absolutely not.

Once I realized where this sudden compulsion came from, I was able to ease up a bit; I went back to checking my balances as needed, with no ill effects. It was a blip on my personal radar, nothing more—until I placed it in the context of my whole career, so much of it spent working in women's magazines. *Maybe what I'd spent the past ten years reading had done something to me too.*

As with any person in any career, working in women's magazines has shaped me—and as with any psychological matter, it's near impossible for the person experiencing it to know how fully she's being shaped by her surroundings. But my stint in finance journalism showed me in stark terms that just because the images I'd been immersed in for years—including that photo I'd tacked to my wall so long ago—failed to inspire any direct action or direct self-loathing, that didn't mean I wasn't affected by what I spent hours reading each day. It had long since become impossible for me to use the bathroom without checking my reflection in the mirror.

Was that the ladymag equivalent of looking at my bank balance? Would I be looking at my reflection dozens of times a day if I'd built a career at, say, *Popular Mechanics*? I'd read enough about eating disorders to ascribe my own bouts of disordered eating to stress and brain chemistry, but now I had to question that. Would the various weight-loss plans I'd tried in adulthood—now protein shakes for breakfast instead of Diet Coke—have been curbed had I opted to work at a news magazine? For that matter, what if I'd not been a member of the media at all but had just been an observer? I used to slip a stick of concealer into my bra on nights out because I was so afraid of going four hours without a touch-up over my acne—would that ever have occurred to me if I'd lived in a world that wasn't plastered with pictures of gorgeous women? I'd grown up with a mother who took care to point out what she called the "trick photography" of women's images in advertising, and I'd gone on to minor in women's studies at college, spending a good deal of time reading about the harm these images did. I'd believed that knowledge had been what gave me that apocryphal Teflon coating. What if it hadn't done any good at all? Worse yet, what if I'd been bracing myself against potential harm from women's magazines at the expense of developing a more critical attitude toward things that *were* actually harming me?

When I look at these two incidents now—the cold-fish thinspo, and the sudden financial self-consciousness—I see them not as polarized to each other but as a reflection of the importance we heap onto media in the first place. The financial compulsions made me see that I was certainly influenced by the materials surrounding me, but in what ways? How much does living in a media-saturated world shape the way women feel about the way we look? Can the billboards and glossy ads we've collectively grumbled about ever be *good* for us? Do we keep buying women's magazines because they make us feel bad, or because they make us feel good, or both? And if we *are* harmed by the tsunami of images out there, is there any way we can protect ourselves from their influence? In short: What's the true relationship between women and images of women?

Everyone Knows Media Images Hurt Women . . . Right?

You'll hardly be shocked to learn that there's plenty of evidence suggesting that idealized images of women—specifically, conventionally attractive, slender women—can be harmful to the actual women who view them. That knowledge doesn't make the facts themselves any less shocking, though. Here's just a sampling: Looking at pictures of models in a women's magazine for just three minutes can decrease women's body satisfaction. The gap between a woman's self-image and the typical beauty standard can predict how concerned she is with her weight—problematic, given that the average fashion model wears a size 0 or 2, while the average American woman wears closer to a size 12. Women who internalize the thin imperative have more body-focused anxiety after looking at pictures of slim models as opposed to pictures of plus-size ones. Exposure to ads featuring thin women can increase symptoms of depression. And while the causes of eating disorders are complex and can't be pinned to any one source, the fact remains that bulimic women report feeling higher levels of pressure from the media to be thin than non-bulimic women.

You've probably heard much of this data before, or at least heard its message, painted in broad strokes. But a more inclusive look at the research on media, women, and self-esteem reveals another dimension. For example, in one study, dieters—women who are sensitive enough to the thin ideal to restrict their food intake—who had looked at pictures of slender women rated the ideal body size as smaller than those who had looked at control photographs or photographs of heavier women. No surprise there, right? Yet they also judged *their own* bodies as being slimmer than other women did. That is, after looking at pictures of thin women, dieters didn't just *want* to be thinner, they actually *believed themselves to be thinner*. In fact, they increased their evaluations of their own overall appearance after looking at photos of slender women. In another study that stands in sharp contrast to the more heavily quoted research, women viewing idealized images experienced a mild euphoria and reported *lower* levels of depression, an effect echoed by participants in yet another study whose self-esteem rose after looking at pictures of moderately thin models.

A note: I generally make a point of not conflating thinness with overall beauty, or body image with appearance self-esteem. I do this not only out of an effort not to reinforce unrealistic body standards but out of an understanding that though we do tend to see slender bodies as being a part of an attractive package, we also delineate body size from beauty. To wit, the cliché *such a pretty face* is often used to describe attractive, overweight women. However, the number of studies that have explored the role of media standards in thinness and body image far outweighs the number of studies that have done the same with overall appearance. So in looking at the scholarship surrounding the connection between imagery and appearance, I've frequently used body image as a stand-in for how a person feels, overall, about her looks. Also, it's important to note that self-esteem—one's overall regard for one's worth as a person—is a different quality from body image, which is more about how a person pictures herself, or himself, when visualizing one's form.

Of course, self-esteem and body image are easily enmeshed with each other. In fact, self-esteem has been shown to moderate the effects of comparing oneself with images, *regardless of the woman's internalization of body ideals*. And women with intact body image are similarly resilient—again, including those who had internalized the thin ideal. In other words, even if a woman believes she should be thin, if her self-esteem and bodily appreciation are solid, she's less likely to have a negative response to pictures of slim models. So despite talk of the damage that beauties on billboards can do, it's not that images *globally* hurt women, but rather that women with shaky self-esteem are susceptible to their potential damage. Problematic? Yes, of course. Cause to paint an entire sex as vulnerable to the media? I'm not so sure. But the assumption that media hurts women's self-image is so entrenched that to suggest otherwise is tantamount to treason to advancing women's issues.

It seems that rather than setting an expectation of harm for all women, we might be better off specifically addressing the concerns of women with low self-esteem and poor body image—but the route there is complicated, and counterintuitive at times. For example, a Canadian study found that while women who were highly invested in their appearance suffered more from idealized pictures than women who were less invested, their reasons for caring about their bodies mattered too. You'd think that women who consider their bodies to be more than just a way to look good would be less vulnerable to media images, right? But women who see their bodies as a way to define themselves may actually feel worse after seeing pictures of thin women than those who see their bodies as vehicles for "appearance management," which is scholar-speak for "looking good." So a *less* holistic, *more* shallow, *more* looks-oriented approach to our bodies might serve us better than earnest attempts to transform our bodies into forms of self-expression. Sort of puts *Extreme Makeover* in a different light.

As for the link between media imagery and women's food intake—including eating disorders—the effect is there, but it's as contradictory as the rest of the data. Remember that study about how dieters felt slimmer after looking at pictures of thin models? It had another component: measuring how media images affect women's food intake. The same dieters who said they felt thinner after seeing pictures of slender women proceeded to eat more cookies than dieters who looked at pictures of heavier women. There's a kind of logic there—if you're dieting and suddenly believe yourself to be thinner, your motivation might well evaporate, so bring on the cookies. But it initially seems to contradict one of the maxims of media criticism: that unrealistic images of women spur disordered eating, particularly the sort associated with restriction or purging. In truth, bulimic women showed equal levels of self-esteem—albeit somewhat depressed self-esteem—as non-bulimic women after looking at images of slender models, and another study showed that while women who *already* had eating disorders overestimated their body size after looking at pictures of thin women, women who didn't have an eating disorder were unaffected. The perception problems triggered by the photographs came after a disordered mind-set was already entrenched. It's a symptom, not a cause.

So the media hurts women (and helps them), particularly weight-conscious women (except sometimes), and may (or may not) play a key role in increased body dissatisfaction (or satisfaction), body depreciation (or appreciation), and eating disorders (perhaps). What gives?

Same!: Women, Images, and Similarity

Let's look at two different ways someone might view a photograph of a conventionally beautiful woman. Woman A and Woman B look at a magazine cover featuring the starlet of the moment, professionally styled and expertly retouched to remove any trace of so-called flaws. Woman A scans her own appearance—pretty face and nice eyes but crooked teeth, skirt not fitting quite right, skin more particleboard than porcelain—compares herself with the woman on the magazine cover, and walks away feeling worse about herself, as it's clear she'll never be able to match the model's impeccable beauty. Woman B—who doesn't look all that different from Woman A—looks at the cover and thinks, *Hey, my hair is roughly her color, and I bet I could style it that way myself if I had a little tutoring. Hell, I'd probably look pretty fantastic too if Annie Leibovitz photographed me!* She aligns herself with the image and walks away feeling better about herself. Taking in an idealized image makes her feel more ideal.

Woman A is engaging in social *comparison;* Woman B in social *identification.* The idea is that if most media images of women are idealized and therefore "upward" on a scale of conventional beauty, some women will compare themselves with these images and feel they fall forever short—while others see the same images and identify with them, thus elevating themselves upward. Does one of these mind-sets sound healthier than the other? It should. In one study, women who scored higher on self-esteem measures had an "identification" response while looking at photos of attractive women, reporting higher bodily satisfaction than they did after seeing pictures of conventionally unattractive women. But those with low self-esteem had the exact opposite response: They felt *worse* after looking at pictures of beautiful women, and *better* after looking at images of unattractive ones. So each of these responses—identification and comparison—works both upward and downward. Show a woman who identifies with images a picture of a not terrifically attractive lady, and she'll feel not terrifically attractive herself. Show the same photograph to a woman who compares herself with images, and she might start to feel not so beastly.

These competing responses explain part of the disparity in the results of various researchers. Working with a sample of women who lean toward comparison or who have low self-esteem will yield far different results than a sample of high-self-esteem women who identify with images. One study designed specifically to test this factor found that simply inducing a mind-set of identification in heavier women prompted those women to temporarily feel more positive about their appearance after viewing slender models, regardless of their personal tendencies toward comparison versus identification. It stands to reason, then, that inducing a temporary mind-set of comparison could nudge women to feel worse about themselves than usual.

Here's where this gets tricky when it comes to researching body image: The easiest and most popular way to measure personality traits and self-assessment is on a numbered point scale (like, "On a scale of one to five, how satisfied are you with your body?"). It's unambiguous, which is usually a good thing in a clinical setting. But asking people to measure themselves in such a quantifiable way is a form of comparison—meaning that all these studies meant to examine women's response to idealized imagery may *incite* negative feelings instead of merely *record* them. A 2006 study measuring women's response to images found that when women reported on their self-esteem using a point scale, their assessments were quite different than when they answered similar questions phrased as free-response queries (like filling in the blank: "My body is _____"). This difference is exacerbated when a woman is primed with images of idealized beauty; that is, if you've just looked at a picture of a woman who is so attractive that she makes a living off her looks, your point of reference temporarily shifts. Even if you usually identify with images, when you're asked to rate your appearance on a scale of one to five and you've just seen a picture that's a five by conventional standards, the explicit invitation to compare yourself induces the comparison mind-set, potentially leading you to rate yourself as less good-looking than you independently believe you are. In this light, even a well-designed study that relies on a point system for gauging women's state of mind becomes flawed. The end result? Data consistently reflects media's negative effect on women, even if it's the data-gathering method, not the visuals themselves, that provokes it. This data then gets heavily reported by media outlets that seek to improve women's lives—as well it should. But in that reporting, we lose the nuances of how we arrived at these dismal statistics. It's a stronger message to say that advertising images hurt women than it is to examine and report the subtler truths about the ways women absorb those images. What we lose along with those subtleties is the fact that a response of suffering is *not* necessarily the baseline of all women. And in trying to raise awareness about the ways idealized imagery can potentially harm us, we wind up not only criticizing an unhealthy relationship with the media but normalizing it too.

If identifying with images brings well-being and comparing oneself with images brings harm, the logical action from an activist standpoint might be to get as many women as possible to identify with images. But there's a roadblock in changing women: The tendency toward social comparison may be determined by fixed personality factors, like neuroticism, so a woman who leans toward social comparison can't just decide to start identifying with images for the long haul. So can the images themselves be changed to induce identification? That is, if more media outlets featured photos that mirror a broader swath of the population—heavier women, shorter women, more women of color, women with wrinkles or uneven teeth or motor disabilities or just a weird *thing* on her nose—would more women start identifying with images and reap the associated benefit in self-esteem?

Certainly some members of the media have tried. In fact, identification is a part of the ersatz science that dictates which photographs are selected for magazine covers. The first time I sat in on a cover meeting—the roundtable collaboration where magazine editors decide what words and images go on the cover—I asked my manager what exactly made a good cover. Her answer wasn't about which image was the most breathtaking, but rather which one had the greatest emotional effect on the reader: "We're looking for the picture that will make a girl think, *I want her to be my best friend.*" (A best friend who happens to be taller, slimmer, and glossier-haired than most, of course.) Some outlets have gone further than simply picking sympathetic-looking models. In 2009, *Glamour* magazine ran a small, otherwise unremarkable photo of a plus-size model with her fleshy belly exposed. Readers wrote in by the dozens lauding the magazine for size diversity, prompting the editors to declare "[a]n ongoing celebration of the so-called imperfections, from nose bumps to gap teeth smiles, that make us all unique" and "[a] promise to give the best plus models not just work, but the same *great* work straight-size models get . . ." *Brigitte*, a German women's magazine, did away with professional models altogether the same year, opting instead to draw models from their reader pool. It was exactly what so many readers and critics of women's magazines had been urging the industry to do for years—combat the supposed epidemic of low appearance esteem by incorporating a broader size range of models, thus demonstrating that you needn't be whippet thin to be stylish and attractive. Show readers more bodies that look like their own, and you'll allow them to more easily project their lives onto the glossy page. Logically, this would not only accomplish a semi-political goal, but it would also increase sales—a happy consumer is a good consumer, right?

Fast-forward to four years later: *Glamour* continues to use plenty of models who are better racial and ethnic reflections of the American population, but the size diversity initiative appears to have taken a backseat. *Brigitte* quietly reversed its no-models policy in 2012. It wasn't that editors had backed down from their principles; it was that readers, quite literally, weren't buying it. *Glamour's* newsstand sales fell nearly 7 percent in the first half of 2010, precisely the time when the initiative should have been bringing in new readers. This drop wasn't unusual at the time among similar publications in a troubled industry, but it was hardly the boon the editors had hoped for. *Brigitte* fared worse, with subscriptions dropping 22 percent after the announcement was made. In the year following the reversal, *Brigitte's* overall circulation increased 10 percent. Even magazines without a formal "real bodies" campaign incorporated more diverse figures into their pages, in hopes of being progressive on this front. They too demonstrate the sales ineffectiveness of the strategy: *Elle's* best-selling cover model of 2012 was a heavily shellacked Katy Perry; its worst-selling issue featured a very pregnant, very nude Jessica Simpson, a celebrity known for championing "real bodies." (Her editorially lauded makeup-free cover for *Marie Claire* in 2010 was another sales dud.) Zooey Deschanel led *Marie Claire* to its second-best sales of 2012 (cover line: "Zooey Deschanel on . . . losing

30 lbs"); its second-worst-selling issue boasted Christina Aguilera, whose ample curves were making headlines at the time (cover line: "'I love my body'"). And the number of people who purchased on newsstands the American *Vogue* issue with Lena Dunham gracing the cover was dwarfed by the number of people who clicked on *Jezebel's* now-infamous post revealing the retouching done on the photos. Robust bodies, it turns out, do not necessarily make for robust sales, regardless of how many letters the editors may get from readers lauding the cause.

Diversity doesn't fare much better when applied to race—but it does get more complicated. People of color have been historically underrepresented in mainstream media. Around 30 percent of Americans are nonwhite, but only around 20 percent of magazine covers feature a person of color. The industry logic on this has usually avoided complicated questions of race in America and instead has stuck to the bottom line: Black cover models don't sell well, editors quietly say to one another. Whether or not this was ever true, today's data is mixed. Beyoncé graced the cover of *Vogue's* top-selling 2013 issue, while Rihanna's November 2012 cover sold 32 percent fewer copies than average on newsstands. With a topic as complex as race in America, pinning low sales on the self-perceived similarity of black and Latina women to cover models would be shortsighted at best. Yet there are few areas as clear-cut in regard to readers' similarity or dissimilarity to models as race—and the lack of direct numbers correlating cover models of color with higher sales doesn't exactly support a case for readers wanting to consume images of their own likeness. In some cases this may well be out of a sense of protectiveness. Black women are far likelier to experience body dissatisfaction when looking at an image of an idealized black woman as opposed to a similar image of a white woman. Couple media underrepresentation of black women with statistics suggesting that black women on the whole tend to have better body image than white women, and it seems as though along with factors like a strong matriarchal tradition and an acceptance of larger body sizes, the relative paucity of black women in the public eye might have inadvertently contributed to this resilience. Certainly this doesn't mean that excluding women of color from mainstream media is a *good* thing in any way, body image or otherwise. After all, black women are hardly exempt from body image issues and other appearance concerns, and Latina women have also been underrepresented, yet their body image is roughly on par with white women's. The lesson here isn't that a lack of media representation is any sort of advantage to women of color, but rather that upping the number of relatable media images won't necessarily result in increased appearance satisfaction, or increased sales, among potential readers.

There's no one direct line of logic that explains which images women are willing to shell out for. The idea that women buy glossy magazines because they make them feel *bad* flies in the face of every sales maxim out there, but how else to explain women's hesitancy to purchase magazines featuring women they could more easily identify with? Logically speaking, aspirational yet relatable images should be the key to high sales. Yet it seems that the best consumer is not the one with eminent confidence in the appeal of her own image, nor the one who slavishly surrounds herself with pictures of idealized beauty that reinforce her own lack thereof. Rather, the best consumer is one who resides in the liminal space between identification and comparison. The consumer who has a defined goal that she doesn't quite know how to achieve—in this case, looking as beautiful as possible—is susceptible to the glamour of role models as well as the sting of inadequacy. The consumer who sees too much of herself in images meant to be aspirational has little more to aspire to; the consumer who believes aspiration is too far out of her reach to even shoot for swipes her credit card in other directions. Indeed, the ideal consumer of the products whose advertisers fund these images— specifically the beauty and fashion industries—is a consumer who sees herself as a *project*. And projects are worth doing only if you think the goal is achievable ... but you just haven't gotten there yet. When a reader of magazines (viewer of images, gazer of websites) experiences identi- fication and comparison *at the same time*, the tension between the two poles creates a gap that the funders of these images—advertisers—are ready and raring to fill.

Killing Us Softly: The Legacy of Media Literacy

When Jean Kilbourne released her first documentary, *Killing Us Softly*, in 1979, it was the only recognized effort linking mass-media images of women to the desire to be thin. That one documentary mushroomed into three additional *Killing Us Softly* films, securing Kilbourne a place in the pantheon of feminists who have changed the way our culture views women. She continues to be one of the most popular campus speakers in the nation (indeed, she's spoken at half of all American universities), and she's served as an adviser to two US surgeons general.

Kilbourne's work was at the forefront of media literacy education surrounding body image. The idea is straightforward: Educate women about the ways idealized imagery may psychologically harm them, and women will be better fortified against absorbing that harm. Kilbourne was specifically targeting high school and college students, but the success of her work expanded the scope of her ideas. Today, in addition to dozens, perhaps hundreds, of university courses on media literacy and body image, there are organizations and branches of larger women's organizations devoted to giving women critical skills for deconstructing media images. About-Face breaks down popular ads and how they depict women. The website for the National Organization for Women features offensive ad images and tells users where to complain about them. The National Eating Disorders Association has an online tool kit containing "Tips for Becoming a Critical Viewer of the Media"; Adios, Barbie critiques everything from makeup campaigns to yoga mat ads to *The Simpsons*.

Media literacy has become so mainstream that the media itself wants in on the action. Numerous women's magazines have run features about image retouching, showing print-worthy photos before and after their photo editors have worked their magic, Sharpie slashes alerting the reader as to where a model's flesh is to be manipulated. Women's websites show videos of their own retouchers overhauling images. Even stock photo services have entire stores of images of retouching in process. Teen media in particular has taken up the charge, in part because of the specific vulnerability of their readers and in part because the readers themselves have spoken up. More than eighty-six thousand people signed a petition started by a fourteen-year-old to demand that *Seventeen* cease retouching its images. Editors responded by releasing a version of the "Body Peace Treaty" that they'd previously drafted for readers to make with themselves, this time writ large—and writ vague—for the magazine itself: "We vow to . . . Never change girls' body or face shapes. (Never have, never will.)"

But perhaps the most widespread media literacy campaign has come from neither nonprofits nor the media but from a more unlikely source: a company firmly entrenched in the actual beauty industry. When Unilever released the first arm of Dove's Real Beauty campaign in 2004, it was downright shocking—ads featuring "real" women, complete with cellulite and short torsos and rolls of flesh previously unseen on billboards, suddenly sprang up everywhere from L.A. freeways to downtown Chicago. Yet the most successful branch of the Dove campaign wasn't strictly an ad but a seventy-five-second video called *Evolution* that shows the process of how ad images are consciously created and manipulated. A pretty but ordinary-looking woman sits down in a photo studio, and in fast-forward we see a remarkable transformation. Hairstylists, makeup artists, lighting directors, the photographer, and photo retouchers coax a billboard-worthy vision from what would otherwise be a rather pedestrian image. "No wonder our perception of beauty is distorted," reads a placard at the end of the video. *Evolution* got more than 12 million views in its first year, and Unilever reported that Dove's overall sales following the video's release rose nearly 6 percent.

Where Dove's media literacy campaign might be measured in dollars, other efforts are measured via more clinical means. Long-term intervention measures, like education and support sessions, have been found to have a significant effect on women's awareness of the beauty ideal, and short-term and long-term interventions alike have been found to decrease women's internalization of that ideal. A study of sixth-grade girls in Canada showed that a year after taking part in a six-session media literacy program, participants had significant increases in body image satisfaction. Similarly, 79 percent of Australian eighth graders who went through a media literacy program had reduced their concerns about their weight, even months after the program's end. The media literacy program developed by sisters Lindsay and Lexie Kite of Beauty Redefined has been proven to help increase participants' self-image, with the number of women reporting negative feelings about their bodies dropping from 50 percent to 12 percent after the multipronged program. And when a group of college women were surveyed about their responses to idealized images, researchers found that most of them were versed in counterarguments surrounding those images.

In a way, though, that's exactly the problem. Women *know* virtually every image we see has been retouched; women *know* that the models gracing billboards and magazine covers have an entire army of beauty workers around them to make them look the way they do. The trouble with media images isn't that women don't have their defenses ready. The trouble is that, certain success stories aside, those defenses aren't very effective. Multiple studies have shown that there's little to no connection between knowing an image is unrealistic and feeling more satisfied with one's own appearance after evaluating it. Teenagers who used critical processing techniques in one study had *less* body satisfaction than their peers, and a meta-analysis of studies on the relationship between media intake and body dissatisfaction found only a small-to-moderate correlation between the two. In a number of studies that point to a degree of success of media literacy programs, critical analysis helped women cut down the extent to which they absorbed the thin ideal—but they remained as dissatisfied with their bodies as they had before. And remember that group of Canadian sixth graders? The participants who'd learned about media literacy felt better about their bodies compared with how they'd felt at the beginning of the study. But girls in the control group who *didn't* go through the media literacy program showed similar improvement in body image as those who did. Maturity, not the program, may have been the key factor in boosting the girls' body image. And a replication study found that participants of the literacy program fared worse: Their self-esteem was actually slightly *lower* at a twelve-month follow-up than it had been prior to intervention.

Media awareness carries an inherent irony. Women who are the most well versed in it may actually be less satisfied with their bodies than their less-aware counterparts, perhaps because that very dissatisfaction can lead to a desire to understand and dismantle beauty standards. And the women who appear to need media literacy the most—women with low self-esteem—are already using some of its techniques, even if they don't know that's what they're doing. In one study, after looking at images of thin models, women with low self-esteem rated personality characteristics as more important to a person's worth than they had before seeing the pictures. Meanwhile, women with higher self-esteem didn't change their opinion. You could see this as evidence that media literacy programs simply don't work—or you could see it as evidence of something that's ultimately more problematic: Women who believe the media is harmful will *behave* as though the media is harmful in order to stay consistent with their beliefs. Absent this belief, they might not organically feel any different after viewing idealized images. But once you're steeped in messages about how damaging those images are, you just might believe you *should* feel differently. In one study, dieters reported feeling significantly more depressed after looking at photos of slender bodies when it was directly implied that there was a connection between images and mood. But when such implications were minimized, so were the reports of emotional darkness. In this light, the more far-reaching that media literacy programs become, the more work they have to do. And the more media literacy decrying images' effects on body esteem is incorporated into our day-to-day lives, sometimes appearing alongside the very same images that purportedly cause the damage, the more we entrench the idea that our response to media images should be one of injury.

There's a related way that media literacy programs may inadvertently perpetuate the negative cycle they hope to sever, which is that the very act of critiquing images means spending more time absorbing them. "Critically viewing idealized media images may increase the extent to which they are processed, thereby increasing body dissatisfaction," write the authors of a 2005 study on social responses to media. Indeed, women in a 2008 study easily compared themselves to models in advertisements when primed to do so—but when they *weren't* prompted, the number of comparisons they made to images plummeted. Turns out the best way to stop absorbing media standards may well be to stop thinking about media standards—a concept echoed by research showing that girls who say they don't notice models' bodies like their own bodies more than girls who apply critical processing to pictures of models. To be sure, some media literacy programs are tuned in to the inherent danger of overexposure when teaching critical skills. Beauty Redefined, for example, gives presentations to community and educational groups using only a minimal number of images in their presentation. Their photos are selected not only for their teachable moments but also with an eye toward avoiding hypersexualization. "We don't use our work as a platform to introduce or reintroduce people to harmful images because we *know* the influence they have," says Lindsay Kite.

But perhaps the most revealing finding on the effectiveness of media literacy lies not in any of its shortcomings but in one of its successes. In one slim yet promising study, people reported feeling worse about themselves when exposed to images of particularly attractive folks—but the effect was ameliorated when they were alerted that the people in the photographs were models, not "real" people. We focus on the unrealistic standards of media images, but we're also aware that the people in those images pay their bills by being beautiful. And just as we expect more from a Broadway performance than we do from the local high school's production of *Our Town*, we understand that the standards are higher for professional beauties as opposed to the girl next door. It's the exaggeration of those standards that lets us dismiss them, even as we might strive for them. Most of us understand that even if we work toward the gold standard of beauty, we're never going to look like a cover girl. But if we try hard enough, maybe we could look like, say, the pretty lady we see at the gym every day or the woman three cubicles down with perfectly shiny hair. *She* manages to look that way, after all, despite having a full-time job, moderate income, and no personal makeup artist—why can't *we*? This sentiment is echoed by findings that show that women prompted to see idealized images as fantasy, not life examples, walked away with a more positive mood and higher regard for their own appearance. Meanwhile, women prompted to take in the same images as a form of social comparison—surprise, surprise—reported the opposite. It's an echo of the media literacy conundrum on the whole: The more we remind women that their celebrity magazines might make them feel bad about themselves, the worse they'll feel. Frame the same magazine as a pleasant diversion and it might become *fun*. Media literacy hardly robs women of their right to bear *Us Weekly*, of course; the images therein are more available than ever. But the increasing focus on the ways media harms us—or rather, *some of* us, though that rarely makes its way into discussions on the matter—contributes to the idea that women's looks are a source of pain, blunting the ways it can be a source of joy. Even, in the case of a juicily free Saturday afternoon spent flipping through a glossy-print fantasyland, a source of entertainment.

Media literacy reminds us about models' professionalization of beauty, and also shows us the unseen professionals that help create the overall effect: makeup artists, hairstylists, personal trainers, Photoshop experts. In this way, awareness campaigns expose what we don't instinctively know, and reinforce what we *do* know, helping us maintain an appropriate skepticism of idealized images. And illumination of the techniques used in image creation is a worthy goal. Despite its mixed legacy, I'd be chagrined if media literacy education suddenly ceased. The first time I read the Beauty Redefined campaign's rallying cry of "You are capable of much more than being looked at," tears sprang to my eyes. Its direct and realistic terms genuinely made me reconsider times I'd prided myself on being looked at, even to my detriment. And whenever various branches of the Dove Real Beauty campaign wriggle their way through my Facebook feed, my cynicism is tempered by the plainspoken joy I see various friends share in response. But the trade-off of pinning our hopes on media literacy campaigns is that we continue to treat media as the focal point for women's dissatisfaction with their looks, when in fact a greater discontent may spring from gazing at the woman standing beside us at the bus stop, not the woman whose body is splayed out on the side of the bus itself. Our best hope for escaping the effects of either might simply be averting our eyes.

Pretty As a Picture: The Crossroads of Images and "Real Life"

The first time I heard someone sympathetic to concerns about appearance—Sunny Sea Gold, a colleague and author of *Food: The Good*

Girl's Drug; How to Stop Using Food to Control Your Feelings—say that she didn't think the media was necessarily responsible for a glut of women's self-image crises, I nodded while thinking, *Bullshit.* "People focus on the images because they're an easy scapegoat," she said. "You can't get angry about genetics, you can't get angry about personality. But you can forever blame and be angry at the fashion industry and the media." Gold was talking specifically about the role of idealized imagery in eating disorders, which are triggered by a complex system of risk factors, including genetics, family environment, cultural environment, personality makeup, and brain chemistry. Her point was that photos of skinny models may be a piece of the eating disorders puzzle, but they're just that—a piece. Now, eating disorders are related to body image, but they're also relatively rare. Yet the overall theory applies to body image and general concerns about beauty: While idealized imagery factors into some women's preoccupation with their appearance, it's nowhere near the root cause.

When Sunny first introduced me to the idea that maybe skinny models weren't to blame for eating disorders, I rebelled against it. It went against so much of what I'd learned in women's studies teachings and my own observations—that is, until I started thinking more about the ways I *actually* related to images, as opposed to the ways I'd retrofitted my experience to match my beliefs. When I think now of the photo I taped up next to my bathroom mirror, I recall the mind-set that led me there: I wanted to be slim and pretty but didn't quite know how to get there, so I followed the hang-up-a-picture bit of advice in hopes that it might be the transformational magic I needed. But even had I begun to look toward that picture as a meaningful aspiration, the image itself hadn't instilled in me the desire to look a certain way. The desire was there before the picture, and while it's naive to think that the glut of images surrounding me played no role in creating that desire, to pin the bulk of it on the media is another form of naïveté. That's not to say we can just ignore the pictures of unattainable beauty that saturate our environment, or even that we *should* strive to ignore them. Critical efforts to educate women about manipulated images can be useful outside the realm of looks and self-esteem—for instance, the more that consumers understand the techniques used to shape their purchasing decisions, the more agency consumers possess. Still, at day's end, the term Sunny used seems fitting: Media images make a convenient scapegoat.

Instead of looking for a scapegoat—or even looking for the actual culprit—we might be better served by looking at why we seek a scapegoat in the first place. One of the strongest predictors of a woman being at risk of internalizing conventional beauty ideals is linking positive expectations to those ideals. In other words, it's not so much that women want to be thinner or prettier than they are; it's that they—we—want a better life. And women who make a mental correlation between an ideal appearance and an ideal life are particularly prone to overestimating the link between the two. A more comprehensive approach to severing that link might be to emphasize actual predictors of life satisfaction: close friendships, ties to one's community, a sense of purpose. When we treat media images as something that universally hurts women, we not only mistakenly assume that all women have a problem with their looks, we make one shared condition—the media—the problem and focus on its solution. This siphons our energies away from looking at other solutions that speak more directly to the cause of many women's dissatisfaction, keeping the beam of critical thinking directed toward media images and the beauty standard at large at the expense of looking at other factors that predict life satisfaction. If we began to more publicly detach beauty from a general sense of "the good life," we might also be better able to see that we often treat our bodies and faces much as we treat the media—as a scapegoat that absorbs the complications of our daily lives.

Amping up resilience in other areas besides critical skills could be similarly helpful. I'm forced to say "could be" because of the conundrum presented by some of the data surrounding media harm and self-esteem. While women with high self-esteem are buffered from potentially harmful effects of the media, concerted efforts to raise self-esteem have mixed results. In fact, the Canadian media literacy study of sixth graders had another component; a different group of students went through a program designed to raise self-esteem. The results were even more unimpressive than those of the media literacy program, with the self-esteem participants showing no change in concern about weight, and a slight drop in perceived academic confidence—even though the students reported positive experiences with the program. While a number of known factors (successful friendships and scholastic competence, for example) contribute to healthy self-esteem, there's no known surefire way of increasing someone's self-esteem.

It's an unsatisfying conclusion: In order to protect herself against the potential harm idealized images can cause, a women needs healthy self-esteem, but there's not a straight path toward getting there. The ability to remain untouched by these images may well begin with the woman herself—an individualistic approach that flies in the face of community-oriented, politicized efforts to change the culture instead of changing the woman. I wince at the thought of heaping the responsibility of any problems surrounding media and women right back onto the individual. But when I look at the handful of ways mainstream culture has tried to address impassioned critiques—and when I see how even good efforts have little effect—I'm forced to wonder exactly what we as a culture can do to spare the women who suffer because of idealized images. At what point do we trust that any individual woman knows what's best for her, whether that be critical processing, avoiding women's magazines altogether, or embracing the aspirational aspect of these images? At what point do we stop asking that media outlets continue to search for ways to reflect their audience in a meaningful way? After all, as consumers we've failed to support magazines that showcase images of "real women." But perhaps if there were a *true* sea change in images of beauty instead of the occasional campaign or diversity showcase, we might see that the women who are hurt by those images have their burden lifted, while women who generally have a positive relationship with those images remain as secure as ever.

Yet perhaps the greatest reason we view media as so omnipotent is not because of its almighty grip on our conscious and subconscious minds, but rather the opposite: its flatness. As social creatures, we cannot help but compare ourselves with those around us—and we cannot help but recognize the humanity of those same people. Mass-media images allow us to be spectators in a way that "real women" do not, because the vitality of the living, breathing person standing next to us bars us from focusing solely on her appearance. We may compare ourselves with her, sure; as we've seen, we're even likelier to compare ourselves with her than with an image. But the fact of a person's existence forces a more holistic vision on the viewer. Despite the visceral power of physical appearance, we remain unable to wholly reduce another human to a set of data. A person's breath, a person's expression, her movements, her voice, her scent—all these work together to resist efforts to flatten her and make her solely an image. But photography is static. It may challenge the viewer, of course, but it is ultimately unable to resist reduction in the way a person can simply by existing. An image channels our desires in a form that resists complication. Humans, on the other hand, have potential to bring new information to the table in every interaction we have with them. There is only so much we can project onto another person; her essence is animate, dynamic. Images have a simplicity that makes them the perfect landing pad for our fears and aspirations. People, they're too complicated. After all, an image has only two dimensions. A person? Depending on whom you ask, infinite.

Still, none of this changes the fact that images do have force in and of themselves—and force in numbers as well. We've elevated images to the point where we begin to understand our actual lives as a series of images, not as life itself—who doesn't know what *pretty as a picture* means? And who among us hasn't remembered an event not by how we experienced it but by how the photos of it turned out? It's perfectly understandable that we do this, as lived experiences are complex. Our relationship with our bodies, our faces, the ways we want to be seen versus the ways we are seen versus the ways we see ourselves—these are some weighty issues, and we can hardly be blamed for seeking a method to easily organize these big-picture questions. Images provide that organization, by giving us something visible that we can funnel our manifold experiences through. They're a shorthand of sorts, a means we can use to interpret life's messier concerns. It is easier to look at our relationship with images—particularly images created not by any one particular person but by an amorphous, pervasive entity, The Media—than it is to look at our relationship with those near-existential questions.

It's exactly because images are a handy interpretative tool for larger issues that we've come to see them as problematic. The fact is, sexism still exists, so to a degree we *need* images of women to be troublesome to help us understand "the woman problem" in a clear way that numbers and anecdotes—and sometimes even our own experiences—can't always provide. We allow images to have power because they serve as a placeholder for our realities. No wonder we have made the media the enemy—for as the saying goes, we have met the enemy, and she is us.

7

"Like" Me

How Social Media and 24/7 Surveillance Are Shaping Women's— and Men's—Self-Image

I'd been casually dating a thirty-year-old, six-foot-three blond computer programmer from northern Brooklyn for a few months when the friend who had set us up asked me to look at her online dating profile to see if it struck the right balance of flattering yet accurate. I read it and sent her a couple of suggestions. Just as I was about to close the browser window, an impulse came over me: Why not do a quick search to see if any thirty-year-old, six-foot-three blond computer programmers in a certain north Brooklyn zip code had an active profile? We hadn't discussed seeing each other exclusively, but I liked him enough to be curious about whether he was wooing other women on alternate nights.

I wasn't particularly surprised to find his profile there and active—I'd looked for it, after all, and it just confirmed what I'd already suspected, that his feelings toward me were lukewarm. No, the real surprise was the profile picture he'd used. I knew him as a dignified-looking professional: well-cut sport coats, clean-shaven, pink-cheeked, teeming with jocular health and a quiet air of prosperity. Like a Kennedy, if the Kennedys had a Brooklyn accent. But his profile photo was something else altogether. Wearing a muscle shirt and a gold chain around his neck, he bore a five o'clock shadow and an expression I'd never seen him wear. Dull-eyed and hazy, he was practically leering at the camera, which I could tell was held by him at arm's length. Had I seen this expression on a stranger on the street, I'd have averted my eyes and quickened my pace. It wasn't threatening per se, but there was an undeniable hint of risk emanating from the man on my screen. In a word, he looked *sleazy*—a quality I'd never witnessed in him. I mean, we shared our first kiss at an art museum. He was as gentlemanly and wholesome as they come.

At the time I was disappointed. Over time, though, my recollection of the episode turned from disappointment to something more like empathy. The photograph spoke to a side of him that remained hidden from the world at large, even from people he'd had a degree of intimacy with. I wondered what it was like for him to take that photo. Had he started out in his usual sport coat and smile? Had he discarded them as not representative of the person he was or the person he wanted to be? Did his smartphone hold dozens of photos of him in that sleeveless shirt, angling to get just the right amount of shadow on his biceps, just the right leer in his usually friendly gaze? Were the casual comments he'd made about his body—how he preferred his coffee with cream and sugar but drank it black to avoid the added calories, how he'd like to quit smoking but was afraid of gaining weight if he did so—somehow related to this display of self-consciousness?

Digital photography and social media have combined to give us the illusion that we have control over our image. And to a point, we do. But when I think back to his profile picture—and to my own selfies, which reveal not so much how I actually look but how I want to be seen—I realize that they're less about asserting control and more about fleshing out the ever-increasing self-consciousness that social media allows. So far I've addressed self-consciousness primarily as a feminine attribute, a result of the mix of glorification and oppression that has marked womanhood for centuries. But the past decade has made it impossible to ignore the ways that digital self-surveillance dances with self-consciousness for *all* of us—including men, who are now subject to the same sort of monitoring that women have been under for many a generation. There's been plenty of ink spilled over the ways that social media has formed us, or, depending on your perspective, the ways it's just doing the same old thing in new ways. Whatever side of the debate you're perched on, it's undeniable that social media has shaped the way we *display* our self-image—and, just possibly, our willingness to cop to our fascination with ourselves. In fact, the debate over whether social media is a blessing or a curse mirrors the debate over whether self-enhancement is something we should revel in or shun. Positivists on each side promise a fuller, more alluring life; naysayers warn of narcissism and manipulation. In each case, there's merit in both positions. And in each case, the phenomenon in question is a stand-in for something else.

The Almighty Image: Online Self-Representation

Before we look at how social media shapes the way we see ourselves, it's worth looking at the phenomenon that drives its visual end. The ubiquity of digital photography allows nearly all of us to see the world as a field of potential images, a mind-set once reserved for people who consciously thought of themselves as photographers. Today we're all photographers—at last count, Americans took 50 billion photos a year. Eighty-six percent of Americans under age twenty-nine posted photos online, seventy-three percent of American households had a digital camera, and Facebook saw its users uploading about a billion photographs each *week*. Combine the ease of digital photography with compatible tools like basic photo-editing programs and the ability to publicly share images via social media, and we've gone from merely "taking pictures" to "making pictures." Mashing public images with original text à la "thinspo," using screenshots from last night's *NCIS* to illustrate today's political point, taking dozens of selfies to get that one perfect portrait—*this* is image creation today. It's accessible to anyone who goes online, shifting the control of the almighty image from professionals to us, the hoi polloi. Considering the ways that imagery is reputed to shape our definition of conventional beauty, it seems a beauty revolution could be at hand.

And in some ways, it is. As an answer to thinspo—images of extraordinarily slender women with supposedly inspirational slogans layered across them, like "Nothing tastes as good as skinny feels"—we now have "fatspo" featuring Rubenesque women, like the "fatkini" meme that shows heavy women proudly strutting their stuff in bikinis, showing that bodily pride isn't limited to the slender. In 2012, lingerie bloggers launched an international discussion about the lack of diversity in bra advertising, with women of color, fat women, small-breasted women, and women with generous bellies and stretch marks posting photos of themselves in lingerie using the hashtag #diversityinlingerie. A number of memes that allow women to casually show themselves as is have cropped up over the years—post a picture of yourself without makeup/with bedhead/#nofilter. And there are countless exposés of the ways photo manipulation shapes the ideal female body, with before-and-after shots revealing how professional retouchers use Photoshop to transform already-beautiful women into creatures of unreal perfection. Even the teenage girl using simplified versions of these programs on her own pictures is gathering an intimate, firsthand awareness of the power of image manipulation in a way that could leave a deeper impression than just the cerebral knowledge that nearly all public photos are retouched.

Images will always have the potential to be points of resistance to mainstream culture. But as with any new technology, glimmers of revolution become absorbed into existing power structures. Take the grassroots campaign for diversity in lingerie advertising, which was co-opted by Lane Bryant's 2015 ad scheme. Plus-size models popped up in ads bearing the #ImNoAngel hashtag (a direct jab at the unreal perfection of the Victoria's Secret Angels campaign); customers were then encouraged to label their own plus-size-and-proud photos with the hashtag. Having women of all sizes featured in lingerie ads was indeed part of the goal behind #diversityinlingerie. But the spirit of rebellion that spurred that grassroots movement was, by necessity, absent once it became a corporate message (and, unsurprisingly, diversity beyond a moderate expansion of body sizes was missing from the company's campaign). The technologies that allow, say, a fat or disabled woman to showcase herself as a beauty are the same technologies that allow corporations with enormous resources—and individuals who support the status quo—to reinforce their place in the attention hierarchy. And by "individuals who support the status quo" I don't just mean people in places of power; I mean anyone who has used a retouching tool to make her own photograph look more conventionally attractive, myself included. When I'm erasing a pimple or filling in a spot where I've bitten off my lipstick, I'm just out to make myself look my best, not out to bolster The Man. The fact remains that even as I'm raising my own awareness of photo manipulation, I'm falling into lockstep with mainstream beauty standards.

At the same time that image creation has been demystified, we've kept up our worship of images. We select images to use as our backgrounds for our computers, to personalize lock screens on smartphones, to identify ourselves on Facebook, and for online commenting. My friends' faces pop up on my phone whenever I receive a text message from them. Even our financial security is influenced by images: To log on to my bank account, I need to confirm a keyword that has a personal association with a picture stored in my bank's database. Becoming as image-oriented as possible seems to be our collective technological goal. Yet despite these seemingly new ways of processing pictures, the ways we treat images are as old as time. Susan Sontag wrote that images have a "primitive status" in our culture, so embedded are they with one of our prime senses, to the point where we begin to conflate images with the objects shown in the images. "The primitive notion of the efficacy of images presumes that images possess the qualities of real things," she writes in *On Photography*, "but *our inclination is to attribute to real things the qualities of an image.*" (Emphasis mine.) On vacation we hunt for a beach that looks like one we saw on a postcard; we say that a woman is so beautiful she "looks like a model." I've heard a friend who survived an emergency plane landing, and another whose water broke at work before she gave birth shortly thereafter, describe the experience as being "like a movie"—extraordinary events being spoken about not as life but as film. And when one of our favorite subjects is ourselves, conflating the image and the object within the image can be risky.

Enter the Internet, a medium in which we're largely represented by images of our choosing. Time and distance allow us to craft our online personae in ways we can't manage in face-to-face interactions. We can carefully curate our interests, our "likes," the information selected to portray the person we believe ourselves to be without betraying ourselves with cues like voice or physical bearing, and we use photos as supporting evidence all the while. With the aid of apps that allow us to retouch those photos, we can curate our faces and bodies too. Social media has the potential to turn online self-presentation into a never-ending project, much in the same way girls and women have turned their own bodies into what historian Joan Jacobs Brumberg calls "the body project"—a chronic endeavor of improving or maintaining one's physical form. The body project is an undertaking that can never truly be finalized: Once your weight is sufficiently controlled, your complexion might erupt; once your complexion is settled, body hair needs tending. The ongoing project of online self-presentation can be much the same—once you've chosen the right profile photo, you might want to tinker with Instagram filters; once you've exhausted those options, you can begin curating just the right selfie set, or food album, or kids' photo collections, and so on. (Some enterprising minds exploit the malleable nature of our digital lives. There's a spate of online dating consultants out there who work with clients to craft online profiles, shaping them as needed according to the responses various profiles receive.)

But our online self-presentation is more complex than crafting one static profile. It's a flexible, fluid presentation that allows us to mete out various clues in the information game of our social selves. Actually, it's a presentation that women are likelier to have mastered than men. Historically, women have been given a palette of social roles—mother, maiden, spinster, whore, for starters—and haven't necessarily been given much choice in which roles they wind up with. Women have more agency now than we did even fifty years ago, but the idea that women have certain roles to fill has largely stayed intact (witness the hand-wringing we still go through over mothers who exit the workforce to raise children versus mothers who stay and "have it all"). What's changed isn't so much the actual stock of social roles but the flexibility we have in filling them, in part thanks to artifice. Add cleavage and teased hair to a woman of a certain age, and instead of a spinster she's now a cougar. For better or worse, a mother can simultaneously appear to fill the whore role if she plays up the MILF factor; same with the virgin, should she start dressing suggestively. It makes sense that many women might use this flexibility online as well, making it natural to promote a panoply of various selves online.

This malleability might be natural, but it can lead to alienation from oneself, particularly if there's a sense that one or more of the selves presented is a front. Simone de Beauvoir defines self-alienation in *The Second Sex*: "[I]t is to prefer a foreign object to the spontaneous manifestation of one's own existence, it is to play at being." And if there's one thing Facebook allows us to do, it's "to play at being." Certainly alienation can accompany online self-presentation, something I learned when I looked at my MySpace profile—this was 2006—and realized that if I met the woman described in it, I wouldn't like her.

At the same time, there's something uplifting about the fluidity available to us online. In fact, a 2011 study found that while people experienced a moderate bump in self-esteem after just looking at Facebook, they experienced a significant self-esteem boost after making some sort of change to their profile. Now, these were people who were already Facebook users, so it wasn't that they perked up upon merely creating an idealized self online—they felt good upon being able to *manipulate* something about their persona. It may well be the static self, not the ever-changing digital self, that breeds doubt. A 2010 study found a negative correlation between self-esteem and manipulation of one's Facebook profile photo—choosing a particularly flattering photo, or using enhancement software—a correlation that disappeared when looking at manipulation of one's own *collection* of photos. In other words, zeroing in on one particular image of ourselves is linked to negative feelings, but sharing a multifaceted vision of the self isn't. In these studies, presenting a fractured self didn't bring the alienation de Beauvoir warned of; it actually reinforced positive feelings about oneself. Acknowledging the natural fluidity of our identity—which social media can help us do—may be a move toward keeping one's self-esteem intact.

Duck-Faced at Chernobyl: The Self-Expression of the Selfie

In my seventeen years as a New Yorker, I've seen plenty on the subway: a man dressed like a horse nowhere near Halloween who kept yelling "giddyap!" and cracking a whip on himself, a woman eating a salad leaf by leaf with an eight-inch chef's knife, the expulsion of various bodily effluvia. Still, among these oddities and horrors, one otherwise commonplace woman stands out in my memory: a stranger who, in 2007, spent the entire subway ride to Queens taking portraits of herself. The general angle was the same each time—shot with the camera held from above, of course—and except for subtle shifts in facial expression and the degree to which her head was cocked, it didn't seem like she was experimenting with self-portraiture as much as she was just mirror gazing, but without the mirror. I was horrified and envious in equal measures. Horrified because of the excessive show of self-absorption, and envious that she was utterly unafraid to do this in public. I'd had a digital camera for a few years by that point (this was before smartphones) and hadn't I taken—and promptly erased, lest anyone see my exercise of vanity—dozens of self-portraits, engineering the most minute aspects of my features, attempting to capture myself at my best?

The stranger's portraiture session stands out to me years later not because it was the only time I'd see this kind of photo shoot but because it was the first. We didn't yet have an appropriate word for what that woman was doing on the subway or for what I'd been doing alone in my apartment, and my hesitancy about this variety of self-portrait was so strong at the time that I'd have flinched had you labeled it with a word as cutesy as *selfie*. Those who would eventually become fluent in the language of the selfie might find my reservations quaint, claiming that the selfie is a clever way to turn introspection outward—but then there are those who would confirm that yes, my little Saturday-night photo shoots were born of vanity, not exploration. On one side of the selfie debate are those who point to selfies as sheer narcissism—of all the things in the world to document with our newfound power to take as many photographs as we like, we're choosing *ourselves*? Worse, we're choosing ourselves in situations where we're the least important thing in the frame. Witness the Tumblr *Selfies at Serious*

Places, a collection of photos plucked from various social media, snapped everywhere from concentration camps to Lenin's Tomb to Chernobyl. (In fact, just as the similar Tumblr *Selfies at Funerals* picked up steam in 2013, President Barack Obama was caught taking a selfie with the Danish and British heads of state . . . at the memorial service for Nelson Mandela.) But even when the setting is neutral, the anti-selfie crowd claims the practice is self-indulgent—or possibly a capitulation to the beauty standard, at least for women. "They're a logical technically enabled response to being brought up to think that what really matters is if other people think you're pretty," Erin Gloria Ryan wrote on *Jezebel*.

Ryan's takedown of the selfie was a response to a glut of selfie defenses from other prominent feminists, most notably *Odd Girl Out* author Rachel Simmons, who wrote in *Slate*, "The selfie suggests something in picture form—*I think I look [beautiful] [happy] [funny] [sexy]. Do you?*—that a girl could never get away with saying. It puts the gaze of the camera squarely in a girl's hands, and along with it, the power to influence the photo's interpretation." Some selfie takers refer to their creations as a "visual diary," while others admit selfies *are* a capitulation to beauty standards—and that that's exactly their appeal. "My selfies are proof that I'm worthy of documentation," says Rana, twenty-eight. "Taking dozens of photos of myself let me see that sometimes I looked pretty hot, which I hadn't really thought before. I'd see my friends looking gorgeous in my Facebook feed and would feel sort of jealous, but when I started playing around with selfies I saw that it was more about picking the right photo. I saw beauty as being more flexible, and that includes my own beauty too." Some point out that damning selfies as narcissistic is an echo of the classic double bind: Reward women for striving to be attractive, but deride them once they cross some invisible line of pride that's hard to detect. Selfies can be a refutation of the idea that womanhood must entail a degree of self-loathing on the appearance front. Seen this way, the selfie is nearly rebellious in its refusal to play along with the good girl's self-deprecation.

My instincts make me lean toward the selfie-as-narcissism side of the argument, but right as the chatter around selfies reached critical mass, I came across the online photo album of a friend who had been recently diagnosed with non-Hodgkin's lymphoma. Her dramatically puffed-up face, and the progression of her shiny elbow-length hair to a pixie crop to the eventual silk scarf encasing her bald head, told a story of physical trials that her words could not. I thought of photographer Nan Goldin's haunting 1984 self-portrait *Nan One Month After Being Battered*, which depicted Goldin's swollen, still-bruised face in the midst of recovering from a violent attack at the hands of her boyfriend. Few would decry my friend's cancer chronicle or Goldin's work as self-indulgent narcissism—my friend because of how effectively the photos depicted the severity of her condition, Goldin because of her skill, artistic approach, and personal-is-political framing. These examples are particularly extreme, but less drastic versions can be seen in selfies taken with a larger goal in mind—daily selfies taken over years to record the process of maturing, or the "ugly selfie" mini-movement, which sees users sending along intentionally goofy or unflattering photos in order to subvert the typical selfie. And what of the #nomakeupselfie movement that caught fire in 2014, which saw legions of women posting photos of themselves without makeup, going against the grain of what's expected of women? In all of these, the selfie captures both a heightened emotional state and a defined physical state; there's something concrete to see, allowing us to then hand tint the portraits with our own essence. It's a meaningful communication for both creator and viewer. The Dove Real Beauty campaign successfully capitalized on this communication with its short film *Selfie*, in which teenage girls teach their mothers the intricacies of taking the perfect selfie, the idea being that bonding over something joyous like self-portraiture can triumph over the negative types of beauty bonding that have marked many a mother-daughter relationship.

The selfie can also educate the mainstream about people usually seen as outsiders. As queer transgender activist Teagan Widmer said in a podcast on the matter, "As someone who's part of a marginalized group, I spent a lot of time not being able to tell my own story. . . . I think self-portraiture allows for a way to challenge that." In the wake of a highly publicized string of police brutality that spurred the Black Lives Matter movement, online activists organized #blackoutday, dedicated to posting and reposting selfies from black Internet users as a show of solidarity. But most selfies floating around cyberspace capture something far more run-of-the-mill—emotions, sure, but nothing more dramatic than what any of us feel day-to-day. And even this judgment is subjective: Am I nodding vigorously at Goldin's early selfies because of her artistic pedigree? Would I find my friend's cancer reports misdirected if I didn't know her? Am I being a hypocrite for considering Widmer's selfies and the faces of #blackoutday as political acts while rolling my eyes at young women sporting duck face?

Even with this consideration, it's tempting to make a simple division: selfies for the sake of telling a larger tale, acceptable; selfies for the sake of showing the world what you look like, narcissistic. It's also a false division. Taken collectively, the selfies of the second kind tell a far larger story of what we as a culture value and what we *think* we value. One of the most widespread defenses of the selfie is that it's a form of self-expression—which it absolutely can be. Yet when I look at selfies en masse, the range of expression seems frustratingly limited. For every selfie that reveals something untold about the subject, there are dozens that reflect a processed identity, that of a wide-eyed, pouty-lipped, cheeks-sucked-in, chin-tilted-down person who just happened to take a casual snapshot at that exact moment. The classic selfie pose is so established that it's garnered a nickname (yep, that's duck face) most often used to describe the expression many young women wear in selfies. The fact that there's such a specific face associated with the selfie tells us that the portrait is less about expressing one's self and more about expressing compliance with the idea of what a young woman is. For all the ways people, particularly women, play with portraiture in the name of discovery, the sea of selfies overwhelmingly supports the beauty standard so many women claim to be tired of. Now, wanting a glimmer of the supposed rewards of beauty is completely understandable, and I'm guessing that the spirit behind most selfie mini-shoots is *fun*, not a plodding takedown of the beauty imperative. But when posting a selfie to Facebook is still the quickest route to hearing that yes, your friends "like" you, to pose it as a subversion of the beauty standard is a long shot. The lioness's share of selfies form a record not of individuality but of adherence to a template of desirability. Few selfies make the subject look, say, acne-ridden or double-chinned; part of the selfie template dictates that you take the photo with the camera slightly above your head, a perspective that slims your face and enlarges your eyes. (We even make our imagined selfies attractive: Online gamers tend to construct avatars with prototypically ideal bodies. And just as in real life, beauty curries favor; players with attractive avatars tend to acquire higher status than players with offbeat representation.) If there's self-expression involved in the prototypical selfie, it's the expression of a wish, not of reality.

But self-expression isn't the only American value that the selfie lays false claim to. It also democratizes the ability to be seen first and foremost through images, something that has previously only been the realm of people surrounded by others who want to photograph them—celebrities. With the selfie we can give ourselves the celebrity treatment. We don't have to settle for a mediocre snapshot taken at a friend's birthday party—we can capture our best angles, in whatever lighting we want, hair carefully arranged, features set in duck face or whatever expression we've decided best showcases our looks. And with the ability to duplicate our photos endlessly, the mass of our own data comes to echo the glut of celebrity images everywhere. We may not be famous, but hallmarks of celebrity previously inaccessible to us are now at our fingertips. As we saw in the previous chapter, much of the power of the celebrity image lies in our tendency to *identify with*, not compare ourselves against, the subject of the photos. Collapsing the identity in the image with your own identity is the logical end point of our fascination with celebrity photos.

Photography is a means of control, specifically control of the subject. When we create images of ourselves, we become both the controller and the controlled—which is ostensibly a good thing, the idea being that it's better to be in control of ourselves than to be controlled by others. But it echoes the idea that women, in viewing themselves, are both the watched and the watcher. "A woman must continually watch herself," writes John Berger in *Ways of Seeing*. "She is almost continually accompanied by her own image of herself. Whilst she is walking across a room or whilst she is weeping at the death of her father, she can scarcely avoid envisaging herself walking or weeping. . . . And so she comes to consider the *surveyor* and the *surveyed* within her as the two constituent yet always distinct elements of her identity as a woman. . . . Thus she turns herself into an object—and most particularly an object of vision: a sight."

It's this that I see when I scroll through legions of selfies: young women, and to a somewhat lesser extent young men, documenting themselves *simply to be looked at.* And not just by others; the selfie nurtures the internal surveyor above all. It's no coincidence that so many selfies are still taken in the mirror, even as most smartphones have features that allow users to see the viewfinder as they snap away. In looking at my own selfies, I see that many of them are indeed mirror shots, probably because of the flattering "mirror face" I make when looking at myself—uncomfortably close to the duck face I'm inclined to deride. If you take a picture of the mirror as you're looking into it, you are literally showing the world how you see yourself. Your external surveyors—other people—now have the exact same perspective as the internal surveyor.

Yet even when we lead others by the hand to that perspective, we cannot dictate how others see us. For that matter, we can't entirely control how we see ourselves. And when our self-image collides with the image others have of us, the clash can hurt. This might be an argument for an unabashed embrace of the selfie—by displaying our self-image to the world, we inherently embrace the risk that it doesn't quite jibe with the image others have of us. And it is a risk indeed. A 2012 study showed that the quickest way to create a bad impression online is to present a version of yourself that contradicts how other people see you. Post a selfie that's too out of sync with the image others have of you and your "friends" might have some puzzled frowns on the other side of the screen. It's akin to the risk a woman takes when she adorns herself with bold red lips and false eyelashes instead of a tasteful mauve and subtle mascara. She's less likely to be forgotten, but she's more likely to be written off as "trashy," because the louder your self-articulation, the greater the chance that someone will disagree with your vision. I'd hesitate to label most selfies as emotionally risky based on their content, but there is an element of risk involved simply in putting forth your vision of yourself. If the gap between how you'd like to be seen and how the rest of the world actually sees you is too vast, you risk seeming a tad delusional at best, and ridiculous at worst.

Case in point of the ridicule that can come when that gap looms wide: the angelic selfie of a "sleeping" woman that went viral in 2012. She'd posted it on Instagram, with a caption about how her boyfriend had taken the snapshot while she was napping. Adorable, right? But then you notice a mirror in the background that reveals that she took the photo herself. It becomes funny then—the pic inspired parodies and memes across the blogosphere—but only to a point. It's funny because we know all too well what went on behind the scenes. And it stops being so funny once we realize *why* we intimately understand her impulse to capture an image of how her beloved sees her, even if he didn't actually see her that way at all. We know because her selfie is just as engineered as our own.

Selfies have potential to be revolutionary, allowing us, the masses, to show ourselves as we want to be seen. They can help us challenge assumptions about beauty standards, visibility, desirability. But until we start flexing that potential instead of treating selfies as an echo of existing power structures, it will remain stunted. Individuals might be able to grab a moment of assertion through them—the triumph of posting an arresting portrait here and there, the assurance that we're worthy of documentation. As a collective, however, those portraits remain a source of comfort, not challenge, for the status quo.

Rate Me: The Male Gaze Turned Inward

While men and women use social media technology in roughly equal numbers, they may use it in somewhat different ways, particularly when it comes to how we visually represent ourselves. Women are nearly three times as likely as men to choose their Facebook profile picture with "looking attractive" as the goal. Men are twice as likely as women to have never changed their profile picture, and less likely to self-promote with photographs—which is just as well, given that viewers of both sexes spend more time looking at profile *pictures* of women and profile *information* of men. All of this corresponds with the notion that generally speaking, people tend to judge women by what they look like and men by what they do.

That's not the whole story, though. Look at a different set of statistics and it seems like men care just as much about how they appear online. For starters, men are likelier than women to digitally touch up the photo they select as a Facebook profile picture. They're also likelier to use a full-body shot than women, who lean toward portraiture. They're as likely as women to have sent a suggestive sext selfie, and, further along the road of surveillance, roughly four times as likely as women to use self-tracking devices that quantify bodily functions (heart rate, calorie expenditure) and daily activities and then enable users to share those results with others. All of these paint men as behaving just as self-consciously as women online. What gives?

Social media itself is part of the riddle, a driving force behind an increase in men's awareness of their looks, not merely a symptom of it. With the expectation that we all have a profile somewhere, complete with photograph—and with online dating services like Tinder exploiting this by creating snap-judgment apps that allow users to swipe away undesirable pictures of potential love interests from a menu of hopefuls—it's understandable that men would enter the rabbit hole of self-surveillance. Certainly they're aware that with the advent of trackable social media, surveillance from others is impossible to avoid, something women have always known. "Apparently, it took the preponderance of closed-circuit television cameras for some men to feel the intensity of the gaze that women have almost always been under," writes critic Madeline Ashby. "It took Facebook. . . . That sense that someone's peering over your shoulder, watching everything you do and say and think and choose? That feeling of being observed? It's not a new facet of life in the twenty-first century. It's what it feels like for a girl."

Not that surveillance is entirely new to men, particularly when it comes to seeing themselves represented. After viewing traditional porn (videos or magazines, as opposed to Internet porn), young men tend to engage in self-surveillance and body monitoring. Throw the Internet into the pornography mix, and the result is the logical consequence of surveillance plus the illusion of interactivity: seeing oneself as an object (which men did *not* report doing after watching traditional porn, only Internet porn). Not that men necessarily mind that new load of objectification. Witness the crop of sexting scandals that emerged once quick, easy photo sharing became the norm. Former congressman Anthony Weiner's bulging boxer-briefs, former congressman Chris Lee's flexed biceps, shock reporter Geraldo Rivera's tough-guy pecs shot—these are images of men eager to embrace the objectifying gaze women have long been under. These are men who wanted to be desired, not for their jobs or income or sense of humor or any of the things that have traditionally given status to men in our culture. These are men who wanted not only to be desired but to literally be seen as desirable. Digital photography makes that easy; easier still is producing what's essentially pornography. Porn isn't exactly interchangeable with images at large; it has a specific purpose that makes it difficult to take our ideas about it and apply those ideas to the way we think about images in general. But its uniquely utilitarian aims make it an interesting study in men's digital self-representation.

Sex researchers have long theorized that while heterosexual men become aroused by watching porn involving women because—at the risk of stating the obvious—they like looking at women, heterosexual *women* can also get hot to trot after watching porn involving women because they identify with the women in them. So speaking very generally, men take pleasure in viewing, and women take pleasure in projecting. The newfound ability to turn oneself into an image complicates that equation. Suddenly you're not just watching other people on-screen; you realize you can put *yourself* on-screen too. "My girlfriend sent me some sexy pictures of herself, and I wanted to send her something too," says Jon, a thirty-two-year-old in Chicago. "I took a picture of my cock. When I saw myself on the screen of my phone, it was like *I* was the guy in those pornos. I still watch porn but this is something I can do anytime." Jon eventually started posting pictures of his penis on Craigslist, asking women to grade him on a school-like A-to-F scale. Women (or people claiming to be women) obliged. "It was nice to hear feedback—if they'd say anything negative it was usually just something about how lame I was for posting, not about how I actually looked, but the thrill was in seeing myself on-screen and knowing that anyone in the world could see it." And if the existence of ratings site RateMyCock.com—and RateMyCock.info, IGuessYourCockSize.tumblr .com, and Cocks.RateMePlease.com, not to mention the virtual garden of genitalia dotting the Craigslist landscape—says anything, this is hardly a quirk particular to Jon. This is an *industry*.

That's not to say that by posting a cock shot, men are suddenly in the same place of surveillance that women have lived in for most of their lives. It's anonymous, for one; it's willful and wanted, unlike much of the feedback stream women receive. But one of the largest differences between how men and women handle self-representation also speaks to one of its biggest similarities—objectification. There's a history of particular groups of men experiencing their own bodies as objects, like bodybuilders, who by dint of their occupation see their bodies as something to be manipulated. But men's alienation from themselves has spread. Referring to themselves by their body parts ("Do you like *me*?" to mean "Do you like my cock?"), experiencing themselves through the mirror (that is, most of the pecs and biceps shots out there), depending on the opinions of others (asking for ratings)—all of these add up to an estrangement from one's own identity. And it's no accident that much of this alienation focuses below the belt. Writes de Beauvoir of the human tendency toward displacing identity onto objects or concepts, "The penis is singularly adapted for playing this role of 'double' for the little boy—it is for him at once a foreign object and himself; it is a plaything, a doll . . ." It's a representation of oneself, but not *quite* oneself. Men are even beginning to commodify their own images. "Looking for pic trade," "Your pic gets mine," and the like pop up on sites like Craigslist, and some dating sites now offer "erotic pic trade" as an option along with "long-term relationship" or "casual dating." The idea of photos as currency comes full circle with the mini-phenomenon known as a "tribute," in which a person sends a man a sexy photo, and the fellow in turn takes a photo of himself masturbating to the picture and digitally returns it to the sender. It's an amalgam of pornography and face-to-face intimacy that was unheard of fifteen years ago.

Yet even with the increasing similarities between the way we're coming to view men and women, there's an overriding difference: the male gaze. The idea of the male gaze has traditionally been that when women are represented in various forms of media, they're shown in a way that presumes the viewer is a heterosexual male—from a perspective that suggests a woman's sexual availability, and as a set of body parts instead of a whole being. What's happening now that more and more men are exercising their desire to be seen is that they're co-opting ways that, until recently, have been reserved for looking at the *female* body. The male gaze peers both ways now, at women, and right back at men. And when the gaze is a novelty, as it is for many men, its limitations aren't necessarily clear. As twenty-eight-year-old Matt says, "I've always thought that if I were a woman I'd be wearing the shortest skirts and low-cut shirts—I'd want to show myself off. Taking photos of myself where I get to show myself off is the next best thing."

Getting feedback may be part of the drive in the growth of men's willingness to post erotic photos of themselves, but the form of feedback desired tells us something too. By asking for "ratings"—A to F, one to ten—men are asking for their sex appeal to be quantified. Certainly women have been assigned quantification by men ("She's a ten"), leading some to conflate quantification with validation. (Indeed, as a counterpoint to RateMyCock.com, there's RateMyBoobs.net, RateMyCups.com, and the free-for-all British site RateMyBits, which encourages users of any sex to "upload boobs or willy.") Still, there's something particularly masculine about this form of measurement. It recalls the "quantified self" movement, which aims to "help people get meaning out of their personal data," according to the website of the movement's founders. Quantified selfers use a variety of tracking devices—body trackers, electronic records, and so on—to record their daily routines, helping them understand everything from what times of day their stress levels spike to how they're frittering away money. By far the largest branch of the quantified self movement is related to the body, with users logging calorie intake and expenditures, heart rate, steps walked, sleep patterns, etc. It's intrinsically related to a practice known as body hacking, as popularized by Timothy Ferriss, author of the number-one *New York Times* best seller *The 4-Hour Body*. Ferriss's advice for a lean, muscular body includes performing two minutes of body-weight squats in restaurant bathrooms just before eating, ingesting specific amounts of caffeine during weekly bouts of binge eating, and weighing one's feces in order to make sure the previous two bits of advice are working as expected. Were the book marketed to women, it would roundly be torn to bits by the feminist blogosphere for encouraging behavior that uncomfortably mimics an eating disorder. (While much of the advice is unisex, the language of chapters on increasing sexual stamina make it clear that the book's primary intended audience is male.) It aims to make men more conscious of their bodies, helping them surveil and monitor their actions, with the idea being that they emerge from their own sea of data new and improved—and more attractive, as implied by the word *datasexual*, which describes quantified selfers who thrive on not only measuring but sharing their data.

In other words, the quantified self movement aims to make men behave a little more like women, asking them to be hyperaware of their bodies without allowing them the playful possibilities of self-adornment in return. Self-improvement, not reinforcing gender norms, is the goal. But the means is uncomfortably familiar.

Welcome to the Dollhouse: Men and the "Grooming" Industry

Back when pretty much the only men wearing makeup were either rock idols or Boy George, I privately came up with the guideline that if any particular piece of bodily care was something women generally performed while men generally didn't, I could safely consider it "beauty work." Nail polish and leg shaving? Beauty work. Nail trimming and hair combing? Basic hygiene. It wasn't perfect, but for a college student beginning to question gender roles, it was a useful guide in helping me determine what parts of my morning routine I might want to examine with a particularly feminist—and mascaraed—eye.

That guideline has begun to crumble. Americans spent $4.8 billion on men's grooming products in 2009, doubling the figure from 1997, according to market research firm Euromonitor; globally, the market grows 9 percent a year. Men's skin care—not including shaving materials—is one of the faster-growing segments of the overall market, growing 500 percent over the same period. As for shaving, sales of various aids skyrocketed: Sales of facial trimmers grew 13 percent in 2012, while sales of body groomers grew 16 percent—unsurprising, considering that multiple studies show that men depilate areas other than their face. (After all, according to Gillette brand manager John Grim, "Women have spoken, and overall they overwhelmingly prefer men who style their body hair.") Nearly 13 percent of all cosmetic procedures are performed on men, and dermatologists are reporting a marked increase in the number of male patients claiming to have sensitive skin. It's unclear how much of the men's cosmetics market is color products (you know, *makeup*), but the appearance of little-known but stable men's cosmetics companies like 4VOO, KenMen, The Men Pen, and Menaji suggests that the presence is niche but growing.

Actually, that's not quite right. It's growing, sure, but it may be more accurate to say that men's makeup is an industry ready for *re*growth. With what fashion historians call "the great masculine renunciation" of the early to mid-nineteenth century, Western men's self-presentation changed dramatically. In a relatively short period, wealthy men went from sporting lacy cuffs, rouged cheeks, and high-heeled shoes to the sober suits and streamlined hairstyles that weren't seriously challenged until the 1960s. The idea was that if men across classes were all to adopt simpler clothes, populist leaders could physically demonstrate their brotherhood-of-man ideals. Whether the great masculine renunciation achieved its goal is questionable, but what it *did* do was take a giant step toward eradicating the nineteenth-century equivalent of the beauty myth for men. At its best, the shift liberated men from aristocratic peacocking so that their energies could be better spent in the rapidly developing business world, where their efforts, not their lineage, would be rewarded (at least in theory). By reducing the number of appearance options available to men, the great masculine renunciation also reduced the burden of choice and the judgments one faces when efforts fall short of the ideal. But in the past half century, Americans have slowly eradicated many of the standards put into place by that movement. Weekend casual wear became appropriate for casual Fridays; casual Fridays became business casual; business casual gave way to the "anything goes" ethos of Silicon Valley and beyond. Skinny jeans started being marketed to men and women alike, extending the need for a slim profile to the heftier sex. The Beatles wig my uncle wore in the late sixties to feign a hip hairstyle that went over the ears is now a laughable relic. At my last office job, two male managers had hair that reached their shoulders.

And this is where things get tricky. In the past decade, the loosening of the male dress code has translated to a broader swath of skin care and cosmetics, partially answering the cries of women who were fed up with paying close attention to hair and makeup while men could get away with little more than a shower and a comb. Even aside from this sauce-for-the-gander thinking, there's something to champion, particularly when looking at the grooming industry's intersection with gender politics: Marc Jacobs in drag on the cover of *Industrie* magazine, above the headline "Mrs Jacobs"; James Franco's juicy makeover for *Candy*, the first magazine aimed specifically at the transgender community.

But a closer look at the actuality of the men's grooming industry shows that there's very little gender play going on. Instead, these products are designed to reinforce notions of conventional masculinity: power, status, and money. Men might be buying more lotion than they did a decade ago, but color cosmetics are still only the tiniest segment of the men's grooming market. And most of those color products are designed to conceal, not enhance. They're not playful in the least, unless legions of men are making a game out of covering their zits with tinted Clearasil. Instead, products with low visibility—and low risk to traditional gender roles—rule the market. Think body washes, shaving accessories, moisturizers, and perhaps the occasional beard rinse. As the group president of Estée Lauder told *Women's Wear Daily* when the company launched a line of Tom Ford skin care products, "This is not [notoriously outrageous] Jean Paul Gaultier with men's makeup. This is a serious, high-ticket men's grooming line with a couple of products with cosmetics benefits to be used in a very masculine way." The biggest risk men are encouraged to take is to dabble in the world of the "metrosexual"—a term coined in order to make it clear that heterosexual men can pay attention to their appearance while retaining their conventional heterosexual masculinity. (According to the word's internal logic, gay men are excluded from being metrosexuals.)

It's not like the companies promoting men's products are pushing the gender envelope either, even when brands are panting to reinvent themselves. When Old Spice needed a new image beyond its dad-smell evocations, Wieden+Kennedy ad agency tapped former NFL wide receiver

Isaiah Mustafa to anchor a gaggle of commercials. At the heart of the campaign was a tongue-in-cheek mocking of masculine tropes, with the muscled Mustafa posturing as "The Man Your Man Could Smell Like" who could do everything from bake birthday cakes to tame horses to ride motorcycles. Other brands deploy a similarly goofy humor: Gillette illustrates its effectiveness against "man-sized odor" by showing sports and landscaping equipment dropping off a man's body as he showers; Dove Men+Care employs a voice-over reminiscent of a 1950s newscaster talking about how to protect one's "multifunctional casing"; the punkish nail polish company ManGlaze dubs its shades names like Mayonnaise (white), Lesbihonest (fuchsia), and Butt Taco (orange, for reasons best left to the imagination).

Of course, not all campaigns for men's products rely on whimsy. But the overwhelming use of humor targeting this market sends a clear message: Men don't really need this stuff after all. It's just a joke, buddy . . . but since you're paying attention, why not try our brand? By simultaneously endorsing and mocking conventional forms of masculinity, product campaigns hit a sweet spot where men can care about their looks without risking the appearance of foppery. Meanwhile, women are presumed to have a self-image too fragile for humor to be an effective beauty marketing tool. I asked a friend who works as an ad copywriter if she'd ever seen a funny beauty ad, and between the two of us we could recall exactly one example of a funny beauty-ish ad aimed solely at women, an online commercial for a tampon delivery service. Which, you'll notice, isn't about beauty, but hygiene. (Incidentally, the commercial went viral, showing that the delicate sex just might be hungry for ads that presume we're resilient enough to laugh at the products that beautify us.)

Strength and aggression are also abundant in masculinity marketing. A smattering of names from various men's products: Facial Fuel, Dude Wipes (not to be confused with the Fresh Richie "wipette" designed for "the modern gentleman and his precious jewels"), Assassin, Combat-Ready Balm, Turbo Wash, Sucker Punch, Camo Concealer, and the nexus of manly product names, Power Rich (a "multitasking supercream" by Dermalogica). And it's no coincidence that the higher up the socioeconomic scale you go, the likelier you are to see tactics other than humor used to sell products to men. Cologne ads tend to use seductive evocation and blatantly posit men's bodies as sex objects, and several high-end brands cloak themselves in science (including an entire skin care line called MenScience). When a product comes too close to mimicking a *beauty* product—as opposed to a *grooming* product, the industry term for man stuffs—it risks becoming feminine. And femininity is something most men can indulge in only if they have a certain amount of security. Not just mental security in their masculinity, but rather the kind of security known as cultural capital, or a person's assets other than money that assure social mobility. Education, language skills, and simple know-how are types of cultural capital—as is physical appearance. The recent increase in men's skin care and cosmetics, rather than simply signaling a relaxation of gender roles, reinforces beauty work as a form of cultural capital. To gender-bend even by wearing something as simple as concealer, most men would need a degree of assurance that their societal position is secure enough that they can flout convention without losing face. (Many a tale from the transgender community will reveal that gender-bending without that assurance can result in isolation, or worse.) The easiest way to get that assurance is through class privilege. Just look at the spokespeople for men's products: Take Hugh Laurie and Gerard Butler, both of whom endorsed L'Oréal's skin care program for men, tellingly called L'Oréal Paris Men's *Expert*. They can use goods originally developed for the ladies because they've transcended the working-class world where heteronormativity is, well, normative. They can demand respect even with a manicure. Your average construction worker, or even your average IT guy, doesn't necessarily have that luxury. It's also not a coincidence that both Laurie and Butler are British, even though the campaigns are aimed at Americans. The "gay or British?" line shows that Americans tend to see British men as being able to occupy a slightly feminized space, even as we recognize their masculinity, making them perfect candidates for telling men to start exfoliating already. NBA basketballers Shaquille O'Neal and Dwyane Wade endorsed Dove's men's skin care; with their sports cred, their masculinity is assured. Same with Kiefer Sutherland's guys'-guy manner working for Axe body spray, musicians Adam Levine and Sean Combs for acne treatment Proactiv, and Bluebeard for the eponymous "beard wash." And if numbers are any indication, companies' reliance on masculine tropes is a thriving success. L'Oréal posted a 5 percent sales increase in the first half of 2011, the time when both Laurie and Butler graced their commercials for the men's line.

It's not like men of any era have gotten out of appearance anxiety scot-free. But when we dropped the suit and the standard men's hairstyle, relegating them to a certain type of man, we also wedged open a Pandora's box of appearance concerns for men. This awareness corresponds with the rising expectation that we all perform self-surveillance now: Pick a Facebook picture, find a good avatar, are you using *that* photo on your dating profile? The greater range of appearance options available to men allows them to fully exploit the idea of personal branding—the packaging of the self as a product, an object to be consumed. Personal branding is cited as a technique to make oneself more memorable, particularly useful in the job marketplace. That is, the packaging of the self, specifically including one's appearance, is increasingly being linked to the workplace—the realm where men have long been told they need to excel in order to have cultural power. By linking career and appearance through the personal branding options that the disappearance of the great masculine renunciation gives men, we create a separate sort of beauty myth for men. And separate but equal can't be what we're striving for.

As a group, men have a power that is hardly shrinking, but it is shifting— and if entertainment like *Breaking Bad, Mad Men,* and the Apatow canon are any indication, that dynamic is being examined in ways it hasn't been before. One way our culture harnesses anxiety-inducing questions about gender identity is to offer us easy, packaged solutions that simultaneously affirm and undermine the questions we're asking ourselves. In fact, that was one of the biggest points of *The Beauty Myth*, which gave voice to the unease so many women feel about that situation—but at its heart it wasn't about women at all. It was about power. It was also an examination of how femininity is so easily reduced to a set of signals and images. What was outside of the book's scope was an examination of how masculinity is reduced just as easily, though because of the breadth of tropes assigned to men, that reducibility isn't quite as clear. The very idea of the beauty myth was that women's appearance became more policed in reaction to women's growing power. I can't help but wonder what this means for men in a time when we're still recovering from a recession in which men disproportionately suffered job losses, and in which the changes prompted in large part by feminism are allowing men a different public and private role. It's a positive change, just as feminism itself was clearly positive for women—yet the backlash of the beauty myth served to counter women's gains.

In the rise of beauty culture for men, it's almost like we've been given another chance to create a space where the accoutrements of beauty can exist at their best, not at their most cynical: as expression of the human joy we share at our ability to decorate ourselves, as portal to the soothing rituals of self-care, as room for experimentation. We also have the chance to examine how the grooming industry markets itself to men in this period of enormous growth—and what we find there can illuminate the ways we treat gendered industries, helping us see with fresh eyes exactly how the schemes of the women's beauty market work. But we're not really seizing that chance. We're just beginning to have conversations about the genuinely enriching possibilities of beauty in women's lives—how it can help us create closer friendships with other women, how it can be a source of self-articulation. But we're giving men the same old scripts. We're content to shunt the possibilities of "hope in a jar" into a reservoir of conventional masculinity, and in doing so, we deny ourselves an opportunity to treat men with a deeper, less misanthropic sensibility. In doing that, we shut down one possible route to bettering the lives of women too.

8

"Don't You Know You're Beautiful?"

The Therapeutic Beauty Narrative

The first time I saw an ad from the Dove Campaign for Real Beauty, I wanted to cheer. Well, I wanted to cheer the first time I saw *coverage* of the Dove Campaign for Real Beauty, as its news coverage was far more widespread than the ads themselves. You may recall this branch of the campaign yourself, from the billboards that dotted highways across the nation and the full-page ads in magazines. A handful of women wearing white bras and underwear stood side by side; all were smiling broadly, some with arms around one another. Notably, the ad featured more than the standard token brown-skinned model—women who appeared to be African American, Latina, and Southeast Asian stood alongside white-skinned women. But the most striking thing about the ads was this: The women weren't thin. Neither were they particularly heavy. It was more that they looked . . . well, like me, and maybe like you, or like any of the "real women" you know with muscular legs, padded bellies, the occasional tat-too, or pockets of wobbly flesh tucked around the spots on women's bodies notoriously labeled "problem areas." And for a change, these bodies weren't on display as *befores* in ads for weight-loss products. In fact, these women weren't presented as needing fixing of any sort. They looked attractive, healthy, and vibrant. They looked *proud*.

It's about time, I thought. Finally, women who resembled the lovely ladies I saw around me every day were being presented as beautiful in their own right. It addressed the grumblings I'd had about unrealistic beauty standards and negative body image and women as projects for upkeep or construction—all my good feminist quibblings with how women's bodies were represented in media. Even when I read deeper critiques of the ads, about how the women's bodies fell short of being truly diverse (where were women with physical disabilities and the women who couldn't fit into size 14 pants?) or about how they were still being used as aspiration, I still applauded Dove. It felt like a company was finally paying attention to the complaints women had been vocalizing for so long. It was like someone there had read *The Beauty Myth*—or maybe just listened to women who were tired of being told their looks were never going to be good enough unless they tried product X—and decided to try to be part of the solution, not part of the problem. Sure, they were still selling wrinkle creams and whatnot, but hey, you've gotta make a living, right?

Other companies and outlets of mainstream culture were becoming increasingly eager to address women's negative relationship with their looks. Several beauty companies jumped on the Dove bandwagon, banking their buck on women being hungry for marketing that acknowledged the complaints women had about the industry. Bookstores welcomed titles like *The Body Image Workbook, Feeling Good about the Way You Look, The Broken Mirror, The Woman in the Mirror, Comfortable in Your Own Skin, The Beauty Bias*, and *When Women Stop Hating Their Bodies*. Songs about women's troubled relationships with looks hit the airwaves: "Beautiful" from Christina Aguilera ("I am beautiful no matter what they say"), "What Makes You Beautiful" from One Direction ("You don't know you're beautiful / That's what makes you beautiful"), "Fuckin' Perfect" from P!nk ("Exchange ourselves and we do it all the time / Why do we do that?"), "Don't You Know You're Beautiful" from Kellie Pickler ("Just the way you are"), and "Just the Way You Are" from Bruno Mars ("Yeah, I know, I know when I compliment her, she won't believe me"), among others.

Was I glad to see a broad recognition of some of the doubts that had plagued me and so many women I knew throughout our lives? Yeah, I was. But the more I heard our doubts about our appeal articulated and re-articulated, my "you go, girl" sentiment began to erode. In fact, my feelings soon looked suspiciously like resentment. Yes, I sometimes felt bad about my looks—like I wasn't ever going to be thin enough, clear-skinned enough, shiny-haired enough, *good* enough to take pride in my appearance. And certainly I'd heard enough similar woes from friends to know that it felt at times like women's relationship with beauty was at a crisis point. Then, of course, there's the boatload of statistics supporting the idea that women don't like what we see in the mirror: surveys saying that one-third of women would be willing to die younger in exchange for the perfect body, or that 93 percent of women feel they should look younger, or, from Dove itself, that 72 percent of girls—*children*—feel "tremendous pressure" to look beautiful.

But. *But.* There was another set of numbers that told a different story. In other studies, nearly two-thirds of women report feeling just fine with the way they look, with more than a quarter of women under thirty rating themselves an eight or above on a one-to-ten scale. While both women and men tend to make self-deprecating judgments regarding body size, they also tend to *overestimate* their attractiveness and sexiness when compared with evaluations of them from others. People are quicker to recognize a digitally beautified image of their face as their own than they are to recognize their *actual* face. And even when we do recognize that one of our traits looks quite different from the gold standard, we have a tendency to devalue that trait—if my hair isn't fantastic, then how much can anyone's hair really matter? These findings reflected a quiet truth I'd long known about myself: For all the days I despaired over the breadth of my thighs or the small colorless mole below my left nostril, there were just as many where I thought I looked just fine. Good, even. Sometimes beautiful. Yet when I began asking other women how they felt about their looks, I heard much of what you'd expect. "I never felt beautiful," says Megan; "I was never the pretty girl," says Erica; "When my husband tells me I'm beautiful, I always correct him," says Cheryl. It wasn't until I started asking more specific questions that the fuller picture emerged. Megan says she never felt beautiful, but when I asked her about the first time she thought about how she looked, she told me about dressing up as Olivia Newton-John for Halloween as a teenager and feeling—and this is her word, not mine—"beautiful." When I asked Erica about the last time she felt good about her looks, her answer was quick: "Yesterday, even though I hadn't showered and was all sweaty and stuff—I just felt pretty. No reason." Cheryl later tells me that *beautiful* is a hard word to apply to herself, because it implies being "at the tip-top of the scale," but says that she feels "pretty" much of the time.

It's no surprise that women might be more eager to highlight their self-doubt than their self-satisfaction. In 2012, the British newspaper *Daily Mail* published a piece by writer Samantha Brick with the headline " 'There Are Downsides to Looking This Pretty': Why Women Hate Me for Being Beautiful." The piece, accompanied by various photos of Brick, detailed the ways her looks had brought her vitriol from women around her, from neighbors ignoring her friendly hellos to female bosses telling her to stop dressing provocatively, though Brick was dressed similarly to other women in the office. "And most poignantly of all," she wrote, "not one girlfriend has ever asked me to be her bridesmaid." It went viral within hours of publication, eventually generating more than five thousand comments, trending globally on Twitter, and landing Brick spots on talk shows on both sides of the pond. Even by the standards of the *Daily Mail*, an outlet known for its clickbait ethos, the response was remarkable, not so much for its volume but for its content. Brick was called "deluded," "deeply paranoid," "awful," "completely batshit," "stunningly annoying," and—surprise!—a "bitch." What's more, readers were quick to set the writer straight, letting her know she was "forgettable" or even "ugly" in appearance. Yes, the piece smacked of arrogance; yes, the *Daily Mail* likely ran it knowing exactly what would happen; yes, Brick's confrontational tone made one wonder whether it was her beauty or her smugness that had earned her the cold shoulder she was bemoaning. But the level of vitriol directed at Brick was so outstanding that it was clear the response was about far more than a single 1,400-word essay. Here was a woman who'd dared to publicly say that she was beautiful—without qualifying it with a catalog of her physical flaws, without any sort of "ugly duckling" backstory, without *apology*—and she was practically being flogged for it.

The Brick incident was just about one woman, of course, or at least it seemed that way on the surface. But echoes of women's furtive pride reverberate everywhere, if you know to keep your ears open for it. Remember, one of the studies we looked at in chapter 5 showed that when pairs of friends disagreed about which one of them is more attractive, more often than not, it was because *both* women privately believed themselves to be the prettier one. But can you think of a single pair of female friends who would openly vie for the title? Not that we delight in our visage only when compared with others. Take selfies, for example. As we saw in chapter 7, the reasons behind snapping a self-portrait are complex, but there's an underlying condition behind sharing a photo of yourself with the entire Internet: You've got to think you look . . . well, if not *fabulous*, certainly not *un*-fabulous. Even the "ugly selfie" has a knowing quality about it, the subtext being, *I can let myself look terrible in this photo, because I don't look terrible most of the time.* If the defenders of the selfie are to be believed, these portraits are young women's way of letting the world know that they think they deserve to be seen—"a tiny burst of girl pride" is how writer Rachel Simmons described them. Then there's the squeaky-wheel cousin of the selfie, the "Am I pretty?" video, in which someone—usually a teenage girl—uploads a video of herself asking her audience to evaluate her appearance. It's wildly upsetting at first glance—are girls really so desperate for assurance about their looks that they'll ask literally *anyone* for feedback? (Guys have their own version—to wit, RateMyCock.com—but they're less likely to inspire pity. Not only are such sites anonymous, but their pornographic sheen makes it clear that the subjects of the photos are getting direct gratification from uploading their own pictures.) When I watched some of these videos, I saw what I expected: fear, tentativeness, yearning, despair. But in other videos, I saw something else. There was pride, eagerness, boldness. There was *play*. Some featured an upbeat pop soundtrack backing a series of still photographs of the subject. In others, she'd be in motion but mugging for the camera, doing everything from duck face to blowing kisses. These girls were clearly enacting prettiness. That alone isn't a sign of blossoming self-esteem, to be sure. But I have a hard time believing that it stems entirely from a hatred for one's own looks.

I don't mean to say that we women secretly think we're the shiznit and that we're pretending to be down on ourselves out of modesty or expectation. Nor am I saying that concerns about women's bodily self-esteem have been entirely overblown—indeed, to say so would be willful blindness to the very real pain that so many of us have felt. The problem isn't that we feel so great about ourselves and are restrained from saying so. The problem is that the expectation of how women regard their looks has been framed so heavily in terms of negativity that we've turned this popular narrative into a tool that can be wielded against the exact population it purportedly serves.

We Shall Overcome: The Therapeutic Narrative

When I listen to the first stories women are willing to share about beauty, there's a recurring arc: Prepubescent girl with well-adjusted bodily esteem meets world; world (in the form of mother, father, media machine, thoughtless dance teacher, etc.) implies she's too fat/gangly/bulb-nosed/narrow-featured to be considered beautiful; girl embarks on rampage of disparaging her looks; girl comes to terms with her appearance and goes back to a place of well-adjusted bodily esteem. There are variations, of course—she might spend the crisis phase being preoccupied with her appearance or ignoring self-presentation altogether. Perhaps she's not fortunate enough to have had the innocent childhood joy of feeling carefree in her body—or to find a place of comfort as an adult. Maybe she's an outlier in this schema altogether, feeling at ease with herself even during the turbulence of adolescence, or just not thinking about it all that much. But the blueprint is there, and if you've spent any time consuming media aimed at women, you've seen it.

There's a name for this sort of general template: the therapeutic narrative. The idea is that Americans have come to frame our experiences, particularly painful ones, in terms of a good story—a narrative. In the ideal therapeutic narrative, the "hero" has overcome anguish in order to reach a place of understanding and acceptance. It's a combination of several schools of thought: creative writing (who doesn't love a good story?), Freudian analysis (thanks to which we now take for granted that our early childhood has vast repercussions in adult life), and psychologist Abraham Maslow's hierarchy of needs, which culminates in self-actualization—a concept with a particular power in American culture, given our historical love of a bootstraps ethos that tells us that all we really need to do to succeed is put our mind to it.

We see the therapeutic narrative at work all the time. Witness women's magazines and their tales of triumph; witness best-seller lists, perennially full of therapeutic fables; witness Oprah. For that matter, witness reality shows like *Top Chef* and *Project Runway*, which regularly shape participants' personal growth as a part of the season's dramatic arc. And if you're anything like me, witness the way you might frame your own tale. Without ever intending to, I've interpreted my personal life as a series of psychological before-and-afters: *before* leaving an unhappy relationship; *after* exiting a period of depression. If you asked me for my life history, it would be less the "I was born in 1976" variety and more a chart of my psychological well-being.

Central to the therapeutic narrative are four things, as outlined by sociologist Eva Illouz: (1) a once-whole, once-healthy self that was damaged by (2) a negative incident or pattern, which (3) leads to suffering. But! Luckily we have (4) self-awareness, the key to returning to one's natural state of pure psychological health through a full understanding of one's "damage." Taking a look at the focus on women's appearance, it's all there: the once-innocent girl, the incident of damage, the bodily self-loathing—and, by the time the tale is told, self-acceptance. The therapeutic beauty narrative is fairly new, even though we've been preoccupied with our bodies for some time. For in order for a story to be widely understood, we need an understanding of what the crisis is, something we didn't widely articulate until twenty years ago. By the time GenXers became cultural movers and shakers, we'd turned *The Beauty Myth* into a best seller and had become fluent in terms like *body image* and *self-love*. We'd identified that there was a problem with women's relationships with their looks, we'd begun to articulate the resultant suffering, and we'd begun to inch toward self-awareness in order to overcome that suffering, with the self-actualization of acceptance as the pinnacle of a woman's relationship to her body. We'd turned our relationship with our looks into a therapeutic narrative. It's actually surprising that it took as long as it did. The term *body image*, after all, was coined by a pupil of Freud's.

The primary purpose of the therapeutic narrative is a streamlining that ultimately enables the storyteller to weave a cohesive tale that the speaker herself is in control of. That simplification has its place, because it can help any of us find meaning in our experiences. For example, when applied to psychotherapy, the therapeutic narrative is often seen by practitioners as an opportunity for patients to examine and re-author troubling parts of their lives. Simplifying our relationship with beauty may have once helped us articulate truths about it. Giving a common language to the toll the beauty imperative can take on self-esteem allows us a measure of solidarity that we might not have had before. But in simplifying, we're forced to edit out pieces that don't fit into the dramatic arc. In an individualized, clinical setting, eliminating the parable's contradictions is acknowledged by therapists as key to successful treatment. Writ large on a cultural scale, that simplification winds up silencing the full experience for the sake of the story. Worse, we silence women whose experiences don't fit the narrative: If a woman is proud of her looks, she's framed either as a role model with a preternatural self-confidence we should all aim to mimic or as plain old vain. (Or if her appearance doesn't align with mainstream beauty norms, she might be seen as heroic—or as foolish.) We keep frank discussion of our experiences in the realm of impolite speech, reinforcing the boundaries of how we discuss beauty. When we do this, we continue to imbue beauty with impalpable powers, and we distance ourselves from our own experiences on the matter, turning parts of our lives that don't fit the legend into outliers instead of incorporating them into the messy chronicle of our lived experience. We become alienated from ourselves.

It's important to recognize that the therapeutic beauty narrative isn't entirely—or even mostly—crafted from fiction. Plenty of young women *do* take a confidence dip around adolescence, particularly around their appearance; plenty of women *do* wrestle with the beauty imperative as adults; plenty of women *do* eventually find some sort of peace with their looks. Plenty never do at all. But even a woman who by and large doesn't fit into the narrative template has likely had moments where she fit into one of its key characteristics: feeling crappy about the way she looks. And the thing is, feeling crappy about the way you look is, to put it mildly, horrible. When I think of moments—some fleeting, some not so much—when I've felt particularly insecure about my looks, it's as though there's a shroud around me that's invisible yet impossible to ignore. My movements become more tentative; my speech becomes slower, thicker, like I'm speaking through a fog. It dictates how long I can hold a smile, and whether I read the smiles of those around me as warmth or mockery; their laughter as embrace or patronization. I have a harder time looking people in the eye. It determines whether I assume the best of people or assume the worst, whether I think I have a reasonable expectation of being listened to or if I'll be dismissed, whether I believe someone is holding my gaze on the street because I'm appealing to look at or because I'm not.

None of these things are related to how I actually look, mind you. It's more that my attitude toward my appearance forms a veil that colors not only how I see myself but how I see the world—and how I expect the world to see me. It has the power to dangerously skew my perspective. That tilt is temporary, sure, but that doesn't lessen the impact of those moments. Being uncomfortable in your skin might well be as uncomfortable as you'll ever be. It stings. It hurts. Most of all, it's *memorable*.

To explain that indelibility, we can look at a little trick of the human mind called "negativity bias." A psychological tic that makes negative experiences stand out more strongly than positive ones, negativity bias shows up in areas well beyond looks and self-esteem. We react more strongly to unpleasant odors than to pleasant ones, we recognize angry faces more quickly than we recognize relaxed faces, and even infants as young as three months old are likelier to remember a non-helpful character than a helpful one. It also happens to dovetail beautifully with the therapeutic beauty narrative. The sheer weight of feeling troll-like etches itself onto one's psyche. Even if the number of times we feel beautiful equals the number of our lesser moments, the impact of ugliness looms larger. The desire to avoid that sensation becomes a powerful force in our memory. We remember that sensation; we carry it with us. The sparkling sensation of feeling delightfully pretty? It feels great, sure. It's also weightless, comparatively speaking, less able to find a foothold in our memory. And if you can't (or don't) remember something, you can't easily incorporate it into your biography. Couple the transient nature of positive experiences with knowledge of the ways our culture reinforces beauty standards, and soon enough you've got something to overcome.

But here's a funny thing about us humans: Even as we lean toward accentuating the negative, we continue to hold out hope for a better future. A 2006 study showed that people tend to rate themselves as being better-looking now than they were in the past—and they expect to be even better-looking in the future. That is, even though our culture equates beauty with youth, people consistently see their future, older selves as being more attractive than their younger selves, and they anticipate getting even better-looking with age. This doesn't make much sense—until you look at theories of human motivation. The idea is that we're motivated to frame our experiences in a way that lets us feel good about our current lives. One way to do that? Put down the self of the past in order to elevate the self of today. In the case of our looks, this tendency falls into lockstep with the "therapeutic" aspect of the therapeutic beauty narrative; that is, if we can report having overcome a past psychic struggle to accept ourselves as is, we can better enjoy the relaxed pleasure of feeling just fine today. In truth, that struggle may be conveniently cherry-picked—I wrote in my diary at age sixteen how glad I was that I'd "finally" learned to accept my body. Never mind that I was still trying to lose weight or that I'd keep trying to do so through much of college—or that the therapeutic myth of the thirtysomething woman I am today paints age sixteen as one of the low points of my self-image. At sixteen, if I was to comfortably inhabit my body for any length of time, I needed to believe I both looked and felt better than I had even months before. That's how I could write with all seriousness on the eve of my seventeenth birthday, "I know I'm not sixteen anymore. I am SO GLAD I'm past all that [with an arrow pointing to turn the page back to an entry made a couple of months earlier about how "You are not attractive, get it through your head"]. *I still want to lose weight though.*"

So the therapeutic beauty narrative works neatly with the ways we think about beauty, sure. But we wouldn't use it to the extent we do if it didn't give us something in return. And one of those things is a convenient scapegoat. Some time ago, a good friend was in the midst of a serious depression. I'd invited her over for dinner, and we were halfway through our second bottle of wine when she let down her guard. She was "a mess," in her words—too messy to maintain her physical and mental health, too messy to leave the man who was neglecting her, which then led into her fears that she might not be able to find someone better. She'd rapidly gained weight and become lax in her self-care. "*Look* at me, who'd want me?" she said. I'd been quiet, preferring to listen rather than give pat reassurance; I knew that when I'd been depressed, such well-meaning utterances felt empty, highlighting the difference between sympathy and empathy. But with the "*look* at me" comment, I turned from empath to viewer, and my knee-jerk reaction was to soothe what little I could: "You're beautiful."

"I *know* I'm pretty," she muttered, quickly, as if she wanted to rush through it to get to the real point of her despair, even if she didn't quite know what that was. It was the first time I'd heard her acknowledge her beauty, but that wasn't what struck me. What struck me was how, when it came down to it, she intuitively understood that her looks had nothing to do with what was going on inside. Sure, she'd indicated that her appearance played a role in her unhappiness, hence my response. But it seemed as though upon hearing my blanket assurance, the puzzle of her depression came into focus, however briefly, and she knew that the words I had to offer weren't the ones she needed. What was actually going on was the sort of amorphous troubles that are difficult, perhaps impossible, to articulate. Hopelessness, depression, emptiness—years later, she'd come to refer to that time as an existential crisis. In the face of something so daunting, is it any wonder that she momentarily chose something simpler—her looks—on which to anchor her pain?

If it's my impulse to be sympathetic when beauty woes are used as a scapegoat, it's my impulse to wince when I look at another motivation women might have for rooting themselves in a position of injury, for in a skeptical light it paints us as childish: It's a way to get affirmation. The easiest way to hear you look fabulous is to put yourself down. As we saw in chapter 5, negating a compliment can be a way to restore a friendship's power balance after it's been temporarily tipped by the weight of a compliment. But that equation is easily inverted. Saying something along the lines of "I look gross" disturbs the power equilibrium in a sadomasochistic way: It lowers the speaker into a position of humility, but it also reliably *elevates* her if the response is a compliment (which, if everyone plays by the rules, it will be). Self-deprecation turns into a form of power—the power to provoke a compliment. It's a power I've deployed myself, and it would be easier for me to believe I didn't know my own motivations in doing so if I didn't have proof, time and time again, of its efficacy.

The ritual of self-deprecation can be seen in full online. The phenomenon of teen "Am I pretty?" videos generated concern aplenty among adults, and with good reason; they can indeed be heartbreaking. But looking at the comments on these videos, it's clear there's something else at play. The responses are almost uniformly positive: "U r pretty!" and "Beautiful!" are standard responses. If the girl posting the video isn't conventionally attractive, users are likely to be supportive in a different way, using softened feedback like "You're a cutie!" or "Who cares as long as you're pretty on the inside," giving compliments on strong features ("Nice lips and complexion"), or offering advice on how she can improve her looks ("Tie hair back, lose glasses"). If comments about her looks *do* turn nasty, other users rally to her defense with barbs like "You should look in the mirror before you call anyone ugly, you're ugly on the inside," "Haters gonna hate," or simply "Why r u such an a**hole?" Comments that question the user's motive, on the other hand, often stay unaddressed. A put-down about one young woman's looks might receive six defensive responses, but questions like "Why do u ask if you're pretty when u know u are?" or "Why are you such an attention whore?" provoke little but silence.

In looking at our motivations to stick with the therapeutic beauty narrative, my goal isn't to say that it's merely a way of avoiding contemplation or of fishing for compliments, or to cast scorn on those who voice their doubts about their own appeal. When we enact this story line, we're not doing it cunningly or cynically; it stems from a place of sincerity and, often, from pain. But when legions of women report such similar experiences about their most intimate psychological wanderings, we must look at how many of those similarities are organic, and how many are a result of what we expect to hear.

The Real Beauty Campaign: Corporate Investment in the Therapeutic Beauty Narrative

If we want to see any sort of narrative in action, we can always look to an industry that depends on a particular demographic of people having a shared experience at the same point in time: advertising. The Dove Campaign for Real Beauty remains the best-known marketing effort to capitalize on the therapeutic beauty narrative, but it wasn't the first. In 1998, the Body Shop launched a campaign featuring Ruby, a plastic doll so named for her Rubenesque figure—think Barbie, but size 16. The tagline of Ruby posters and billboards: "There are 3 billion women who don't look like supermodels and only 8 who do," frequently accompanied by the Body Shop slogan of "Know your mind, love your body." Six years later, Unilever unleashed the Dove Campaign for Real Beauty, and a slew of others followed. In 2011, mineral-makeup company Bare Escentuals unveiled a set of commercials in which they stated that they'd "set out to find the world's most beautiful women . . . without ever seeing their faces." Women showed up at the casting call and filled out questionnaires about themselves, which were given to the minds at Bare Escentuals. The company then cast the women based solely on the basis of their questionnaires, choosing representatives not for their looks but for their inner beauty. Inner beauty showed up a few years later as well, with the Inner Beauty Challenge, a campaign sprouting from Benefit Cosmetics' partnership with a suicide prevention nonprofit. Followers were urged to follow a seven-day program designed to help young women "focus on the positive, have fun, and embrace your INNER beauty." As an incentive, Benefit gave away a cosmetics package each day of the challenge; to enter, users just had to upload a photo or video of themselves taking that day's action (day four: "Show the love," day five: "Get real"), marking it with the designated hashtag—and, according to the site's legal disclaimer, giving Benefit the right to use the photos and videos in whatever way the company saw fit.

The same year Bare Escentuals experimented with blind casting, Make Up For Ever debuted a series of print ads of young women taking what appear to be selfies, with the tagline "You're looking at the first unretouched make up ad." Indeed, a notary public certified that the images were free of retouching. Aerie, the lingerie branch of American Eagle and a fashion line for young women, followed suit in 2014 with ads featuring models' bodies as is, complete with moles, waistline creases from bending, tan lines, veins—all things that would normally be edited out of photos, particularly for a lingerie line. All this followed a spate of editorial retouching awareness campaigns in various magazines: *Marie Claire*'s 2010 unretouched cover featuring Jessica Simpson sans makeup; side-by-side before-and-after photos of Aisha Tyler in *Glamour*, complete with the actress's commentary on what it was like to see herself whittled away; *Seventeen*'s pledge to readers to never alter girls' bodies on its pages.

Not that the "you go, girl" approach was left to visuals alone—take L'Oréal's famous slogan, "Because We're Worth It." Stila Cosmetics heralds its foundation collection with "Face It . . . You're Beautiful." And then there's the tagline for the Bare Escentuals blind casting campaign, particularly baffling given the emphasis on the models' personalities: "Pretty is what you are. Beauty is what you do with it." Meanwhile, Benefit took it a step further with what functioned as a sort of meta-campaign for its They're Real! mascara. The idea is that the consumer is so used to fakery in the beauty industry that having a product that gives the *illusion* of fakeness while actually being authentic is downright seditious. Or maybe it was just a play on the name of the company's hydrating concealer: Fakeup.

Some of these tactics might seem daring. Revolutionary, even. Finally, the corporate world seemed to be listening, giving thoughtful responses to the demands made by critics and everyday skeptics. Maybe feminism and commercialism could work together after all. The key here, though, is that these tactics *seem* daring—until you take a closer look. Bare Escentuals' blind casting, for example, appears to be taking a radical risk. But the pool of women at the casting call was composed entirely of models and actresses—professional beauties, hardly leaving the company in danger of casting an Oscar the Grouch look-alike based on her inner beauty. That campaign, and Benefit's Inner Beauty Challenge, conveniently get to have it both ways by entwining inner and outer beauty: Sell a product designed to beautify consumers on the outside, while responding to critiques of the beauty industry as shallow and opportunistic by showcasing the ways women's internal qualities make us radiant. Then there's the no-Photoshop ads. The Make Up For Ever campaign stakes its claim on a "what you see is what you get" model, with the implicit promise being that since the woman in the ad wasn't airbrushed, the consumer can have a reasonable expectation of looking as good as she does. The product being peddled? High-definition foundation—which was developed to make its wearers look good on camera. The idea isn't that Make Up For Ever finds retouching to be deceptive; the idea is that their makeup will make you look retouched. The ads *strengthen* the cultural power of retouching, while getting to appear as though they're dismantling it. As for the slogans, they're a part of a tradition of co-opting feminist or otherwise woman-friendly language. Just as Virginia Slims' "You've Come a Long Way, Baby" rendered cigarettes as a progressive choice for women, "Because I'm Worth It," by L'Oréal's open acknowledgment, was designed to capitalize on "a new spirit of feminism." (It was changed to "Because You're Worth It" after *The Beauty Myth* was published, and to "Because We're Worth It" in 2009, in what the *Wall Street Journal* termed "an effort to appear more inclusive.")

But the biggest schism between the process and the result comes from the most widely known campaign of this ilk. Dove's entire Campaign for Real Beauty hinges on one central idea: Women have been systematically told that they're never going to look good enough, they've internalized that belief as truth, and it's high time that changed. To support this thesis, Dove commissioned a global study of 3,200 women ages eighteen to sixty-four, led by prominent names in the field of beauty and self-esteem—Dr. Nancy Etcoff, author of *Survival of the Prettiest*, and Dr. Susie Orbach, author of *Fat Is a Feminist Issue*. Among the most repeated findings of the 2004 study (Dove commissioned a follow-up in 2011): Only 2 percent of women worldwide would describe themselves as beautiful. Eleven percent of American women believe they are "much/somewhat less beautiful" than other women, and physical appearance was one of the least satisfying areas of all women's lives, universally ranking below family, friends, health, and romance. And more than two-thirds of women "strongly agree" that media and advertising set an unrealistic physical standard for women.

It's compelling data. Paired with empowering images of women of various shapes, colors, and ages—and, of course, the Dove logo—it makes for compelling advertising.

But in the very study that Dove relies on for these compassion-churning statistics, there's a lot more going on. That bit about how only 2 percent of women worldwide would describe themselves as beautiful? This was the survey question that finding was derived from: "Which ONE of the following words, if any, would you be most comfortable using to describe the way you look?" The options: natural, average, attractive, feminine, good-looking, cute, pretty, beautiful, sophisticated, sexy, stunning, gorgeous. From the words on that list, 2 percent of respondents chose "beautiful"—hardly how that finding was spun in the campaign. In fact, 17 percent of women "strongly disagree" with the statement "I do not feel comfortable describing myself as beautiful." In other words, at least 17 percent of women *would* describe themselves as beautiful, were they able to choose more than one word on the list.

Other findings from the paper were similarly obscured by the public arm of the campaign. Sixty percent of American women in the study defined themselves as weighing too much; more than 60 percent of American women actually *do* weigh too much, according to the Centers for Disease Control and Prevention. (The question of how much weight actually affects health is up for debate, but modern medical wisdom still tends to stick with long-established guidelines regarding what's "too much." If there is actually an obesity crisis, it's not one of erroneous perception.) Seventy-seven percent of American women reported being "somewhat" or "very" satisfied with their physical attractiveness and beauty. As for comparing themselves with others, 11 percent of American women find themselves less beautiful than other women—and 17 percent find themselves *more* beautiful than others. When comparing their general physical attractiveness with other women's, American respondents rated themselves even higher, with 25 percent saying they were more attractive than their peers. Most women plopped themselves smack-dab in the middle, with 71 percent of American respondents self-reporting as "average in beauty," 63 percent as "average in overall physical attractiveness." Here's the thing: By definition, most of us *are* average. *Thinking of your looks as average does not constitute a self-esteem crisis.* What might *generate* a self-esteem crisis? Thinking of yourself as average when you're getting the message that it's sort of pathetic that you don't think of yourself as beautiful.

None of this is to say that the beauty industry is somehow more manipulative than any other—cherry-picked wording and zeitgeisty slogans are hallmarks of advertising across the board. What unites these campaigns is their underlying reliance on the therapeutic narrative. Once upon a time, the basic formula for selling cosmetics was straightforward, if distasteful: dampen women's self-image by implying they're not quite good enough as is, then raise it with the promise of the product. Create a problem; offer a solution. What the new ilk of campaigns does is basically skip the first step, then zoom ahead to the "solution" of the product, or simply buoy the viewer's emotions and associate the product with that heightened feeling. However overblown women's self-esteem crisis might be, most humans are familiar with the sensation of being unhappy in front of the mirror. Dove singles out that feeling, then provides us with a path back to wellness. It takes what companies used to do implicitly (suggest that there's a problem) and makes it explicit (we all *know* there's a problem—and here's a solution!). In both tactics, the advertisers presume that there's something about the woman that needs fixing, whether it's her ability to live up to the beauty standard or her inability to reconfigure her emotional life to a heightened standard. Campaigns targeting women's interior lives take the dissatisfaction women have with the beauty industry and sell it right back to us under the guise of well-being. It seems as though the brands have simply done a good job of connecting with the consumer by responding to malcontent—which they have. But there's a less savory suggestion here too: Women can band together to complain about the beauty industry, they can organize to raise awareness of marketing tactics that depend on a weakened sense of self, their consciousness can reach the tipping point, and *their criticisms can still be used to bolster the beauty industry*. Companies get to appear to be standing alongside their critics while continuing to ultimately reinforce the narrative that garnered the criticism in the first place.

I don't mean to be entirely cynical about the beauty industry's embrace of criticisms directed toward it. After all, these companies are just doing what companies do: trying to sell goods to as many people as possible. And as the overwhelming response to the Dove campaign showed—as I write this, its most recent video has more than 66 million views—women *are* hungry for marketing that acknowledges the darker side of beauty without directly contributing to it. Hell, *I'm* hungry for it, despite any cerebral misgivings I might have. My initial reaction to the unveiling of the Dove Campaign for Real Beauty was, after all, joy. Even after I'd become critical of the campaign, its various branches worked on me. Remember the viral video where women described themselves to a criminal sketch artist, and a stranger then described those women to the same artist, and you saw the vast difference between the two portraits? The first time I saw it, I got teary. Campaigns reliant on the therapeutic beauty narrative are often effective, for one of the very reasons that it took hold in the first place—negativity bias. When we see an attractive but pedestrian woman play down her physical highlights, only to see them illuminated in the eyes of a stranger, it speaks to those moments when a woman's relationship with her own looks is best described as wounded. Watching another woman's eyes light up upon seeing a kinder interpretation of her appearance, we get to heal along with her.

The trouble with these campaigns isn't that they're manipulative; they're no more so than any advertising. It's that they're easily mistaken for altruism. As my friend Mary puts it, "It's like Dove expected fat women to be grateful to them just for acknowledging that they exist." When we assign goodwill to companies for repurposing our own discontent and selling it back to us, it doesn't just mean that we're rewarding them for ostensibly listening to women's longstanding critiques of the beauty industry. It means that we're doing their work for them.

The Mystification of Beauty

Corporate leveraging of the therapeutic beauty narrative may be trouble-some, but it's on the individual level that we see the narrative's great-est effects. For starters, it can be used as a tool in the romantic arena, by setting up women as damsels in distress who can be rescued in the form of compliments (or, more insidiously, the compliment-insult hybrid known as the neg). But its deeper snarls show up in women's relation-ships with one another—and with themselves. It asks that women go from enacting the beauty standard to enacting stories *around* beauty: to post #nomakeupselfies, for example, or to "like" the latest branch of the feel-good Dove campaign, continuing to rally women's energies around our looks without giving the topic more than a cursory makeover. More important, it turns beauty into a trait that can never be fully acknowledged publicly, meaning it can never be fully discussed. We discuss *aspects* of beauty, wide-ranging ones at that—the nuts and bolts of creating the per-fect ringlets, the intersection between happiness and its inimitable glow, our whispery fears that we're never going to be quite enough. But when so much of our relationship with our looks is framed in terms of a predeter-mined fable, that discussion has limits. This lends beauty the veil and power of the untouchable, the unreal, the inarticulable. By forming a template that's difficult to stray from, the therapeutic narrative streamlines the lived experience of beauty, rendering parts of it mute while simultaneously im-buing other parts of it with more power. That is, it keeps beauty mystified.

To be sure, beauty and *mystery* can be related. (What sort of character pops into your mind with the phrase *a mysterious woman*? Ten bucks says she's a looker.) But when we go through the act of *mystifying* something, we obscure our true relationship with it. Mystifying beauty can keep a woman who views herself as having finished her therapeutic arc from recognizing where she might still need some growth—and it can keep another woman from *ever* feeling as though she's finished the narrative, entangling her in an ongoing drama of self-improvement.

Part of the purpose of mystification is maintaining a sense of awe or idealism. If you get too close to the object or concept being mystified, you'll begin to see its flaws. Mystifying beauty keeps it unreal, making it something none of us can ever *quite* possess, not *really*. It will forever be something to work toward, a riddle to be decoded, perhaps with the help of experts (which beauty culture ensures there's never a shortage of). It takes beauty out of our hands and puts it in the realm of the future, making it as tantalizing as anything that's just out of one's own reach. It's an echo of part of what makes beauty troublesome in the first place: No matter how pretty you become, it's never going to be pretty enough. The irony is that even though the therapeutic beauty narrative reinforces the mystification of beauty, part of the narrative itself depends on the idea of successfully *de*mystifying beauty. (Exhibit A: the abundance of before-and-after Photoshop exposés aiming to help women see the illusions of media images.) In the proper arc, the storyteller learns something key about beauty that doesn't diminish the meaning of the beauty standard at large but that makes it less important *to her*. Perhaps she learns that outer beauty isn't what really counts, or, à la Dorothy's ruby slippers, discovers that she's had it all along. That work can be valuable in its own right. But it also serves to make us believe that we've seen through beauty's tricks, which distracts us from seeing the larger machinations at play. It keeps us from questioning the base purpose of the impossible beauty standard, prevents us from asking who benefits when women spend such enormous amounts of energy on enhancing themselves, inhibits us from embracing the subversive possibilities of beauty culture—ideas that must be reckoned with if we can ever truly relish beauty as a lived experience.

Beyond manipulation and mystification, there are a host of other fall-outs of the therapeutic beauty narrative. It normalizes a chronically diseased relationship with our appearance, a condition that should be seen as *ab*normal. It paints women as passive, particularly as consumers—*poor things, at the mercy of the big bad beauty industry*. It can temper the joy so many women report finding in the act of beautification. It robs women of the opportunity to create their own idiosyncratic reports about their relationship with their looks—and it robs them of the opportunity to drop their own myths altogether. But perhaps the biggest trouble with the ways the therapeutic beauty narrative plays out with the individual is exactly that—it reinforces our status as *individuals,* not as parts of a collective. When Naomi Wolf published *The Beauty Myth* in 1991, it generated a national conversation about the beauty imperative. Amid the flood of pent-up frustrations about everything from the dieting industry to cosmetic surgery to airbrushed ads, one of the book's crucial points was largely lost in the discussion surrounding it: The beauty myth was created in part to keep women concerned with their individual, personal troubles, in order to divert attention from the larger problems facing women as a group.

In 1993, my father, a longtime civil servant, handed me a college scholarship application for children of federal employees. The crux of the application was a short essay about the Biggest Problem Facing America Today. At the time, an unusual number of issues directly affecting young women were a part of the national conversation: the Family and Medical Leave Act, the Student Loan Reform Act, the establishment of volunteer organization AmeriCorps, the Clinton attempts at health care reform, and the beginning of a string of murders of ob-gyns who performed abortions. The topic I chose? Women feeling insecure about their looks. My interest has always lain within the "personal" end of "the personal is political" discussion, but today it strikes me how willing I was to overlook sexual equality laws in the workplace, equal pay, reproductive rights, access to higher education, or any other national issue. Granted, at seventeen years old I was a teenager, a member of a solipsistic demographic hardly known for its nuanced understanding of that whole "personal is political" bit. Still, twenty years later, much adult discussion of the beauty myth sticks strictly to the personal (often including my own work on the matter, to be sure) instead of extending to the sexist power structures that established it in the first place. Body image workbooks and workshops, personal essays in women's magazines about triumphing over self-loathing, therapists who specialize in women's appearance dissatisfaction—all these may give the individual a much-needed boost, but for the most part that's where it ends. Yes, we need an intimate knowledge of the ways the beauty myth affects each of us on the individual level before we can dismantle it and focus on truly advancing women's power. In no way am I suggesting that women should sacrifice their own psychological well-being in order to take on the world at large. Indeed, the most politically active women I know are those who have a balanced perspective on their looks, either because they've worked toward that balance or were fortunate enough to be born with it. As feminist fashion blogger and personal style consultant Sally McGraw says about her own work, "The point is not to feel pretty. The point is that you're already pretty, and once you've accepted that, you free up an enormous amount of mental space for other things." Freeing up that space is crucial, and we need knowledgeable guides like her to get there.

But believing that the best way to cultivate our power is to direct our attention toward psychological healing is only half the story. If we fail to bridge the beauty myth's individual impact and its larger political reverberations, we remain isolated—and women's isolation has been a driving force behind the beauty myth all along.

CONCLUSION

Skin Deep

Looking Beyond Beauty

On the morning of July 5, 1942, a young Jewish woman in Amsterdam named Margot Frank received a call-up notice from the Schutzstaffel ordering her to report to a labor camp. Her father told Margot and his younger daughter, Anne, of a long-arranged plan: The family was to go into hiding. July 16 had been the target date, but with Margot's sudden call-up notice, there was no time to spare. "Margot and I started packing our most important belongings into a schoolbag," Anne wrote in her famous leather-bound journal on July 8. "The first thing I stuck in was this diary, and then curlers, handkerchiefs, schoolbooks, a comb and some old letters. Preoccupied by the thought of going into hiding, I stuck the craziest things in the bag, but I'm not sorry."

Allow me to point out what strikes me here: *Anne Frank packed curlers.* Yes, curlers were more de rigueur in 1942 than they are today; it was probably less like packing lipstick and closer to packing, say, dental floss, or the comb she also tucked into her bag. Yes, she was probably in shock and automatically packed as she might for a sleepover at a friend's house, not for going into hiding for an indefinite period during wartime. Yet that's exactly what hooks me about this bit of reportage. In the midst of a waking nightmare, in the midst of one of the greatest horrors this world has seen, this particular thirteen-year-old reached not for "the craziest things" but for something that could potentially provide familiarity, routine, a pastime, and some semblance of normalcy. She reached for an emblem of beauty.

At best it would be disingenuous to claim that perspectives on beauty are an essential takeaway from the diary of Anne Frank. At worst it would be so dismissive of her legacy as to exit the realm of integrity. Please rest assured that I'm making no such claim. What I am saying is that her instinct to grab her curlers offers a testament to the anchor that beauty rituals can become for us. Whether, given more time, she would have categorized curlers as an essential item worth bringing along in one of the two bags she toted to Prinsengracht 263, we don't know. We know only that with a mere few hours of notice—during which Anne had to select which clothing she could layer without attracting too much attention on the streets of Amsterdam, say good-bye to her cat, try not to distract her parents from the pressing tasks at hand, and begin to process the notion of living a life hidden away—curlers were instinctively deemed indispensable enough to take on the journey with her. After her diary, they were the second thing she listed packing.

Amid the crucial moral education Anne Frank gave us with her diary lies another, smaller lesson that isn't as important but is just as human: Beauty matters. Indeed, throughout this book, I have laid out some of the ways beauty matters to all of us. But I find myself wanting to conclude it with a different assertion—that it needn't matter. I mean that in the expected feminist ways, to a degree—that we shouldn't use beauty as a stand-in for personal worth, that we shouldn't judge others by it. Yes, of course, all that. But what I mean more specifically is that I would like to see us no longer treat beauty as a goal—including the goal of having convinced ourselves that we're awash with it, or that we've reached the end of our own therapeutic beauty narrative. The costs of treating beauty as an achievement can include the expected—emotional pain, financial drain—but also the brand of self-talk that sees us talking ourselves into its embrace. We ask women today not only to be beautiful but to *feel* beautiful. It's arguably a more noble goal than simply looking pretty, but it's asking women to regulate their private lives, and it's not exactly an easy task either. Our assurances to ourselves that we've achieved an ideal relationship with the way we look aren't so different from what *No More Dirty Looks* coauthor Alexandra Spunt terms "chasing the beauty dragon": that never-ending pursuit of *just* the right product, *just* the right look, *just* the right fix. Both quests see us chasing something elusive, and something made ever more compelling by its elusiveness. And both contain an inherent promise—that once we finally capture it, we can rest at last.

It's a powerful promise. And judging from the rare occasion that I've actually caught the dragon for a moment (most recently in the form of a heavenly eyeliner that actually stays put all day), fulfilling that promise can even impart genuine satisfaction, at least for a moment. Still, chasing the beauty dragon—and chasing its cousin, the seductive serpent who can magically make us feel beautiful too—is chasing an illusion. It's chasing a static vision of ourselves that fails to capture the fluctuations that mark us as human.

"I think there's a lot of pressure on women to have bodies that are exceptional," body image blogger Kate Fridkis told me when I interviewed her about her pregnancy memoir, *Growing Eden*. "That are 'better' than normal. That go beyond—fitter, leaner, boobier, more dramatic, tighter, you know. I've definitely wanted to look 'better' than normal. Better than myself. But it turned out, with my pregnancy and the birth of my baby, that normal was exactly what I needed to be. It was awesome that I was ordinary. And my ordinary body was awesome." In a country that prides itself on its national exceptionalism, the idea of personal exceptionalism holds a special allure. When Kate linked personal exceptionalism with the pursuit of beauty, its truth resonated too loudly with me to ignore. I started mentally cataloging the ways I'd tried to be exceptional—from my scholastic achievements as a kid to a sudden goal of deadlifting two hundred pounds—and wondered if wanting to be exceptional just for the sake of being exceptional was all that different from wanting to be beautiful. Then I wondered whether having exceptional appearance esteem fit into the same category.

I won't lie. Were a fairy godmother to offer me a bulletproof self-image, or even the easy, relaxed, and consistent confidence that I've seen in a handful of women I know, I'd take it. In a heartbeat, I'd take it. I'd take it for myself, and I'd take it for you, so that I could then sit down and give you a point-by-point guide of how to get there yourself. The thing is, my confidence will never be bulletproof; my self-image will never be free of every pockmark. There are women who thrive in this arena. I am not one of them. *They are exceptional.*

What I can tell you may not be exceptional, but it is the truth: The greatest moments of serenity I've had in my life are not the times when I've felt beautiful but when beauty was the furthest thing from my mind. Some might call it engagement or flow—I just know that when I am in a state of presence, all parts of me are summoned. I could be hiking or lifting weights or sharing a conversation with a spellbinding thinker or doing anything that severs the loop of self-consciousness that is constantly, *constantly*, aware of how I look. In those moments, there is no part of me that's left to watch myself doing or being, no part that's monitoring from the sidelines. In those moments, it doesn't occur to me to step outside of myself and play my own observer.

I'd love to be able, at this point, to give you a manual for how this trick is done, or, at the very least, tell you how I've managed to do it. But I can't, because I haven't. I started writing about beauty in part because I wanted to figure out why I'd feel fine about my looks one day and terrible the next. I've figured that out, to a degree—in a nutshell, it's because like so many women, I tend to use my appearance esteem as a barometer for my overall well-being—and that's helped even things out a bit. Still, it hasn't stopped completely, and I don't expect it will. And even though I know all about that nagging little trick called negativity bias and understand that I'm likelier to remember the tough moments more than the neutral or positive ones, that doesn't make the times when I feel crappy any easier.

Through my blog, I regularly get letters from women, particularly young ones, asking for my advice on how to stop that crappy feeling. My answer has shifted since I first began writing about beauty. At one point I'd suggest cognitive-behavioral techniques like recognizing black-and-white thinking, at other times I'd encourage them to put pen to paper. To those who seemed most deeply troubled, I said, with as much compassion as I could, *You need help beyond what I can offer*. All of those responses might have been helpful. Perhaps none of them were. I don't know.

Here is what I tell them now: The best way I've found to work through my own times of self-doubt is not to work through them at all, but rather to simply *sit* with them. At one point, I would attempt to convince myself that my moments of thinking I looked terrible were a mirage—that I looked just fine, and hadn't I been downright pleased with my reflection just the other day? Other times, I'd try to distract myself, or I'd do something concrete to actually look better, like deep-condition my hair. Sometimes I'd even just plain old give in, moping about feeling sorry for myself—woe is me, stretch mark-y, ruddy-complected, split-ended *me*. All of these coping mechanisms have their place. Sometimes I might be able to talk myself into feeling more even-keeled. Sometimes I'd forget once I became involved in something more engaging. Sometimes I'd have a good sulk and wake up the next day feeling just fine. But none of those actions allowed for stillness. None of them allowed me to fully experience the discomfort I was feeling. Once I began to just *be* with that sensation and accept it—not as my doom but as one moment among many—the illusion that it was my looks that were causing me discomfort could lift, allowing whatever might have been underneath to be revealed. Becoming comfortable with discomfort might seem like the longer, harder path. It's not. It's a shortcut to being able to more clearly see the quieter shifts that my mind—and perhaps yours—makes throughout the course of a moment, a day, a lifetime. It's a shortcut to clarity.

You may be thinking, *Well, that's nice, but isn't this a book about beauty?* Yes, it is. But now that I answer the classic meet-and-greet question of "What do you do?" with "I write about the ways beauty shapes women's lives," I've learned how woefully incomplete that answer is. In fact, I eventually started saying "The ways *appearance* shapes women's lives," because so often, the response I'd receive after using the word *beauty* would be something like, "But what do you mean by *beauty*?" After which the person would go on to offer her or his own definition of the word. Maybe something about charisma or spirituality or vague talk of "glow" or, worse, inner beauty. The first few times I heard such a response, I'd sort of inwardly roll my eyes and just wait for the person to finish—yes, of *course*, beauty encompassed more than just looks, I *knew* that, but that wasn't the point of my work. This push for a more holistic definition of beauty reeked of a grab for political correctness or an attempt at seeming deep. I suppose I'd rather be surrounded by people with that mind-set than by people whose concept of beauty was more superficial, but that didn't stop me from privately finding that line of response to be hopelessly canned.

But it kept happening. I tried to find a pattern in the kinds of people who pushed me for a fuller definition of beauty: a quiet but wicked-tongued schoolteacher, a devoutly Christian woman I knew from high school, a personal trainer who'd once flexed his muscles onstage as a bodybuilder, a massage therapist I once shared Thanksgiving with, an earnest Quaker lesbian, a Moroccan expatriate with a brilliant smile, an ex-boyfriend who had an almost magical power to heal my headaches by touch. Some were women, some were men; some were conventionally beautiful, others not necessarily; some were political activists, some watched *Real Housewives* without a hint of apology. At least two of the women had undergone cosmetic surgery; another two had shaved off all their hair at one point, in hopes of discovering what life was like without that particular veil of femininity. There was no pattern among them, beyond the fact that they'd all crossed paths with me. I had to reckon that it *wasn't* a nice bit of bullshit, that it *wasn't* a line, that it *wasn't* an attempt to seem particularly philosophical. As much as many of us might bemoan hallmarks of contemporary American culture that make us seem like a superficial people—the reality TV shows, the quick fixes, the Hot or Not–type websites, the best beach bodies—the truth is, we are a people hungry for a more complete way to consider beauty and what it means.

The investigation of physical beauty can be a route toward examining those larger meanings of beauty—issues that ultimately matter more, something I'm happy to admit even as I'm sitting here writing a book about what's skin-deep. The way I reconcile my focus on the visual, physical side of beauty with my belief that it's often a smoke screen for larger concerns is to look at where the two meet and to follow *that* trail wherever it might lead.

One such trail rests just two tiers away from me in my family tree. My maternal grandmother died when I was eleven, and my memories of her are vague at best. They have a blurred sensation to them—a contrast to so many other, more vivid family memories I have from that age. As an adult, I've come to understand that blurriness as symptomatic of the alcoholism that ultimately killed my grandmother. I'm not sure if I ever saw the woman I called Nanny sober, but it didn't really matter to me as a child. Nanny might slur her words, Nanny might fall down, Nanny might do weird things like take aside the five-year-old me and give me a twenty-dollar bill that my mother would make me return because she knew Nanny couldn't afford it outside of the beery haze that gave her comfort. None of that mattered to me. That was just Nanny. Her disease altered my mother's family—my family—in ways that none of the survivors will ever fully untangle. It never obscured her affection for me.

I knew my grandmother only in the way children know their grandparents; she was more an abstract idea of "grandmother" to me than she was an individual. It wasn't until my twenties that I got to know my other three grandparents as people—a gift from each of them that Nanny was never able to give. I've had to come to know her through a combination of objects and other people's recollections. A brass-jazz record that seemed out of place in my grandparents' small collection would reveal that her favorite vacation was the time she stashed the kids away and went to New Orleans for a long weekend with my grandfather. My mother telling me of the afternoon the two of them took refuge from the stifling Oklahoma heat by holing up in the bedroom and reading poetry. Thin strands of her continue to show up in my own life: My aunt would claim that the fact that I became a writer traces back to Nanny, who had worked on her high school's newspaper, and my mother once expressed surprise when I mentioned I'd ordered a pineapple malt at a diner, as that was my grandmother's favorite.

To know my grandmother, though, I'd have to know her alcoholism. The way I'd pieced it together through the bits I grasped at over the years, I'd learned that she hadn't drunk much during my mother's youth, but by the time my mother's two youngest siblings were teenagers, she was drinking, and heavily. The four children in the family had grown up with two entirely different mothers, it seemed. I heard about a New Year's Eve party my grandparents hosted sometime around 1970, and how that seemed to trigger something previously buried within her. As I understood it, she started drinking at that party—rather, she started drinking differently— and after it, she never stopped.

But as happens with family stories that are told in staccato over a lifetime, that wasn't exactly what happened. My uncle came of age after her disease had set in. One day, well into my thirties, I asked him why my grandmother, as I romantically put it, had "picked up the bottle and never stopped." "It wasn't like that," he said. She'd tried to quit, it turns out; in fact, she'd tried a lot. She had periods of sobriety, even attending support groups. But as is so often the case with a person who has gone past the point of functional alcoholism into the kind of drinking that can kill someone, those periods were never long enough. And then, almost as an afterthought, he told me one more way she'd tried to quit. If she'd gone long enough without drinking, she'd give herself a reward: She'd take herself to the beauty parlor and have her hair done.

When I think of the excruciating hours that my grandmother endured after making the decision of sobriety—*maybe this time it would work*—I picture my able-bodied Nanny walking much like a newborn calf, legs trembling, step unsure, working tremendously hard just to get out of bed. Perhaps she wouldn't even have enough in her to put on a clean nightgown, as every molecule of energy she had was devoted to the exquisite waiting of sobriety, waiting until one day had gone by without a drink—one day at a time—only to wake up again the next morning and realize that those legs were just as shaky as they had been the day before. I picture her on those endless days, wearing the psychic nakedness of a person recalibrating her relationship to the world around her, marking time through anything that allowed her to know that time had indeed passed: the sunlight moving from one side of the kitchen to the other, the coffee going cold. I picture her forging a shaky scaffolding built of painstaking minutes and hours, a scaffolding that had crumbled once and that would crumble again and again, but maybe not today.

And then—then I picture her on the days when her head was held a little higher, her hope sailing with a bit more billow. I picture her dialing the number for her hairdresser and asking for a noon appointment; I picture her walking into the salon and being greeted by name; I picture her receiving the care of a half friend/half stranger, her hair being shampooed, the curlers placed. I picture her looking in the mirror and seeing not only the middle-age woman she was but also a pretty, dark-haired young woman with cat's-eye glasses, a victory roll, and all the world ahead of her. I picture her sitting under one of those over-the-head hair dryers and reading something like *Life* magazine. I picture the reward of an afternoon spent alone, or near alone, in contrast to a lifetime spent caring for others, a lifetime spent amid a bevy of siblings and, later, children. Being surrounded all the time by family can be a slow, loving torture for someone as introverted as she was. An afternoon of solitude, for her, was self-care.

I don't want to overlook what one could easily take as the moral of this story: This particular reward—and all of her rewards, for there were others—wasn't ultimately enough for her to stop drinking. She died in her mid-fifties; her liver was done. It isn't a neat story or a tale of redemption or a heartwarming yarn on which to end a book about beauty. But for me, its ending isn't what matters. What matters to me is what went through her mind as she performed the crude psychic striptease that even temporary sobriety requires for the late-stage alcoholic. She could have reached for any number of things as her self-given reward—a new scarf, an afternoon spent reading the poetry she so loved, one of those pineapple malts. She chose beauty. The power of beauty and self-care didn't keep her from self-destruction. *But she believed it might.*

You could take from this that beauty is ultimately a mockery of true self-care, or you could take from this that the power of beauty is its potent promise. I don't draw conclusions about my grandmother's failed attempts at sobriety from this one morsel of information. And if the focus on the tangible aspects of beauty is a smoke screen for the larger concerns for our lives, that still leaves me unsatisfied. It doesn't provide answers to the riddles of my grandmother's addiction. All it does is pave a tender, meandering route toward the most vulnerable aspects of her interior life. It is not the end point; it is not the key. That doesn't make it any less valuable to me.

One of the most succinct definitions of physical beauty I've heard was something like this: *I know something is beautiful if I want to keep looking at it*. In other words, beauty is fascination—and fascination of any sort is the quickest route to engagement or flow or whatever you want to call that state of not thinking but of *being*. Take the glee of beauty, and take its malcontents too—and when those moments of dissatisfaction arise, I urge you to see them in the larger vision of your life. Both the joys and pains of pursuing beauty hold the potential for something more lasting. Finding a great lipstick is a treasure that's doubled when a potential new friend comments on it; a feeling of hopelessness upon looking in the mirror can be an alert to a more pressing concern that your energies would be better spent addressing.

For those of us who are intrigued by beauty and the way it intersects with our lives, my hope is that we can take that fascination and use it as a portal to a larger enthrallment, not as a spectacle to be cordoned off and simply seen. Beauty is just the entryway to a more lasting place of enchantment. Which doors you open are up to you.

Acknowledgments

No BOOK IS WRITTEN alone, and this one is no exception. Thank you to Brandi Bowles of Foundry Literary + Media, who has been not only an excellent agent but also an advocate and trusted adviser throughout the entire conception and execution of this book. I was fortunate to benefit from a small coterie of editors at Simon & Schuster. Molly Lindley acquired the book and held my hand through its first draft, and I am forever grateful for her guidance, and for the opportunity she afforded me. Sydney Tanigawa skillfully shepherded the manuscript through a revision. Senior editor Karyn Marcus expertly saw it through to completion, along with publishing assistant Megan Hogan, whose editorial eye and steadfast handling of this first-time author is enormously appreciated. Thank you to the entire Simon & Schuster team who worked on *Face Value*: Jonathan Karp, Cary Goldstein, Clarissa Marzán, Amanda Lang, Richard Rhorer, Ebony LaDelle, Kristen Lemire, Allison Har-zvi, Beth Maglione, Ellen Sasahara, Jackie Seow, Julia Prosser, and Alison Forner. Senior production editor Christine Masters and copy editor Stephanie Evans are a copy dream team. Megan Beatie of Megan Beatie Communications has been invaluable in putting *Face Value* into the world; I'm fortunate to have a publicist who "gets it."

There are too many people in my life who have influenced me in some way to name here. A woefully incomplete list: Rob Elder, Alexis Tomarken, Jennifer Goldstein, Nicole Kristal, Sarah Szpaichler, Chris O'Brien and his fantastic collection of tiki music, Rich Melo, Mary Duffy, Stacia Jensen, Paige Swartley Christiansen, Christy Upton, Jenny Epel Muller, Sarah Frye

Valencius, Navin at The Rock, Annie Tomlin, Allegra Felter, Kathleen Baxter, Craig Fitzpatrick (and Henry and Audrey too), Abigail Pesta, Michael Matassa, Lori Katzin, Rachel Aydt, "Weedy Sea Dragon," Tim Heffernan, Lisa Ferber, Eden Di Bianco, Chris Lukasik, Tara Roberts, Mary Dixon, Josh Weinstein, Megan Cahn, Sarah Kilkenny (to whom I owe a pedicure), Anne Voorhees, Rob Williams, Leah Zibulsky, and Andrew Loughnane. Erin McCaffrey Nenadich is as generous as she is skilled. Geraldine Sealey and Bradley Rife were the first people to tell me that I could write not just a book, but this book.

Thank you to my trusted core of chapter readers, who also happen to be top-notch friends: Mary Potts Howard, Lindsay Goldwert, and Jennifer Stewart (whose suggestion, which I scribbled on a folded scrap of paper while sitting on her couch one Friday night, became the title of this book).

Jennifer Hawthorne supported me in crucial ways by being a blessedly flexible manager at Rodale; without her I wouldn't have been able to focus on my work in the ways I have. Janet Owens taught me the fundamentals of writing, and Marc Herring taught me that unless I learned to think, any writing skill I might possess would be useless.

I'm thankful to the entire *The New Inquiry* team, particularly Sarah Leonard, the inimitable Rachel Rosenfelt, and Malcolm Harris, who suggested I come on board in the first place. And without the support, intellectual guidance, patience, perpetual faith in my abilities, and generous library policy of Rob Horning, this book, quite simply, would not exist. I owe him tremendously.

The best part of writing *The Beheld*, the blog that led to this book, has been the people it has enabled me to connect with, many of whom had a direct impact on this book. Caitlin Constantine, Kjerstin Gruys, Virginia Sole-Smith, Kory Stamper, Virginia Postrel, Phoebe Maltz Bovy, Charlotte Shane, Alana Massey, Kate Fridkis, Mara Glatzel, Lindsay and Lexie Kite, Cristen Conger, Meli Pennington, Danielle Meder, Rebekah Westrum, and Tatiana Christian continually challenge me simply by thinking, creating, and writing in the ways they do. Rachel Hills does the same, and was a valued source of support for me during the entire book process. Sally McGraw is a rock star.

This book largely owes its existence to my New York family. Frankie Morningstar-Plumb and Simon Bonaparte both provided solace and levity. Andrew Plumb's continually out-of-the-box thinking spurred my own, and his willingness to rigorously work through the fuzzier parts of my thinking allowed me to crystallize parts of the manuscript that had been troubling me for months. Cameo Morningstar played a number of roles in my life during the writing of this book: reader, editor, chauffeur, personal trainer, publicist, cheerleader, co-conspirator, wine expert, witch, sister, muse, friend. Her imprint is all over these pages, and they are better for it, as I am better for knowing her. And I will honor the ways of Zack Katzin—a man of few words—by simply saying that his world-class sandwiches fueled my brain through the writing of this book, and that his unflagging belief in me carried me through times when my own belief sagged. As a writer, I could not ask for a more supportive partner. If I harbor any "positive illusions" surrounding our life together, I'll happily keep them.

My family of origin: My uncles, Dave Killam, Joe Madrano, Michael Coleman, and Kent Whitefield, have supported me with a combination of curiosity, reading suggestions, and software. Each of my aunts— Marsha Killam, Devota Madrano, Michele Whitefield, and Tricia White- field Coleman—has taught me something distinct about beauty through my life, and each of them is on these pages in some way. A particular thanks to Kent, Michele, and Trish for giving me their blessing to write about Patricia Gaskill Whitefield, my maternal grandmother, whose story is more theirs to share than mine. My paternal grandmother, Jacqueline Madrano, remains fundamental to my understanding of beauty, and the many hours I passed "playing makeup" at her vanity are paying off here. I'm grateful to my brother, Noah Whitefield-Madrano, for his confidence in my abilities, for sharing the writer gene with me, and for simply being who he is. My parents, Dan Madrano and Deborah Whitefield, have given me an invaluable gift since day one: support so innate that I've never even thought to question its existence. Without that bedrock, I wouldn't have begun to think about writing a book, let alone followed through. *Thank you* doesn't come close to expressing my appreciation, but those words are the clearest ones I have. *Thank you.*

Most of all, though, my gratitude is with the women who have shared their stories about beauty with me, both before this book was ever conceived and during its creation. You shared your tenderness with me, which has been a treasure, both as a writer and a person. Humbly, gratefully, thank you.

Notes

Introduction: Beyond the Beauty Myth

6   *hearing from women all across the Eastern Bloc:* Slavenka Drakulić, *How We Survived Communism and Even Laughed* (New York: HarperPerennial, 1993), 31.

1: The Pencil Test

12   *"Influence on Smile Attractiveness":* Burçak Kaya and Ruzin Uyar, "Influence on Smile Attractiveness of the Smile Arc in Conjunction with Gingival Display," *American Journal of Orthodontics and Dentofacial Orthopedics* 144 (2013): 541.

12   *"Facial Beauty in Personnel":* Nese Caki and Betul Solmaz, "The Effects of Facial Beauty in Personnel Selection: A Field Work in Retail Sector," *Procedia: Social and Behavioral Sciences* 84 (2013): 1203.

12   *"Individual Differences in Perceived Facial":* Oshin Vartanian, Vinod Goel, Elaine Lam, Maryanne Fisher, and Josipa Granic, "Middle Temporal Gyrus Encodes Individual Differences in Perceived Facial Attractiveness," *Psychology of Aesthetics, Creativity, and the Arts* 7 (2013): 38.

13   Survival of the Prettiest: Nancy Etcoff, *Survival of the Prettiest: The Science of Beauty* (New York: Doubleday, 1999).

14   *"[O]ur thoughts and our behaviors":* Ibid., 24.

14   *"Not only was I not close to the ideal":* Author interview on background, November 11, 2012.

14   *"I calculated my ratio in college":* Author interview on background, March 4, 2013.

15   *"symmetry does not solely determine perceived attractiveness":* Judith H. Langlois, Lori A. Roggman, and Lisa Musselman, "What Is Average and What Is Not Average about Attractive Faces?" *Psychological Science* 5 (1994): 214–20.

15   *opposite a piece about blood banks for vampires:* Susan Jimison, "Men Marry Women for Their Hips!"; Aurelia Oencea, "Blood Banks for Us, Too! Demands Lady Vampire," *Weekly World News*, November 30, 1993.

15 *"academic urban legend"*: Jeremy Freese and Sheri Meland, "Seven Tenths Incorrect: Heterogeneity and Change in the Waist-to-Hip Ratios of *Playboy* Centerfold Models and Miss America Pageant Winners," *The Journal of Sex Research* 39 (2002): 133.

16 *also found results contrary to the original report:* M. Voracek and M. L. Fisher, "Shapely Centerfolds? Temporal Change in Body Measures: Trend Analysis," *BMJ: British Medical Journal* 325 (2002): 21.

16 *mattered more to men than waist-hip ratio:* L. G. Tassinary and K. A. Hansen, "A Critical Test of the Waist-to-Hip Ratio Hypothesis of Female Physical Attractiveness," *Psychological Science* 9 (1998): 150.

16 *A headline from* Glamour's *website:* Erin Meanley, "Dressing for Men? Avoid the Empire Waist," *Glamour* (blog), last modified September 24, 2008, accessed January 30, 2014, http://www.glamour.com/sex-love-life/blogs/single-ish/2008/09/dressing-for-men-avoid-the-emp.html.

17 *more face-like because of their regularity:* I. Penton-Voak and D. I. Perrett, "Consistency and Individual Differences in Facial Attractiveness Judgements: An Evolutionary Perspective," *Social Research* 67 (2000): 219.

17 *features close to the mean size of populations studied:* J. Pollard, J. Shepherd, and J. Shepherd, "Average Faces Are Average Faces," *Current Psychology* 18 (1999): 98.

17 *might gravitate toward a more baby-faced man:* I. Penton-Voak and D. I. Perrett, "Female Preference for Male Faces Changes Cyclically: Further Evidence," *Evolution and Human Behavior* 21 (2000): 39.

17 *analyzing five earlier studies measuring the impact of looks:* Daniel Hamermesh, *Beauty Pays* (Princeton, NJ: Princeton University Press, 2011).

18 *composite face may be appealing because it is* familiar: Langlois, Roggman, and Musselman, "What Is Average": 214–20.

18 *change their ratings after seeing . . . peers' estimation:* J. Zaki, J. Schirmer, and J. P. Mitchell, "Social Influence Modulates the Neural Computation of Value," *Psychological Science* 22 (2011): 894.

19 *perceived health and attractiveness far outweighed the actual connection:* S. M. Kalick, L. A. Zebrowitz, J. H. Langlois, and R. M. Johnson, "Does Human Facial Attractiveness Honestly Advertise Health? Longitudinal Data on an Evolutionary Question," *Psychological Science* 9 (1998): 8.

20 *Dr. Satoshi Kanazawa of the London School of Economics:* Khadijah Britton, "The Data Are in Regarding Satoshi Kanazawa," *Scientific American* (blog), last modified May 23, 2011, accessed October 9, 2012, http://blogs.scientificamerican.com/guest-blog/the-data-are-in-regarding-satoshi-kanazawa.

20 *The student union called for his dismissal:* Ian Sample, "LSE Academic's Claim 'Black Women Less Attractive' Triggers Race Row," *The Guardian*, May 19, 2011.

20   *He was let go from* Psychology Today: "Psychology Today Agrees to Remove
     Controversial Author Satoshi Kanazawa from Website," ColorOfChange.org,
     last modified June 1, 2011, accessed October 10, 2012, http://colorofchange.org
     /press/releases/2011/6/1/psychology-today-agrees-to-remove-controversial-au.

20   *temporarily banned by his employer:* "Dr Satoshi Kanazawa—Findings of Internal
     Review and Disciplinary Hearing," London School of Economics, last modified
     September 14, 2011, accessed October 10, 2012, http://www.lse.ac.uk/news
     AndMedia/news/archives/2011/09/Kanazawa.aspx.

20   *"may have been flawed" . . . "political correctness":* Ibid.

21   *"At one point, evolutionary psychologists":* David Perrett, interview by author, Oc-
     tober 19, 2012.

21   *his own book on the science of attraction:* David Perrett, *In Your Face: The New Sci-
     ence of Human Attraction* (Basingstoke: Palgrave Macmillan, 2010).

21   *She's quick to point out that there's evolutionary psychology:* Kathryn Clancy, inter-
     view by author, February 21, 2013.

23   *moderate cosmetics use makes women appear more likable:* Nancy L. Etcoff, Shan-
     non Stock, Lauren E. Haley, Sarah A. Vickery, and David M. House, "Cosmetics
     As a Feature of the Extended Human Phenotype: Modulation of the Perception
     of Biologically Important Facial Signals," *Plos One* (October 3, 2011).

23   *women's eyes and lips are darker than men's:* Richard Russell, "A Sex Difference
     in Facial Contrast and Its Exaggeration by Cosmetics," *Perception* 38 (2009):
     1211.

24   *"Can Being Attractive Make You Bad at Math?":* Marci Robin, "Can Being At-
     tractive Make You Bad at Math?" *NewBeauty* (blog), last modified February 11,
     2011, accessed August 29, 2012, http://www.newbeauty.com/blog/dailybeauty
     /4336-can-being-attractive-make-you-bad-at-math/.

24   *"Are Good Looks Problematic for Women?":* Rick Nauert, "Are Good Looks Prob-
     lematic for Women?" *Psych Central*, last modified February 7, 2011, accessed
     October 14, 2012, http://psychcentral.com/news/2011/02/07/are-good
     -looks-problematic-for-women/23225.html.

25   *"More Beautiful Than Most? Your Higher Salary Makes You Happier":* "More Beau-
     tiful Than Most? Your Higher Salary Makes You Happier," *Psych Central*, last
     modified March 31, 2011, accessed October 14, 2012, http://psychcentral.com
     /news/2011/03/31/more-beautiful-than-most-your-higher-salary-makes-you
     -happier/24894.html.

25   *the study established a correlation, not causation:* Daniel S. Hamermesh and Jason
     Abrevaya, "Beauty Is the Promise of Happiness?" NBER Working Paper No.
     17327 (The National Bureau of Economic Research, NBER Papers in Labor
     Studies, August 2011).

25 *"Beauty and Its Neural Reward Are in the Eye of the Crowd"*: Christian Jarrett, "Beauty and Its Neural Reward Are in the Eyes of the Crowd," *British Psychological Society,* last modified March 4, 2011, accessed October 14, 2012, http://bps-research-digest.blogspot.com/2011/03/beauty-and-its-neural-reward-are-in-eye.html.

25 *the study was about how the brain calculates* value: Zaki, Schirmer, and Mitchell, "Social Influence": 894.

25 *"A Perfect Body? Women Would Swap a Year of Life"*: Jo Willey, "A Perfect Body? Women Would Swap a Year of Life," *Express,* last modified March 31, 2011, accessed October 14, 2012, http://www.express.co.uk/news/uk/237783/A-perfect-body-Women-would-swap-a-year-of-life.

25 *more than two-thirds of women in the survey*: Phillippa Diedrichs, Nicole Paraskeva, and Alice New, "The Succeed Foundation Body Image Survey" (University of the West of England for The Succeed Foundation, March 24, 2011).

25 *gave a 2008 lecture*: David Brown, "What's Wrong (and Right) with Science Journalism" (lecture, University of Iowa, October 8, 2008), *The American Scholar,* last modified September 1, 2009, accessed October 18, 2012, http://theamericanscholar.org/science-reporting-and-evidence-based-journalism/.

25 *"But for science writing . . . makes an anecdote evidence"*: Ibid.

26 *"Meeting eyebrows, held so beautiful by the Arabs"*: Johann Kaspar Lavater, *Essays on Physiognomy* (London: B. Blake, 1840), 389. It's an amusing read, for gems like his pronouncement that "From the hair alone we may know the man" and his eight rules of stupidity: "Every countenance is stupid in which the eyes are discernibly more distant from each other than the breadth of an eye."

27 *"We . . . suspect the WHR"*: Tassinary and Hansen, "A Critical Test," 155.

27 *three of the Big Five in personality testing*: S. Penton-Voak, N. Pound, A. C. Little, and D. I. Perrett, "Personality Judgments from Natural and Composite Facial Images: More Evidence for a 'Kernel of Truth' in Social Perception," *Social Cognition* 24 (2006): 607. The study's title is a clue to its conclusion: There is indeed evidence that there's a "kernel of truth" behind the idea that we can accurately assess people's character by their face. People were able to perceive personality by photos with above-chance accuracy, but the accuracy is low nonetheless.

27 *study looked at how desire for certain personality traits*: A. C. Little, D. M. Burth, and D. I. Perrett, "What Is Good Is Beautiful: Face Preference Reflects Desired Personality," *Personality and Individual Differences* 41 (2006): 1107.

28 *Galton started collecting and merging photographs*: Francis Galton, "Composite Portraits Made by Combining Those of Many Different Persons into a Single Figure," *Nature* 18 (1878): 97–100.

28   *Galton coined the word* eugenics: Francis Galton, "Eugenics: Its Definition, Scope, and Aims," *The American Journal of Sociology* 10 (July 1904).

28   *categorization of people has a historic link to eugenics:* Rebecca L. Davis, *More Perfect Unions: The American Search for Marital Bliss* (Cambridge, MA: Harvard University Press, 2010).

28   *eugenics-minded competition . . . emphasized familial pedigrees:* Daylanne K. English, *Unnatural Selections: Eugenics in American Modernism and the Harlem Renaissance* (Chapel Hill, NC: The University of North Carolina Press, 2004). For more on this bit of history and its implications, see Lili Loofbourow's work at http://millicentandcarlafran.wordpress.com/2010/05/18/miss-usa-why -beauty-pageants-matter-again.

28   *another group of specially selected citizens:* "Nazi Racial Science," United States Holocaust Memorial Museum website, accessed January 4, 2013, http://www .ushmm.org/research/research-in-collections/search-the-collections/bibliography /nazi-racial-science.

31   *"In our culture . . . There's a desire to quantify your appeal":* Charlotte Shane, interview by author, March 30, 2011.

33   *"My tastes are different than what's thrown at me":* Author interview on background, November 11, 2013.

33   *"Beauty can be looked at rationally":* David Perrett, interview by author, October 19, 2012.

2: Hotties, Foxes, and Cankles

40   *"In this changing world, the 'sweet girl' ":* Harper's Bazaar, July 1936; *Nursing World* 97 (1936).

40   *Bella was the 58th most popular baby name . . . Beau, 270th for boys:* "Top 10 Baby Names for 2013," Social Security Administration, accessed February 12, 2014, http://www.ssa.gov/OACT/babynames/.

40   *A partial offering of girls' names . . . Cullen:* Baby Center database, accessed February 2014, http://www.babycenter.com/baby-names.

41   *"The beauty department is the only place":* Author interview on background, January 28, 2011.

41   *it can become an all-encompassing label:* Another way that job titles reflect the way we see beauty: With smaller post-recession magazine staffs comes job collapse, and the tasks of beauty editor and health editor often wind up going to one person. The fact that it's beauty and health that often become conflated and not, say, beauty and fashion, is telling in regard to the mainstream view toward women's health.

42 handsome *was used as a compliment for both sexes:* John Trusler, *The Distinction between Words Esteemed Synonymous in the English Language, Pointed Out, and the Proper Choice of Them Determined* (London: self-published, 1783).

43 *A study of personal ads revealed that 45 percent of straight women:* Celia Shalom, "That Great Supermarket of Desire: Attributes of the Desired Other in Personal Advertisements," in *Language and Desire: Encoding Sex, Romance, and Intimacy,* ed. Keith Harvey and Celia Shalom (New York: Routledge, 1997).

43 *"We all like to think we are attractive":* Ibid., 199.

43 *"its use to describe a woman implies":* Ibid., 201.

45 *the most frequent configuration:* R. K. Herbert, "Sex-Based Differences in Compliment Behavior," *Language in Society* 19 (1990): 201.

45 *Women use more words than men do when issuing a compliment:* Ibid.

46 *what language researchers call "comment history":* Ibid.

46 *treat compliments from other women as gateways:* Janie Rees-Miller, "Compliments Revisited: Contemporary Compliments and Gender," *Journal of Pragmatics* 43, no. 11 (September 2011): 2673–2688.

47 *happens only 10 percent of the time:* Herbert, "Sex-Based Differences in Compliment Behavior."

48 *a whopping 66 percent of the time:* Ibid.

49 *Hochschild terms the "emotion work":* Arlie Hochschild, *The Managed Heart* (Berkeley: University of California Press, 1983).

49 *" 'You look nice' or 'you look pretty' just don't cut it":* Author questionnaire on background, March 17, 2012.

50 *women are likelier to notice . . . compliments from partners:* A. M. Doohan and V. Manusov, "The Communication of Compliments in Romantic Relationships: An Investigation of Relational Satisfaction and Sex Differences and Similarities in Compliment Behavior," *Western Journal of Communication* 68 (2004): 170. Interestingly, Doohan and Manusov found that the number-one topic of compliments reported between partners was neither appearance nor skill but emotions (such as "You make me feel amazing"). In other words, the number-one way people said their partners complimented them wasn't technically with a compliment at all.

51 *"[Y]ou only need a euphemism if you find the truth distasteful":* Marilyn Wann, *FAT! SO?: Because You Don't Have to Apologize for Your Size* (Berkeley: Ten Speed Press, 1998), 20.

51 FUPA: Fat upper pussy area. You're welcome.

51 Love handles, *a term that originated around 1970:* Merriam-Webster Unabridged, s.v. "love handles," accessed February 8, 2013, http://unabridged.merriam -webster.com/unabridged/love%20handles.

52 *"His girlfriend grabbed the rolls around his middle"*: Neil Solomon, *Dr. Solomon's Easy, No-Risk Diet* (New York: Coward, McCann & Geoghegan, 1974), 26.

53 *"We have terms like* sexual harassment*"*: Gloria Steinem, "Words and Change," *Outrageous Acts and Everyday Rebellions* (New York: Holt, Rinehart and Winston, 1983), 149.

54 *Before the UK's Sex Discrimination Act . . . describe the office environment:* Chris Kennedy, " *'La Crème de la Crème'*: Coercion and Corpus Change—An Example from Recruitment Advertisements," in *Change and Language: Papers from the Annual Meeting of the British Association for Applied Linguistics*, ed. Hywel Coleman and Lynne Cameron (Clevedon, UK: The British Association for Applied Linguistics in association with Multilingual Matters Ltd., 1994). Recruiters showed a perhaps unwitting consciousness of the ways they sought good-looking candidates. An ad placed just before the law took effect reads, ". . . this is my last, last advertisement on behalf of other male chauvinist pigs, for 'attractive, elegant, charming, and intelligent career girls . . .' "

55 *painting the word* Gilda *on the side of it:* Jane Caputi, *The Age of Sex Crime* (Bowling Green, OH: Bowling Green University Popular Press, 1987).

55 *Russia used to regard its word for beauty . . . can be bought and sold:* I. Belyakova, "Transformations in the Lexical Field of Beauty in the Russian Language As a Result of Westernization of Russian Culture" (lecture, 4th Annual International Conference on Literature, Languages & Linguistics, Athens, Greece, July 2011).

55 f-bomb *was first included in* Merriam-Webster *in 2012:* Mark Memmott, " 'F-Bomb' Added to Dictionary," *The Two-Way*, National Public Radio, August 14, 2012, accessed February 25, 2013, http://www.npr.org/sections/thetwo-way/2012/08/14/158749187/f-bomb-added-to-dictionary.

56 *one of the newest appearance-centric words:* Kory Stamper, interview by author, February 25, 2013.

56 *"Since the second wave":* Ibid.

58 *the annual "No Fat Talk" week initiated by the Tri Delta sorority:* Olivia M. Smith, "Campaign Targets 'Fat Talk,' Negative Body Images," CNN, last modified October 21, 2010, accessed September 14, 2015, http://www.cnn.com/2010/LIVING/10/21/no.fat.talk.week.

3: Lipstick Isn't Cubist

61 *not all women wear makeup (though the majority in America do):* Global Industry Analysts, Inc., *Color Cosmetics—A Global Strategic Business Report* (San Jose, California, April 2010).

61 *seventy women answer questions about their makeup usage:* Rodolphe Korichi, Del-

phine Pelle-de-Queral, Germaine Gazano, and Arnaud Aubert, "Why Women Wear Makeup: Implication of Psychological Traits in Makeup Functions," *Journal of Cosmetic Science* 59 (2008): 127.

61   *they fell into three groups:* Ibid.

62   *valued themselves and their makeup was reflected:* Ibid.

63   *Women are consistently rated as more attractive:* R. Mulhern, G. Fieldman, T. Hussey, J. L. Lévêque, and P. Pineau, "Do Cosmetics Enhance Female Caucasian Facial Attractiveness?" *International Journal of Cosmetic Science* 25 (2003): 199.

63   *"Wearing makeup allows me to look":* Author questionnaire on background, June 28, 2013.

63   *"I like the ritual":* Author questionnaire on background, June 25, 2013.

63   *"I never got in the habit of it":* Author questionnaire on background, November 19, 2011.

64   *"I'm an actress at heart":* Author interview on background, June 27, 2013.

64   *"Like chugging a Red Bull":* Author questionnaire on background, June 25, 2013.

64   *women report feeling more self-confident when wearing makeup:* Thomas F. Cash and Diane Walker Cash, "Women's Use of Cosmetics: Psychosocial Correlates and Consequences," *International Journal of Cosmetic Science* 4 (1982): 1.

64   *"Yes, I've tried that stuff that 'feels like nothing' ":* Author questionnaire, November 19, 2011.

64   *women who were wearing makeup had lower signs of physiological stress:* Rodolphe Korichi, Delphine Pelle-de-Queral, Claire Delmas, Francis Vial, Germaine Gazano, and Arnaud Aubert, "Does Facial Makeup Regulates [sic] Emotions in Stressful Situations? Psychological, Behavioural and Physiological Approaches," *Integration of Cosmetic Sciences* 25 (2008).

65   *"I use [makeup] to show the world who I truly am":* "MY CONFESSION + How I Use Makeup to Blend In to Stand Out! Cassandra Bankson & Dermablend," YouTube video, 2:04, Dermablend Professional: Camo Confessions, posted by "Cassandra Bankson," March 10, 2014, accessed August 13, 2014, https://www.youtube.com/watch?v=_kds9UHseOk.

65   *makeup can make* other *people see its wearer as more confident:* Rebecca Nash, George Fieldman, Trevor Hussey, Jean-Luc Lévêque, and Patricia Pineau, "Cosmetics: They Influence More than Caucasian Female Facial Attractiveness," *Journal of Applied Social Psychology* 36 (2006): 493. Participants were also perceived to be healthier and to have more earning potential than women without makeup.

65   *It can also drive others to find her more competent:* Juliette Richetin, Jean-Claude Croizet, and Pascal Huguet, "Facial Make-Up Elicits Positive Attitudes at the Implicit Level: Evidence from the Implicit Association Test," *Current Research in Social Psychology* 9 (2004): 145.

65   *she's approached more frequently by men:* Nicolas Guéguen, "Brief Report: The Effects of Women's Cosmetics on Men's Approach: An Evaluation in a Bar," *North American Journal of Psychology* 10 (2008): 221.

65   *she may get more tips from her male customers:* Céline Jacob, Nicolas Guéguen, Gaëlle Boulbry, and Renzo Ardiccioni, "Waitresses' Facial Cosmetics and Tipping: A Field Experiment," *International Journal of Hospitality Management* 29 (2010): 188.

65   *People exposed to pictures of makeup-wearing women:* P. Pössel, S. Ahrens, and M. Hautzinger, "Influence of Cosmetics on Emotional, Autonomous, Endocrinological, and Immune Reactions," *International Journal of Cosmetic Science* 27 (2005): 343.

66   *Some Latina women may have a particularly good grasp of this:* Rosie Molinary, interview by author, September 23, 2011.

66   *"Wearing my hair textured":* Author interview on background, June 6, 2013.

66   *"I don't like the idea that my hair is political":* Britt Julious, "We Are Not Our Hair," WBEZ 91.5 blog, last modified April 3, 2013, accessed July 12, 2014, http://www.wbez.org/blogs/britt-julious/2013-04/we-are-not-our-hair-106452.

67   *"I wear [makeup] every day":* Author interview on background, June 7, 2015.

67   *"A new haircut is a butch accessory":* Kelli Dunham, interview by author, February 16, 2011.

67   *"I want to do what women do":* Author questionnaire on background, June 25, 2013.

68   *Women's pupils are slightly larger than men's:* Juan A. Sanchis-Gimeno, Daniel Sanchez-Zuriaga, and Francisco Martinez-Soriano, "White-to-White Corneal Diameter, Pupil Diameter, Central Corneal Thickness and Thinnest Corneal Thickness Values of Emmetropic Subjects," *Surgical and Radiologic Anatomy* 34 (2012): 167.

68   *skin that's a shade lighter than that of their male counterparts:* Richard Russell, "A Sex Difference in Facial Contrast and Its Exaggeration by Cosmetics," *Perception* 38, no. 8: 1211–1219.

68   *Never mind that men don't actually find reddish labia more alluring:* Sarah E. Johns, Lucy A. Hargrave, and Nicholas E. Newton-Fisher, "Red Is Not a Proxy Signal for Female Genitalia in Humans," *Plos One* (April 6, 2012).

69   *Desmond Morris theorized the connection:* Desmond Morris, *The Naked Ape: A Zoologist's Study of the Human Animal* (New York: Dell Publishing, 1967).

69   *"Match your lipstick to the color of your labia":* Sleeping Beauty, directed by Julia Leigh (2011, DVD).

69   *ovulating women wore more makeup:* Nicolas Guéguen, "Makeup and Menstrual Cycle: Near Ovulation, Women Use More Cosmetics," *Psychological Record* 62 (2012): 541. Participants also reported spending more than two additional minutes applying cosmetics than they did when not ovulating, and to positive effect: Makeup artists judged that ovulating women did a better job of putting on makeup than the same women did when not ovulating.

69   *men have been shown to be quicker to approach makeup-wearing women:* Guéguen, "Brief Report."

70   *women's heads tend to be larger in proportion to the neck:* Anita N. Vasavada, Jonathan Danaraj, and Gunter P. Siegmund, "Head and Neck Anthropometry, Vertebral Geometry and Neck Strength in Height-Matched Men and Women," *Journal of Biomechanics* 41 (2008): 114.

71   *men* did *do more of that peacocking than most do today:* Robert Ross, *Clothing: A Global History* (Cambridge, UK: Polity, 2008).

71   *a projected $265 billion: Global Beauty Care Products Industry 2012–2017: Trend, Profit, and Forecast Analysis, September 2012* (Birmingham, UK: Market Publishers, September 1, 2012).

73   *"[A] given social front tends to become institutionalized":* Erving Goffman, *The Presentation of Self in Everyday Life* (New York: Doubleday Anchor, 1959), 27.

74   *indeed Miss Manners herself:* Judith Martin, *Miss Manners' Guide to Excruciatingly Correct Behavior (Freshly Updated)* (New York: W.W. Norton & Company, 2005).

74   *A "dark secret," in Goffman's terms:* Goffman, *The Presentation of Self*, 125.

74   *"[A] team whose vital secrets are possessed":* Ibid., 143.

75   *in 2015 the New York City transportation system ran a series:* "Clipping? Primping?" MTA website, accessed July 9, 2015, http://web.mta.info/nyct/service /CourtesyCounts.htm#CLIPPING?PRIMPING?.

75   *"I'm the one who puts it on every day":* Author interview on background, November 6, 2011.

75   *"does not present* herself": Simone de Beauvoir, *The Second Sex* (New York: Bantam, 1970), 502.

76   *cosmetics can decrease heart rate, calm the nervous system:* S. Barkat, T. Thomas-Danguin, M. Bensail, M. Rouby, and G. Sicard, "Odor and Color of Cosmetic Products: Correlations between Subjective Judgments and Autonomous Nervous System Response," *International Journal of Cosmetic Science* 25 (2003): 273.

76   *increase the ability to feel pleasure:* A. Abriat, S. Barkat, M. Bensafi, C. Rouby, and C. Fanchon, "Psychological and Physiological Evaluation of Emotional Effects of a Perfume in Menopausal Women," *International Journal of Cosmetic Science* 29 (2007): 399.

76   *barely wore makeup during her stints . . . "the world treats me differently":* Miyoko Hikiji, interview by author, June 13, 2013.

78   *Baker Hyde's yearlong cosmetics-free experiment:* Phoebe Baker Hyde, *The Beauty Experiment: How I Skipped Lipstick, Ditched Fashion, Faced the World Without Concealer, and Learned to Love the Real Me* (Boston: Da Capo, 2012).

78   *Rachel Rabbit White's "No Make-Up Week":* Rachel Rabbit White, "No Make-Up Week," *Rachel Rabbit White* (blog), last modified September 2010, accessed October 21, 2011, http://www.rachelrabbitwhite.com/projects/no-make-up-week.

78 *Women's self-esteem is shown to be consistently lower than men's:* Daniel Clay, Vivian L. Vignoles, and Helga Dittmar, "Body Image and Self-Esteem Among Adolescent Girls: Testing the Influence of Sociocultural Factors," *Journal of Research on Adolescence* 15 (2005): 451.

78 *the same age when body consciousness begins:* A. Feingold and R. Mazella, "Gender Differences in Body Image Are Increasing," *Psychological Science* 9 (1998): 190.

78 *"I guess you could call it insecurity":* Author questionnaire on background, June 25, 2013.

79 *"14 Women Tell Us Why They Wear Makeup":* Augusta Falletta, "14 Women Tell Us Why They Wear Makeup," *Buzzfeed,* last modified March 26, 2015, accessed April 4, 2015, http://www.buzzfeed.com/augustafalletta/stop-saying-women -wear-makeup-to-get-dudes#.yhReDG8m29.

79 *"It's fun in the same little-girl way":* Author questionnaire on background, June 25, 2013.

79 *were instructed in skillful makeup application:* Victoria Sherrow, *For Appearance' Sake: The Historical Encyclopedia of Good Looks, Beauty, and Grooming* (Westport: Greenwood, 2001).

79 *Darlene Jespersen was fired . . . sided with Harrah's:* Jespersen v. Harrah Operating Company, 444 F.3d 1104 (9th Cir. 2006).

80 *Melanie Stark, who worked in the music department:* Caroline Davies, "Harrods 'Ladies' Code' Drives Out Sales Assistant," *The Guardian,* July 1, 2011.

80 *women report feeling more self-confident and more sociable:* Cash and Walker Cash, "Women's Use of Cosmetics."

80 *Their body image is better when they're wearing makeup:* Thomas F. Cash, Kathryn Dawson, Pamela Davis, Maria Bowen, and Chris Galumbeck, "Effects of Cosmetics Use on the Physical Attractiveness and Body Image of American College Women," *The Journal of Social Psychology* 129 (1989): 349.

80 *mood improves on nearly all measures after a visit to the hairdresser:* A. Picot-Lemasson, G. Decocq, F. Aghassian, and J. L. Lévêque, "Influence of Hairdressing on the Psychological Mood of Women," *International Journal of Cosmetic Science* 23 (2001): 161.

80 *heavy makeup wearers have been found to be more pro-feminist:* Thomas F. Cash, "Not Just Another Pretty Face: Sex Roles, Locus and Control of Cosmetics Use," *Personality and Social Psychology Bulletin* 11 (1985): 246.

80 *a decrease in signs of stress after applying cosmetics:* Korichi, Pelle-de-Queral, Delmas, Vial, Gazano, and Aubert, "Does Facial Makeup Regulates [sic] Emotions."

81 *"Whenever you find that you are on the side of the majority":* Mark Twain, *The Wit and Wisdom of Mark Twain,* ed. Bob Blaisdell (Mineola, NY: Dover Publications, 2013), 153.

83 No More Dirty Looks: Siobhan O'Connor and Alexandra Spunt, *No More Dirty Looks: The Truth About Your Beauty Products and the Ultimate Guide to Safe and Clean Cosmetics* (New York: Da Capo Lifelong Books, 2010).

84 *"We want you to go wild"*: "The Clean-Makeup Challenge—Join Us!" No More Dirty Looks website, last modified February 21, 2011, accessed February 21, 2011, http://nomoredirtylooks.com/2011/02/the-clean-makeup-challenge -join-us/.

84 *"We had people privately e-mailing"*: Siobhan O'Connor, interview by author, April 30, 2011.

85 *women were judged negatively in occupations that are stereotyped by sex*: Allegra C. Wiles, "More Than Just a Pretty Face: Preventing the Perpetuation of Sexual Stereotypes in the Workplace," *Syracuse Law Review* 57, no. 3 (2007): 657.

87 *US cosmetics industry continues to grow to the point of $58.3 billion*: Simon Pitman, "Contraction of US Cosmetics Industry Set to Rebound by 2014," *Cosmetics Design*, last modified January 13, 2011, accessed November 23, 2015, http:// www.cosmeticsdesign.com/Business-Financial/Contraction-of-US-cosmetics -industry-set-to-rebound-by-2014.

87 *"I'll wear it if I have to"*: Author questionnaire, November 6, 2010.

87 *"It's like, who am I, to think you should look at me?"*: Author questionnaire, February 6, 2011.

4: The Eye of the Beholder

90 *"I'm pretty much attracted to someone or I'm not"*: Author interview on background, February 15, 2014.

93 *Men reported valuing physical attractiveness . . . high earning potential*: D. M. Buss, "Sex Differences in Human Mate Preferences: Evolutionary Hypotheses Tested in 37 Cultures," *Behavioral and Brain Sciences* 12 (1989): 1.

93 *heterosexual women are likelier . . . to gussy themselves up*: Doug P. VanderLaan and Paul L. Vasey, "Mate Retention Behavior of Men and Women in Heterosexual and Homosexual Relationships," *Archives of Sexual Behavior* 37 (2008): 572.

93 *the more conventionally attractive . . . "resource display"*: David M. Buss and Todd K. Shackelford, "From Vigilance to Violence: Mate Retention Tactics in Married Couples," *Journal of Personality and Social Psychology* 72 (1997): 346.

93 *men were likelier to pursue . . . whose profile it was paired with*: Peter Michael Bak, "Sex Differences in the Attractiveness Halo Effect in the Online Dating Environment," *Journal of Business and Media Psychology* 1 (2010): 1.

93 *"I wish I had more time to put into my appearance"*: Author interview on background, June 6, 2013.

94 *researchers found little correlation between people's stated preferences*: P. W. Eastwick and E. J. Finkel, "Sex Differences in Mate Preferences Revisited: Do People Know What They Initially Desire in a Romantic Partner?" *Journal of Personality and Social Psychology* 94 (2008): 245.

95 *Men who meet society's definition of conventionally good-looking:* Alan Feingold, "Matching for Attractiveness in Romantic Partners and Same-Sex Friends: A Meta-Analysis and Theoretical Critique," *Psychological Bulletin* 104 (1988): 226.

95 *as much as we say that opposites attract:* Gian C. Gonzaga, Belinda Campos, and Thomas Bradbury, "Similarity, Convergence, and Relationship Satisfaction in Dating and Married Couples," *Journal of Personality and Social Psychology* 93 (2007): 34.

95 *Theories on why . . . somewhat resemble ourselves:* L. Lee, G. Loewenstein, D. Ariely, J. Hong, and J. Young, "If I'm Not Hot, Are You Hot or Not? Physical Attractiveness Evaluations and Dating Preferences As a Function of One's Own Attractiveness," *Psychological Science* 19 (2008): 669. Weird-looking rock star dudes and supermodels, take heed: The study authors also found that men were less likely than women to be affected by their own conventional attractiveness when pursuing people to date.

95 *people who rate themselves as highly attractive . . . not terrifically attractive:* R. Matthew Montoya, "I'm Hot, so I'd Say You're Not: The Influence of Objective Physical Attractiveness on Mate Selection," *Personality and Social Psychology Bulletin* 34 (2008): 1315.

96 *Men given positive general information:* V. Swami, A. Furnham, T. Chamorro-Premuzic, K. Akbar, N. Gordon, T. Harris, J. Finch, and M. J. Tovée, "More Than Just Skin Deep? Personality Information Influences Men's Ratings of the Attractiveness of Women's Body Sizes," *Journal of Social Psychology* 150 (2010): 628.

96 *rated the subjects of* the exact same photos *as more:* Gary W. Lewandowski Jr., Arthur Aron, and Julie Gee, "Personality Goes a Long Way: The Malleability of Opposite-Sex Physical Attractiveness," *Personal Relationships* 14 (2007): 571.

96 *recorded evidence that this sensation isn't unusual:* Kelly Fudge Albada, Mark L. Knapp, and Katheryn E. Theune, "Interaction Appearance Theory: Changing Perceptions of Physical Attractiveness through Social Interaction," *Communication Theory* 12 (2002): 8.

96 *people with better education . . . objectively good-looking partner:* Julie H. Carmalt, John Cawley, Kara Joyner, and Jeffery Sobal, "Body Weight and Matching with a Physically Attractive Romantic Partner," *Journal of Marriage and Family* 70 (2008): 1287.

98 *think of ourselves as better-than-average drivers:* Iain A. McCormick, Frank H. Walkey, and Dianne E. Green, "Comparative Perceptions of Driver Ability—A Confirmation and Expansion," *Accident Analysis & Prevention* 18 (1986): 205.

99 *75 percent of heterosexual married folks . . . landing at 8.06:* Montoya, "I'm Hot": 1315.

99 *people consistently rate their partners as more attractive than other people do:* Pieternel Barelds-Dijkstra, "Positive Illusions about One's Partner's Physical Attractiveness," *Body Image* 5 (2008): 99.

99 *people in relationships tend to see other people as less attractive:* Simone M. Ritter, Johan C. Karremans, and Hein T. van Schie, "The Role of Self-Regulation in Derogating Attractive Alternatives," *Journal of Experimental Social Psychology* 46 (2010): 631.

99 *committed women* remember *the faces of:* J. C. Karremans, R. Dotsch, and O. Corneille, "Romantic Relationship Status Biases Memory of Faces of Attractive Opposite-Sex Others: Evidence from a Reverse-Correlation Paradigm," *Cognition* 121 (2011): 422.

99 *rated their relationships as more satisfying were likelier:* Ian S. Penton-Voak, Angela C. Rowe, and Jenna Williams, "Through Rose-Tinted Glasses: Relationship Satisfaction and Representations of Partners' Facial Attractiveness," *Journal of Evolutionary Psychology* 5 (2007): 169.

99 *the stronger the illusion . . . longer the pairing is likely to last:* Sandra L. Murray and John G. Holmes, "A Leap of Faith? Positive Illusions in Romantic Relationships," *Personality and Social Psychology Bulletin* 23 (1997): 586.

100 *both men and women engage in positive illusions . . . regardless of how committed they are to the partnership:* F. M. Gagné and J. E. Lydon, "Identification and the Commitment Shift: Accounting for Gender Differences in Relationship Illusions," *Personality and Social Psychology Bulletin* 29 (2003): 907.

100 *lesbians and gay men engage in positive illusions:* Terri D. Conley, Scott C. Roesch, Letitia Anne Peplau, and Michael S. Gold, "A Test of Positive Illusion versus Shared Reality Models of Relationship Satisfaction among Gay, Lesbian, and Heterosexual Couples," *Journal of Applied Social Psychology* 39 (2009): 1417.

100 *women may be likelier than men to derive a sense of identity:* S. E. Cross, M. Morris, and J. S. Gore, "Thinking about Oneself and Others: The Relational-Interdependent Self-Construal and Social Cognition," *Journal of Personality and Social Psychology* 82 (2002): 399.

100 *"I'm sure there are men who hire escorts":* Charlotte Shane, interview by author, March 30, 2011.

101 *men en masse consistently rate women as being better-looking:* Mitja D. Back, et al., "Why Mate Choices Are Not As Reciprocal As We Assume: The Role of Personality, Flirting and Physical Attractiveness," *European Journal of Personality* 25 (2011): 120. The main purpose of this study was actually to find out if the people we're attracted to tend to be attracted to us. Researchers found that though flirting was indeed reciprocal in a speed-dating situation, thus leading participants to believe that attraction was mutual, people actually weren't all that great at picking out people who liked them back. And while men who believed themselves to be good-looking were choosier than other men were, that correlation didn't hold true for women. So much for the idea that women are the picky ones, eh?

101   *"I like to look at them"*: Author interview on background, October 25, 2013.

101   *Lesbian Chic: Appearance and Queer Women*: For this section I've looked specifically at experiences and research particular to queer women, but much of the rest of the chapter should also be seen as being relevant to women who date women. I've tried to be specific in stating "men" where I mean men (men who date women, that is), indicating the orientation of heterosexual women when research findings apply solely to them, and using "people" when I'm referring to concerns that apply more broadly.

102   *the majority of American adults identify as heterosexual*: Gary J. Gates, "How Many People Are Lesbian, Gay, Bisexual, and Transgender?" (The Williams Institute at University of California School of Law, April 2011), accessed February 11, 2013, http://williamsinstitute.law.ucla.edu/wp-content/uploads/Gates-How -Many-People-LGBT-Apr-2011.pdf.

102   *"I don't have to worry about hiding from the male gaze"*: Author interview on background, February 22, 2014.

102   *"I really felt that [my first girlfriend] saw me for me"*: Author interview on background, February 24, 2014.

102   *"When things ended with this one woman"*: Author interview on background, February 22, 2014.

102   *"I really think women can look at your shoes and lose interest"*: Nicole Kristal, interview by author, April 30, 2011.

103   *many are stumped when it comes to identifying a distinctly bisexual look*: Nikki Jane Hayfield, "Bisexual Women's Visual Identities: A Feminist Mixed-Methods Exploration" (doctoral thesis, University of the West of England, 2011).

103   *it can make bi women invisible to one another*: Bi advocate Amy Andre has offered this solution: "[W]e need a bisexual haircut! I think the bi community needs to come together and decide on one hair style, and that will be *the* bi hair style. Then, we need to be able to advertise the fact that that is the bi hair style, so that people can recognize us—but, of course, never harass us or act violently towards us." Amy Andre, "What Does a Bisexual Look Like?" *The Bilerico Project* (blog), last modified September 27, 2011, accessed February 2014, http://www .bilerico.com/2011/09/what_does_a_bisexual_look_like.php.

103   *describes herself as a clothes hoarder . . . "yes, I'm 'really' gay"*: Author interview on background, August 29, 2014.

104   *lesbians internalize conventional beauty norms less*: Sherry M. Bergeron and Charlene Y. Senn, "Body Image and Sociocultural Norms: A Comparison of Heterosexual and Lesbian Women," *Psychology of Women Quarterly* 22 (1998): 385.

104   *they're at similar risk as straight women*: Letitia Anne Peplau, David A. Frederick, Curtis Yee, Natalya Maisel, Janet Lever, and Negin Ghavami, "Body Image Satis-

faction in Heterosexual, Gay, and Lesbian Adults," *Archives of Sexual Behavior* 38 (2009): 713.

104   *truth is likely a synthesis of the two:* Caroline J. Huxley, Victoria Clarke, and Emma Halliwell, " 'It's a Comparison Thing, Isn't It?' Lesbian and Bisexual Women's Accounts of How Partner Relationships Shape Their Feelings about Their Body and Appearance," *Psychology of Women Quarterly* 35 (2011): 415.

104   *lesbians tend to find bodies with a higher BMI more attractive:* Charlotte N. Markey and Patrick M. Markey, "Gender, Sexual Orientation, and Romantic Partner Influence on Body Image: An Examination of Heterosexual and Lesbian Women and Their Partners," *Journal of Social and Personal Relationships* 31 (2014): 162.

104   *portly lesbians are likelier to think of themselves as overweight:* Ibid.

105   *bisexual women report less workplace discrimination:* Caroline Huxley, "Lesbian and Bisexual Women's Experiences of Sexuality-Based Discrimination and Their Appearance Concerns," *Psychology & Sexuality* 4 (2013): 7.

105   *their answers had nothing to do with queer visibility:* Author e-mail interview on background, joint response, September 6, 2014.

106   *The Game, the 2005 best seller chronicling:* Neil Strauss, *The Game* (New York: ReganBooks, 2005).

106   *Sample negs from an online pickup artist forum:* Vince Lin, "Ultimate Negs Collection," *PUA Lingo* (blog), last modified October 1, 2012, accessed February 4, 2013, http://www.pualingo.com/ultimate-negs-collection.

106   *it was the lead of Strauss's 2004 New York Times essay:* Neil Strauss, "He Aims! He Shoots! Yes!!" *The New York Times*, January 25, 2004.

107   *the "Dear Girls" meme of 2011:* "Dear Girls," Know Your Meme, last modified June 2015, accessed February 8, 2013, http://knowyourmeme.com/memes/dear-girls.

107   *"I watched this friend of mine":* Kristal, interview by author, April 30, 2011.

108   *women report being more aware of the presence:* Eve-Anne M. Doohan and Valerie Manusov, "The Communication of Compliments in Romantic Relationships: An Investigation of Relational Satisfaction and Sex Differences and Similarities in Compliment Behavior," *Western Journal of Communication* 68 (2004): 170.

109   *"I'd stayed up the whole night":* Author interview on background, August 13, 2012.

109   *"It was proof I wasn't ever":* Author interview on background, February 22, 2014.

109   *Similarly, twenty-six-year-old Rebecca has no problem:* Author questionnaire on background, March 13, 2012.

110   *"This might be strange, but I've noticed":* Author interview on background, October 27, 2013.

111   " '[F]alling in love' is no more than the process": Shulamith Firestone, *The Dia-*

lectic of Sex: The Case for Feminist Revolution (New York: William Morrow, 1970), 132.

112   *it's the engineered facial expression:* Author interview on background, March 13, 2012.

113   *"It wouldn't occur to me to think a woman had deceived me":* Author interview on background, February 2, 2014.

115   *"My girlfriend has apologized":* Author interview on background, February 15, 2014.

115   *"She's gone out with one too many assholes":* Author interview on background, November 11, 2013.

115   *"Are we talking about my perception of women":* Author interview on background, February 2, 2014.

5: The Prettiest Girl in the Room

120   *she took Andersen's neutral account of the relationship:* Carolyn Turgeon, *Mermaid: A Twist on the Classic Tale* (New York: Broadway Books, 2011).

120   *"You have these two beautiful protagonists":* Carolyn Turgeon, interview by author, March 1, 2011.

121   *"Once I learned that someone else being pretty":* Author interview on background, October 27, 2013.

121   *Women are likelier to use indirect aggression on a beautiful woman:* Maryanne L. Fisher, "Female Intrasexual Competition Decreases Female Facial Attractiveness," *Proceedings of the Royal Society B: Biological Sciences* 271 (2004): S283.

121   *While men were likelier to accept . . . if the profile came from a plainer one:* Shaojung Sharon Wang, Shin-Il Moon, Kyounghee Hazel Kwon, Carolyn A. Evans, and Michael A. Stefanone, "Face Off: Implications of Visual Cues on Initiating Friendship on Facebook," *Computers in Human Behavior* 26 (2010): 226.

121   *Mean-girl behavior toward particularly attractive girls:* Maria Agthe, Matthias Spörrle, Dieter Frey, Sabine Walper, and Jon K. Maner, "When Romance and Rivalry Awaken," *Human Nature* 24 (2013): 182.

121   *ovulating women rate other women's faces:* Fisher, "Female Intrasexual Competition."

122   *Satisfaction with one's own appearance:* Steven Arnocky, Shafik Sunderani, Jessie L. Miller, and Tracy Vaillancourt, "Jealousy Mediates the Relationship between Attractiveness Comparison and Females' Indirect Aggression," *Personal Relationships* 19 (2012): 290.

122   *conventionally beautiful women don't do anything different:* J. A. Simpson, S. W. Gangestad, P. N. Christensen, and K. Leck, "Fluctuating Asymmetry, Sociosexuality, and Intrasexual Competitive Tactics," *Journal of Personality and Social*

Psychology 76 (1999): 159. Male strategies included making direct comparisons between themselves and competitors, and putting down their competitors.

122 *women who don't make such comparisons:* Arnocky, Sunderani, Miller, and Vaillancourt, "Jealousy Mediates the Relationship."

122 *"Most of the time I feel pretty":* Author interview on background, October 27, 2013.

122 *independent reviewers estimate how much makeup . . . wore the same amount of makeup:* Pamela C. Regan, "Cinderella Revisited: Women's Appearance Modification As a Function of Target Audience Sex and Attractiveness," *Social Behavior and Personality* 39 (2011): 563. The researchers also noted that women's decreased use of cosmetics when expecting to meet an unattractive man might be a signal of the role male beauty plays in romance—they theorized that women toned down their makeup in order to lessen the possibility of piquing the man's interest.

123 *"I might be different from other women you're interviewing":* Author interview on background, November 19, 2013.

123 *her cooperative living situation precluded the competition:* Author interview on background, November 19, 2013.

124 *"It was hard being best friends with Sherry":* Author interview on background, June 7, 2013.

124 *acknowledges that she was "a bit of a catch":* Author interview on background, June 7, 2013.

124 *women who judged themselves as less attractive than their friend:* April Bleske-Rechek and Melissa Lighthall, "Attractiveness and Rivalry in Women's Friendships with Women," *Human Nature* 21 (2010): 82.

124 *"It was like, what is this girl doing in my freak zone":* Author interview on background, October 27, 2013.

127 *the more satisfied we are with a friend:* Marian M. Morry, "Relationship Satisfaction As a Predictor of Similarity Ratings: A Test of the Attraction-Similarity Hypothesis," *Journal of Social and Personal Relationships* 22 (2005): 561.

127 *similarities are one of the most reliable ways to predict a friendship's strength:* Miller McPherson, Lynn Smith-Lovin, and James M. Cook, "Birds of a Feather: Homophily in Social Networks," *Annual Review of Sociology* 27 (2001): 415. Similarities included demographic similarities (like race, sex, age, and education, with sex having the smallest impact on how people form friendships) as well as value-based similarities, like politics. The researchers noted that people often misperceived the attitudes and values they shared with friends, believing that they shared values that in truth were simply not discussed.

127 *female friends are rated by neutral parties as being more equal:* Bleske-Rechek and Lighthall, "Attractiveness and Rivalry": 82.

127 *"I've always been friends with women I felt were"*: Author interview on background, October 27, 2013.

129 *the more demographically similar a woman is to her female friends . . . report less envy*: Stephanie McKee, Heather J. Smith, Aubrey Koch, Rhonda Balzarini, Marissa Georges, and Matthew Paolucci Callahan, "Looking Up and Seeing Green: Women's Everyday Experiences with Physical Appearance Comparisons," *Psychology of Women Quarterly* 37 (2013): 351–365.

129 *"My friend Jess is the sexiest woman I know"*: Author interview on background, January 28, 2011.

129 *good-looking people have indeed been found to be roughly 10 percent happier*: Daniel S. Hamermesh and Jason Abrevaya, "Beauty Is the Promise of Happiness?" NBER Working Paper No. 17327 (The National Bureau of Economic Research, NBER Papers in Labor Studies, August 2011).

129 *good-looking men benefit from this more*: James Andreoni and Ragan Petrie, "Beauty, Gender and Stereotypes: Evidence from Laboratory Experiments," *Journal of Economic Psychology* 29 (2008): 73–93.

130 *particularly attractive women may even be penalized*: Stefanie K. Johnson, Kenneth E. Podratz, Robert L. Dipboye, and Ellie Gibbons, "Physical Attractiveness Biases in Ratings of Employment Suitability: Tracking Down the 'Beauty Is Beastly' Effect," *Journal of Social Psychology* 150 (2010): 301.

131 *"otherwise inchoate longings an object of focus"*: Virginia Postrel, *The Power of Glamour* (New York: Simon & Schuster, 2013), 36.

131 *"I have a friend who always looks amazing"*: Author interview on background, November 22, 2013.

133 *Hundreds of salons nationwide*: Professional Beauty Association website, accessed July 27, 2012, https://probeauty.org/cutitout.

133 *fundamental inequalities between the sexes*: Manicure-pedicure services in particular point to another inequality: class and race. A 2015 exposé series in the *New York Times* by Sarah Maslin Nir called attention to widespread labor abuses in the industry: pay far below the minimum wage, no overtime compensation, charging workers to ply their trade. It was enough to make me decide to stop patronizing nail salons of this variety. The problems of the industry warrant attention far greater than a footnote, but labor issues of this sort are beyond the scope of this book. It's a story very much worth following; you can begin by following the progress of New York Healthy Nail Salon Coalition on Facebook and elsewhere.

134 *"It's not like we go get pedicures"*: Author interview on background, October 27, 2013.

134 *physical appearance was one of the most frequently mentioned qualities*: Sandy Sheehy, *Connecting: The Enduring Power of Female Friendship* (New York: William Morrow, 2000).

134 *"Mariana is always so playful with her makeup":* Author interview on background, November 21, 2013.

134 *who complimented a total stranger at a party on her hair:* Author interview on background, November 2, 2013.

135 *"There's something safe about makeup":* Author interview on background, October 27, 2013.

135 *"Grooming yourself can be a way of saying":* Lisa Ferber, interview by author, December 7, 2010.

136 *A 2011 study…friends or randomly paired strangers:* T. Vaillancourt and A. Sharma, "Intolerance of Sexy Peers: Intrasexual Competition among Women," *Aggressive Behavior* 37 (2011): 569.

136 *record the facial expressions of the study participants:* Ibid.

137 *"[W]omen are bound together by a kind of immanent complicity":* Simone de Beauvoir, *The Second Sex* (New York: Bantam, 1970), 511.

137 *"With other women, a woman is":* Ibid., 512.

138 *doesn't remember the last time someone tried to engage her:* Kelli Dunham, interview by author, February 16, 2011.

138 *"I catch myself using compliments and makeup talk":* Author interview on background, October 27, 2013.

138 *"That's the province of":* Author interview on background, October 27, 2013.

138 *negative correlation between how much a woman talks with her friends:* P. Giles, "Peer Influence and Body Dissatisfaction amongst College Sorority Women" (thesis, University of Arkansas, August 2013).

140 *"I grew out of it, that's all":* Author questionnaire, February 6, 2011.

142 *"Much has been written recently about the 'child within'":* Terri Apter and Ruthellen Josselson, *Best Friends: The Pleasures and Perils of Girls' and Women's Friendships* (New York: Harmony Books, 1999), 135.

143 *women's most frequent response … negate the compliment:* R. K. Herbert, "Sex-Based Differences in Compliment Behavior," *Language in Society* 19 (1990): 201.

143 *Comic Amy Schumer brilliantly satirized:* "Compliments," *Inside Amy Schumer*, aired May 14, 2013.

144 *generally agree on which one is considered more attractive:* Bleske-Rechek and Lighthall, "Attractiveness and Rivalry": 82.

145 *many obese women report compensating:* Carol T. Miller, E. D. Rothblum, D. Felicio, and P. Brand, "Compensating for Stigma: Obese and Non-Obese Women's Reactions to Being Visible," *Personality and Social Psychology Bulletin* 21 (1995): 1093.

145 *"I love my friends for who they are":* Author interview on background, October 27, 2013.

145 *"I don't think about it all that much":* Author interview on background, November 10, 2013.

145 *"I might be different from other women"*: Author interview on background, November 11, 2013.

6: Who's Afraid of the Big Bad Media?

152 *Looking at pictures . . . can decrease women's body satisfaction:* Emily A. Hamilton, Laurie Mintz, and Susan Kashubeck-West, "Predictors of Media Effects on Body Dissatisfaction in European American women," *Sex Roles* 56 (2007): 397. Body mass index had no effect on body satisfaction, incidentally.

152 *The gap between a woman's self-image and the typical beauty standard:* S. S. Posavac and H. D. Posavac, "Predictors of Women's Concern with Body Weight: The Roles of Perceived Self-Media Ideal Discrepancies and Self-Esteem," *Eating Disorders* 10 (2002): 153.

152 *Women who internalize the thin imperative:* Emma Halliwell and Helga Dittmar, "Does Size Matter? The Impact of Model's Body Size on Women's Body-Focused Anxiety and Advertising Effectiveness," *Journal of Social and Clinical Psychology* 23 (2004): 104.

152 *Exposure to ads featuring thin women:* G. R. Bessenoff, "Can the Media Affect Us? Social Comparison, Self-Discrepancy, and the Thin Ideal," *Psychology of Women Quarterly* 30 (2006): 239.

152 *bulimic women report feeling higher levels of pressure:* Lori M. Irving, "Mirror Images: Effects of the Standard of Beauty on the Self- and Body-Esteem of Women Exhibiting Varying Levels of Bulimic Symptoms," *Journal of Social and Clinical Psychology* 9 (1990): 230.

152 *in one study, dieters . . . after looking at photos of slender women:* Jennifer S. Mills, Janet Polivy, C. Peter Herman, and Marika Tiggemann, "Effects of Exposure to Thin Media Images: Evidence of Self-Enhancement among Restrained Eaters," *Personality and Social Psychology Bulletin* 28 (2002): 1687.

152 *women viewing idealized images experienced a mild euphoria:* Philip N. Myers Jr. and Frank A. Biocca, "The Elastic Body Image: The Effect of Television Advertising and Programming on Body Image Distortions in Young Women," *Journal of Communication* 42 (1992): 108.

152 *self-esteem rose after looking at pictures:* Dirk Smeesters and Naomi Mandel, "Positive and Negative Media Image Effects on the Self," *Journal of Consumer Research* 32 (2006): 576.

153 *self-esteem has been shown . . . internalization of body ideals:* April M. Jones and Justin T. Buckingham, "Self-Esteem As a Moderator of the Effect of Social Comparison on Women's Body Image," *Journal of Social and Clinical Psychology* 24 (2005): 1164.

153 *women with intact body image:* Emma Halliwell, "The Impact of Thin Idealized Media Images on Body Satisfaction: Does Body Appreciation Protect Women from Negative Effects?" *Body Image* 10 (2013): 509.

153 *women who were highly invested in their appearance:* K. Ip and J. L. Jarry, "Investment in Body Image for Self-Definition Results in Greater Vulnerability to the Thin Media Than Does Investment in Appearance Management," *Body Image* 5 (2008): 59.

154 *bulimic women showed equal levels of self-esteem:* Irving, "Mirror Images."

154 *women who* already *had eating disorders:* K. Hamilton and G. Waller, "Media Influences on Body Size Estimation in Anorexia and Bulimia. An Experimental Study," *British Journal of Psychiatry* 162 (1993): 837.

155 *Woman A is engaging in social* comparison: Kathy Wilcox and James D. Laird, "The Impact of Media Images of Super-Slender Women on Women's Self-Esteem: Identification, Social Comparison, and Self-Perception," *Journal of Research in Personality* 34 (2000): 278. Another interesting finding of the study: Women who were more responsive to emotional cues were likelier to feel bad about themselves after looking at pictures of particularly slender women, while women who were less responsive to emotional cues felt *better.*

155 *women who scored higher . . . those with low self-esteem had the exact opposite response:* Jones and Buckingham, "Self-Esteem As a Moderator": 1164.

156 *inducing a mind-set of identification in heavier women:* Esther K. Papies and Kim A. H. Nicolaije, "Inspiration or Deflation? Feeling Similar or Dissimilar to Slim and Plus-Size Models Affects Self-Evaluation of Restrained Eaters," *Body Image* 9 (2012): 76.

156 *A 2006 study measuring:* Smeesters and Mandel, "Positive and Negative Media Image Effects," 576.

157 *tendency toward social comparison may be determined:* Frederick X. Gibbons and Bram P. Buunk, "Individual Differences in Social Comparison: Development of a Scale of Social Comparison Orientation," *Journal of Personality and Social Psychology* 76 (1999): 129.

158 *prompting the editors to declare:* Genevieve Field, "Oh. Wow. These Bodies Are Beautiful," *Glamour,* November 2009.

158 *did away with professional models altogether:* Sonja Pohlmann, "Aschenputtels Abgang," *Der Tagesspiegel,* last modified September 7, 2012, accessed September 17, 2013, http://www.tagesspiegel.de/medien/frauenmagazine-aschenputtels-abgang/7103706.html.

158 Brigitte *quietly reversed its no-models policy:* Ibid.

158 Glamour's *newsstand sales fell nearly 7 percent:* Audit Bureau of Circulations Fas-Fax, August 2010.

158   Brigitte *fared worse, with subscriptions dropping 22 percent:* Pohlmann, "Aschenputtels Abgang."

158   *overall circulation increased 10 percent:* Gruner + Jahr *Brigitte* media kit 2014, accessed February 18, 2014, http://www.gujmedia.com/print/portfolio/brigitte/circulationcoverage/ (page no longer available).

158   Elle's *best-selling cover model . . . its worst-selling issue featured:* Erik Maza, "Best and Worst Sellers at the Newsstand," *Women's Wear Daily,* March 12, 2013.

158   *editorially lauded makeup-free cover:* John Koblin, "The Cover Story: The Best (and Worst) Sellers of 2011," *Women's Wear Daily,* December 27, 2011.

158   *Zooey Deschanel led* Marie Claire *to its:* Erik Maza, "September's Cover Set," *Women's Wear Daily,* July 1, 2013.

159   *its second-worst-selling issue boasted:* Erik Maza, "Twentysomethings, TV and 'Twilight': The New Three T's of Newsstand Sales," *Women's Wear Daily,* August 8, 2012.

159   *dwarfed by the number of people who clicked on* Jezebel's: *Vogue* media kit, accessed September 21, 2015, http://www.condenast.com/brands/vogue/media-kit/print. Total circulation: 1.2 million. Jessica Coen, "Here Are the Unretouched Images from Lena Dunham's *Vogue* Shoot," *Jezebel* (blog), last modified January 17, 2014, accessed September 21, 2015, http://jezebel.com/here-are-the-unretouched-images-from-lena-dunhams-vogu-1503336657. Views: 2,130,070.

159   *30 percent of Americans are non-white:* Lindsay Hixson, Bradford B. Helper, and Myoung Ouk Kim, *The White Population: 2010,* US Census Bureau, September 2011, accessed September 12, 2013, http://www.census.gov/prod/cen2010/briefs/c2010br-05.pdf.

159   *only around 20 percent of magazine covers feature a person of color:* David Carr, "On Covers of Many Magazines, A Full Racial Palette Is Still Rare," *The New York Times,* November 18, 2002.

159   *Beyoncé graced the cover of:* Charlotte Cowles, "Beyoncé and Dead People Sell Magazines, Nicki Minaj Does Not," *The Cut, New York Magazine* website, last modified August 12, 2013, accessed September 12, 2013, http://nymag.com/thecut/2013/08/beyonce-and-dead-people-sell-mags-minaj-doesnt.html (page no longer available).

159   *Rihanna's November 2012 cover sold 32 percent fewer:* Maza, "Best and Worst Sellers."

159   *Black women are far likelier to experience body dissatisfaction:* Cynthia M. Frisby, "Does Race Matter? Effects of Idealized Images on African American Women's Perceptions of Body Esteem," *Journal of Black Studies* 34 (2004): 323.

159   *black women on the whole tend to have better body image:* Beth L. Molloy and Sharon D. Herzberger, "Body Image and Self-Esteem: A Comparison of African-American and Caucasian Women," *Sex Roles* 38 (1998): 631.

160   *Latina women have also been underrepresented, yet their body image is roughly:* M. Altabe, "Ethnicity and Body Image: Quantitative and Qualitative Analysis,"

International Journal of Eating Disorders 23 (1998): 153. Underrepresentation of Latinas in the media may have another effect: the streamlining of Hispanic culture. As Rosie Molinary, author of *Hijas Americanas*, says, "When I was eighteen, if I said to someone I was Puerto Rican, they'd say, 'Puerto what?' I grew up in South Carolina, and there weren't other Latinas around. So I thought [young Latinas] were going to say that it was so much easier to come of age now when there were Latinas in the media—and that ended up not being the reaction at all. Instead, they talked about how it created a really hard standard for them. I was getting 'Puerto what?' but fast-forward to young women now, and if they say they're Puerto Rican and happen to be Afro-Latina, so they're black Puerto Rican, people are like, 'Why don't you look like Jennifer Lopez?' Because in the media there's a bit of a poster girl for each country. You're Mexican, it's Salma Hayek; you've got Jennifer Lopez for Puerto Rico, Eva Mendes for Cuba. If you're African American, there's not just one African American actress to compare you to; if you're white, there's not just one white woman to be compared to." Rosie Molinary, interview by author, September 23, 2011.

161　*she's spoken at half of all American universities:* "Full Bio," Jean Kilbourne, accessed September 20, 2013, http://www.jeankilbourne.com/bio.

161　*About-Face breaks down popular ads:* About-Face website, accessed September 24, 2013, http://www.about-face.org.

161　*features offensive ad images and tells users:* "Ads," NOW Foundation website, accessed September 21, 2015, http://now.org/now-foundation/love-your-body/ads/.

161　*online tool kit containing:* "Tips for Becoming a Critical Viewer of the Media," National Eating Disorders Association website, accessed September 24, 2013, https://www.nationaleatingdisorders.org/tips-becoming-critical-viewer-media.

161　*Adios, Barbie critiques everything from:* Adios, Barbie website, accessed September 24, 2013, http://www.adiosbarbie.com.

162　*More than eighty-six thousand people signed a petition:* Julia Bluhm, "Seventeen Magazine: Give Girls Images of Real Girls!" change.org, accessed September 21, 2015, https://www.change.org/p/seventeen-magazine-give-girls-images-of-real-girls.

162　*"We vow to . . . Never change girls' body or face shapes":* Christine Haughney, "Seventeen Magazine Vows to Show Girls 'As They Really Are,'" *The New York Times*, July 3, 2012.

162　*"No wonder our perception of beauty is distorted":* "dove evolution," YouTube video, 1:14, directed by Tim Piper and Yael Staav for Ogilvy and Dove, creation and concept by Mike Kirkland and Tim Piper, posted by "Tim Piper," October 6, 2006, accessed September 13, 2013, https://www.youtube.com/watch?v=iYhCn0jf46U.

162 Evolution *got more than 12 million views:* Jack Neff, "Unilever Unleashes 'On-slaught' on Beauty Industry," *Advertising Age,* October 2, 2007.

162 *Unilever reported that Dove's overall sales:* "Ready for Their Close-Up," *National Post* (Canada), last modified August 23, 2007, accessed September 13, 2013, http://www.nationalpost.com/story.html?id=e2e95710-bd0a-46c5-8208 -725975e9ec88.

162 *significant effect on women's awareness ... decrease women's internalization:* R. Watson and L. M. Vaughn, "Limiting the Effects of the Media on Body Image: Does the Length of a Media Literacy Intervention Make a Difference?" *Eating Disorders: The Journal of Treatment & Prevention* 14 (2006): 385.

162 *participants had significant increases in body image:* Gail L. McVey and Ron Davis, "A Program to Promote Positive Body Image: A 1-Year Follow-Up Evaluation," *The Journal of Early Adolescence* 22 (2002): 96.

162 *eighth graders who went through a media literacy program:* Susan J. Paxton, Eleanor H. Wertheim, Angela Pilawski, Sarah Durkin, and Tracey Holt, "Evaluations of Dieting Prevention Messages by Adolescent Girls," *Preventive Medicine* 35 (2002): 474–491.

163 *media literacy program developed by sisters:* Lindsay D. Kite, "Healthy Media Literacy: Bridging Critical Media Literacy and Health Literacy to Promote Positive Body Image and Health" (dissertation, University of Utah, 2013).

163 *most of them were versed in counterarguments:* Renee Engeln-Maddox, "Cognitive Responses to Idealized Media Images of Women: The Relationship of Social Comparison and Critical Processing to Body Image Disturbance in College Women," *Journal of Social and Clinical Psychology* 24 (2005): 1114.

163 *little to no connection between knowing an image is unrealistic:* Renee Engeln-Maddox and Steven A. Miller, "Talking Back to the Media Ideal: The Development and Validation of the Critical Processing of Beauty Images Scale," *Psychology of Women Quarterly* 32 (2008): 159.

163 *Teenagers ... had less body satisfaction:* R. A. Botta, "Television Images and Adolescent Girls' Body Image Disturbance," *Journal of Communication* 49 (1999): 22.

163 *between media intake and body dissatisfaction found only a small-to-moderate correlation:* Michael P. Levine and Sarah K. Murnen, "Everybody Knows that Mass Media Are/Are Not (Pick One) a Cause of Eating Disorders: A Critical Review of Evidence for a Causal Link between Media, Negative Body Image, and Disordered Eating in Females," *Journal of Social and Clinical Psychology* 28 (2009): 9.

163 *critical analysis helped women cut down ... as dissatisfied with their bodies:* L. M. Irving and S. R. Berel, "Comparison of Media-Literacy Programs to Strengthen College Women's Resistance to Media Images," *Psychology of Women Quarterly* 25 (2001): 103.

163 *girls in the control group who* didn't *go through the media literacy program:* McVey and Davis, "A Program to Promote Positive Body Image."

163 *self-esteem was actually slightly* lower *at a twelve-month follow-up:* G. L. McVey, R. Davis, S. Tweed, and B. F. Shaw, "Evaluation of a School-Based Program Designed to Improve Body Image Satisfaction, Global Self-Esteem, and Eating Attitudes and Behaviors: A Replication Study," *International Journal of Eating Disorders* 36 (2004): 1.

163 *Women who are the most well versed in it:* Engeln-Maddox and Miller, "Talking Back to the Media Ideal."

164 *women with low self-esteem rated personality characteristics . . . didn't change their opinion:* R. L. Bergstrom, C. Neighbors, and J. E. Malheim, "Media Comparisons and Threats to Body Image," *Journal of Social and Clinical Psychology* 28 (2009): 264.

164 *In one study, dieters reported feeling:* Mills, Polivy, Herman, and Tiggemann, "Effects of Exposure," 1687.

164 *"Critically viewing idealized media images":* Engeln-Maddox, "Cognitive Responses to Idealized Media Images of Women," 1114.

164 *easily compared themselves to models . . . comparisons they made to images plummeted:* Michael Häfner, Odile Jagsch, Anja Kund, Sonja Mager, Philippe Türk Pereira, and Anja Zimmerman, " 'The Female May Feel Male': Defending against the Adverse Consequences of Exposure to Idealized Media Images," *Journal of Social and Clinical Psychology* 27 (2008): 778.

165 *girls who say they don't notice models' bodies:* Renée A. Botta, "For Your Health? The Relationship between Magazine Reading and Adolescents' Body Image and Eating Disturbances," *Sex Roles* 48 (2003): 389.

165 *"We don't use our work as a platform to introduce":* Lindsay Kite, e-mail interview by author, October 15, 2013.

165 *the effect was ameliorated when they were alerted:* Chris Bale, "Attractiveness and Self-Esteem: A Test of Sociometer Theory" (thesis, University of Central Lancashire, 2010).

165 *women prompted to see idealized images as fantasy . . . higher regard for their own appearance:* Marika Tiggemann, Janet Polivy, and Duane Hargreaves, "The Processing of Thin Ideals in Fashion Magazines: A Source of Social Comparison or Fantasy?" *Journal of Social and Clinical Psychology* 28 (2009): 73.

167 *"People focus on the images because they're an easy scapegoat":* Sunny Sea Gold, interview by author, April 12, 2011.

168 *strongest predictors of a woman being at risk of internalizing:* Renee Engeln-Maddox, "Buying a Beauty Standard or Dreaming of a New Life?" *Psychology of Women Quarterly* 30 (2006): 258.

168 *A different group of students went through a program:* McVey and Davis, "A Program to Promote Positive Body Image."

7: "Like" Me

174 *Americans took 50 billion photos a year ... billion photographs each week:* Risto Sarvas and David M. Frohlich, *From Snapshots to Social Media* (London: Springer, 2011).

175 *lingerie bloggers launched an international discussion:* Elisabeth Dale, "New Push for Diversity in Lingerie," *Huffington Post* (blog), last modified August 21, 2013, accessed August 28, 2013, http://www.huffingtonpost.com/elisabeth-dale/new -push-for-diversity-in_b_3788356.html.

175 *Plus-size models popped up in ads bearing the #ImNoAngel hashtag:* Roo Ciambriello, "Lane Bryant Bashes Victoria's Secret With 'I'm No Angel' Campaign," *AdFreak, AdWeek* website, last modified April 8, 2015, accessed April 12, 2015, http://www.adweek.com/adfreak/lane-bryant-bashes-victorias-secret-im-no -angel-campaign-163944.

176 *images have a "primitive status":* Susan Sontag, *On Photography* (New York: Anchor, 1990), 155.

176 *"The primitive notion of the efficacy of images":* Ibid., 158.

177 *"the body project":* Joan Jacobs Brumberg, *The Body Project* (New York: Vintage, 1998).

177 *online dating consultants:* Abby Ellin, "The Dating Coach Is In ($125/Hour)," *The New York Times,* September 27, 2007.

178 *"[I]t is to prefer a foreign object":* Simone de Beauvoir, *The Second Sex* (New York: Bantam, 1970), 502.

178 *people experienced a moderate bump in self-esteem . . . some sort of change to their profile:* A. L. Gonzales and J. T. Hancock, "Mirror, Mirror on My Facebook Wall: Effects of Exposure to Facebook on Self-Esteem," *Cyberpsychology, Behavior, and Social Networking* 14 (2011): 79. The study also measured people's self-esteem after participants looked in the mirror; self-esteem, on average, decreased after a mirror glimpse. Given that the study found that people's self-esteem was leveraged by Facebook if they adjusted their profile, I can't help but wonder if the same logic applies to adjusting the image one sees in the mirror. Maybe this is part of the positive effect makeup has on self-esteem—adjusting one's social profile in a more visual sense.

178 *negative correlation between self-esteem . . . collection of photos:* S. Mehdizadeh, "Self-Presentation 2.0: Narcissism and Self-Esteem on Facebook," *Cyberpsychology, Behavior, and Social Networking* 13 (2010): 357.

179 Selfies at Serious Places: @heyfeifer, *Selfies at Serious Places* (blog), accessed November 14, 2013, http://selfiesatseriousplaces.tumblr.com/.

180 Selfies at Funerals: @heyfeifer, *Selfies at Funerals* (blog), http://selfiesatfunerals .tumblr.com.

180   *President Barack Obama was caught taking a selfie:* Christine Hauser, "'Selfie' of Obama Was Misinterpreted, Photographer Says," *The New York Times,* December 11, 2013.

180   *"They're a logical technologically enabled response":* Erin Gloria Ryan, "Selfies Aren't Empowering. They're a Cry for Help," *Jezebel* (blog), last modified November 21, 2013, accessed December 12, 2013, http://jezebel.com/selfies -arent-empowering-theyre-a-cry-for-help-1468965365.

180   *"The selfie suggests something in picture form":* Rachel Simmons, "Selfies Are Good for Girls," *Slate,* last modified November 20, 2013, accessed December 12, 2013, http://www.slate.com/articles/double_x/doublex/2013/11/selfies_on _instagram_and_facebook_are_tiny_bursts_of_girl_pride.html.

180   *"My selfies are proof that I'm worthy of documentation":* Author interview on background, January 8, 2013.

181   *what of the #nomakeupselfie movement:* Roo Ciambriello, "How a 'No Makeup Selfie' Trend Suddenly Became a Cancer Awareness Effort," *AdFreak, AdWeek* website, last modified March 24, 2014, accessed July 9, 2015, http://www .adweek.com/adfreak/how-no-makeup-selfie-trend-suddenly-became-cancer -awareness-effort-156480.

181   *its short film:* "Selfie," YouTube video, 8:03, in partnership with the Sundance Institute, directed by Cynthia Wade and produced by Sharon Liese, posted by "Dove US," January 19, 2014, accessed July 9, 2015, https://www.youtube.com /watch?v=BFkm1Hg4dTI.

181   *"As someone who's part of a marginalized group":* Teagan Widmer, "Nia King & Teagan Widmer: The Great Selfie Debate," *Youngist,* last modified June 19, 2013, accessed July 28, 2013, http://youngist.org/nia-king-teagan-widmer -the-great-selfie-debate/#.VgBk1WTBzGc.

181   *#blackoutday, dedicated to posting and reposting selfies:* Yesha Callahan, "#BlackOutDay Takes Over Social Media," *The Root* (blog), last modified March 6, 2015, accessed July 10, 2015, http://www.theroot.com/blogs/the_grapevine /2015/03/_blackoutday_takes_over_social_media.html.

183   *Online gamers tend to construct avatars:* Robert Andrew Dunn and Rosanna E. Guadagno, "My Avatar and Me: Gender and Personality Predictors of Avatar Self Discrepancy," *Computers in Human Behavior* 28 (2012): 97.

183   *players with attractive avatars tend to acquire higher status:* Shao-kang Lo, "The Impact of Online Game Character's Outward Attractiveness and Social Status on Interpersonal Attraction," *Computers in Human Behavior* 24 (2008): 1947.

183   *"A woman must continually watch herself":* John Berger, *Ways of Seeing* (London: Pelican, 1972), 46.

184 *the quickest way to create a bad impression online:* S. Hong, E. Tandoc Jr., E. A. Kim, B. Kim, and K. Wise, "The Real You? The Role of Visual Cues and Comment Congruence in Perceptions of Social Attractiveness from Facebook Profiles," *Cyberpsychology, Behavior, and Social Networking* 15 (2012): 339.

185 *"sleeping" woman that went viral in 2012:* "Caught Me Sleeping/Bae Caught Me Slippin," Know Your Meme, last modified January 2015, accessed December 19, 2013, http://knowyourmeme.com/memes/caught-me-sleeping-bae-caught-me-slippin.

185 *men and women use social media technology:* Joanna Brenner and Aaron Smith, "72% of Online Adults Are Social Networking Site Users," Pew Internet & American Life Project, last modified August 5, 2013, accessed January 8, 2014, http://www.pewinternet.org/Reports/2013/social-networking-sites/Findings.aspx.

185 *choose their Facebook profile picture with "looking attractive":* Michele M. Strano, "User Descriptions and Interpretations of Self-Presentation through Facebook Profile Images," *Cyberpsychology: Journal of Psychosocial Research on Cyberspace* 2 (2008): article 5.

185 *viewers of both sexes spend more time:* G. Seidman and O. S. Miller, "Effects of Gender and Physical Attractiveness on Visual Attention to Facebook Profiles," *Cyberpsychology, Behavior, and Social Networking* 16 (2013): 20.

186 *men are likelier than women to digitally touch up:* N. Haferkamp, S. C. Eimler, A. M. Papadakis, and J. V. Kruck, "Men Are from Mars, Women Are from Venus? Examining Gender Differences in Self-Presentation on Social Networking Sites," *Cyberpsychology, Behavior, and Social Networking* 15 (2012): 91.

186 *likelier to use a full-body shot:* Ibid.

186 *have sent a suggestive sext selfie:* Amanda Lenhart, "Teens, Adults and Sexting: Data on Sending/Receiving Sexually Suggestive Nude or Nearly Nude Photos by Americans," Pew Internet & American Life Project, last modified October 23, 2010, accessed January 9, 2014, http://www.pewinternet.org/Presentations/2010/Oct/Teens-Adults-and-Sexting.aspx.

186 *to use self-tracking devices that quantify bodily functions:* Matthew Cornell, "Is There a Self-Experimentation Gender Gap?" *Quantified Self,* last modified December 17, 2010, accessed January 7, 2014, http://quantifiedself.com/2010/12/is-there-a-self-experimentation-gender-gap.

186 *"Apparently, it took the preponderance of closed-circuit television":* Madeline Ashby, "The New Aesthetics of the Male Gaze," *Dangerous to Those Who Profit from the Way Things Are* (blog), last modified April 4, 2012, accessed May 6, 2012, http://madelineashby.com/?p=1198.

186 *men tend to engage in self-surveillance and body monitoring:* Laura Vandenbosch and Steven Eggermont, "Sexualization of Adolescent Boys: Media Exposure and

Boys' Internalization of Appearance Ideals, Self-Objectification, and Body Surveillance," *Men and Masculinities* 16 (2013): 283–306.

187   *"My girlfriend sent me some sexy pictures"*: Author interview on background, January 14, 2013.

187   *not to mention the virtual garden of genitalia*: Dick pics are so common that writer Madeline Holden started CritiqueMyDickPic.tumblr.com to, well, critique dick pics. Private reviews are available for ten dollars. It's genius.

188   *bodybuilders, who by dint of their occupation*: Alan M. Klein, "Man Makes Himself: Alienation and Self-Objectification in Bodybuilding," *Play & Culture* 5 (1992): 326.

188   *"The penis is singularly adapted"*: de Beauvoir, *The Second Sex*, 43.

189   *"I've always thought that if I were a woman:"* Author interview on background, November 11, 2013.

189   *"help people get meaning out of their personal data"*: "About the Quantified Self," accessed September 12, 2013, http://quantifiedself.com/about.

189   *Ferriss's advice for a lean, muscular body*: Timothy Ferriss, *The 4-Hour Body: An Uncommon Guide to Rapid Fat-Loss, Incredible Sex, and Becoming Superhuman* (New York: Harmony, 2010).

190   *Americans spent $4.8 billion on men's grooming products*: Andrew McDougall, "Men's Grooming on the Rise in North America," CosmeticsDesign.com, last modified September 13, 2010, accessed September 14, 2013, http://www.cosmeticsdesign.com/Market-Trends/Men-s-grooming-on-the-rise-in-North-America.

190   *globally, the market grows 9 percent a year*: "Men's Grooming Market Research," Euromonitor International, accessed December 2, 2011, http://www.euromonitor.com/mens-grooming.

190   *growing 500 percent over the same period*: Ibid.

190   *Sales of facial trimmers grew . . . sales of body groomers grew*: Andrew McDougall, "You're So Vain: Men's Grooming Market Booming," CosmeticsDesign.com, last modified August 8, 2012, accessed January 8, 2014, http://www.cosmeticsdesign.com/Market-Trends/You-re-so-vain-Men-s-grooming-market-booming.

190   *multiple studies show that men depilate*: Michael Scott Boroughs, "Body Depilation among Women and Men: The Association of Body Hair Reduction or Removal with Body Satisfaction, Appearance Comparison, Body Image Disturbance, and Body Dysmorphic Disorder" (dissertation, University of South Florida, January 2012); Susan A. Basow and Katherine O'Neil, "Men's Body Depilation: An Exploratory Study of United States College Students' Preferences, Attitudes, and Practices," *Body Image* 11 (2014): 409.

191   *"Women have spoken, and overall"*: Andrew McDougall, "Men's Grooming? The Best a Woman Can Get, as Gillette Changes Tact," CosmeticsDesign.com, last

modified April 3, 2013, accessed January 8, 2014, http://www.cosmeticsdesign
.com/Market-Trends/Men-s-grooming-The-best-a-woman-can-get-as-Gillette
-changes-tact.

191   *13 percent of all cosmetic procedures:* "ISAPS Global Statistics," International Soci-
ety for Aesthetic Plastic Surgery, 2014 survey, last modified July 8, 2015, accessed
November 23, 2015, http://www.isaps.org/Media/Default/global-statistics
/July%202015%20ISAPS%20Global%20Statistics%20Release%20-%20Final.pdf.

191   *number of male patients claiming to have sensitive skin:* K. Vanoosthuyze, P. J. Zup-
kosky, and K. Buckley, "Survey of Practicing Dermatologists on the Prevalence of
Sensitive Skin in Men," *International Journal of Cosmetic Science* 35 (2013): 388.

191   *Western men's self-presentation changed dramatically:* Robert Ross, *Clothing: A
Global History* (Cambridge, UK: Polity, 2008).

192   *"This is not [notoriously outrageous]":* Samantha Conti, Julie Naughton, and Pete
Born, "Tom Ford Driving Into Men's Skin Care," *Women's Wear Daily*, June 21,
2013, accessed January 8, 2014.

8: "Don't You Know You're Beautiful?"

199   *one-third of women would be willing to die younger in exchange for the perfect body:*
Jo Willey, "A Perfect Body? Women Would Swap a Year of Life," *Express*, last
modified March 31, 2011, accessed October 14, 2012, http://www.express.co.uk
/news/uk/237783/A-perfect-body-Women-would-swap-a-year-of-life.

199   *93 percent of women feel they should look younger:* Alison Caporimo, "What's
Beautiful Now: The Allure American Beauty Survey," *Allure* website, accessed
February 14, 2014, http://www.allure.com/beauty-trends/2011/american
-beauty-census#slide=2.

199   *72 percent of girls—children—feel "tremendous pressure" to look beautiful:* "Surprising Self-Esteem Statistics," Dove website, accessed February 14, 2014,
http://www.dove.us/Social-Mission/Self-Esteem-Statistics.aspx.

199   *women under thirty rating themselves an eight or above:* Melissa Dahl, "Most of
Us Think We're Hotter Than Average, Survey Says," *Today* website, last modified September 8, 2010, accessed October 23, 2013, http://www.nbcnews
.com/id/39044399/ns/health-skin_and_beauty/t/most-us-think-were-hotter
-average-survey-says/#.Vfs6bLxVikp. (Original MSNBC/Elle study no longer
available.)

199   *tend to overestimate their attractiveness:* Ngaire Donaghue and Nicole Smith,
"Not Half Bad: Self and Others' Judgements of Body Size and Attractiveness
across the Life Span," *Sex Roles* 58 (2008): 875. The study specifically compared
overall aesthetic judgments with body size comparisons. People tend to overes-

timate their body size; that is, regardless of what others think about their body size, they find their bodies to be less ideal than what we as a culture have heralded as beautiful. But when researchers found that the tendency to self-deprecate didn't extend to people's judgments of their physical appeal on the whole, they theorized that people's overestimation of their own body size is less a reflection of generalized self-esteem and more a reflection of "the lack of information about what 'normal' bodies look like."

199   *quicker to recognize a digitally beautified image of their face:* Nicholas Epley and Erin Whitchurch, "Mirror, Mirror on the Wall: Enhancement in Self-Recognition," *Personality and Social Psychology Bulletin* 34 (2008): 1159. Study participants extended this generosity to enhanced photos of friends' faces, but not to a relative stranger's face. Consider it another example of rose-colored glasses.

199   *we have a tendency to devalue that trait:* Jack L. Powell, Mala L. Matacin, and Anne E. Stuart, "Body Esteem: An Exception to Self-Enhancing Illusions?" *Journal of Applied Social Psychology* 31 (2001): 1951.

199   *"I never felt beautiful":* Author interview on background, March 27, 2011.

199   *"I was never the pretty girl":* Author interview on background, November 14, 2010.

199   *"When my husband tells me I'm beautiful":* Author questionnaire on background, November 6, 2010.

200   *published a piece by writer Samantha Brick:* Samantha Brick, " 'There Are Downsides to Looking This Pretty': Why Women Hate Me for Being Beautiful," *Daily Mail,* April 2, 2012.

201   both *women privately believed themselves to be the prettier one:* April Bleske-Rechek and Melissa Lighthall, "Attractiveness and Rivalry in Women's Friendships with Women," *Human Nature* 21 (2010): 82.

201   *"tiny burst of girl pride":* Rachel Simmons, "Selfies Are Good for Girls," *Slate,* last modified November 21, 2013, accessed December 18, 2014, http://www.slate .com/articles/double_x/doublex/2013/11/selfies_on_instagram_and_face book_are_tiny_bursts_of_girl_pride.html.

203   *Central to the therapeutic narrative:* Eva Illouz, *Cold Intimacies: The Making of Emotional Capitalism* (Cambridge: Polity, 2007).

204   *body image, after all, was coined by a pupil of Freud's:* Paul Schilder, *The Image and Appearance of the Human Body* (Abingdon: Routledge, 1950).

205   *react more strongly to unpleasant odors:* Avery Nelson Gilbert, Alan J. Fridlund, and John Sabini, "Hedonic and Social Determinants of Facial Displays to Odors," *Chemical Senses* 12 (1987): 355.

205   *recognize angry faces more quickly:* Christine H. Hansen and Ranald D. Hansen, "Finding the Face in the Crowd: An Anger Superiority Effect," *Journal of Personality and Social Psychology* 54 (1988): 917.

205 *likelier to remember a non-helpful character:* J. Kiley Hamlin, Karen Wynn, and Paul Bloom, "Three-Month-Olds Show a Negativity Bias in Their Social Evaluations," *Developmental Science* 13 (2010): 923.

206 *people tend to rate themselves as being better-looking now:* Geoffrey Haddock, "Do I Get Better-Looking Each Day? Changes in Self-Perceptions of Attractiveness As a Function of Temporal Perspective," *European Journal of Social Psychology* 36 (2006): 761.

208 *If comments about her looks do turn nasty:* For an in-depth look at one particularly troubling aspect of young women and social media, see Gillian Bolsover, "Constructing the Virtual Body: Self-Representation, Self-Modification, and Self-Perfection in Pro–Eating Disorder Websites" (dissertation, London School of Economics, 2010).

209 *the Body Shop launched a campaign featuring Ruby:* Stuart Elliott, "The Body Shop's Campaign Offers Reality, Not Miracles," *The New York Times*, August 26, 1997.

209 *Bare Escentuals unveiled a set of commercials:* Tanzina Vega, "Beauty Might Not Be Blind, but the Casting Call Was," *The New York Times*, September 1, 2011.

209 *Inner Beauty Challenge:* Inner Beauty Challenge, accessed December 4, 2013, http://innerbeautychallenge.com.

210 *Make Up For Ever debuted a series of print ads:* David Gianatasio, "Beauty Brand Tries Unretouched Makeup Ads," *AdFreak, Ad Week* website, last modified March 21, 2011, accessed December 4, 2013, http://www.adweek.com/adfreak/beauty-brand-tries-unretouched-makeup-ads-126927.

210 *featuring models' bodies as is:* Ashley Lutz, "American Eagle Stopped Airbrushing Lingerie Models and Sales Are Soaring," *Business Insider*, last modified November 3, 2014, accessed November 18, 2014, http://www.businessinsider.com/aerie-lingerie-ads-without-photoshop-2014-11.

211 *"an effort to appear more inclusive":* Christina Passariello, Max Colchester, "L'Oréal Slogan Must Prove Worth Anew," *The Wall Street Journal*, last modified November 15, 2011, accessed January 22, 2014, http://online.wsj.com/news/articles/SB10001424052970204323904577037720293895982.

211 *Dove commissioned a global study of 3,200 women:* Nancy Etcoff, Susie Orbach, Jennifer Scott, and Heidi D'Agostino, *The Real Truth About Beauty: A Global Report*, September 2004.

211 *Only 2 percent of women worldwide . . . media and advertising set an unrealistic:* Ibid.

212 *This was the survey question that finding . . . "comfortable describing myself as beautiful":* Ibid.

212 *Sixty percent of American women . . . "average in overall physical attractiveness":* Ibid. In fact, globally—with the exception of Japan—71 percent of women reported being "somewhat" or "very satisfied" with their looks. In Japan, though, only 23

percent of respondents reported being "somewhat satisfied"—and 0 percent reported being "very satisfied."

212 *more than 60 percent of American women actually* do *weigh too much:* Centers for Disease Control and Prevention, "Nutrition, Physical Activity and Obesity: Data, Trends and Maps," accessed January 12, 2016, https://nccd.cdc.gov /NPAO_DTM/Default.aspx.

218 *personal style consultant Sally McGraw:* Sally McGraw, "You Can Do It," *Already Pretty* (blog), last modified October 24, 2011, accessed December 8, 2014, http://www.alreadypretty.com/2011/10/you-can-do-it.html.

Conclusion: Skin Deep

219 *On the morning of July 5, 1942:* Anne Frank, *The Diary of a Young Girl: The Definitive Edition* (New York: Bantam, 2011).

219 *"Margot and I started packing":* Ibid., 53.

221 *"I think there's a lot of pressure":* Kate Fridkis, e-mail interview by author, November 2013.

Index

About the Author

Autumn Whitefield-Madrano's writing has appeared in *Marie Claire*, *Glamour*, *Salon*, *Jezebel*, the *Guardian*, and more. She created *The Beheld*, a blog examining questions behind personal appearance. Her work on the ways beauty shapes women's lives has been covered by the *New York Times* and the *Today* show. She lives in Astoria, New York, and will tell you her beauty secrets if you tell her yours.